THE RISE OF PROFESSIONALISM

Magali Sarfatti Larson

THE RISE OF PROFESSIONALISM

A Sociological Analysis

UNIVERSITY OF CALIFORNIA PRESS
Berkeley • Los Angeles • London

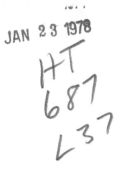
University of California Press
Berkeley and Los Angeles, California

University of California Press, Ltd.
London, England

ISBN 0-520-02938-0
Library of Congress Catalog Card Number: 74-30533
Printed in the United States of America

To my parents,

Amedeo and Pierangela Sarfatti

Contents

Acknowledgments

This book grew out of my doctoral dissertation; I therefore wish to express my gratitude to the National Science Foundation and to the Danforth Foundation for their support while I was working on my thesis. The Kent Fellowship which the Danforth Foundation awarded me from 1972 to 1974 meant much more to me than just financial help.

Sentimental acknowledgments are extremely gratifying for an author, but the reader seldom finds them interesting. The following people will know with how much sentiment I wish to thank them: they are, first of all, my teachers at the University of California, Berkeley: Arthur L. Stinchcombe, Robert Blauner, W. R. Ellis, and Neil Smelser. One of my first and finest teachers, Kalman H. Silvert, died an untimely death as I was finishing this writing. I would have anxiously awaited his response to this work; now, I can only record my intellectual debt and my admiration. Among the many friends and colleagues who endlessly listened, read, suggested, and edited were Andrew Scull, Fred Block, and Charles D. Kaplan, whose intellectual support went far beyond the writing of this book; and also Jeffrey Escoffier, Ann Beuf, Carole Joffe, Arlene K. Daniels, Ted Reed and my students in the seminar on the sociology of professions at the University of Pennsylvania. My debt with Richard Fitzgerald is greatest in regard to the American chapters. Ronald Grele's acute comments on the first draft and his broad historical knowledge helped me greatly, as did Alain Touraine's incisive reading. Last but not least, I wish to thank my editors at the University of California Press, Grant Barnes and Gene Tanke for their help and support, as well as Mrs. Miranda Reinis, for her perfect and patient typing.

My son Antonio was born a few months before I started writing this book. Naturally, he did all that was in his power to prevent me from doing so. I should therefore thank, most of all, the people who helped me with such devotion and good grace to hold Antonio in check. My indebtedness to my parents and to my husband, for this as well as everything else, is of the kind that cannot even begin to be stated here.

M. S. L.
University of Pennsylvania

Introduction

My interest in the professions was initially awakened by practical experiences. During a strike of college teachers in the sixties, the accusation was heard that these professors were behaving "like longshoremen." Later, I was told by the organizers of a union of employed architects in the San Francisco Bay Area that most of their potential members resisted unionization, as something "unprofessional." Somehow, architectural employees, most of whom can be laid off without prior notice from one day to the next and are paid hourly wages often lower than those of semiskilled laborers in construction unions, believed that unionization would further reduce their dignity and their prospects as working people. I began asking myself, "what's in a name?" What made professors and architects—not to mention physicians, lawyers, and engineers—feel that the tactics and strategy of the industrial working class would deprive them of a cherished identity? What is there, in the attributes of a profession, that compensates for subordination, individual powerlessness, and often low pay?

In most cases, social scientists provide an unequivocal answer: professions are occupations with special power and prestige. Society grants these rewards because professions have special competence in esoteric bodies of knowledge linked to central needs and values of the social system, and because professions are devoted to the service of the public, above and beyond material incentives.

The list of specific attributes which compose the ideal-type of profession may vary, but there is substantial agreement about its general dimensions.[1] The cognitive dimension is centered on the body of knowledge and techniques which the professionals apply in their work, and on the training necessary to master such knowledge and skills; the normative dimension covers the service orientation of professionals, and their distinctive ethics, which justify the privilege of self-regulation granted them by society; the evaluative dimension implicitly compares professions to other occupations, underscoring the professions' singular characteristics of autonomy and prestige. The distinctiveness of the professions appears to be founded on the combination of these general dimensions. These uncommon occupations tend to become "real" communities, whose members share a relatively permanent affiliation, an identity, personal commitment, specific interests, and general loyalties.[2]

These communities are concretely identified by typical organizations and institutional patterns: professional associations, professional schools, and self-administered codes of ethics. It is not clear how much "community" would exist without these institutional supports; yet these supports are features that occupations which aspire to the privileges of professional status can imitate, without possessing the cognitive and normative justifications of ''real'' professions.[3]

In fact, the professional phenomenon does not have clear boundaries. Either its dimensions are devoid of a clear empirical referent, or its attributes are so concrete that occupational groups trying to upgrade their status can copy them with relative ease. For instance, it is often emphasized that professional training must be prolonged, specialized, and have a theoretical base. Yet, as Eliot Freidson ironically points out, it is never stated *how* long; *how* theoretical, or *how* specialized training must be in order to qualify, since all formal training ''takes some time,'' is ''somewhat specialized,'' and involves some attempt at generalization.[4] The service orientation is even more problematic: it is, undoubtedly, part of the ideology and one of the prescriptive norms which organized professions explicitly avow. Yet the implicit assumption that the behavior of individual professionals is more ethical, as a norm, than that of individuals in lesser occupations has seldom, if ever, been tested by empirical evidence. Finally, it is true that most established professions rank high on the prestige scale of occupations, although they rank lower than positions of institutional or de facto power, such as Supreme Court Justice or cabinet member in the federal government.[5] Such rankings reflect synthetic evaluations, which fact makes it impossible to ascertain the weight assigned to the ''professional'' characteristics of competence and disinterestedness in such judgments; prestige may well be accorded on grounds that have nothing to do with the professions' distinctiveness, such as the high income and upper-middle-class status of many professionals.

Profession appears to be one of the many ''natural concepts,'' fraught with ideology, that social science abstracts from everyday life. The most common ideal-type of profession combines heterogeneous elements and links them by implicit though untested propositions—such as the proposition that prestige and autonomy flow ''naturally'' from the cognitive and normative bases of professional work. Many elements of the definition reproduce the institutional means and the sequence by which the older professions gained their special status. Others do not seem to take notice of empirical evidence or even of common knowledge about the professions; for instance, the notion of professions as ''communities'' does not fit very well with the wide discrepancies of status and rewards which we know exist within any profession. It is also somewhat disturbing to note that competence and the service ideal play as central a role in the sociological ideal-type as they do in the self-justification of professional privilege.

The elements that compose the ideal-type of profession appear to be drawn from the practice and from the ideology of the established professions; medicine, therefore, as the most powerful and successful of these, should approximate most closely the sociological criteria of what professions are and do. This is undoubtedly one of the reasons for the centrality of medicine in the sociology of professions. And yet empirical studies of medical practice challenge the validity of the sociological model at almost every step: they question, for instance, the effectiveness (and even the existence) of colleague control;[6] they show that ''ascribed'' characteristics of the clientele are at least as important as ''universalistic'' or scientific methods of diagnosis and therapy;[7] they show that in medicine as well as in the law, a practitioner's status is as closely related to the status of his clientele as to his own skill.[8] Historical studies of nineteenth-century medicine, moreover, destroy the notion that "regular" physicians had, in general, any more competence than their "irregular" competitors.[9] In brief, these ideal-typical constructions do not tell us what a profession is, but only what it pretends to be. The "Chicago School" of sociology—represented, most notably, by Everett C. Hughes and his followers—is critical of this approach, and asks instead what professions actually do in everyday life to negotiate and maintain their special position. The salient characteristics of the professional phenomenon emerge, here, from the observation of actual practices.

In his pathbreaking analysis of medicine, Freidson does much to clarify the nature of professional privilege and the processes by which it is asserted. His examination of the "archetypal" profession leads him to argue that "a profession is distinct from other occupations in that it has been given the right to control its own work." Among other occupations, "only the profession has the recognized right to declare . . . 'outside' evaluation illegitimate and intolerable."[10] This distinctive autonomy is, however, only technical and not absolute. Professions ultimately depend upon the power of the state, and they originally emerge by the grace of powerful protectors. The privileged position of a profession "is thus secured by the political and economic influence of the elite which sponsors it."[11]

Freidson's analysis has important implications. First, the cognitive and normative elements generally used to define profession are undoubtedly significant; but they should not be viewed as stable and fixed characteristics, the accumulation of which gradually allows an occupation to approximate the "complete" constellation of professional features. These cognitive and normative elements are important, instead, because they can be used (with greater or lesser success) as arguments in a process which involves both struggle and persuasion. In this process, particular groups of people attempt to negotiate the boundaries of an area in the social division of labor and establish their own control over it. Persuasion tends to be typically directed to the outside—that is, to the relevant elites, the potential public or publics, and the political authorities. Conflict and struggle around who shall be included or excluded mark the process of *internal* unification of a profession.

Second, an account of the process by which professions emerge illuminates the fact that professions *gain* autonomy: in this protected position, they can develop with increasing independence from the ideology of the dominant social elites. The production of knowledge appears to play a more and more strategic and seemingly autonomous role in the dynamics of these special occupations. If professions obtain extended powers of self-evaluation and self-control they can become almost immune to external regulation. The fact remains, however, that their privileges can always be lost. If a profession's work or actual performance "comes to have little relationship to the knowledge and values of its society, it may have difficulty surviving."[12] Revolutionary social change should therefore have profound implications for professional practice because it affects, in both relative and absolute terms, the social status that established professions had achieved in previous regimes.[13]

In the central part of his study, Freidson examines the potential for producing *ideology* that is inherent in the status of profession. This potential exists not only because cognitive and normative elements are used ideologically, as instruments in an occupation's path toward professional status, but also because, once reached, this structural position allows a group of experts to define and construct particular areas of social reality, under the guise of universal validity conferred on them by their expertise. The profession is, in fact, allowed to define the very standards by which its superior competence is judged. Professional autonomy allows the experts to select almost at will the inputs they will receive from the laity. Their autonomy thus tends to insulate them: in part, professionals live within ideologies of their own creation, which they present to the outside as the most valid definitions of specific spheres of social reality.

In a sense, the more traditional view of the professions starts where Freidson arrives after a long process of analysis. Talcott Parsons writes, for instance:

> The importance of the professions to social structure may be summed up as follows: the professional type is the institutional framework in which many of our most important social functions are carried on, notably the pursuit of science and liberal learning and its practical application in medicine, technology, law and teaching. This depends on an institutional structure the maintenance of which is not an automatic consequence of belief in the importance of the functions as such, but involves a complex balance of diverse social forces.[14]

Yet in most cases, the "ideal-typical" or institutional approach tends to emphasize the functional relations of professions with central social needs and values, at the expense of the "complex balance of diverse social forces" which supports such relations. The functional importance of the professions appears to explain the historical continuity of the oldest among them, medicine and the law. The evolution of these two, and the professionalization of other occupations, pertains to general dimensions of "modernization"—the advance of science and cognitive rationality and the progressive differentiation and rationalization of the division of labor in industrial societies.

While the attributes of special status and prestige imply that the professions are linked to the system of social stratification, the emphasis on the cognitive and normative dimensions of profession tends to separate these special categories of the social division of labor from the class structure in which they also are inserted.[15] In particular, the ethics of disinterestedness claimed by professionals appear to acquit them of the capitalist profit motive. The ideal-typical approach seldom takes account of the concrete historical conditions in which groups of specialists have attempted to establish a monopoly over specific areas of the division of labor. The class context in which authority is delegated and privileges are granted to these particular occupations tends to be neglected. Thus, while Freidson's analysis emphasizes that a profession must gain support from strategic social or political groups, the institutional approach suffers from a tendency to present professions as categories which emerge from the division of labor in unmediated connection with society as a whole.

Both sociological ideal-types and the self-presentation of professions imply that the professions are independent from or at least neutral vis-à-vis the class structure. Professionals can be viewed as themselves constituting a class—especially if class is reduced to its indicators, socioeconomic status and occupation. But the emphasis on the professions' cognitive mastery and the implication of "class neutrality" place them, rather, in the stratum of educated and "socially unattached" intellectuals whom Karl Mannheim described in these terms:

> Although they are too differentiated to be regarded as a single class, there is, however, one unifying sociological bond between all groups of intellectuals, namely, education, which binds them together in a striking way. Participation in a common educational heritage progressively tends to suppress differences of birth, status, profession, and wealth, and to unite the individual educated people on the basis of the education they have received. . . . One of the most impressive facts about modern life is that in it, unlike preceding cultures, intellectual activity is not carried on exclusively by a socially rigidly defined class, such as a priesthood, but rather by a social stratum which is to a large degree unattached to any social class and which is recruited from an increasingly inclusive area of social life.[16]

Mannheim's notion that cultural life in capitalist societies was becoming "increasingly detached from a given class" contrasts sharply with the Marxist tradition.[17] Marxist thought concedes to intellectuals a measure of autonomy and detachment from any predetermined social group, but it sees those attributes as a potential which remains within the confines of a class society. In the same perspective, intellectual products either break with the dominant ideology (by a self-conscious effort of their authors), or remain within its bounds.[18] The social function of intellectuals is normally that of consciously articulating, propagating, and organizing culture and ideology, giving them internal coherence and realistic flexibility. For Antonio Gramsci, intellectuals—a category that includes practically all "intellect workers"—are "organically" tied to the class whose interests are actually upheld by the intellectuals' work and productions. Intellectuals are obviously of strategic importance for the ruling class, whose power cannot rest on coercion alone but needs to capture the "moral and intellectual direction" of society as a whole. A revolutionary class must secrete and develop its own "organic" intellectuals in order to challenge the hegemonic power of the ruling class and strengthen the "counter-hegemonic" consciousness of the masses. A complex historical formation includes, however, intellectuals whose function in the "organization of culture" is not as directly linked to the maintenance of ruling class hegemony. Gramsci calls them "traditional" intellectuals: their organic ties to the ruling class have been lost, because they remained attached to a class which itself has lost its central position of power; other, more vital groups of intellectuals have superseded them in the creation and transmission of ideology. The relative social superfluity of "traditional" intellectuals enhances their isolation within institutions that are relatively autonomous from the state and the predominant fractions of the ruling class. "Traditional" intellectuals thus tend to constitute closed, caste-like bodies, which are particularly difficult for a revolutionary movement to co-opt or absorb. Defending corporate vested interests, they speak for abstract intellectual freedoms, for the independent service of disembodied knowledge and "pure" ideas. Examples of "traditional" intellectuals would be the clergy (in an increasingly secularized society), certain branches of the professoriat, and, in Gramsci's analysis of the Italian South, the legal "caste" tied to a landowning class which has not risen to national power.[19]

This outrageous oversimplification of Gramsci's analysis of the intelligentsia suggests, at least, why I think that analysis is so relevant for understanding the position and functions of professions in a class society. Different professions, and different groups *within* a profession, form different ties with a ruling class which itself consists of changing coalitions. The model of profession which emerges from most sociological ideal-types appears to confer upon the established professions the seal of "traditional intellectuality." Historical continuity is not only implied; it is deliberately and actively sought in the attempts by organized professions to give themselves a culture with roots in a classic past. The caste-like appearance of established professions is reinforced by their jealously defended autonomy and their guild-like characteristics. Yet this "traditional" presentation is contradicted by the professions' involvement in the everyday life of modern societies and also by the proximity to power of many professional elites. The contradiction is resolved if we recall that the "organic" or "traditional" character of a category of intellectual workers is not a static feature, but the outcome of a complex historical situation and of ongoing social and political conflicts.

It is clear, at this point, that Gramsci's perspective on the intelligentsia complements Freidson's account of how a particular occupation rises to the status and power of profession. As it rises, an occupation must form "organic" ties with significant fractions of the ruling class (or of a rising class); persuasion and justification depend on ideological resources, the import and legitimacy of which are ultimately defined by the context of hegemonic power in a class society; special bodies of experts are entrusted with the task of defining a segment of social reality, but this trust is also to be understood within the broad confines of the dominant ideology. One could say that the professions seek special institutional privileges which, once attained, steer them toward relatively "traditional" intellectual functions. But the need to defend these privileges, and particularly the professions' immersion in the everyday life of their society, counteract this tendency towards "traditionalism." Not surprisingly, the appearance of detachment and "pure" intellectual commitments is more marked in academic circles than in the consulting professions. However, one may ask with Freidson how far a profession (or an academic discipline) can move toward the "traditional" role and still retain social support; for, indeed, "traditional" intellectuals have little relationship to the predominant forms of knowledge and concerns of their society.

These brief comments on the literature suggest how the initial focus of my research began to shift as I looked at what contemporary sociology has to say about professions, and as I tried to relate the problem of professions to the more general problem of intellectuals in a class society. It appeared to me that the very notion of profession is shaped by the relationships which these special occupations form with a type of society and a type of class structure. Professions are not exclusively occupational categories: whatever else they are, professions are situated in the middle and upper-middle levels of the stratification system. Both objectively and subjectively, professions are outside and above the working class, as occupations and as social strata. In the first half of the nineteenth century, many professionals may have shared the life conditions of small artisans and shopkeepers; changing work conditions in our century may be drawing increasingly large numbers of professionals closer to a proletarian condition. The fact remains that individual professional status is still undeniably a middle-class attribute and a typical aspiration of the socially mobile children of industrial or clerical workers. The internal stratification of professions cannot be ignored; but the market of labor and services within which professionals operate is structurally different from the labor market faced by less qualified workers. Their relative superiority over and distance from the working class is, I think, one of the major characteristics that all professions and would-be professions have in common.

Another general point emerges from the sociological literature on professions: most studies implicitly or explicitly present professionalization as an instance of the complex process of "modernization." For professions, the most significant "modern" dimensions are the advance of science and cognitive rationality, and the related rationalization and growing differentiation in the division of labor. From this point of view, professions are typical products of modern industrial society.[20] The continuity of older professions with their "pre-industrial" past is therefore more apparent than real.

Modern professions made themselves into special and valued kinds of occupations during the "great transformation" which changed the structure and character of European societies and their overseas offshoots. This transformation was dominated by the reorganization of economy and society around the market.[21] The characteristic occupational structure of industrial capitalism and its characteristic mode of distributing rewards are therefore based on the market. Weber, in particular, defined the ability to command rewards in the marketplace as a function of both property and skills, and the possession of skills may be seen as a typically "modern" form of property.[22] A contemporary sociologist observes that "to characterize the occupational order as the backbone of the reward structure is not to ignore the role of property, but to acknowledge the interrelation between the one and the other."[23] And he adds: "Broadly considered, occupational groupings which stand high in the scale of material and symbolic advantages also tend to rank high in the possession of marketable skills. . . . To be sure, positions which rank high in expertise generally attempt to maintain or enhance their scarcity, and thus their reward-power, by various institutional means . . . it is no simple matter for an occupation to restrict its supply in this way."[24]

My intention is to examine here how the occupations that we call professions organized themselves to attain market power. I see professionalization as the process by which producers of special services sought to constitute *and control* a market for their expertise. Because marketable expertise is a crucial element in the structure of modern inequality, professionalization appears *also* as a collective assertion of special social status and as a collective process of upward social mobility. In other words, the constitution of professional markets which began in the nineteenth century inaugurated a new form of structured inequality: it was different from the earlier model of aristocratic patronage, and different also from the model of social inequality based on property and identified with capitalist entrepreneurship. In this sense, the professionalization movements of the nineteenth century prefigure the general restructuring of social inequality in contemporary capitalist societies: the "backbone" is the occupational hierarchy, that is, a differential system of competences and rewards; the central principle of legitimacy is founded on the achievement of socially recognized expertise, or, more simply, on a system of education and credentialing.

Professionalization is thus an attempt to translate one order of scarce resources—special knowledge and skills—into another—social and economic rewards. To maintain scarcity implies a tendency to monopoly: monopoly of expertise in the market, monopoly of status in a system of stratification. The focus on the constitution of professional markets leads to comparing different professions in terms of the "marketability" of their specific cognitive resources. It determines the exclusion of professions like the military and the clergy, which do not transact their services on the market.[25] The focus on collective social mobility accentuates the relations that professions form with different systems of social stratification; in particular, it accentuates the role that educational systems play in different structures of social inequality.

These are two different readings of the same phenomenon: professionalization and its outcome. The focus of each reading is analytically distinct. In practice, however, the two dimensions—market control and social mobility—are inseparable; they converge in the institutional areas of the market and the educational system, spelling out similar results but also generating tensions and contradictions which we find, unresolved or only partially reconciled, in the contemporary model of profession.

The image or model of profession which we commonly hold today, and which we find as well in social science, emerged both from social practice and from an ideological representation of social practice. The image began to be formed in the liberal phase of capitalism, but it did not become "public"—that is, commonly understood and widely accepted—until much later. Not by accident, the model of profession developed its most distinctive characteristics and the most clearcut emphasis on autonomy in the two paramount examples of laissez-faire capitalist industrialization: England and the United States. In the Anglo-Saxon societies (and, one could add, in Anglo-Saxon social science) the image of profession is one which implicitly accentuates the relation between professional privilege and the market. Profession is presented, for instance, as the antithesis of bureaucracy and the bureaucratic mode of work organization. The development of professions (and of their image) was, in a sense, less "spontaneous" in other European societies with long-standing state bureaucracies and strong centralized governments. For instance, engineering emerged in Napoleonic France as a *corps de l'état,* and this model has informed the aspirations of other professions, such as architecture; the Prussian legal profession was reformed by direct and repeated state intervention and remains to this day closely supervised and regulated by the state; Westernized medicine was similarly created in Tsarist Russia by the political authority.[26] The model of profession should be closer in these cases to that of the civil service than it is to professions in England or, especially, in the United States. For this reason, I believe it should present its "purer" features in the Anglo-Saxon countries.

In the United States, in particular, the model of profession has acquired a singular social import. It shapes, for one thing, the collective ambitions of occupational categories which in other countries could never hope to reach the status of profession. The extension of professionalization reflects, among other things, the particular openness of the American university to new fields of learning and the widespread access to higher education in American society.[27] Basing occupational entry on university credentials does not lead, in other words, to excessive social exclusiveness. Furthermore, professions are typical occupations of the middle class, and the vision of American society and culture as being essentially "middle class" is not challenged as strongly as it is in Europe by the alternative and autonomous vision of a politicized working class. The strategy of professionalization holds sway on individuals and occupational categories which are inspired elsewhere by the political and economic strategies of the labor movement.

To limit my analysis of profession and professionalization to England and the United States is not entirely an arbitrary choice, but it is a restrictive one. My account of the establishment and the meaning of professional privilege can in no way be generalized. However, because it is based on societies in which the professional model has developed the most freely out of the civil society, and where it structures the diffuse perceptions and aspirations of large numbers of people, it may help to illuminate efforts and representations which, in other societies, are less systematically tied to the model of profession than they are in the United States and England.

Finally, my historical account of professionalization is relevant to the experiences with which I started. The model of profession emerged during the "great transformation" and was originally shaped by the historical matrix of competitive capitalism. Since then, the conditions of professional work have changed, so that the predominant pattern is no longer that of the free practitioner in a market of services but that of the salaried specialist in a large organization. In this age of corporate capitalism, the model of profession nevertheless retains its vigor; it is still something to be defended or something to be attained by occupations in a different historical context, in radically different work settings, and in radically altered forms of practice. The persistence of profession as a category of social practice suggests that the model constituted by the first movements of professionalization has become *an ideology*—not only an image which consciously inspires collective or individual efforts, but a mystification which unconsciously obscures real social structures and relations. Viewed in the larger perspective of the occupational and class structures, it would appear that the model of profession passes from a predominantly economic function—organizing the linkage between education and the marketplace—to a predominantly ideological one—justifying inequality of status and closure of access in the occupational order. This book is concerned with exploring that passage.

PART I

THE ORGANIZATION
OF PROFESSIONAL MARKETS

Chapter 1

THE HISTORICAL MATRIX
OF MODERN PROFESSIONS

PRE-INDUSTRIAL ANTECEDENTS

Before the industrial revolution, the profile of the free practitioner was defined for lawyers and physicians, and, to a lesser degree, for architects as well.[1] But even the profession of law—which was the first to disengage itself, in the fourteenth century, from the tutelage of the Church—had not yet developed the stable and intimate connection with training and examinations that came to be associated with the professional model during the nineteenth century. This dependence on "objectively" legitimized competence is characteristic of the modern professions; it dates from the "great transformation" which became visible in England toward the end of the eighteenth century. The ethical concept of work which professions inherited from the Reformation is not much older. Professions are, therefore, relatively recent social products. However, a few elements from their pre-industrial past are important to recall, for they suggest why the post-revolutionary societies became a fertile ground for the professions' development and multiplication.

Specialization of function and the creation of special bodies of practical or theoretical knowledge are a function of the accumulation of resources. In preliterate societies, according to Wilbert Moore, the specialized services that are performed outside of kinship structures are those clearly connected with the "salience of the knowledge or skills for individual or collective welfare."[2] But, even before the appearance of writing, "salience" cannot be understood outside of the limits which the preservation of a given social order imposes on the possible definitions of "individual and collective welfare." Therefore, as soon as we consider class societies, the development of specialized roles and functions is broadly determined by the structure of inequality from which it is inseparable: dependent upon the unequal distribution of wealth, power, and knowledge, the institutionalization of specialized functions itself contributes to the unequal distribution of competence and rewards.

The emergence of the state differentiates the advisers of the rulers from the mass of the ruled. Writing, which allows the accumulation and transmission of knowledge on an unprecedented scale, is monopolized by a caste of scribes with special power. In general, all the special bodies of knowledge that appear in a class society can be monopolized by their creators-possessors. Moreover, the fruits of their application are also a monopoly: in effect, the services that rest on cognitive specialization are almost exclusively reserved to the small literate elites on whom the specialists depend for their existence.[3] Their association with elite groups is obvious for the law profession, and also for architecture in the great empires: although architects in Rome were often drawn from the class of slaves, architecture, whether private or official, was considered by Cicero and Vitruvius as "one of the learned professions for which men of good birth and good education are best suited."[4] As for medicine, given the universal need for healing and the ineffectiveness of most therapies, it was more sharply stratified and divided by the social position of the practitioners' clienteles than by the origins of the techniques that were applied.[5]

The distinction between "specialists for the elite" and "practitioners" for more popular clienteles became far clearer with the rise of institutionalized centers of learning, that is, with the rise of the universities in medieval Europe. With some exceptions, the medieval origins of the older professions show a bifurcation between university and guild. The universities had started as associations of students and teachers, or "guilds of learning," but they soon came under the dominating influence of the Church. Secularization gradually emancipated law and medicine from this tutelage. But the association with the university and, especially, the knowledge of Latin, distinguished the "learned" professions from the craft guilds that developed in the towns between the eleventh and the thirteenth century. The links with the Church, presumably, increased the aura of mystery surrounding the professions' esoteric knowledge, while Latin clearly associated them with the world of the elites. Their specialized counterparts in the guilds—scriveners, common lawyers, apothecaries, barber-surgeons, master-masons, millwrights—had relatively more democratic origins and clienteles. Some of these specialists appear, much later, in noble or rich households in a master-servant relationship with their aristocratic patrons.[6] As a rule, however, the common practitioners of the craft guilds appeared together with the urban markets of medieval Europe as free artisans and tradesmen. Their orientation was primarily commercial—that is, geared to a market of services. In England, these pre-professional specialists survived the decline of the craft guilds and, as the "lower branches" of medicine and the law, played a dynamic part in the nineteenth-century constitution of the modern professions.[7]

Two aspects of the professions' pre-industrial past deserve to be emphasized, for they illustrate well the continuity of form and discontinuities of substance between traditional and modern professions. First, from their pre-industrial days, the professions were closely bound to the stratification system. For the learned professions, establishment and social standing were equivalent to their association with the elites and with the state.[8] But until almost the nineteenth century, we cannot speak of an internal stratification of the professions, for "common" and "learned" practitioners inhabited different social worlds. Even though they practiced in related fields, the rigidity of the stratification system prevented the constitution of unified areas within the social division of labor. Thus, there were limitations to what their association with the dominant class could ensure for the learned professions: ensconced in the world of elites, they did not compete with their plebeian rivals and could have only weak claims against them. As Eliot Freidson remarks for medicine, passage through a university or membership in a guild gave physicians the means to distinguish themselves from other kinds of healers. These institutional links, however, did not establish their superiority in the eyes of a broad public; by themselves, these marks of distinction were not sufficient to monopolize the healing function. The favor of an elite did not necessarily bring with it wide public support.[9] To equip themselves for the conquest of public confidence was one of the main tasks of the professions during the "great transformation." Both logic and historical evidence indicate that the heirs of the pre-industrial professional elites were not the main actors in this effort: secure in their privileges, they had no urgent reason to become the vanguard of the modern process of professionalization.[10]

A second point, intimately related to the first, concerns the medieval association of the learned professions with the Church and the university: from this association, the established professional elites derived a clear notion that what distinguished them from traders and artisans was, chiefly, a "liberal education"—that is to say, an education fit for a gentleman, based more on classical culture than on practical skills. The latter had always been acquired through varied forms of apprenticeship, traditionally viewed as an extension of the education conducted within the family.[11] The social position and contacts of the family from which a youth set forth to be apprenticed to a father-like master defined the kind of master, and therefore the kind of training, he got. General culture was a further statement about rank, a way of acceding to the cultural province of an elite.

This conception of liberal education also affected the democratic United States, through its British heritage, and especially through the clergy's enormous influence on higher education: since education bore a clearly religious stamp, the study of the classics seemed useful and practical for the perpetuation of what was the moral and intellectual core of colonial community life.[12] Higher education was essentially classic, aimed at the formation of clergymen and gentlemen who would *later* acquire a trade, despite the efforts of men such as Franklin and Jefferson to give education a more practical and more secular imprint.

Thus, although formal education appears early in the professional constellation, its import changes radically with the assertion of a modern form of professionalism. The established professional elites could indeed secure their social position through their gentlemanly education, which symbolized their claims on social status; to claim superior competence was based on a different use of education and certification. The rise of a system of formal education which includes basic pre-professional instruction and practical training was crucial: it reorganized and superseded apprenticeship, thus signaling the triumph of a new conception of professionalism over the old one. From dependence upon the power and prestige of elite patrons or upon the judgment of a tightly knit community, the modern professions came to depend upon specific formal training and anonymous certificates.[13]

THE RISE OF MODERN PROFESSIONALISM

In the Anglo-Saxon world at the beginning of the nineteenth century, the recognized gentlemanly professions were, in practice, only three: divinity, and its recent offshoot university teaching; the law, which filled, with the exception of architecture, most of the relatively prestigious specializations that could be considered "professional" before the industrial revolution; and the profession of medicine.[14] In England, the three traditional professions were hierarchically divided into higher and lower branches. The hegemonic social position of the landed gentry reserved the careers in government and the military to those with family connections. In the professions, connections with eminent practitioners were more useful than connections with the Court, the Parliament, and the ecclesiastic hierarchy; but they similarly restricted the mobility of the middle orders and reinforced the predominance of patronage.[15]

The French Revolution had sharply signified, for France and for the world, that careers were to be open to talent. But even in France, except for the military in wartime and the government, the opening was more ideological than real until 1830 and the industrial take-off.[16] Both the rise of the modern professions and the reform of the civil service (which in Britain became a fact only after the Medical Act of 1858 and the 1855 report of the Civil Service Commission) were crucially linked to the use of the competitive examination system. This move by merit against birth and patronage was closely connected to the political fortunes of the middle classes and, in England, to the electoral reform of 1832. The democratization should not be overestimated; however, the constitution of modern professions and the emergence of a pattern of professional career represented for the middle classes a novel possibility of *gaining status through work.*[17]

The modern model of profession undoubtedly incorporates pre-industrial criteria of status and pre-industrial ideological orientations. Any concrete historical process, such as the first phase of modern professionalization, inextricably binds together elements which, analytically, pertain to different and even antithetic structural complexes. The collective project of professionalization, furthermore, has its roots in a time of radical and rapid change: the men involved in this project were the "carriers of social structure" and they carried the imprint of changing historical circumstances. Their product, however, was an innovation—if nothing else, because it reorganized and transferred into a new social world parts and patterns of the old.

The general circumstances which imprinted the first phase of professionalization were roughly the same for all the professions. Like most other forms of social organization, professions emerged together in a spurt which Carr-Saunders calls "a wave of association." This can be shown by considering the dates at which national professional associations were founded—not because the professional association is an equivalent of profession, but because it indicates the maturity of the professional project. In England and in the United States, to which I am limiting my analysis, the principal professional associations were formed in the span of two generations. In England, of the thirteen contemporary professions listed by Harold Wilensky as "established" or "in process," ten acquired an association of national scope between 1825 to 1880—a fifty-five year span. In the United States, eleven of the same thirteen were similarly organized into national associations in forty-seven years, from 1840 to 1887 (see Appendix Table 1).

The professions that were formed in America were clearly inspired by their European models—especially the British, in the beginning—but, obviously, there were structural differences between the New World and the old which account for many differences in the professional process and in the emergent pattern. Nevertheless, both in England and in the United States, modern professionalization is connected with the same general historical circumstances: it coincides, that is, with the rise of industrial capitalism, with its early crises and consolidation and, toward the end of the nineteenth century and the beginning of the twentieth, with the evolution of capitalism toward its corporate form.

In a seminal essay on organizations and social structure, Arthur Stinchcombe elaborates the proposition that a given society determines the "social technology" available for the invention of new organizational forms. Organizations with these new forms tend to appear, therefore, at the time when it is precisely possible to found them and when they can function effectively with their new structure. Effectiveness reinforces the tendency to institutionalize an organizational form; hence, organizational structures which were invented "at the right time" tend to become relatively stable. For Stinchcombe, the "social technology" available includes preeminently the "economic and technical conditions," which determine what *resources* will be available to the creators of new organizations. To these factors I would add ideological conditions, which, among other things, limit the alternatives available or imaginable and are a most important determinant of the motivation to organize. Ideological conditions are particularly relevant in the case of those organizations which, like the professions, aim at "increasing the amount of trustworthiness among strangers" in order to market expert advice.[18]

The type of resources mobilized by the professional project* had a determining impact on the resulting organizational and ideological structure. These resources were heterogeneous, for the available "social technology" mixed elements pertaining to the social division of labor with elements pertaining to status stratification in a time of rapid and fundamental social change.

Stinchcombe's analysis relates organizational capacity at a given time with certain basic societal variables which have a positive effect on both the "motivation to found organizations" and the "chances of success of new organizational forms." As a consequence, the rate at which new organizational forms appear tends to increase. These basic societal variables are "literacy, urbanization, money economy, political revolution, and previously existing organizational density."[19] That most of these general conditions greatly improved in England after 1830, and in America some decades later, hardly needs to be belabored.

It is true that education in England was hardly something to boast about, despite the survival of the parish schools and the liveliness of the Scottish universities. Eric Hobsbawm calls English higher education before 1848 a "joke in poor taste" and

---

*According to Webster, "project" means "a planned undertaking." As the term is currently used in sociological analysis, it does not mean that the goals and strategies pursued by a given group are entirely clear or deliberate for all the members, nor even for the most determined and articulate among them. Applied to the historical results of a given course of action, the term "project" emphasizes the coherence and consistence that can be discovered ex post facto in a variety of apparently unconnected acts.

adds that "special fears discouraged the education of the poor."[20] But literacy, at least, must have been common in the coarse business circles painted by Dickens. The conditions of the working poor were tragic, both before and after the repeal of the Poor Act; however, the political and cultural vitality of the working class, so admirably documented by E. P. Thompson, indirectly attests to the spread of literacy.[21] The Charter of 1839 was signed by 2,283,000 persons, and that of 1842 by 3,317,702.[22] The self-serving efforts of the middle classes to discipline the poor also afford indirect evidence of the spread of literacy: in 1787, "Robert Raikes estimated that a quarter of a million children were attending Sunday schools. . . . By 1833, the number . . . had increased to a million and a half."[23] In 1851, the year in which the urban population first outnumbered the rural, there were in England about 76,000 men and women, both laymen and religious, who described themselves as schoolteachers.[24] Primary education did not become compulsory until 1880, for children up to the age of ten.

In America, the public system of education began to take shape after 1860. By 1880, however, there were only 8.7 percent illiterates among native whites older than ten years—a fact which undoubtedly attests to the unreliability of statistics, but also probably to some progress in the spread of literacy in previous years.[25]

Besides literacy, the fantastic development of road networks, railways, the telegraph, the organization of a postal system, the multiplication of newspapers and periodicals, attest that the industrialized countries were accomplishing in the second half of the nineteenth century a qualitative leap in actual and potential communications.

Some facts are too well-known to bear much elaboration: the nineteenth-century industrial revolutions were preceded and then accompanied by an unprecedented acceleration in the annual rates of population growth. The shift in the distribution of labor from agriculture to manufacturing contributed to the sustained growth of towns and cities. The revolutionary transformation of the mode of production entailed an increase in the rate of growth of the gross national product that had no historical precedent. In other words, the term "industrial revolution" presupposes the transformation of agriculture and a revolutionary increase in agricultural productivity; it implies a correlation with a demographic revolution, with urbanization and with the sustained growth of aggregate measures of national wealth.[26]

Politically, the Anglo-Saxon countries had not experienced and would not experience (if we grant the American Civil War the status of a special political phenomenon) the revolutionary intensity that France had known and that the major European states would know as well in 1848 and thereafter. But the middle classes had won extended political rights in England in 1832, and by 1840 the United States had already experienced the disruptions of independence and the impact of Jacksonian democracy, which achieved, in most states, free suffrage for white males.

In France and in the United States outside the South, before the middle of the nineteenth century the larger concentrations of wealth were no longer in the hands of landowners. In Britain, despite the lingering economic predominance of the peerage, the income of peers depended more and more on the economic enterprises of the bourgeoisie. Hobsbawm warns, however, that the social transformation should not be exaggerated. The ranks of the middle classes were still quite thin: from 1801 to 1851, the number of people earning more than 150 pounds annually passed in

Britain from about 100,000 to about 340,000. Given the large families of the time, this means that approximately a million and a half persons, or about 7 percent of the total population, enjoyed this status. "Naturally," says Hobsbawm, "the number of those who sought to follow middle-class standards and ways of life was very much larger." But the rich among them were few. Hobsbawm thinks that those with incomes above 5000 pounds per year could not have numbered much more than 4,000, including the peerage, and he adds: "the proportion of 'middle-classes' in other countries was not notably higher than this, and indeed was generally rather lower."[27]

The modern professions were spawned, thus, by incomplete but nonetheless awesome developments. The possibility of organizational creation had arisen for them, as well as for the industrial bourgeoisie that was "shaping the world in its image." But the resources for the professional project were still limited, as attested by the narrowness of their potential middle-class clientele—which was the only imaginable one, besides the traditional elites. In England, the working masses, for the most part living close to abject poverty, inhabited the "other nation," outside the ken of bourgeois "civilization." And although the market for professional services was potentially larger in the United States, it was in fact limited by other factors: the newness and dispersion of Western settlements, the ideological resistance everywhere, the modesty of the average standards of living. Emerging themselves with an emergent social order, the professions first had to create a market for their services. Next, and this was inseparable from the first task, they had to gain special status for their members and give them respectability. The organizational devices they used reflected both the new and the traditional social order, drawn as they were from two different worlds.

Chapter 2

THE CONSTITUTION
OF PROFESSIONAL MARKETS

The emergence of professional markets in the competitive phase of capitalism was an accessory development in a much more formidable transformation. In structure and ideology, the emerging modern professions foreshadowed much that could be realized in practice only in our century, when capitalism entered its corporate phase. In the first half of the nineteenth century, however, when professions began to organize and reform themselves, they were part of a world that was being subverted and reshaped by "the utopian endeavor of economic liberalism to set up a self-regulating market system."[1] These words, as well as the very expression "great transformation," are Karl Polanyi's; the general thrust of his brilliant interpretation is well known:

> For a century, the dynamics of modern society was governed by a double movement: the market expanded continuously but this movement was met by a countermovement checking the expansion in definite directions. Vital though such a countermovement was for the protection of society, in the last analysis, it was incompatible with the self-regulation of the market, and thus with the market system itself.[2]

Now it is customary to say that professions are "those occupations in which *caveat emptor* cannot be allowed to prevail and which, *while they are not pursued for gain,* must bring to their practitioners income of such a level that they will be respected and such a manner of living that they may pursue the life of the mind."[3] It would be tempting, then, to consider the professions as expressions of Polanyi's "countermovement" and thus account for their paradoxical position: for they are, in fact, one of the distinctive features of industrial capitalism, even though they claim to renounce the profit motive and appear to some as "a mere survival of the medieval guild."[4] But such an account would not only be too simple; it would also incorporate uncritically much of the professions' appearances and ideological self-conceptions.

A first step to render modern professions sociologically intelligible is to reflect on their historical origins: professions were and are means of earning an income on the basis of transacted services; in a society that was being reorganized around the centrality of the market, the professions could hardly escape the effects of this reorganization. The modern model of profession emerges as a consequence of the necessary response of professional producers to new opportunities for earning an income. A collective effort was needed on the part of the actual or potential sellers of services to capture and control expanded markets. For this, new forms of eliciting and guaranteeing the buyers' preference and trust had to be devised and implemented.

From this point of view, the constitution of modern professional markets represents one more instance of social reorganization around the "cash nexus," since a market society means that the money bond has become a predominant principle of social cohesion.[5] The motor of the transformation was the revolutionary affirmation and extension of the capitalist mode of production: after its first steps had been duly protected by state and monopoly privileges, capitalism—that is, its entrepreneurial leaders and intellectual spokesmen—rejected all traditional restrictions to the indispensable development of competitive markets.

The professions were in a special position: unlike the early capitalist industries, they were not exploiting already existing markets but were instead working to create them.[6] The most lucrative markets were small and monopolized: through patronage and frozen corporate privileges, castes of traditional professionals controlled the access to universities and guilds, and thereby to elite clienteles. Below these guarded grounds, competition was keen. The task of professional organizers was twofold: to open the ranks of traditional professional elites by direct or indirect attack upon their gatekeeping institutions; and to organize the expanded markets opened by urbanization and by the relative enrichment of certain publics.

Ancien régime privileges had hindered, though never stopped, the rise of a new class and the disintegration of the old social order. Where political revolution smashed the privilege of guilds and corporations, as it did in France, new warrants of professional worth had to be devised swiftly. Where change was more gradual, as in England, the traditional professional elites had more time to respond and adjust; nevertheless, their insufficient arrangements for controlling an expanding profession and an expanding market had to be replaced. Even if the institutional mechanisms that emerged seemed less new than in post-revolutionary societies, or less effective than those imposed from above by a centralized state, they still served analogous functions with regard to the widened market for professional services. The secular processes that prepared bourgeois hegemony had also altered the pre-industrial social matrix of the professions: for one thing, urbanization had already begun to dissolve in the eighteenth century the "interfusing of family, community, and profession which for long remained typical of nineteenth-century villages, small towns, and even urban neighborhoods."[7] Elite clienteles could always confer special status to their favored practitioners, as they still do in our day; they could not, however, serve as guarantors for every profession, nor deliver to their protégés the means to conquer wide and anonymous publics.

COMMUNITY-ORIENTED AND MARKET-ORIENTED SOCIETY

In the United States and England, as in most other European societies, the professional modernization that started in the nineteenth century was oriented toward a society in which community and aristocratic tradition were no longer sufficient to guarantee credit and credibility. The ideal-typical passage from community-oriented to market-oriented society gives similar contours to the task faced by professional reformers. Concrete historical contexts in turn, determine what resources are available for such an effort, sharpening the contours of the general model and marking the limits of its usefulness.

In late eighteenth-century England, economic and social transformations had only begun to encroach upon the well-guarded bastions of the traditional professional elites. Yet the existence of a national market and the success of the English Revolution of 1688 had signaled the definitive dissolution of the feudal order since the seventeenth century.[8] The advance of bourgeois society in the wake of the structural transformations of the economy could not have left unaffected the conditions of professional practice.

The official professional elites of the Royal College of Physicians or the Inns of Court, centered in London, had monopolized since ancient times the right to license medical practitioners or to call lawyers to the bar. The rise of the "middle orders," however, had multiplied the numbers of practitioners who were in the lower branches, and thus excluded from the institutionalized sanctions of professional status. Medical practitioners of lower standing practiced chiefly in the provinces, outside the jurisdiction of the traditional corporations, and they worked in expanding though bitterly competitive markets. From the sixteenth century on, there is evidence, both in England and abroad, of a growing number of medical men. By the seventeenth century, extensive practices were bringing substantial wealth to an elite of London physicians, while lower down in the social hierarchy apothecaries were practicing medicine and setting themselves apart from shopkeeping druggists. In the eighteenth century, the apothecaries' standing as bona fide medical practitioners was recognized, even though their clientele as well as their status were quite modest, compared to those of the Royal College fellows, or the licentiates, or the increasingly prestigious surgeons.[9]

In the law, attorneys and solicitors—an amalgamated class, for all practical purposes—were reaching in this century the position they occupy at present in the English legal system. The Inns of Court discouraged their membership and excluded them from the bar, unless they abandoned their practice in the lower branch for at least two years before being called. However, the already expanding business of representing and counselling the government's various departments fell entirely into the hands of attorneys and solicitors. Strengthened by their new respectability, they had begun to organize in voluntary societies since the first decades of the eighteenth century. "Complaints were made", we are told, "of the number of attornies; and the difficulty of applying any measure of discipline was increased by the existence of 'vagabond attornies', that is, attornies with no fixed address."[10] To this, Parliament responded with the regulatory act of 1729. Formed in the 1730s, the Society of Gentlemen Practisers in the Courts of Law and Equity, in turn, took up supervision and enforcement of the act's provisions against unworthy attorneys as one of its main tasks.

Toward the end of the eighteenth century, pressures for professional organization were mounting. The most significant and longer-lasting of these movements came from outside the small worlds of the traditional professional corporations. With the decline of amateur and clerical practitioners, professional callings had become full-time specialized vocations. Urbanization and improved communications were breaking the isolation of the large numbers of provincial practitioners.[11] Expressing the general movement of the bourgeoisie for national reform, the organizational efforts of the new professional societies were centrally concerned with regulating competition, and therefore with the terms of access to the marks of professional fitness. As demands for entry or recognition increased, the traditional professional bodies tended to respond by making membership more exclusive. Both the Inns of Court and the Royal College of Physicians reasserted the privileges of Oxford and Cambridge graduates, even though the two ancient universities could hardly be commended for their standards of legal or medical education.[12] Passage through the hallowed English universities—from which Catholics, Dissenters and all but a few poor commoners were excluded, either de jure or de facto—was, if nothing else, a test of social fitness. In fact, the elite professionals of the traditional corporations tended to reserve entry into their ranks to those whom they considered social peers.

Thus, despite the existence of a minority of very successful middle class practitioners, the "first-class" marks of professional distinction were practically monopolized by aristocratic or quasi-aristocratic elites. That these marks were significant for the successful practitioners in the "lower branches" of medicine and law is shown by the leading role they took in the efforts to democratize the government of the traditional corporations. The bulk of the rising professional middle class was even more seriously damaged by the traditional monopolies over professional titles. Beyond the local sphere in which reputations were established, there were few recognized guarantees of competence and probity. Without these visible signs, respectable common practitioners found themselves helpless against the competition of the unscrupulous and the inept, who proliferated in unregulated markets. Their problems were sometimes acknowledged by the traditional corporations but seldom acted upon with determination. The position of the professional middle class was improved almost solely by the organizational efforts of their own leaders and of their own voluntary associations, which moved both against traditional monopolies over titles and licenses to practice, and against the competition of disreputable "colleagues."

Such pressure to break the closed ranks of a professional caste did not arise in America until much later. There had been great progress in higher education and the importation of British professional models in the eighteenth century, but the colonies remained poor, provincial, and sparsely populated. In a decentralized setting, the nine American colleges that existed before the Revolution could not hold the same consecrating power that Oxford and Cambridge held, despite their intellectual and political liveliness. These colleges gave a gentlemanly seal to those many graduates who did not enter the professions; the more numerous graduates who entered the ministry, most especially, or the law, or lastly medicine, constituted an elite among professionals. In the two secular callings, those practitioners who had studied abroad were an elite of the elite.[13] The bar, in particular, had risen to great power and prestige during the eighteenth century: from being an occupation of "mostly pettifoggers and minor court officers . . . who stirred up litigation for the sake of the petty court fees," it had become in urban centers a social and political elite which matched the clergy in importance and tended toward closure.[14] The Revolution purged the bar of its best practitioners, democratizing it, on the whole, but also setting back the general standards of a profession based on apprenticeship and creating a wide gap between the urban legal elites, who shaped the new republic's institutions, and the mass of a growing profession.[15]

But the existence of urban and Eastern professional elites did not mean that they constituted the apex of a recognized professional hierarchy. The difference between cities that looked to Europe and hinterland communities created almost unbridgeable chasms in all professions and trades. In remote frontier areas, geographic isolation assured a de facto monopoly to the lone attorney or physician; it must, however, have been a short-lived advantage, since isolation and decentralization also made self-appointment easy and thus made competition keener. Moreover, professional practice in eighteenth-century America most often was a part-time avocation, except for clergymen, one of whom each township was legally required to support in the old settlements, and who often doubled as part-time lawyers or healers. But even the clergy, which enjoyed in smaller towns the undisputed position of an intellectual elite, was prevented by denominationalism and decentralization from forming a united hierarchy. The clergy, besides, was unable to maintain its lifetime tenure and traditional social standing, as economic development and its sequel of regional depressions shook the foundations of stable community life.[16]

Thus even if decentralization, social mobility, and religious tolerance kept the American professional hierarchy much more open and fluid than in England, the differential sanction of different communities also distinguished in the United States the established urban professionals from the upstarts, the "learned" from the empirics, the gentle from the coarse, and soon, the native sons from the striving immigrants as well. Yet in an expanding social context, restricted professional monopolies could not hold for long. Whether it was the challenge against corporate privileges characteristic of professional modernization in England, or the decline of community warrants which affected both England and the United States, the breakdown of particularistic legitimations demanded the organization or the reconstruction of the competitive professional markets that were emerging in urban centers. In all walks of life, the industrial revolution was separating work and training from the household and from the community. Professional work was becoming a *full-time* means of earning a livelihood, subject to the dictates of capitalist competition for income and profit. To insure their livelihood, the rising professionals had to unify the corresponding areas of the social division of labor around homogeneous guarantees of competence. The unifying principles could be homogeneous only to the extent that they were universalistic—that is, autonomously defined by the professionals and independent, at least in appearance, from the traditional and external guarantees of status stratification. Thus, the modern reorganization of professional work and professional markets tended to found credibility on a different, and much enlarged, monopolistic base—the claim to sole control of superior expertise.

THE ORGANIZATIONAL TASK

The "great transformation" presented the professional "entrepreneurs" with expanding and "free" markets: despite the profound differences in social structure among the national societies that underwent the transformation, the general task of professional organization had similar structural requirements. It was substantively different, however, from the task that industrial entrepreneurs had confronted.

First, for a professional market to exist in a modern sense, a distinctive "commodity" had to be produced. Now professional work, like any other form of labor, is only a *fictitious* commodity; it "cannot be detached from the rest of life, be stored or mobilized," and it is not produced for sale.[17] Unlike craft or industrial labor, however, most professions produce intangible goods: their product, in other words, is only formally alienable and is inextricably bound to the person and the personality of the producer. It follows, therefore, that *the producers themselves have to be produced* if their products or commodities are to be given a distinctive form. In other words, the professionals must be adequately trained and socialized so as to provide recognizably distinct services for exchange on the professional market.

Second, in the formative period, most of the markets for professional services had to be created, for the existing markets were unstable and far from unified; common standards of what this unique commodity—intangible services—meant, and even of what needs it served, were lacking. For a secure market to arise, the superiority of one kind of services had to be clearly established with regard to competing "products." The various professional services, therefore, had to be *standardized* in order to clearly differentiate their identity and connect them, in the minds of consumers, with stable criteria of evaluation. A tendency to monopoly by *elimination* of competing "products" was inherent in this process of standardization; for if other standards of evaluation were allowed to prevail, the preference of the public could not easily be reclaimed away from older "consumer loyalties." Professional entrepreneurs, not unlike their counterparts in industry, were therefore bound to solicit state protection and state-enforced penalties against unlicensed competitors—that is to say, those producers of services whose training and entry into the market they had not controlled. However, no amount of coercion could force a clientele to switch allegiances and seek professional services which it did not even know it needed— at least not in the form that the leaders of professional reform were giving to those professional services. To establish in the public at large common bases for an evaluation of both need and professional competence was, therefore, an ideological task to which the rising professions actively contributed; but obviously, its magnitude was such that it could not be advanced by their efforts alone—ideological persuasion ultimately depended on the completion of the general social shift to a new "symbolic universe."[18] In consequence, the road that the professional reformers had mapped in the liberal phase of capitalism could not be traveled to the end with the "social technology" they had available.

Third, because the standardization of professional services is bound to the production of producers—that is to say, to education—it depends upon inducing new recruits to accept the economic and social sacrifices of training. Hence, at least a moderate guarantee that the recruits' educational investment would be protected had to be sought from the beginning. In a market situation, the guarantee against risks incurred tends to take the form of monopoly, or at least of special protection by the public authorities. In this case, the nature of the products and the state of their markets were such that only the state, as the supreme legitimizing and enforcing institution, could sanction the modern professions' monopolistic claims of superiority for their "commodities." The attitude of the state toward education and toward monopolies of competence is thus a crucial variable in the development of the professional project.

In sum, creating professional markets required, as in every other case, establishing social credit or, to paraphrase Durkheim, creating non-contractual bases of contract. Because of the pre-existing competition, this task demanded strong and quasi-monopolistic protective devices. Because of the unique nature of the products to be marketed, and because their use value to the large public was as uncertain as it was new, control had to be established first "at the point of production": the providers of services had to be controlled in order to standardize and thus identify the "commodity" they provided. For this, a cognitive basis was crucial. The *kind* of knowledge that each profession could claim as distinctively its own was therefore a strategic factor of variation in their organizational effort. However, a cognitive basis of any kind had to be at least approximately defined before the rising modern professions could negotiate *cognitive exclusiveness*—that is, before they could convincingly establish a teaching monopoly on their specific tools and techniques, while claiming absolute superiority for them. The proved institutional mechanisms for this negotiation were the license, the qualifying examination, the diploma, and formal training in a common curriculum. The typical institutions that administered these devices were, first, the guild-like professional association, and later the professional school, which superseded the association in effectiveness.

Obviously, none of this was in itself an organizational invention. The guilds of merchants that sprang up in eleventh-century Europe were also voluntary associations tending toward the monopolistic control of a *new* form of trade. The craft guilds, which were organized everywhere by the thirteenth century, were also devices for establishing social credit in a phase of rapid development of small commodity production. In that historical situation, the merchant guilds moved from de facto monopoly to a right acknowledged by lords and cities. The assembling of producers along craft lines was encouraged by the public authorities as a means of regulating the new urban markets. That the craft guilds later strove to emancipate themselves from the municipal tutelage probably had more to do with the politics of the medieval cities than with the dynamics of professionalism.[19] Nevertheless, the survival of the guild form in the midst of the industrial revolution no longer appears paradoxical: it suggests, rather, that associations of "free" producers backed by public authorities and tending toward monopoly are a general feature in the constitution of new markets based on free skilled labor.

What was genuinely new in the strategy adopted by professional reformers for constituting and controlling their markets was neither the tactical devices they employed, nor even their institutional forms, but the particular combination of these elements into a specific structure. The kinds of market warrants that were needed by the modern professional entrepreneurs had, in turn, new and vastly significant structural implications. These warrants ultimately rest upon the predominance of formal training over various forms of apprenticeship. They attain their full effectiveness when the production of professional producers is conducted within monopolistic systems of education: in their modern form, these systems appear to match rewards with merit by means of formally universalistic criteria of recruitment and promotion. This appearance legitimizes both monopoly and the hierarchical organization of educational systems.

The establishment of national systems of public and compulsory education was in some cases led "from above" by "enlightened" autocratic states; in others it was the piecemeal outcome of diverse ideological and political struggles. In the latter instances, it coincided with the bourgeoisie's conquest of social hegemony.[20] In England, the first industrial society, it was the middling professional men who led the public negotiation of cognitive exclusiveness, in their effort to unseat the traditional professional elites and to separate themselves from the trades. Their progress involved nothing less than the creation of a graded system of comprehensive education and the reorientation of its higher-level institutions. It was hindered by the peculiarities of England's stratification system and by the persistent ideological influence of its aristocracy.[21]

The formidable task of setting up the educational apparatus of bourgeois hegemony involved the whole structure of each society and was shaped by each society's historical development. It necessarily concerned more numerous and diverse social forces than the narrow professional sector of the middle classes. What varied nationally and historically were the particular balances achieved between the upper classes, the clergy, sectors of the industrial bourgeoisie, *ancien régime* intellectuals, and the "organic" intellectuals of the capitalist class, including the professional reformers and organizers.[22] However, the structures that emerged were analogous beneath the surface: *insofar as they were modern,* all levels of the new educational systems were spawned by capitalist industrialization. Determined by the specific class structure of each capitalist society, they determined it in turn, functioning as the characteristic instruments of legitimation of the mature capitalist order. The professions contributed their own specific amalgams of old and new ideological structures to the emerging systems of national education. They were obviously not the only ones to do so, but they led the way in asserting the crucial social function of credentialing systems.

To recapitulate and complete the steps of this analysis: the passage from restricted monopolies of practice to the organization and control of expanded and competitive markets was a necessary one for the professional sectors of the middle class, seeking to improve their position in the emergent stratification systems of capitalist society. Their task presupposed the abandonment—deliberate or involuntary—of the restrictive corporate warrants of professional credibility. It tended toward the reconstruction of monopoly on the universalistic principles dictated by the new dominant ideology. The crowning of this monopolistic project appears to be a set of legally enforced monopolies of practice. However, the actual effectiveness of such sanctions depends on the parallel construction of a "monopoly of credibility" with the larger public. The conquest of official privilege and public favor was, for the professions, a double *external* task of ideological persuasion, which had an *internal* precondition: the unification of the corresponding areas of the social division of labor under the direction of a leading group of professional reformers. The crucial means for this unification, and therefore the concrete core of the professions' organizational task, was systematic training—or, in my terms, the standardized and centralized production of professional producers.

Traditional professional elites had monopolized the marks of distinction conferred by universities. But the actual content of their education, in relation to professional practice, was not that important: protected by traditional corporate privileges, the old professional elites did not need to submit their specific "commodities" to the test of market competition. Market competition, on the other hand, determines the necessary centrality of both training *and* the content of training in the structure of modern professions. The importance of *cognitive* exclusiveness in the control of expanded professional markets suggests some additional remarks.

The industrial revolution and the consolidation of capitalist social systems created new areas of practice and new occupational roles. The application of science to industry and to practically every other area of life gradually and constantly changed the cognitive bases of the social division of labor. It is logical to assume that their structural position in the division of labor gave an advantage to certain occupations: from the point of view of cognitive exclusiveness, those professions or professional sectors which had the opportunity of appropriating and standardizing *new* bodies of knowledge should have been favored in the creation of a distinctive "commodity" and in the attainment of a monopoly of competence. New techniques should be susceptible of monopolization by their inventors or first users: the novelty of a knowledge should therefore facilitate the task of erecting protective boundaries around it.

Professions, however, were not always in control of new knowledge relevant to their practice, for the good reason that much of it was produced by outsiders—researchers in related scientific fields, and also practical men in politics, in business, and in the arts. A profession's cognitive base can evolve in complete independence from the profession itself and from its production of professional producers, *until the production of knowledge and the production of producers are unified into the same structure*. Or, in other words: the link between research and training institutionalized by the modern model of university gives to university-based professions the means to control their cognitive bases. Once again, the emergence of modern systems of education—and here, in particular, the transformation of their higher branches into centers for the production of knowledge—appears as the central hinge of the professional project.

The monopolistic and standardized production of professional producers is a necessary step in the march toward market control, but it is by no means a sufficient one: indeed, the structure of the market in which a profession transacts its services does not depend on the profession's action and intentions—or at least not until the profession gains considerable social power. The structure of a particular profession market is determined by the broader social structure which shapes the social need for a given service and therefore defines the actual or potential publics of a given profession.

In conclusion, to view professional modernization as a project of market control underlines the central role of the state in the development of this project, most particularly its function of sponsoring monopolistic education systems. This point of view explains the crucial importance of two components: the professional project combines them into one complex structure, even though their character and evolution can be, until then, totally independent from each other. Those components are the potential market for a professional service, on the one hand, and on the other, the cognitive basis to which this service is or can be tied.

In the next chapter I will consider in some detail the characteristic market situation of medicine: everywhere, it was one of the first professions to strive for internal unification, although it could not become until much later the leading model of professional power and success. This analysis will lay the ground for a paradigmatic view of the constellation of elements which can increase a profession's chances of attaining market control. A comparison of medicine with engineering will then allow me to explore the interplay between market structure and the cognitive basis of a profession.

Chapter 3

AN ANALYSIS OF MEDICINE'S PROFESSIONAL SUCCESS

To analyze the structure of the market for medicine we must ask how the nature of the medical "commodity" determines, at least in part, the size of the market, the typical modes of exchange, the intensity and variety of competition, and the attitudes of the public authorities toward regulation. Secondly, we must ask how changes in the nature of the commodity affected the chances of success of the professional entrepreneurs who were attempting to unify and control the medical market.

THE MARKET FOR MEDICAL SERVICES

The first and most obvious fact to consider is that the market for medicine is based on a vital and universal need: its potential for expansion is therefore unlimited, at least in principle. The general ideological climate of Western societies has favored the functions medicine claims to serve; the value of individual life, rooted in the Judaeo-Christian religious tradition, and individualism in general, have formed one of the strongest ideological dimensions of the post-feudal world. However, the actualization of this potential depended, for medicine, on factors other than the possible size of the market.

To begin with, the paying clientele in the nineteenth century was still quite narrow. But with more people becoming moderately affluent, and the already affluent getting richer, the perception that the practice of medicine was profitable to at least *some* physicians encouraged entry into the field.[1] The appearance of a market in urban centers, and, particularly in America, in rural areas as well,[2] set in motion the mechanisms for the standardized production of producers outlined in the preceding chapter. In England, the main problem was to tie the serious forms of training that the "lower branches"—surgeons and apothecaries—were organizing in their schools and teaching hospitals to a title of uniform prestige. In America, the absence of restrictive corporate monopolies, such as that of the British Royal College of Physicians, permitted an unbridled expansion of the supply of physicians. Proprietary schools, with requirements as lax as their curricula were brief, proliferated in the first two-thirds of the nineteenth century, rapidly substituting their diplomas for the license which medical societies had granted in most states since the eighteenth century.[3] After 1825, competition for students among these schools led to a general decline of standards and requirements. The schools, nevertheless, had a powerful effect which apprenticeship by itself could never have attained: they induced a rapid growth of the profession, while standardizing medical practice to an extent as yet unknown.[4]

However, the state of medical science in the first half of the century and its particular lack of distinction in the United States implied that standardization was conducted on the basis of mostly ineffective therapies and unfounded pathological theories. The total freedom of the market and the ease with which schools could be set up institutionalized, in America, the characteristic sectarian divisions of its medicine. The "regular" doctors who founded the American Medical Association in 1847 and controlled most state societies, as well as many exclusive elite groupings, were not distinguished by any pragmatic superiority of the savage therapies which were their trademark; their advantage was relative—general education and social rank—and it differed from that of the corporate English physician only because it was not institutionalized. In the second quarter of the nineteenth century, the rise of homeopathic medicine brought this relative superiority to an end: homeopathy, indeed, was an attack by equally "genteel" doctors upon the standard therapies used by the "regulars."[5] Unlike previous sectarian movements, such as Thomson's herbalism or Sylvester Graham's health prescriptions, homeopathy conquered urban middle-class and upper-class clienteles in the United States, as it had done in Europe. It became, therefore, the primary target of the "regular" medical organizers.

American indifference to basic science appears to have played a large role in the lack of medical research during most of the nineteenth century.[6] Its effects on the medical professional were compounded by the repeated assertion, on the part of the state legislatures, of every American's "inalienable right to life, liberty, and quackery."[7] But even where scientific medicine had arisen and begun its growth early in the century—that is, chiefly in France and in Germany—it did not produce valid therapeutic results until the 1880s and 1890s. Medical practitioners were, therefore, almost as reticent toward science, as impotent against their rivals in the field, and as disunited as their American counterparts. It would therefore be misleading to assume, as is often done, that the market for "real" medical services expanded gradually, by a process of cumulative expansion of its "scientific nucleus."[8] The universal need for health services could be beneficially tapped if, and only if, the satisfaction of the need could be connected in the mind of the public with *one type* of service.[9] The "premodern" situation could not be overcome by medicine so long as consumers, when they changed providers, also changed medical commodities: in such a situation, we cannot speak of *one* market for medicine, but of many, and the sector controlled by the regulars was, at that, a relatively small one. In fact, until the end of the century, the fastest growing "medical" market was that of patent medicines, produced outside of any respectable medical persuasion.

Considering this situation, it is not surprising that medical graduates—most particularly in the United States, where it was so easy to overproduce them—were very often poor and frustrated up to the end of the nineteenth century.[10] The universal need for medical services represents a tremendous asset for a category of professional producers only *after* they have succeeded in establishing a monopolistic hold on their market. Until then, the universality of the need operates in reverse, breeding competition.

Thus, the second feature of the market for medical services was its extreme competitiveness. In England, the most significant axis of competition was between the "lower branches" and the higher rungs of the profession—until 1858, when the Medical Act established a single national register of physicians. But in England as elsewhere, the proliferation of medical commodities shows, on the one hand, that the need for health services had been activated by various forces, chief among which was the transformation in ways of life brought about by urbanization.[11] On the other hand, this proliferation reflects a market situation fragmented into many incompatible definitions of the commodity to be sold.

Urbanization aggravated the economic and intellectual effects of competition: it fostered incursions into a rival's practice, price cutting, advertising, professional defamation, and the like. The situation was particularly critical in the United States: there were no medical schools of wide renown, and the public authorities, perhaps as a consequence, granted medical societies the right to issue licenses but were "unwilling to enact laws which would have deterred unlicensed practitioners."[12] The chief aim of the first medical societies was to create some distinctive trademarks by means of licensure and restrictions upon membership. They hoped to limit competition by reducing the supply of "real" doctors, by standardizing medical fees, and by adopting and enforcing codes of professional etiquette. From the 1820s on, the multiplication of proprietary medical schools not only killed in the bud the societies' monopolistic efforts; it also institutionalized the competition between different paradigms of healing, thus reducing the field of operation for all graduate practitioners.[13]

The associations, nevertheless, had begun the task continued by the schools— that is, the separation in the public's eyes between "graduate" physicians and "uneducated" or unlicensed empirics. They had also begun to provide a focus for the practice of medicine, atomized by the isolation or the competitiveness of solo practice. Local and regional societies of all persuasions managed to introduce a modicum of regulation and intraprofessional courtesy, while positions on the licensing boards gave prestige to their incumbents. Later, professorships in the schools became real "passports to business," providing medical faculties with central positions in networks of apprentices, former students, and patient referrals. In the United States in particular, the founding of societies, licensing boards, and schools had effects quite independent of these institutions' actual scientific worth: their existence constructed an occupational role-image for the "doctor" and preserved it in the public's eyes even when the withdrawal of public confidence in official medicine was at its highest. According to Richard Shryock, in the second half of the nineteenth century, most laymen had nothing but contempt for medical science, while holding their own family doctor in great respect.[14]

The extreme competitiveness of the medical field is important from the point of view of market organization: it has the paradoxical effect of spawning and spurring constant efforts to regulate competition by controlling the supply of producers, the interaction between them, and the very process of production.

Furthermore, in a situation where official medicine was no more successful in curing disease than its rivals, it could still rely on traditional mechanisms to establish trust. Thus, the family doctor could maintain his prestige, in the face of widespread disbelief in medicine's therapeutic soundness, because he appeared, first of all, as the man to whom one went for help with *private* problems. His medical effectiveness was probably much less important than his parental attitude, his wisdom, his willingness to provide detached yet personalized help. Like the irregular practitioners, he too was backed by the force of community traditions; furthermore, to the reliance of rituals of help, he could add the prestige of middle-class status and at least the semblance of scientific capacity.

Expert advice, when it is given in a private interpersonal situation, can always readily draw upon extraprofessional sources of credibility and legitimation. Thus, all professions contain elements that appear more starkly and more coherently in the role of the priest. In a secularized society, the family doctor of old is one of the most direct inheritors of the role of the religious minister or priest. Modern medicine, however, more than any other profession, illuminates how functionally rational elements of legitimation—scientific expertise and proved technical superiority in healing—blend with traditional, irrational, or substantively rational supports.[15] What is to be stressed here is that medicine is relatively exceptional in this sense, because of the persistently private and purely individual basis on which professional services are provided.

The privacy of the consulting room makes the physician's services impenetrable to public scrutiny: in the actual transaction itself, the patient faces the physician alone.[16] The patient, therefore, must rely exclusively on his own uninformed judgment since, indeed, the information he has about the effectiveness of the services he is getting is always indirect or ex post facto: he can judge his doctor only through the subjective assessments and experience of other patients, through the realization that he is not getting any better (or that he is not improving fast enough), through non-functional factors of confidence, or through the judgment of other doctors. This last aspect is perhaps the most significant, for it is here that professional etiquette and the informal organization of the medical profession turn against the layman.[17] The profession is outraged by malpractice suits and rejects, of course, the most logical attempts by patients to have something to say about a doctor's fees or his competence. Yet, as Eliot Freidson has shown, the privacy of solo practice is also impenetrable to colleague review. Beyond the requirements of a degree, obtained no matter how many years ago, there is little more that the profession expects of its members and little more that it controls.[18]

Moreover, the patient's anxiety about what may be, to him, matters of life or death leads him to make an emotional investment in the doctor-patient relation. Since there is a general tendency to attribute to one's doctor quasi-charismatic powers, uncritical acceptance of his expertise is frequent: a patient wants to believe that somebody can help.

These considerations on the typical mode of exchange in the medical market point to a third market characteristic: because of the permanently individual and private nature of the actual transaction, the sum of individual consumers are not, and most probably cannot, be organized. This market situation maximizes the effectiveness of association among the producers.

I have emphasized, however, that the medical market, like all other professional markets, ultimately depends on ideological sources of social credit. On the one hand, in the act of consultation, the doctor can appeal to interpersonal factors of confidence in order to bolster the individual patient's belief in his professional competence. On the other hand, general public belief in the profession's superior skills has to be deep and widespread enough to motivate the sum of individual choices which result in consultation with a physician. Thus, medicine appears to depend more than other professions on the general state of the public's ideology about the nature and functional attributes of healing. Legally enforced monopoly, however, can compensate for lack of widespread public confidence, and at the least it reinforces the ideological bases of trust. In this respect, medicine is particularly well served by the nature of the service it provides.

The fourth characteristic of the medical market is, in effect, the relatively greater readiness of public authorities to facilitate monopolistic control over practice by those professional healers who appear more effective, or at least more convincing, than others. The fact that medicine operates in an area of vital concern for the individual and for the community compels the state to intervene. Once scientific medicine had offered sufficient guarantees of its superior effectiveness in dealing with disease, the state contributed willingly to the creation of monopoly by means of registration and licensing. Indeed, only in a quasi-monopolistic situation can the producers be supervised and a minimum of "professional" competence obtained. Thus, because of the saliency of the medical function, monopolistic tendencies received state sanction long before the rise of modern medicine, as an expression of the state's efforts to regulate and standardize health practices: "Most European governments felt the need, at least by the sixteenth century, for some regulation of medical practice. The College of Physicians in London, the *collegium-medicum* of German cities, the *tribunal de protomedicato* in Spain, were all granted some control over licensing practitioners, the inspection of drugs, and the like."[19] These premodern associations became more concerned with the protection of their monopoly than with the reliable production of professional producers; their entrenchment accounts in large part for the dynamics of emergence of modern professions in post-feudal societies.

What is significant here, though, is that the vital importance of public health always kept open to the profession of medicine a privileged conduit to governmental backing for its monopolistic claims. The recurrence of epidemics was a most powerful factor in reviving the periodically faltering interest in public health; in order to exploit this potential, medicine, as I have emphasized before, needed more than a market situation favorable to monopoly. It needed a dramatic demonstration that its services were more likely than those of other healers to solve persistent health problems. But even this was not enough: scientific medicine, indeed, was not the

patrimony of any sect, but the "product of convergent influences of diverse antecedents" into a wholly new school.[20] Often the resistance of regular medicine to
bacteriology required an intervention of the state *against* established sectors of the
profession, on the side of popular demand and of public health movements in which
laymen often outnumbered physicians.[21] For medicine to appropriate the new discoveries, the bulk of the profession had to be socialized to the new tools. This required, in effect, that one or more generations of physicians be formed along new
and homogeneous standards of training.

Until that time, the state's interventions on the side of "regular" medicine should
be seen more as a political response than as a matter of encouraging the best product
in a vital market. Since "regular" doctors tended to be, precisely, those of higher
social status, they were naturally heard with more favor and more often appointed
to public positions—a fact which appeared to give governmental sanction to their
definition of the medical "commodity."[22] Social movements, however, could
elicit from the state different political responses: the public health movements are
one instance, and another is the movement by the "lower" corporate orders in
England against the entrenched upper-class physicians—their victory with the
Medical Act of 1858 can be interpreted as a victory of the middle class against aristocratic privilege.

State sponsorship, in short, is not sufficient to give a profession autonomous
control over all its potential market. In the best of cases, state sanction can eliminate
competitors, but it cannot force consumers to consume, except in minimal and
routinized areas, such as compulsory vaccination. Medicine's privileged position
with relation to the state was perfunctory, therefore, until the profession succeeded
in unifying itself around a demonstrably superior definition of the medical "commodity" and in guaranteeing a reliable production of producers. This process,
which I have called the *negotiation of cognitive exclusiveness,* was inseparable from
the production and progress of medical knowledge.

All the learned professions were tied, in principle, to one organizational base for
the transmission of knowledge: the traditional university.[23] Until its reform was
achieved, the university hindered rather than helped the production of systematic
scientific and technical knowledge. In this respect, medicine had a further advantage over the other learned professions: the centrality of its function had made it
necessary for the state to support public hospitals. This was an alternative institution which could serve as an integrative focus for the profession, and could be used
in the production and transmission of medical knowledge. It appears, in fact, that
the number of large hospitals was one of the main reasons why Paris became the
world's capital of medical science in the first half of the nineteenth century. Over-
coming the *ancien régime* guild barriers, these hospitals brought together surgeons
and physicians, thus allowing the physicians to incorporate the localized structural
pathology, which surgeons always had spontaneously applied, and to start the scientific study of specific diseases.[24] Not surprisingly, countries such as the United
States, in which hospitals were for a long time unfit for scientific research, lagged
far behind in medical discoveries.[25]

In sum, the market for medical services appears to have distinctive features which derive from the saliency and universality of the need it serves. The potential for unlimited expansion, the extreme competitiveness before the market was successfully monopolized, as well as the readiness of the state to act as sponsor for the dominant (or most "trustworthy") sector of the profession, flow from the nature of the need. In turn, the individual nature of the need determines the persistently interpersonal character of the *actual* transaction of services. This aspect explains the typical, albeit not unique, influence of interpersonal factors of trust, and also the insulation of the professional producer from *direct* scrutiny in his actual performance. Regulation and control of actual professional practice are therefore situated "before" and "after" the process of consultation rather than during its actual occurrence. Control of the "product" is typically indirect. The individualized mode of consumption, the vital nature of the need, as well as the influence of non-functionally rational and subjective factors of confidence, make it unlikely that the consumers will be able to exercise this control.

None of these factors is, in itself, sufficient to guarantee either professional autonomy or monopolistic market control to the dominant sector of the profession. Each of them, and all of them combined, are conditioned by the possibility of negotiating cognitive exclusiveness, which is a crucial *intervening* variable. Once this exclusiveness was achieved, the structure of its market gave medicine what I consider to be an exceptional and unparalleled capacity for monopolistic control: characteristics which favor a sellers' market controlled by the producers were particularly coherent in the case of medicine. This can best be illustrated by contrast with another profession which, during the nineteenth century, was also dealing in new and rapidly changing professional "commodities."

A COMPARATIVE CASE: ENGINEERING

It would seem at first glance that the profession of engineering should have had few competitors to fight: the industrial revolution having so transformed its function and its cognitive base, the profession should have been able to grow smoothly along with its market, cumulatively producing new knowledge and controlling its application. From this hypothetical point of view, the pressure to articulate a monopoly would have been lower than in medicine; on the other hand, the low level of competition (in America, for instance, the demand for civil engineering services largely exceeded the supply until the 1840s), and the novelty of the area of practice should have facilitated professional control of the market. In a rapidly changing technological environment, it would be logical to assume that the devisers of technological innovations would have "naturally" obtained cognitive exclusiveness. If the engineers had indeed been so favored with regard to this crucial intervening variable, their autonomy in defining the content of their work should have been high; their "natural" monopoly over new knowledge should, in fact, have maximized the positive factors—of whatever nature—in their professional market situation.

This view is misleading. To show why, we must consider the general character of the professional service involved.[26] The first difference from medicine is that engineering was not—and emphatically *is* not today—a functionally homogeneous area of the social division of labor. True, all branches of engineering (even, indirectly, the most abstract contemporary specialties, such as systems analysis) fall in a general category which Daniel Calhoun calls coordinators or "devisers of physical objects." In this broad category, the varieties of engineers keep company with "architects, building tradesmen, artists, mechanics."[27]

Among the technical devisers of a pre-industrial age, the specialized military engineer, of long European ancestry, and the architect, born of the Renaissance, carried their identity into the industrial era. Civil engineering drew much of its manpower from the specialized military corps, while overlapping, in some cases, with architectural practice. However, the task of building an infrastructure of public works for industrial expansion transformed the role and far exceeded the old pools of skilled labor.[28] Mechanical engineering was much more clearly a product of the industrial revolution. Its origins, like those of mining engineering, were entrepreneurial. Its elite was constituted, in America, by creative and innovative manufacturers who were at the heart of the particular social and cultural tradition of the machine shop.[29] Despite the egalitarian mobility myths which remained for a long time attached to the shop, this entrepreneurial elite most often came from upperclass Northeastern families and carried to its calling the social sanctions and security of its origins.[30] In the 1830s and 1840s, railway shops became an extension of shop culture, as well as a principal breeding ground for mechanical engineers and the first area in which the very title came into general usage.The repair and supervision of railroad machinery, however, blurred the clear stereotype of the combined entrepreneur and technological creator produced by the machine shop: at one end, the "superintendent" of motive power had a foot into management and vied for autonomy with non-technical executives; at the other, engine drivers appropriated the term "engineer," thus eroding in the public's mind its gentlemanly connotations.[31]

There was not, therefore, *one* earlier type out of which the modern engineer developed, nor one single functional area, as in the case of healing, but different specializations which *separately* gave rise to present-day engineering specialties—as well as to architecture, its derivations, and numerous "instrument-making" crafts which never reached or even aspired to the status of professions.

The second basic difference between engineering and medicine is that the physical nature of the engineer's professional product immediately involves the possibility that the buyer be a different person from the consumer: if nothing else, a physical object or a physical arrangement can be transmitted to or exchanged with consumers other than the original buyer. The relation between the technical deviser and the buyer of his services is typically quite different from that which prevails when buyer and consumer are fused, and so is the set of potential loyalties and responsibilities from which the technical deviser may have to choose. At the beginning of the industrial revolution, technical devisers were either self-employed as craftsmen or manufacturers, or employed by governments in their military apparatus, by proprietors of economic units, or, sometimes, by collections of local notables, as in the early

American public works. Government service, as well as the fusion of entrepreneurship with technical expertise, reduced the chances of potential conflict between responsibility to the buyer or employer and responsibility to the consumer; however, the increasing scale of the projects undertaken and the concentration of means of production progressively reduced the entrepreneurial role of engineers; the possibility of conflicting loyalties therefore tended to become a normal ingredient of the engineer's work situation.

The physical nature of the product also implies that it can be seen, examined, and copied. The jealous defense of industrial secrets stands to show that these secrets could be stolen without too much difficulty, and also that expertise drawn from empirical practice is tied to the *pace* of change: a rapid rhythm of technological innovation appears to guarantee the technical deviser's skills against routinization. So long as technical expertise did not derive from the methodical application of theory— chiefly physics—to engineering problems, it was mainly the complexity and scale of a project, as well as the pace of technological change, that served to justify claims of superior competence. In America, both formal engineering education and theoretical work lagged behind Europe—particularly France and Germany—until late in the nineteenth century. Apprenticeship was for generations the main source of engineering skill:[32] canals and machine shops, mines, railroads, and later the new electric, automotive, and radio industries, were principal suppliers of first-rate engineering talent. Especially in the first phase of industrialization, the gap between workmen and engineers seemed possible to bridge, as witnessed by the flowering of mechanics institutes and correspondence courses, characterized by a stronger commitment to the ideology of open mobility than to the diffusion of scientific knowledge.[33] In fact, the long predominance of apprenticeship preserved the control of gentlemanly elites—entrepreneurial, in mechanical and mining engineering, or quasi-managerial, in civil engineering.

This dominant empirical component is not what distinguishes engineering from other American professions. Apprenticeship was the accepted pattern in most other occupations, including medicine and law, during the first half of the nineteenth century. What is distinctive is that the average engineer emerged from this early phase as a *salaried professional,* in Europe as well as in the United States. Independent consultation and entrepreneurship were not the typical modes of practice, although elites of the profession exaggerated both their significance and their accessibility.[34] In themselves, however, the dependent conditions of practice need not have introduced a principle of heteronomy at the very core of the engineer's role. This heteronomy was instead a consequence of the nature of the organizations for which the engineer typically worked—that is, relatively large-scale economic enterprises in a capitalist society. Within this context, the function of the engineer was dual, at once technical and economic. Cost being an inherent criterion of the "rightness of the technical solution," the civil engineer was expected to advise on the practicability and profitability of new projects, and sometimes he was also expected to engage in promotional activities. In the United States, after the depression of 1837, the main attacks on the hiring of internal-improvements engineers focused on their unreliable cost estimates and on their defense of unreasonable expenditures—that is, on *economic* aspects of their task.[35] Obviously, the engineers did not ignore the fact: in the 1880s, the President of the American Society of Mechanical Engineers declared: "we must measure all things by the test, *will it pay?*"; and an eminent Columbia professor candidly defined engineering as the "science of making money for capital."[36]

The economic component of the engineer's function appears as a wedge of "other-directedness" in his role which overrode the independence he could derive from technical expertise. On the other hand, the economic component also appears to have played an indirect part in the upgrading of functions, which created the engineer's role and his possibilities of career. The assimilation of the engineer to the interests of project sponsors or entrepreneurs—and, later, his promotion to managerial or quasi-managerial functions within a bureaucratic context—were a crucial difference between the emerging role of the engineer and "less gentle" forms of technical devising.[37] Thus from the profession's formative period, even before the giant corporations became the main employers of engineers, we find a situation in which professional status appears to derive as much from organizational mobility as from technical expertise.

These considerations all point toward one overriding characteristic of the market for engineering services, which only becomes more dominant with the standardization and institutionalization of training; this characteristic is the inherent *subordination* of the engineers' market.

In all circumstances, the services of the specialized technical deviser are more likely to be mediated than those of a profession which provides intangible services; the nature of the service increases the probability that the relation between professional and user or consumer (as distinct from the buyer or employer of professional services) will be *indirect*. Thus even when the ultimate products of professional work are, indeed, destined for every man (as is the case, in theory, for public works), they are mediated by *functionally specific and organized clienteles,* which are much more frequently employers (buyers of labor) than clients (buyers of services). The modern engineer rises in the context of industrial capitalism, in which the mediation of technical devising by specific bodies becomes permanent subordination to organized and increasingly complex economic enterprises. Thus in the late nineteenth and early twentieth centuries, American civil and electric engineering societies developed tentative codes of ethics, as bargaining assets in potential conflicts with their sponsors or employers; the mechanical engineering association, by contrast, did not see the need for a code of ethics until much later. The intimate ties of the mechanical engineering elite with capitalist entrepreneurs undoubtedly explain this attitude. The reasons given are interesting, however, for they refer in fact to the structural differences between engineering and other professions. The first major reason was that the buyers of engineering services did not need special protection: "If there was one thing the average American considered himself, it was a mechanic, and as such he was qualified to judge engineering design and correctness."[38] Business clients and employers, moreover, knew quite well what they wanted and how they wanted it done. It was argued, furthermore, that the engineer's works were checked by the very laws of nature: while "men in other professions may blunder or play false with more or less impunity . . . the mistakes of the engineer are quick to find him out and proclaim his incompetence. He is the one professional man who is obliged to be right."[39]

Two factors that help an association of producers maximize its effectiveness were either weak or absent in the case of engineering. First, the advantage which the seller of professional services has over the ordinary individual buyer is reduced to a minimum by the engineer's dependence on knowledgeable or at least powerful employers or clients, even though this advantage can easily be used against lay consumers.[40] Second, the nature of the product implies that the public really can obtain more direct evidence about the professional's capacity than in the case of medicine, while the state can regulate and supervise the products, rather than the producers themselves. By their nature, the engineer's services and their end products are visible; what removes them from the public eye is, in fact, the mediation of a "buyer" who is distinct from the "user" and is, in many cases, a *private* capitalist enterprise. No matter how vigorously or successfully the engineering profession might have organized to secure its market and face its employers, it could not have *controlled* its professional market because that market was inherently subordinate. Though strategic for industrial growth, the services of the engineer were subordinate to general considerations of accounting and business profit. Thus, while the medical market depended, of course, on the general increase in standards of living, the market for engineering services depended almost totally on industrial investment and on the business cycle.[41] In the case of medicine, the power of the profession depended, in theory, on the elimination of competitors: monopoly was necessary in order to benefit from an expanding market. But once monopoly or near-monopoly was achieved, the power of the profession grew as the market sector under its control expanded. In a subordinate professional market, monopoly, though important, does not play the same part: it cannot compensate for the ups and downs of the larger market, which may determine the contraction of the demand for professional services. Expansion—that is, a balance of supply and demand favorable to the profession—does not give a profession like engineering controlling powers, but only a better bargaining position.

Faced with a market structure so unfavorable to monopolistic claims, engineers should have concentrated on what they could, after a point, control: namely, the production of producers, and in particular, the advantageous adjustment of supply to demand. Here, however, the profession has faced another difficulty: as pointed out, the various branches of engineering emerged from areas of practice which had not been *autonomously* defined by the profession. The technical devisers in engineering controlled new and rapidly changing cognitive areas; yet, in practice, their fields of action were created by processes of economic development in which the expert technician intervened either as entrepreneur or in a subordinate capacity. The specialists, as such, did not decide who would be taken into training, nor did they control the principal rewards. The acquisition of theoretical bases and the methodic systematization of empirical knowledge defeated apprenticeship and gave to educators their usual leadership in professionalizing efforts. But even though the profession had gained control over the production of producers, it had not unified its cognitive basis, except at a very general level, nor freed it from external determination. Today, the attempts by the academic sectors of engineering to create a common cognitive basis are successfully resisted by the practitioners and their employers. Thus despite the engineer's role in defining new knowledge or new applications of knowledge, the essential element of autonomy remains weak in this profession. The attempts to standardize the "production of producers" independently of industry's predefinitions simply reveal again the inescapable structural subordination of the professional market.

The "strong" market characteristics of medicine were not sufficient in themselves to ensure monopolistic control. Cognitive exclusiveness appeared to be the intervening factor which maximized the effectiveness of each market characteristic and of all of them combined. The analysis of engineering shows, in turn, that autonomy in defining the content of work—or the control over new cognitive areas—does not by itself compensate for the structural subordination of the professional market. The subordination of the engineer's role submits the selection of the technical problem and the criteria that are brought to bear in its solution, at least partially, to heteronomous considerations. Autonomy is chiefly gained *outside* the professional role, by acceding to positions of command or responsibility in the *dominant* market.

In the concluding words of Daniel Calhoun's study, the American civil engineer before the Civil War appears already as the typical professional of a transitional stage, "between an earlier proprietary society and an emerging industrial, corporate society."[42] Tied to a peculiar kind of business market and to persistent entrepreneurial forms, the elite of mechanical engineering maintained for a long time the myths of the "proprietary society." By the beginning of the twentieth century, however, the growing numbers of mechanical engineers, as well as their colleagues in mining and, most particularly, in the newer fields of electricity, radio, and automobile production, had never known any other condition than salaried employment in bureaucratic organizations. Professionalism meant for them that a salaried and subordinate position should be conceded as much deference and prestige as the independent professional whose image was crystallized in the general ideology. Their professionalizing project was dominated, in Edwin T. Layton's words, by "an obsessive concern for social status," and was marked as well by specific ideological attempts which exalted the *expertise* of this dependent professional and made it the base of a grandiose social role.[43] As the first modern professional to emerge within a large-scale economic organization, the engineer stands in sharp contrast to the medical doctor; his profile also anticipates later professional forms, in which the "model" provided by medicine may be fading.

This analysis of engineering establishes a general and important point: the *subordination of a professional market minimizes the effects of cognitive exclusiveness.* It also suggests which conditions of knowledge facilitate the constitution of a specific area of competence. The rapidity of change in the cognitive basis is important, for it prevents the routinization of technical skills. The visibility of a profession's accumulated skills and achievements, its "demonstration effect" vis-à-vis the public at large and its specialized clients, is a potent resource for ideological persuasion. Medicine, incidentally, acquired this resource much later than engineering: in the 1840s the popular negative judgment about medicine was influenced by the tangible achievements of physical science, as if the public tacitly asked "where were the medical equivalents of the steam engine or the telegraph?"[44] Finally, the increasingly firm ties which engineering established with scientific theory magnified the cumulative aspect of engineering's achievements by making them a part of general scientific knowledge. This gave some credibility to "the engineers' claim to be the agents of progress and enlightenment."[45] On the other hand, the monopolization of scientific education by colleges and universities made the possession of scientific training into a crucial element of distinction between professional engineers and mere technical devisers.

Turning now to a more systematic examination of the cognitive basis for professional claims to market monopoloy, I will try to show not only that medicine was favored by its market structure but also that it was exceptionally well equipped to establish its claim to cognitive exclusiveness.

THE COGNITIVE CONDITIONS OF PROFESSIONAL MONOPOLY

The technical and cognitive conditions for the emergence of profession are so abundantly treated by the sociological literature that I will indicate only those factors which, in my framework of analysis, facilitate market control and standardization.

Wilensky observes that "if the technical base of an occupation consists of a vocabulary that sounds familiar to everyone (social science and the arts of administration) or if the base is scientific, but so narrow that it can be learned as a set of rules by most people, then the occupation will have difficulty claiming a monopoly of skill or even a roughly exclusive jurisdiction."[46] But even a body of knowledge that is both esoteric and theoretical—and therefore difficult to routinize—is still not a sufficient condition for the control of a competitive market. Take, for instance, the case of the Protestant ministry in America: despite the undeniable existence of an esoteric body of theological knowledge, and despite the rise of separate seminaries from 1784 on, the established denominations could not protect themselves from the challenges of the evangelist movement. Similarly, the law was not protected from outsiders until the institutionalization of formal teaching and qualifying bar examinations.[47]

I have suggested that the "best" cognitive basis for a monopoly of competence is one which reveals, or activates, or maximizes the favorable characteristics of a professional market. It must be specific enough to impart distinctiveness to the professional "commodity"; it must be formalized or codified enough to allow standardization of the "product"—which means, ultimately, standardization of the producers. And yet it must not be so clearly codified that it does not allow a principle of exclusion to operate: where everyone can claim to be an expert, there is no expertise.

I have also indicated that change in the cognitive basis is a necessary component, for it prevents excessive routinization and therefore maintains the relative inaccessibility of expertise. At the same time, change must not be so rapid nor so fragmentary that it forecloses the possibility of socializing the aspiring experts into a unified and unifying body of knowledge. Furthermore, change, to be legitimate, must be perceived as progress. Were it not so, it could (and ultimately would) be perceived simply as the deliberate manufacture of pseudo-expertise, a device for excluding the non-initiated.

These considerations point in the direction of a type of cognitive activity which is esoteric, yet formalized and standardized enough to be, in principle, accessible to all who would undergo prolonged training. This activity is also characterized by a tendency to cognitive consensus among its practitioners; its products result either from periods of continuous cumulative growth or from discontinuous, revolutionary changes in the consensual norms that define the goals and the forms of cognition. In any case, both the cumulative and the qualitatively discontinuous achievements are recognized as progress. *This cognitive activity is science.* In Thomas Kuhn's words, "We tend to see as science *any field in which progress is marked. . . .* If we doubt, as many do, that non-scientific fields make progress, that cannot be because individual schools make none. Rather, it must be because there are always competing schools, each of which constantly questions the very foundations of the others".[48]

The sociological content of Kuhn's approach to a scientific production is relevant for the analysis of professions.[49] An apparent tautology, which needs to be explained, sums up a central part of his interpretation: science is inseparable from a perception of progress because it is the exclusive product of specialized communities of scientists. The perception of progress presupposes a tacit acceptance of what problems are worth solving or what goals are worth reaching. Scientific communities, says Kuhn, are characterized by sets of shared tacit understandings, which he calls scientific paradigms. A paradigm is not an abstract system of explicit rules, but *a practice,* accessible through a long process of socialization. The guidelines of this practice are embodied in concrete examples of successful scientific inquiry, which include "law, theory, application, and instrumentation together," and are learned by replication. These examples are "concrete puzzle-solutions" which contain the promise that all the remaining problems proposed within a paradigm can, indeed, be solved. Because their shared definitions of reality are based on relatively uniform and standardized practices, scientists work toward and reach cumulative results: normal science consists of converging attempts to solve the same puzzles, to elaborate, articulate, and adjust the same paradigm. Mature scientific communities are thus distinguished by a structural tendency to paradigmatic unification, which excludes those who engage in a different practice and therefore have different standards of what is relevant and different perceptions of what constitutes progress.

Because scientists are the only producers of science, the lay public has no other choice but to accept, *without sharing them,* their definitions of scientific practice and scientific progress. Scientific communities can define autonomously the standards of correct practice. Their exceptional autonomy and singular degree of integration have a sociological condition: "the unparalleled insulation . . . from the demands of the laity and of everyday life" which Western societies have conceded them. As Kuhn observes, "Just because he is working only for an audience of colleagues, an audience that shares his own values and beliefs, the scientist can take a single set of standards for granted."[50]

Thus, at the limit, scientific communities are their own market: scientists are simultaneously the producers and the main consumers of their products. Because their practice is relatively independent from all external factors except financial sponsorship, it *appears* to be solely determined by the state of each discipline and by its internal tradition of research. If cognitive consensus breaks down, the autonomy and insulation of the scientific professions facilitates the resolution of the crisis, that is, the striving toward reintegration of an area of work under new paradigmatic standards.[51] The task of persuasion is arduous, but limited, nevertheless, to a very narrow community which shares a life commitment and basic norms of interaction. For Kuhn, persuasion cannot supplant the "act of faith" which is, ultimately, at the heart of a "paradigm switch." But in this too, the scientific communities have an advantage: because of their autonomy and insulation, they can *afford* to convert, even if the new paradigm is only "at the start, largely a promise of success discoverable in selected and still incomplete examples."[52]

By definition, the consulting professions do not have such freedom. Their market is an *open* market, in the sense that it necessarily includes a *lay* clientele, no matter how specialized and organized it may be. Because the consulting professions "survive by providing to a varied lay clientele services that are expected to solve practical problems," even their most scientific sectors depend on practical, external considerations.[53] The inquirers in the fields of applied (or applicable) science do not address themselves to "puzzles" posed by the internal evolution of a paradigm, nor do they concentrate on 'insoluble' anomalies. The sociologist of science Joseph Ben-David observes: "For the professional physiologist and pathologist seeking to understand bodily functions in physical and chemical terms, the statistical inquiry of Ignaz Semmelweis into the etiology of puerperal fever made no theoretical sense. And initially, the same applied to the discovery by Pasteur and others of the bacterial causation of illness."[54]

For these fields which receive their problems from everyday life, Ben-David proposes the name of "quasi-disciplines." By definition, they cannot attain the insulation which characterizes scientific communities. Furthermore, the practitioners who carry the results of "quasi-disciplinary" research into everyday practice tacitly evaluate a new technology of work in terms of its market potential. The paradigmatic standards under which the research has been conducted are not important, if its practical effects are demonstrably valid. Thus in his study of nineteenth-century American physicians, William Rothstein convincingly argues that the conflict between medical sects hinged on the effects of different therapies, and not on theoretical incompatibilities between systems. Where therapies were demonstrably valid—as was the case with smallpox vaccination or the quinine cure of malaria—all the medical sects adopted them.[55]

The significant differences between pure scientific disciplines and quasi-disciplines cannot be ignored. The problem, however, is to discern how a scientific basis can be an advantage to a profession in its attempts to secure market control. Leaving aside the obvious—the superiority of the scientific method over prescientific approaches for knowing and mastering physical aspects of reality—a scientific basis appears to offer the best potential for the unified and standardized production of professional *producers*. After all, quasi-disciplines also follow scientific methods and tend, themselves, toward paradigmatic unification—their practice and, to a much lesser extent, the use of their products, require a broad scientific basis. What professions obtain from this basic training in pure science has no *immediate* bearing upon their practice; but the passage through broad scientific training puts the future professionals through one first phase of effective unification and standardization. Also, as in any other case, longer training periods complete or perfect this standardization by selectivity and by deepening the effects of socialization. No less importantly, basic scientific training provides a clear principle of separation from the exclusion of the "non-standardized," empirically trained professionals. For instance, in the 1870s, when American engineering programs were not yet producing the majority of American engineers, the teaching of mathematics—a subject which the shops could not teach—had already opened a growing cleavage between shop-trained professionals and school graduates.[56] The understandably heated arguments of the shop-men and other defenders of practical skills against what they saw as an exclusive and practically useless emphasis on mathematics cannot hide that they had already lost the battle.

The sociological center of the process of unification is the system for the production of producers. The broad scientific moorings of the "quasi-disciplines" *require,* as Abraham Flexner pointed out for medicine, affiliation with the modern university. At the same time, these scientific bases *qualify* a profession for affiliation more readily than any other, in a world where science is the cardinal system of cognitive validation and legitimation. Entry into the university gives any profession a core of educators; because of the university's apparent universalism and independence from lay demands and private interests, these educators are in the best position to defend the universalistic guarantees of professional competence and to legitimize the professionals' claim of autonomy and monopoly. As professionals themselves, they are interested in the market in which their products—the graduates—will have to secure income and status. In the modern university, which centralizes the production of knowledge as well as that of producers, *scientific* educators control and produce a constantly changing body of knowledge. The cumulative change characteristic of normal science makes the passage of aspiring professionals through the centers for the standardized production of producers *compulsory,* not only because of a legislative fiat but "naturally," because these centers monopolize new knowledge. Lawyers and architects, for instance, produce professionally relevant new knowledge in their practice; but the bulk of relevant new knowledge in medicine, optometry, engineering, and the like is produced by research. Changes in the cognitive basis of professional practice no longer appear arbitrary, but are determined by the internal logic of scientific inquiry and are *legitimized as progress*.

This effect can be grasped by illustrating its opposite—a deliberate attempt to change a technology of work in order to give an advantage, among other things, to the standardized products of formal schooling. From the 1880s on, American engineering educators had advocated the adoption of the metric system. Unlike the manufacturers, they had nothing to lose from such a switch; quite the contrary. As the historian Monte Calvert remarks: "What could be more of a boost to the status of the college-trained engineer than for him to possess a new and arbitrarily determined system of measurement? What could better assure his ascendancy over the boy from the shop? Knowledge of the metric system could become, like calculus, a badge of the formally trained."[57] Metric conversion could make complex calculations immediately accessible to the average technical school graduate, thus destroying one of the few advantages that experience gave to those trained on the job. But the arbitrariness of the change denied legitimacy to the educators and graduates' stance, which was of course ardently opposed by the engineering-entrepreneurs and their allies.

In sum, the tendency toward paradigmatic unification—inherent in scientific communities and determined in large part by their insulation—is extended to the consulting professions when they connect themselves with a "quasi-discipline" and with the quasi-monopolistic center for the production of new knowledge—namely, the modern university. A profession's capacity for standardizing training and research within the confines of normal science and for excluding competing paradigms is not only greatly augmented by its connection with science; it is also given the ultimate legitimation of an objective, independent, incontrovertibly more effective inquiry, which opens up the possibility of unlimited progress.

The evolution of medicine concretely and exactly illustrates the impact of a scientific foundation on a professional field. The "pre-paradigmatic" situation lasted for most of the nineteenth century. Attempts by "regular" physicians to unify the profession tended to take the form of arbitrary exclusive practices against other practitioners. In the United States, where the near-total freedom of the market had encouraged proliferation, physicians attempted to institutionalize one particular orthodoxy by founding schools, in both the physical and the intellectual sense. "The United States and Canada," wrote Flexner in 1910, "have in little more than a century produced 457 medical schools, many, of course, short-lived, and perhaps 50 still-born; 155 survive today."[58] Until the foundation of the Johns Hopkins graduate school of medicine in 1893, America had no training center that could even remotely be compared to those in Germany, or even in Paris or Edinburgh. For a long time, external considerations were given more weight than unsupported and unsystematic "scientific" convictions—as shown, for instance, by the clash between contagionists and anticontagionists (the latter strenuously supported by commercial interests opposed to quarantine) over how to deal with the epidemics of yellow fever and cholera during the first decades of the nineteenth century.[59] This situation was obviously not unique to the United States. In Europe, however, institutional affiliation—with hospitals, in England and France; with research institutions connected with universities, as was often the case in Germany; or in conflict with the academy, as happened in France—had given a potent weapon to groups of scientifically oriented physicians and scientists interested in medical problems. These organizational nuclei gave both continuity and coordination to the attacks on traditional medicine, while providing the researchers with the situation of relative insulation necessary for autonomous scientific production. By the middle of the nineteenth century, writes the historian of medicine Richard Shryock, "a monistic pathology and a related therapeutics were no longer tolerated in regular medicine . . . medicine had come of scientific age."[60]

Clinical and pathological studies had been coordinated; physiology had been established on a firm scientific footing by Claude Bernard in Paris and by Helmholtz's group in Berlin; the numerical method inaugurated by Pierre Louis in the 1830s had laid the grounds for modern medical statistics and large-scale investigations in matters of public health; new drugs and new instruments, heretofore unused, such as the achromatic microscope, had been incorporated into practice or research, while the threat of epidemics had led to great developments in the administrative infrastructure concerned with public health. The stage was set for the incorporation of the bacteriological discoveries begun in the 1870s. The research branch of modern medicine was approaching paradigmatic unification by that time, even though practice lagged far behind.

One significant example of this unification is the case of the Viennese doctor Rokitansky, who had been one of the foremost representatives of the French scientific approach to medical problems. Despite this background, he ended up, inexplicably, with a speculative theory of humoral pathology—a clear regression to the monistic systems of the past. Shryock observes that a mere fifty years earlier, Rokitansky's fame would have sufficed to found another school on his theoretical system. But in the 1850s, the young Rudolf Virchow, who was still an obscure pathologist, examined the theory, found it a "monstruous anachronism" and it was abandoned, even by the author himself. "There was in fact no other choice," says Shryock, "unless he wished to take both himself and his theory without the pale of the medical profession."[61]

The emergence of shared criteria of validity and reliability within a sector of the medical profession constituted a major advance toward control of the market. By unifying its cognitive basis, medicine was emancipating itself from the support of its sponsoring elites. It had also acquired the instruments necessary for standardization of the services it provided; and standardization tied every transaction to the superiority, soon to be definitively proved, of the scientific medical "product." In Freidson's words, the accomplishments of modern surgery and, in particular, modern bacteriology "created a qualitative break with the past, making possible for the first time the predictable and reliable control of a wide spectrum of human ills by virtually any well-trained practitioner of the occupation, not solely by a great clinician."[62]

Both the internal and external preconditions for market control had been achieved. Internally, medicine had found independent means to put its house in order. As the example of Rokitansky shows, the charismatic clinician was no longer immune to challenge by comparatively obscure colleagues: both leaders and rank-and-file member of the profession were subjected to the tacit rule of accepted and transcendent cognitive norms. Externally, medicine had acquired independent means—means autonomously elaborated within the profession—of convincing both government and the public of its superior therapeutic effectiveness. The triumph of scientific medicine marked the end of medical sectarianism. In the United States, from the mid-1870s on, the states reinstituted licensing, entrusting it this time to those medical schools which were proving capable of producing the new breed of medical practitioners.

What was still needed, in fact, to reach the power and scientific capability of today's medicine was the thorough modernization of training in schools and hospitals. This process was the most rapid and complete in the United States—perhaps, as Shryock suggests, because previous efforts at medical reform had failed and modern centers for the production of producers had to be created practically from scratch. The influence of the 1910 Flexner Report on Medical Education helped concentrate medical training in a few centers (Flexner had recommended 31, out of the existing 155), and it transformed most medical schools in a single decade. In a parallel development, from 1913 on the major hospitals began to modernize, in large part as a result of the American College of Surgeons' policy of approval or disapproval of existing facilities. From a backward and provincial state, American medicine, after the "bacteriological revolution," started on its way to practically unparalleled professional power.

We need not enter here into the factors that gave American medicine an amount of corporate power apparently unmatched in other societies; medicine is an exceptionally powerful profession everywhere, and I want to emphasize the *exceptional character of medicine's professional success.* Medicine alone entered a market which, for a long time and in most places, approached the ideal conditions for attainment of monopoly, with a scientific product to sell. No other "old" profession serving unspecialized and unorganized clienteles had, at the same time, a potentially limitless market and an organic connection with science and scientific technologies of work.

Freidson's view that medicine, because of its preeminence among all other occupations, "has come to be the prototype upon which occupations seeking a privileged status today are modelling their aspirations," needs to be examined in the light of the preceding analysis.[63] In the first place, the model provided by medicine appears impossible to duplicate, because the market conditions facing the "new" professions are markedly different from those encountered by medicine at the end of the last century. Secondly, Freidson himself suggests a criterion of profession which adds another dimension to medicine's exceptionalism. He argues, in fact, that the status of profession is relative to that of other occupations and inseparable from their subordination to professional dominance in a structured work setting.[64] He proceeds to show that physicians define the content of practice and even the content of training for a host of allied and highly skilled occupations, such as nurses, anesthetists, therapists, laboratory technicians, radiologists, chiropractors, and the like. Now, all professions—and perhaps all specialized occupations—gain what E. C. Hughes calls the power to "delegate dirty work."[65] But it is difficult to find a profession, other than medicine, that dominates a role set constituted in large part by highly skilled and highly prized occupations, often regarded themselves as professions by their members and by the public. Indeed, with the questionable exception of the military, no profession except medicine *controls a complex organization* such as the modern hospital, which by virtue of its advanced bureaucratic and technological base continuously spawns new and highly skilled specializations.

In other parts of his work, Freidson analyzes professional autonomy as founded not on dominance in an area of the division of labor, but on control over the technical content of work. But does not every specialized occupation involving some skill command "the exclusive competence to determine the proper and effective method of performing some task?"[66] There is no better supporting evidence than the help-lessness most of us feel in dealing with plumbers or auto mechanics. Professions, however, are granted the power to determine the *scope of the service*. Despite the increasing specialization of all professions, we give professionals, however reluct-antly, much broader discretionary powers than we give a craftsman. Who would take at his word a mechanic who recommends a valve job when he is asked to change the oil? Yet, many people find themselves incapable of resisting a surgeon who recommends an operation, or a lawyer who advises against going to court.[67] As Freidson brilliantly shows in the case of medicine, a profession, "in developing its own 'professional' approach . . . changes the definition and shape of problems as experienced and interpreted by the laymen."[68]

This discretionary power, which goes far beyond mere technical autonomy, derives from monopoly: a monopoly of competence legitimized by officially sanc-tioned "expertise," and a monopoly of credibility with the public. Of the two, the first is more important: it leaves the public without legal or credible alternatives, and it restricts the control by outside agencies over the actual ethicality of the trans-action of professional services.

I have analyzed the emergence of the professional model in the liberal phase of capitalism as the outcome of a project tending toward market control. The autonomy of technique is a central element in the negotiation of cognitive exclusiveness, but *it is only one element in a structure* which comprises both the profession's market and the profession's resources for market control. In order to understand how the autonomy of technique extends into other areas and comes to function as a principle of exclusion and a mark of distinction, it must be seen in the context of a profes-sion's efforts to achieve market monopoly. We are back, therefore, to the unique combination of advantages which medicine enjoyed in this regard.

This singularity of medicine is important. For, indeed, to choose it as an occupa-tional model when neither the advantages of its market structure, nor in many cases the advantages of its cognitive basis, can be reproduced, in an *ideological* choice. As such, it suggests the general ideological functions of the professional model. I can only argue here that autonomy of technique is inseparable from the privileges on which it is founded and into which it extends; and if it is true that medicine pro-vides the standard model of professionalization, it is because of those very privi-leges, which for other occupations represent the prize at the end of the road.

There is one final aspect which makes medicine distinct: in a secularized society, medicine serves the most directly the "sacred" value of life. Of all the professions, it appears to have the strongest claims to an ideal of service and devotion to human welfare. This view is widespread. It constitutes a massive capital of social credit on which medicine draws. This capital was accumulated, in part, by actual results and by the active participation of some sectors of the profession in the public health movements of this century and the last. However, if such a generalized image is used in justification of a market monopoly, it becomes a double-edged sword: when people are motivated to seek a physician's services because they believe only a physician can help them, and when they also believe that they have a right to health care, the implicit contradiction between service function and market structure becomes very clear. As one author remarks, "Doctors have convinced the public that they alone are competent to give good medical care, but then are unwilling or unable to make good on the expectations they create."[69]

The universality of the need it serves gave medicine unique advantages in its quest for market monopoloy. It also made it into one of the principal diffusors of the stereotyped image of profession among the public. The contradiction between the use value and the market value of the service renders the profession of medicine particularly vulnerable to challenge, if ever the lay clienteles could overcome their characteristic atomization and attack medicine's corporate power politically, with the strength of a social movement. This potential for challenge is particularly significant today: the *general* demystification of the professional model and of its ideological functions may, indeed, begin with the attack on the archetypal profession of medicine.

Chapter 4

STANDARDIZATION OF KNOWLEDGE AND MARKET CONTROL

The structure of the professionalization process binds together two elements which can, and usually did, evolve independently of each other: a body of relatively abstract knowledge, susceptible of practical application, and a market—the structure of which is determined by economic and social development and also by the dominant ideological climate at a given time.

The standardization or codification of professional knowledge is the basis on which a professional "commodity" can be made distinct and recognizable to the potential publics. This effect is never direct, but mediated by the process of training: cognitive standardization allows a measure of uniformity and homogeneity in the "production of producers." Cognitive commonality, however minimal, is indispensable if professionals are to coalesce into an effective group.

What makes the codification of knowledge so important from the point of view of the professional project is that it depersonalizes the ideas held about professional practice and its products. It sets up a transcendent cognitive and normative framework within which, ideally, differences in the interpretation of practice and in the definition of the "commodity" can be reconciled. The formalization of the cognitive base of a profession has a powerful effect on professional unification because it allows a deeper and more thorough standardization of the production of producers than would otherwise be possible. Let me briefly examine the reasons for this.

The condition for the unification of a professional area is, obviously, that there be a group of professionals ready to champion the propagation of one "paradigm," and that this group have enough persuasive or coercive power to carry the task through. The task is immensely easier when knowledge is depersonalized by formalization, for all depersonalized knowledge tends to become objectified, if not "objective." This means that the validity of this knowledge appears to transcend the particular circumstances and subjective preferences of the groups that produce it (or reproduce it, by use or transmission). The more formalized the cognitive basis, the more the profession's language and knowledge appear to be connotation-free and "objective." Hence the superiority of a *scientific* basis for professional unification: as pointed out in the preceding chapter, it not only produces a more formalized language but also links a profession to the dominant system of cognitive legitimation. A scientific basis stamps the professional himself with the legitimacy of a general body of knowledge and a mode of cognition, the epistemological superiority of which is taken for granted in our society. The connection with superior cognitive rationality appears to establish the superiority of one professional "commodity" *independently* of the interests and specific power of the group or coalition which advocates this definition. The monopolistic professional project is legitimized, therefore, by the appearance of neutrality.

The argument up to now implies an assumption of linear cumulative advance toward the objective and ideological advantages which derive from standardized knowledge and cognitive rationalization. This assumption can be dispelled by considering the internal dynamics of cognitive unification, and the changing tension between standardized knowledge and elements of professional practice which cannot be reduced to average or standard form.

From its beginning, the professional project of organization for a market necessarily involves attempts to formalize a body of knowledge. However standardized, knowledge is applied by individual professional producers; it is therefore inseparable from the cognitive makeup and whole personality of these individuals. This implies three things: first, the social characteristics which professionals share at a given time will influence the extent and the direction of standardization, for they will be related to the criteria of exclusion and inclusion articulated by a particular professional group. Second, the group of producers who takes the leadership of the professional project will define, as well, the areas that are not amenable to standardization; they will define, that is, the place of unique individual genius and the criteria of talent "that cannot be taught." Third, the place of individual talent, or personal charisma, in the practice of a vocation, will change during the process of unification of a profession. Nontransferable skills and individual genius appear to be linked to cognitive *indetermination* (or, in other words, to what cannot be standardized in the cognitive basis and in the practice of a profession).

In a brilliant analysis of French medicine, the sociologists H. Jamous and B. Peloille propose an interesting cognitive definition of profession. While any productive activity implies a measure of indetermination, professions are "occupations . . . whose indetermination/technicality ratio, intrinsic to the systems of production, is generally high."[1] While technicality represents the "means that can be mastered and communicated in the forms of rules," indetermination covers those "means that escape rules and, at a given historical moment, are attributed to the virtualities of the producers."[2] Because indetermination allows secrecy, control over productive skills tends to remain in the hands of individual masters, who can therefore pick and choose the apprentices with whom they are willing to share their secrets. Cohesion among the producers comes, essentially, from the corporate defense of privileges rooted in the monopoly of "secret" skills and from the cultural tradition generated by the social structures of corporate defense. Such, roughly, is the pattern of the guild.[3]

In terms of Jamous and Peloille's analysis, the dialectics of indetermination and codification are a central dimension of work. Inherent in every productive activity is a tendency to codify and rationalize production. In the analytical framework I have proposed, the structural need for such rationalization in a professional area of production is both revealed and maximized by orientation to a market of services. The necessity of rationalization and standardization is, in fact, one of the traits that distinguishes the modern guild-like professions from their *ancien régime* predecessors. Both historically and logically, standardization appears to have a democratic potential: because it reduces the margin of indetermination and secrecy, standardization broadens the possibilities of access to a body of technical and cognitive skills. It tends, therefore, to be advocated by those who are excluded from the occupational privileges based on secrecy.

Such was the case of the French clinicians who, in the wake of the 1789 Revolution, dethroned the medical guilds and the healing orders from the hospitals. Less than a century later, they were themselves confronted with the rise of bacteriology. To this, the clinical establishment responded by accentuating indetermination and by equating professional excellence with virtualities which they alone claimed to possess and they alone could recognize and judge: to the new scientific medicine, they opposed the irreplaceable role of "bedside experience" and the subjectivity which "real" medicine demands.[4] Jamous and Peloille argue that this is a general and even recurrent pattern in the history of occupations and that it generally involves three partially overlapping phases:

> In the first, both the professional ideology put out by the dominant members and the struggles develop around the conditions governing the existence, in the activity in question, of scientific rationality or transferable techniques. In the second, it is the role played by the latter, as the means of attaining the results, which is saturated with ideology and which is at the center of each confrontation. Finally, in the third, it is the social function of the activity and of production which becomes primarily the object of conflict and of ideological rationalizations.[5]

Without endorsing the arbitrary division into phases, which it may be difficult to generalize, the first two appear to coincide with Kuhn's pre-paradigmatic stage: the dynamics of paradigm competition generate unification efforts and narrow a field by limiting the alternative definitions that can be given of it.[6] It is at this point of cognitive unification that the dialectics of indetermination and standardization become visible, as the expression of internal conflicts for control of the organizational project and of the professional market. The phase of professional organization in which standardization becomes a central issue obviously implies that a measure of cognitive commonality has already been achieved within each conflicting group. It also implies that organizational bases already exist.

Indeed, if commonality of cognitive understandings among the professional producers is envisaged as a continuum, extreme cognitive disunity, at one end, can only reinforce itself: the appearance of original talents and new interpretations of the field would, indeed, multiply disparate personality cults. With an organizational base, however, personal followings can become institutionalized into "schools," while the visibility, centrality, and resources of the organization determine the influence of individual genius. Such appears to have been the case of medical "marginals" such as Sir Astley Cooper at St. Guys, Pierre Louis, François Magendie, and Claude Bernard in the Parisian hospitals, Louis Pasteur in his laboratory, or Johannes Muller and Carl Ludwig in the German research institutes.

The case analyzed by Jamous and Peloille, however, suggests an analogy with Kuhn's stage of "paradigm confrontation" precisely because it is an extreme case: the rationalization inherent in the "bacteriological revolution" involved a view of medicine which negated the dominant role of the clinicians. As Jamous and Peloille point out, "the affirmation of an essentially clinical definition of medicine . . . has the function of delaying as long as possible this differentiation [between theoretical and practical medicine] which tends to turn the clinical doctor into one who simply applies medical knowledge."[7] Resolution of the conflict required what was, in fact, a true coup de force of the government: the 1953 Debré Reform, enacted "from above" with lay participation.

Indeed, what made the conflict so deep in the case of French medicine was the coincidence between a paradigmatic change and a clearcut situation of power: for a long time the clinicians controlled all the strategic positions in the Faculty and in the hospitals, while the biologists were either subordinates on their staffs, relatively marginal academics, or researchers "outside the circuit" in a few independent institutes.

In America, the effects of the "bacteriological revolution" were different: they could only be appropriated and utilized for professional superiority by the few medical schools which had the means—that is, the money for full-time faculties, laboratories, libraries, and teaching hospitals—and the image of devotion to the public welfare which alone could justify philanthropic or, later on, governmental investments. Scientific medicine did not threaten an already established and recognized medical hierarchy: in fact, it had the unintended consequence of creating a hierarchy and an elite within the medical profession.[8]

Not all cases of advancing rationalization and standardization of the cognitive basis of a profession involve conflict. If leadership in the rationalizing effort is taken by practitioners who are already recognized as eminent within a relatively stable hierarchy, the emergent standards, far from displacing them, codify elements of their own practice and of its implicit or explicit theory. What may happen, over time, is that the readjustment in the "indetermination/technicality ratio" results in a redistribution of functions which respects the existing hierarchy: the elites gradually delegate the most standardized areas of practice and research to subordinate groups, which may be added "at the bottom" of the professional hierarchy.[9]

A different resolution of potential conflict is suggested by the emergence and secession of specialties: this process can be seen as involving efforts of codification of a new area, or as the articulation of a sub-paradigm by a group of professionals. Because such groups do not attack the core with which the dominant professional group identifies, they are not "forced into" the existing hierarchy: rather, they branch out and generate their own professional stratification, parallel but not subordinate to the pre-existing system. The creation of a new field or subfield may be a solution for newcomers in a crowded field controlled by conservative elders.[10]

The general "crisis of legitimacy" analyzed by Jamous and Peloille may be a very particular case; it illuminates, nevertheless, the general dynamics of the professional structure: elements of cognitive rationality are used in a profession's project of market control, in its internal conflicts of power, and in its collective assertion of status. Cognitive rationality cannot be formally treated as an isolated attribute of profession, for it never appears in its pure form; it is always embodied in the institutions for professional training, selection, and control and is often evident in the midst of political struggle. The correspondence between advancing cognitive rationality and the process of unification and overarching organization of a profession can be illustrated indirectly, by looking at the changing context within which individual reputations are established, since the attribution of talent always reflects the state of organization of a profession.

A first step toward the subordination of individual talent to the unity of the professional field comes with the emergence of organizations with "profession-wide" significance: the incumbent of a high-ranking role in such an organization may be viewed as talented merely because of the position he occupies. "Amtcharisma"— the fusion of organizational status with personal reputation—has the effect of depersonalizing talent. Thus, a position on a licensing board or on a board of health helped the reputation of American physicians before the rise of scientific medicine, despite the persistence of sectarian disputes. Professional societies, in fact, implicitly count on this effect of organizational affiliation to attract members and keep them under control.

Advances in the unification and standardization of professional knowledge have a different effect, which the French clinicians rightly feared: "theoretical" and "practical" knowledge become distinct. The organization of centers for the production of knowledge sharpens this bifurcation and tends to subordinate the practitioners, who "apply" knowledge, to those who produce it. This subordination is magnified when the centers of cognitive production become, as well, the principal agencies of professional training.

As the codification of knowledge advances, apprenticeship is superseded, or at least necessarily preceded, by formal training. A profession's dependence on formal institutions of training enhances the role of educators, who are increasingly identified with the theoretical rather than the practical side of the profession. As the educators themselves develop a consciousness of their interests and become concerned with professional autonomy and professional privileges, their role increases in the profession as a whole. A growing number of future practitioners is exposed to their influence and formed by a body of knowledge which educators define and to which they often contribute directly. They are the first members of the profession to discern "budding talent" and to attribute it on the basis of "theoretical" ability. A presumption of talent in later professional practice derives from the reputation of the institution where a professional has been trained. Educators, obviously, have more control over training institutions than practitioners do. The attribution of talent, therefore, depends in large part on the structural position of educators; at the same time, it tends to increase the likelihood that educators will be recognized as spokesmen for the profession as a whole.[11]

A different effect comes from the concentration of increasing numbers of professionally trained individuals in the production of theoretical knowledge. On the one hand, such concentration accelerates the apparently autonomous evolution of the cognitive basis. On the other hand, it increases the tendency toward specialization. Theoretical distinction tends to overshadow practical talent *at the same time* that it tends to become more esoteric, granted to specialists by specialists and fully meaningful only in their circles.

While specialization restricts the scope of individual genius, the basic cognitive unification achieved by the profession as a whole legitimizes this specialized talent: individual reputations cannot be dismissed as mere personality cults, for they are granted by professional peers whose credentials allegedly stamp them as superior (though standardized) talents. In fact, all accepted professionals increasingly tend to come from the centers which monopolize the production and transmission of knowledge, and also the production of producers. The credentials of the average producer purport to mean that he has achieved at least standard mastery over a standardized body of knowledge, which is now recognized as more valid than its competitors. When these standardized professional talents recognize one of their peers as exceptional, their judgment cannot be questioned without questioning the very bases of professional privilege—or, from the inside, *without questioning the profession's internal stratification.*

Thus, at the level of theoretical production, colleague sanction of individual talents becomes more legitimate *at the same time* that it becomes narrower and less accessible to general review.[12] The closed corporate basis on which academic eminence is achieved appears more autonomous than eminence in consulting practice: heteronomous, extra-professional elements always enter the latter. Today, beyond a narrow local sphere, the media intervene to maximize the heteronomy. The divergence between the practical and the theoretical or academic sectors of a profession is accentuated by the apparent insulation of the latter: they may, indeed, claim the privilege of making the only "authentic" reputations because of their superior autonomy and "purity" of motives. However, when a profession has reached the phase in which it can claim standardized cognitive superiority, it is hard on its unity "toward the outside world" to denounce altogether an "eminent" *licensed* practitioner as a fraud or a quack. Professional repudiation of heteronomous reputations, therefore, tends to not be asserted in public.

This discussion has emphasized the point of view that the standardization allowed by a common and clearly defined basis of training is far more important for the unification of a profession than the more diffuse subcultural aspects, which are often underscored as major aspects of the socialization process and arbitrarily distinguished from the cognitive and technical basis.[13] This basis defines the common language and the tacit knowledge that distinguish a profession as a whole from the laity. *It is, in fact, the main support of a professional subculture.* Those professions that do not have such a solid support tend, by contrast, to create and emphasize pure mannerisms (including cognitive ones, such as unnecessary jargon or unjustifiably esoteric techniques or "pseudo-paradigmatic" changes).

Furthermore, as a profession strengthens its ties with formal institutions of training, it *also* obtains a base of broader subcultural standardization: the professional school or the university spawn a subculture of their own, to which relatively large numbers of apprentices are exposed. Thus, cognitive standardization appears to be one crucial, if not the most crucial, variable in the sequence which, passing through the rise of monopolistic centers of training, leads to credentialed professionalization and market control.

While cognitive standardization is a most powerful generator of deeply shared cultural assumptions, the reverse does not appear to be true: pre-existing cultural homogeneity does not itself breed efforts at cognitive unification of a professional area. For instance, the American physicians or lawyers who met in exclusive societies (of different degrees of formality) during the first half of the nineteenth century did not appear to be too interested in raising the *average* quality of the professional producers by standardizing and rationalizing training. The doctors were more interested in establishing homogeneity by elitist exclusiveness—that is to say, in reserving the benefits of organizational affiliation to their social peers—than in propagating their particular definitions of medical practice and medical science.[14] The historian Daniel Calhoun suggests that these groups' *visible* attempts to monopolize marks of distinction left the disunited professions without defense against the Jacksonian ideological attack on privilege, embodied, so it appeared, in the licensing statutes.[15] Presumably, the cultural and social uniformity of these very small groups of professional men was much higher than it could be today. Yet Calhoun reports several cases in which individual talent (or deviance, as it were) could not be accommodated by these small societies, for this would have endangered a unity based more on extra-cognitive similarities than on paradigmatic or quasi-paradigmatic tendencies.[16]

Only with the rise of formal training institutions and standardized training can professions—or more precisely, the associations or elite groups which act as their spokesmen—begin to assume that there is a commonality, however, minimal, among their members. For one thing, the training centers make a first selection among professional aspirants. Toward the end of a professionalization process, regulation of intraprofessional competition becomes "normal." It would be tempting to argue that such things as fee tables, codes of etiquette, and the like transfer competition from the sphere of practice to that of training, in the form of competition for grades and recommendations in undergraduate and graduate training. The available evidence indicates, however, that the correlation between a student's academic achievements and his subsequent success in practice is low and tending to zero.[17]

What training centers appear to do for practicing professions is, among other things, to provide them with effectively socialized average members: members, that is, who recognize a profession's hierarchy and, implicitly, the criteria of success on which it is founded, because they themselves have often already entered the professional networks on which success so largely depends.[18] This socialization is fundamental precisely because it touches the average member of a profession, and not only its elites: it could not, therefore, be founded on the capricious variation of professional subcultures, even if these corresponded to an accepted professional hierarchy. Its homogeneizing and unifying effects depend upon the standardized body of knowledge to which the average student has been exposed and which is socially accepted as superior to the knowledge acquired outside, by experience on the job or in an avocation. In this manner, the average professional producer comes equipped with at least a minimal sense of the *cognitive superiority* which he shares with all other professional producers and which distinguishes all of them from the laity. Monopoly of training and credentialing establishes and institutionalizes this clear dividing line between professional and layman, a line which is seldom challenged or even questioned by the internal conflicts within a profession. Minimal professional solidarity is founded on this sense of shared expertise: while it does not legitimize the internal hierarchy of a profession for its practitioners, at least it legitimizes in their eyes the social division of labor. It is only in generalized crises of legitimacy in the larger society that such order comes to be questioned.

DIMENSIONS OF MARKET CONTROL

In the long and unfinished process of establishing and securing market control, the various professions have different resources available. The analysis of medicine and engineering has identified some of these resources. Their importance for a particular profession at a given time can only be established empirically; it is possible, however, to indicate which conditions are the most favorable to the professional project of market control for each of the structural elements which this project intertwines. The following list recapitulates problems that have been discussed in the preceding pages:

1. The nature of the service that is marketed. (The more salient, the more universal, and the less visible the service, the more favorable the situation is for the profession.)

2. The type of market. (The less competitive the market, the more favorable the situation; but also, the more competitive the market the more the profession is compelled to organize along monopolistic lines. The more independent the market from the capital and goods market, the more favorable the situation is for the profession.)

3. The type of clientele. (The more "universal" and the less organized the clientele, the more favorable the situation is for the profession.)

4. The cognitive basis. (The more standardized and better-defined the cognitive basis, the more it permits the attainment of visibly "good results"; the more esoteric the body of knowledge and the more it approaches a new paradigm, the more favorable the situation is for the profession. Today, these conditions can almost be summarized by saying: the more scientific the cognitive basis, the more favorable the situation is for the profession.)

5. The "production of producers." (The more institutionalized its forms, the more standardized the process, the more it is under the profession's control, the more favorable the situation is for the profession. Indeed, if the demand for services is large and stable, the profession can regulate the supply through its control of admission and thus maximize its power position on the market.)

6. The power relations. (The more independent the professional market from other markets, the more the state is compelled to protect the public by eliminating

the incompetent or less competent professionals, the more favorable the situation is for the profession. Although a powerful sponsoring elite appears to be a favorable condition, in itself it can produce a secure but *dependent* situation for the profession.)

7. The affinity with the dominant ideology. (The more a profession's particular ideology coincides with the dominant ideological structures, the more favorable the situation is for the profession.)

In the preceding chapter, I have attempted to show that, on all counts, medicine was in a favorable position or gradually attained it. Because of this exceptional situation, medicine appears *both* as a prototype and as an exception: it presents a *complete* professional structure and also a "natural" sequence of attainment of monopoly. As Freidson observes, a profession's authority is at its highest "when the number of its members is small in relation to demand and when the clientele is unorganized."[19] Such a monopolistic "seller's market," furthermore, allows a profession to artificially increase the scarcity of the supply. But *demand* is more difficult to manipulate, and few professions can count, like medicine, on unlimited demand. For this reason, most professions attempt to reach an institutional market, which functions "not by the whims of workers and employers, but by rules, both formal and informal. These rules state which workers are preferred or even which employers must buy in this market if they are to buy at all. Institutional rules take the place of individual preference in setting the boundaries."[20]

This model of an institutional market points to the shortcut by which monopoly is sought. The preceding analysis has traced the "natural" genesis of a monopoly in a market of services. One of the central tenets of this analysis has been that, in this kind of market, control must first be instituted at the point of production of the producers; for this reason some degree of cognitive standardization is indispensable to market control. Once the pattern of professional monopoly is established, and above all, once the academic systems have risen as the recognized monopolizers of cognitive legitimation, the university provides the best justification of the claim for an institutional market: monopolizing training is important, but monopolizing it at the university level brings a built-in legitimation of monopoly in terms of cognitive superiority. As we shall see later, this is the shortcut attempted at present by most professionalizing occupations: a legitimized cognitive monopoly appears, indeed, as the best protection a specialized occupation can have against challenges from the lay public.

In a perfect market situation, the sovereignty resides, theoretically, in the consumer. The professions ultimately depend on the public's willingness to accept and legitimize the superiority of their knowledge and skills. The singular characteristic of professional power is, however, that the profession has the exclusive privilege of defining *both* the content of its knowledge and the legitimate conditions of access to it, *while the unequal distribution of knowledge protects and enhances this power*. Even in the case of monopolies that are artificially established by legal decree because the profession's cognitive exclusiveness is shaky, the associations of professional producers always strive to define the content of public relation. One author remarks that "some professional associations have also developed into pre-liminary arenas of public government, in which a large part of the most important law affecting the profession is first formulated."[21]

As in any exchange situation in which power is unequally distributed, the risk of exploitation and abuse is extremely high in the case of these powerful occupa-tions. The professions, however, claim that transactions in the professional markets are radically different from those in the laissez-faire commodity markets; in the latter, caveat emptor is the rule, while in the former, professional work ethics and the ideal of service justify the consumer's trust. In fact, the argument gives norma-tive sanction to an objective reality: the average lay buyer of professional services is compelled to trust the seller because he normally does not have any other stan-dards of evaluation than the judgment of competence passed on the professional by his colleagues (and, in the more or less remote past, by the academic system and by official licensing boards, in which the profession itself is always influential and often dominant). It remains to be examined whether these distinctive markets for services include structural aspects which might account for the fact (or the belief) that professions, in the words of William J. Goode, "can, but typically do not, exploit."[22]

A STRUCTURAL APPROACH TO
THE PROFESSIONAL PHENOMENON

I began by proposing a deductive model of the organizational task which the modern professions faced as they attempted to establish control over their markets in a transformed world. In a sense, this was a guess that certain forces and dimen-sions became determinant in the historical context of the first professionalization movement. This guess was necessary to map the complex reality of the profes-sional phenomenon. With this model in mind, I proceeded then to look at the market situation of medicine, and, by contrast, that of engineering. Of all the professions which exchange services on a market, medicine is, today, the one which most peo-ple are likely to encounter: the universal need that medicine serves makes it the principal agent for diffusing professional stereotypes among the lay public. Not surprisingly, a sociology of professions which tends to abstract its concepts from everyday life almost inevitably supports its theories with evidence drawn from medicine and tends to take it as a parameter for other aspiring occupations.[23]

At almost every step of the analysis, however, we recognized the exceptional nature of this "archetypal" profession. Precisely because medicine was exception-ally favored in its project of market control, it reveals with clarity the elements which a "complete" professional structure must combine. I do not mean by this that "com-plete" professions should exhibit all or a number of the disparate attributes that are visible in medicine, or that they should inevitably strive to replicate them. I mean that a successful project of professionalization, one that comes close to attain-ing the goals of market monopoly, social status, and work autonomy, must be able to combine certain structural elements. The necessity of these elements was not abstracted from the contemporary situation of an exceptionally powerful profession, but deductively established and constructed into an analytical framework. A provisional map of the professional phenomenon has now begun to emerge.

If we view professionalization as a collective project which aims at market control, it appears, first, that this organizational effort brings together structural elements of different origins, which follow independent lines of evolution. On the one hand, we have a specific body of knowledge, including techniques and skills; on the other, a market of services. Both elements have specific boundaries and specific structural characteristics in each profession; both vary nationally and historically (even though, today, the conditions of production and exchange of scientific knowledge tend to internationalize the cognitive content and cognitive structure of professions with a scientific basis). The structure of a professional market is determined by the larger social structure within which it is situated. The stage of economic development, the volume and distribution of national income, the class structure and ethnic composition, the average standard of living, the nature of the state and its policies, and ideology—including a variety of cultural traditions—define the potential, the characteristics, and the dynamics of a profession's market.

I cannot even begin to outline here the social conditions in which knowledge of various kinds is historically produced: this is the subject of the sociology of knowledge and of its various specializations concerned with science, with law, and with the arts. Obviously, the conditions of practice in a professional field, whether they are institutionalized or not, determine what will be considered cognitively and technically relevant in all the broad spectrum of socially available knowledge at a given time.[24] Relatively diffuse philosophical and esthetic outlooks also undoubtedly have an influence.[25] The very breadth and variety of the cognitive, technological, and ideational materials which may become relevant to a professional practice indicate that they can be produced independently from the profession which consciously or unconsciously incorporates them. The modern professional project, however, *tends* to integrate the production of knowledge with professional practice.

The core of the professionalization project is the production of professional producers; this process tends to be centered in and allied with the modern university. The university also tends to become the major center for the production of professionally relevant knowledge. Both of these processes—the producing of practitioners or researchers and the producing of knowledge pure and applied—tend to become increasingly integrated and coherent within the modern university. Training and research increasingly depend on the same institutional structure. Their evolution is at least partially subject to common conditions and is at least partially articulated with the larger society by the same institutional and extra-institutional mediations. Within the university, considerations derived from professional practice (influenced, that is, by the structure and conditions of a professional market) come to bear upon professional training; these practical considerations have a more or less direct influence upon the determination of what constitutes professionally relevant knowledge and even upon the production of this knowledge. Thus, in its modern sense, profession appears to be a structure which links the production of knowledge to its application in a market of services: the training institutions are the empirical arena in which this linkage is effected.

Secondly, the professional project tends toward the monopolization of opportunities for income in a market of services or labor and toward the monopolization of status and work privileges in an occupational hierarchy. The necessary means to these ends is the control and monopolization of relatively standardized professional education. The institutionalized production of professional producers mediates and reveals the contradictions inherent in the structure of the professional project.

Let us briefly recall the general lines of this analysis: in the context of the "great transformation," elite or community patronage was insufficient to guarantee the position and competence of growing numbers of practitioners in expanding markets. As these traditional warrants declined, two movements became visible. Their character and respective importance vary as a function of the larger social structure within which the specific professional projects developed. One movement attacks the privileges of exclusive groups of traditional professionals and their de facto or institutionalized monopolies over marks of professional distribution; simultaneously, the other movement attempts to regulate competition by reconstructing monopoly on different and much broader bases of control. The monopolistic goal of the professional project, which demands regulation and control of access to the professional market on the supply side, contradicts, therefore, the democratization potential inherent in the expansion of professional markets and in the challenge to corporate privileges.

Control of a market of professional services requires the monopolization of competence and the demonstration that this competence is superior to others. It is ideologically necessary for the legitimation of monopoly that instruction—the acquisition of competence—appear to be accessible to all who seek it and are able to assimilate it. This meritocratic legitimation does not become central to the dominant ideology until bourgeois hegemony is consolidated and an "open," though hierarchical, system of education is set in place; it is, however, present in the modern professional project from its inception. The production of professional producers cannot be arbitrarily limited by standards extraneous to a profession's functions. Closure is justified only in terms of the special skills acquired by professional producers who have been freely admitted to training and judged by universalistic criteria. These criteria refer to virtualities of the person which appear to be randomly distributed or else are the result of effort and moral virtues—such are intelligence, studiousness, dedication, perseverance, and general culture as the result of prior efforts.

For this ideological legitimation to be effective, meritocratic access to the educational system must have a semblance of reality. The growth of public investments in education and the expansion of enrollments at the higher levels confirm this appearance and are partly sustained by ideological necessity. Professions, as the occupational roles which most closely tie educational credentials to occupational function, bring a significant and realistic reinforcement to the meritocratic legitimation of social inequality. However, from the monopolistic point of view which is that of the professional project, the necessity of maintaining universalistic and objective appearances in the educational system involves some risks. For one thing, the mark can easily be overshot: the overproduction of professional producers may cause the price of professional services or labor to fall, and result in unemployment or under-employment of specialized and highly trained labor. This recurrent possibility jeopardizes the professional promise of social status: professional education and professional occupations become less certain means of securing social prestige and upper-middle class standards of living.[26] In the long run, the attractiveness and the general social prestige of professional roles can be adversely affected.

Obviously, the risk of overproduction of professional producers can be handled by making the standards of admission into training increasingly stringent and by manipulating licensing examinations. Professionals with vested interests in main-taining the price of their services or labor and the social prestige of their calling make up the standards for both schools and licensing boards. The question, however, is for how long this reduction of supply can be publicly justified by the "pure objec-tivity" of meritocratic standards, especially when the cost of training also tends to increase. As the monopolization of competence becomes more visible, it is also more likely that it will be challenged, especially if the reduction of supply restores the privileges of professional roles. Besides, by comparison with most other jobs and occupations, professional callings always appear as relatively privileged forms of work: the social pressure for admission to professional training does not arise from realistic assessments of the average conditions of work or the absolute char-acteristics predominant in a specific profession at a given time. It is influenced, rather, by traditional and stereotyped images of the professionals' position in the occupational structure as a whole; it responds, that is, to an ideological evaluation of available opportunities in a society. Because of the open and universalistic ap-pearance of the educational system, it is at this level that the monopolistic goal of the professional project enters into visible contradiction with the democratizing and rationalizing dimensions potentially defined by the market orientation. The exclusiveness inherent in any project which tends to assert and secure collective social status aggravates the contradictions.

Finally, in its historical development, the professional project mobilized hetero-geneous ideological means to justify its claims. As I have repeated, universalistic and meritocratic legitimations could not become immediately predominant, de-pendent as they were on the development of apparently open national systems of education. Traditional claims of disinterestedness and public service, integrated into the ideological model of profession, contradict the market orientation of the professional project and the monopolization of competence to which it necessarily tends. Ideologically, these claims deny the invidious implications of monopoly and are used to stave off possible attacks.

In the next chapter I shall examine the origins and substance of these traditional ideological resources. After completing the historical analysis of the development and evolution of the professional model (in Chapters Seven through Ten), I will return, in conclusion, to a closer analysis of the structure, functions, and contradic-tions of profession and professionalism.

Chapter 5

MARKET AND ANTI-MARKET PRINCIPLES

To evaluate the divergences between the market toward which the first modern professions strove and the larger, self-regulating market that was becoming dominant at the time of the profession's emergence, we must return briefly to Karl Polanyi's thesis. The rise of industrial capitalism is characterized, for Polanyi as well as for Marx, by the generalization of commodity exchange and by the ideological appeal to the principle of equivalence of exchange. Legitimation of the new social order is sought in the ideological construction of reality based on this principle of apparent equivalence.[1] Polanyi writes: "The double movement . . . can be personified as the action of two organizing principles in society. . . . The one was the principle of economic liberalism, aiming at the establishment of a self-regulating market, relying on the support of the trading classes, and using largely laissez-faire and free trade as its methods."[2]

The violence which this functionally rational principle of organization does to all the other instances of social practice and to the immemorial fusion of the economic function with other levels of practice, such as the symbolic, the religious, and the political, evokes a parallel and simultaneous countermovement, based on "the principle of social protection aiming at the conservation of man and nature as well as productive organization, relying on the varying support of those most immediately affected by the deleterious action of the market—primarily, but not exclusively, the working and the landed classes—and using protective legislation, restrictive associations, and other instruments of intervention as its methods."[3]

One tempting objection can be immediately disposed of: the professions' reliance on the state to control the access to their markets was and is justified in terms of the protection of the consumer. However, once state-backed monopoly was obtained, it represented the ultimate sanction of market control by a group of professional "producers" and a proved means, thereafter, of protecting themselves against *undue* interference by the state. Indeed, reliance upon the state was not merely a pattern borrowed by the nineteenth-century professions from the medieval guilds, but also the means by which the ascending bourgeoisie had advanced toward a self-regulating market. In Polanyi's words, "The road to the free market was opened and kept open by an enormous increase in continuous, centrally organized, and controlled interventionism. . . . There was nothing natural about laissez-faire . . . laissez-faire itself was enforced by the state . . . [it] was not a method to achieve a thing, it was *the thing to be achieved*."[4]

But, is not the persistent corporate nature of the professions antithetical to the liberal "utopia"? Does it not place the professions on the side of those supporting the "countermovement"? The answer is ambiguous and it largely exceeds the bounds of the market ideal-type which I have heretofore applied to the professions.

I have argued that the organizations of producers which we call professions were indispensable for the constitution of new markets of mainly intangible and rather exceptional products. Corporatism was necessary, though not sufficient, to impose one "definition of the product" as the best and to give it legal sanction. Similarly, corporate class action was necessary to bring about state action in favor of laissez-faire. But this last course was not entered into by the English industrial bourgeoisie until after it had effectively used protectionist laws to achieve the definitive subordination (or elimination) of its economic rivals. At the time of the Anti- Corn Law movement, besides, the bourgeoisie had already been politically enfranchised by the electoral reform of 1832, which was a beginning acknowledgement of bourgeois economic supremacy.

The industrial bourgeoisie had relied, in its rise, on state protectionism and on direct coercion by the state against the proletariat and other categories of the poor. Only after its triumph did the bourgeoisie mobilize for the ideological conquest of the proletariat and the establishment of hegemony.[5] But direct coercion does not make any sense in the conquest of a market that is essentially constituted by ideological definitions. Nor, on the other hand, could professions, as a minor sector of the rising class, mobilize the necessary coercive powers. In other words, their rise depended most crucially on ideological persuasion.[6] Therefore, the continuity of corporate control over the producers was necessary to ensure ideological uniformity around one "definition of the product" and vigilance against ever-resurgent counter-definitions.

PROFESSIONS AND THE
IDEAL OF COMMUNITY

In the older modern professions, as we know, corporate control ultimately succeeded in regulating competition and in establishing some standards of group behavior. This kind of control was not stabilized, however, until after the achievement of cognitive exclusiveness, that is to say, until after the professions had unified their respective areas of the social division of labor. The regulation and organization of market-oriented practice in the professions that consolidated toward the turn of the century stood in contrast to the anarchy of the commodity markets and of capitalist production. Therefore, Emile Durkheim could see in the organization of the professions not only the modern expression of the medieval corporation, but also the social model that would produce the ethics and rules needed by a complex division of labor, and thus save modern society from the chronic anomie rooted in its economy.[7]

If the professions appeared to Durkheim as capable of generating organic solidarity, it is because they possessed some of the characteristics of community which, in their traditional form, were declining in the larger society. William Goode describes the special community of profession by the following traits:

(1) Its members are bound by a sense of identity. (2) Once in it, few leave, so that it is a terminal or continuing status for the most part. (3) Its members share values in common. (4) Its role definitions vis-à-vis both members and non-members are agreed upon and are the same for all members. (5) Within the areas of communal action there is a common language, which is understood only partially by outsiders. (6) The community has power over its members. (7) Its limits are reasonably clear, though they are not physical and geographical, but social. (8) Though it does not produce the next generation biologically, it does so socially, through its control over the selection of professional trainees, and through its training processes it sends these recruits through an adult socialization process.[8]

In preceding pages I have emphasized the essential import and importance of cognitive unification for professional commonality. I have suggested that professional identity is experienced as shared expertise and therefore involves a sense of at least cognitive superiority with regard to the layman or the irregular practitioner. Indeed, the whole process of setting up a monopolistic market of services, based as it is on *articulating and enforcing principles of inclusion and exclusion,* could be simultaneously envisaged as the setting up of a *partial* community. As Goode implies in his fourth point, professions are characterized by a minimal equality among the members in precisely that aspect which is of maximum concern to the organization: namely, the definition of an occupational role, with its prerequisites and prerogatives. In mature professions, exclusion is principally centered in the educational system, which operates a brutal (and continuing) selection among potential recruits; the profession itself can thereafter emphasize inclusion and operate *in the mode* of a community. Although control of "community affairs" is most frequently vested in elites that are difficult to dislodge, the minimal equality among members allows the profession to maintain solidarity. The ideology of participation among equals contributes to legitimize the internal hierarchy and the division of labor within the profession.[9]

Although Durkheim presented the corporation as an industry-wide assembly of *both* employers and employees, he was well aware of the fact that organic solidarity could not emerge unless the "abnormal" forms of the division of labor were eliminated. For this, equality of opportunities was an indispensable, though minimal, prerequisite.[10] The associations of *free* professionals could thus appear to Durkheim as embodying a necessary "nomic" function and as authentic occupational communities because they were based on minimal equality and were therefore minimally legitimate in the eyes of their members. This minimal equality was grounded on the deeply inequalitarian structure of opportunities of the larger society and was, furthermore, only minimal: it coexisted with forms of internal stratification and elite control which replicated more general social conditions. Nevertheless, they were associations of producers with minimally shared attributes and common interests *which did not cut across class lines:* they belonged, therefore, to the genus "trade-union" and not to the genus "industry-wide corporation." Why then, should we treat the association of free professionals as something distinct from its model, the craft union? The first and obvious reason is that the craft union always operated in a subordinate market, where it never controlled either the social and economic conditions of work nor, after mechanization, its technical content. Furthermore, at the beginning of the twentieth century, the craft union was well into its decline, reflecting the increasing subordination and alienation of industrial labor.[11]

What gave the solidarity of professional producers its typical significance in this early phase, then, was that they were *autonomous*. In a market society where labor is a commodity, these associations of free producers had arisen, in fact, in order to *constitute and control* a new type of market. This fundamental aspect modifies the "anti-market" potential of their corporate solidarity. The atypical "community of profession" did not extend its nomic functions beyond the boundaries of its own market position: the solidarity of the professional producers was seldom, if ever, mobilized to advocate or help the organization of their own consumers. Thus, on the consumer side, the ideal professional market closely approximates the atomistic liberal model, while on the producers' side, with all due qualifications, it presents an analogy with the rise of corporate capitalism against the consequences of anarchic competition.[12] If it is true, besides, that "the professions sought to use the state to achieve greater autonomy for themselves vis-à-vis nongovernmental pressures, and sometimes they even used government to protect themselves from government,"[13] then the goal was clearly laissez-faire for the producers, although on the model of liberal pluralism. Thus although the professional community, based on solidarity and on a shared set of cognitive and normative rules, may be seen as part of the reaction against the market, its aims were formulated within a market orientation: the professions' appeal to non-contractual social relations was aimed, in fact, at promoting certain kinds of contractual transactions.

Underlying the preceding arguments is the assumption that *one* sector (even more, a subordinate sector) of the rising class does not by itself define the dominant ideology: its own ideological constructions are therefore subsumed under the cover of the dominant ideology. From the market point of view that has been too greatly emphasized up to now, the rise of the professions appears as one more phase of capitalistic rationalization. My emphasis on the separation from traditional community bases, on the standardization of services, on the standardized "production of producers," on the rational foundations of knowledge, on the links with science and technology, should have made this point abundantly clear. Thus, as Parsons has noted, today's professions share with business certain "elements of the common institutional pattern": reliance on functional rationality embodied in science and in its applications; authority based on functional specificity; predominance of universalistic criteria in the relationship with clients and in the judgment of occupational achievement.[14] The "community of profession" was both an agent and a product of rationalization. It cannot be denied, however, that professions, at least ideologically, espouse anti-market principles. The insulation from the larger society provided by the corporate structure contributes to the survival of these principles, but it does not generate them. We must look elsewhere for their origins.

THE SERVICE IDEAL REVISITED

Because the rise of the professions depended so largely on the establishment of social credit, they had to appeal to general ideological structures. One was the principle of rationalization itself, embodied in the scientific ethos and in the rational authority of technical expertise. But in the nineteenth century, this ideological appeal could not provide a general basis of legitimation. The utilitarian ethos was much more widespread, especially amidst the industrial bourgeoisie, which was the obvious base for an expanding professional market. However, to bank on it, the professions had to show incontrovertibly "good results" and this was not always possible, or did not become possible until late.[15] In any case, for results to be judged good, criteria common to those used by the profession (or dramatic demonstrations) had to become available to the public. Furthermore, age-old fears of professional abuse had to be overcome. For this, trust in the probity and ethicality of the professional practitioners had to be convincingly established—ethicality being, in Freidson's words, "prerequisite for being trusted to control the terms of work without taking advantage of such control."[16]

The crusading efforts of some professionals—both scholars and practitioners—attempted to spread among the public not only a respect for knowledge but for "the *values* of science as ingredients of social and economic reform and as professional ethics."[17] This "connection between the scientific movement, social mission, and professionalism" was conspicuously absent in Germany and particularly vigorous in Britain and in the United States.[18] But even there, it was still an embryonic theme, embodied in few practices and submerged, besides, in the continuing social dislocations and dreadful human costs of the competitive phase of capitalism. The scientific legitimation still appealed only to small enlightened minorities, even within the professions themselves.[19]

Therefore, the only general ideological structures on which professional ethicality and social credit could be convincingly established were those inherited from the passing traditional order. They were antithetical to the principles of the acquisitive society, although it should not be forgotten that, ultimately, an appeal to these ideological structures was paradoxical, for "the guaranteeing of competence and integrity in a laissez-faire economy, has an economic basis: it guarantees the continuous saleability of professional services."[20] Two main ideological "sources" can be distinguished.

The first, as Polanyi would have it, was a self-protective reaction of a society subverted and dislocated by industrial capitalism. The regard of the professions (or some individuals within them) for the public interest can be connected with this source.

Before the industrial and democratic revolutions, as we know, the public of the three learned professions—law, medicine, and the ministry (which subsumed university teaching)—was almost exclusively composed of the rich and the aristocracy. The industrial revolution and its sociopolitical consequences brought about the possibility of opening up new markets for services. This opening was far from representing a fundamental democratization of the professional markets, either on the producers' or on the consumers' side. As we shall see in the next chapter, the process of professionalization was also a project of collective mobility: the clienteles toward which the leading professional reformers naturally looked were the happy few, or not quite so few, who benefited from the industrial revolution. The professional sector of the middle classes aspired to gain at least as much prestige as the most acceptable commoners (or, in America, the successful businessmen) within this social stratum. This social ambition colored the professional project; it is likely to have inspired the motivation of most of the professionals who responded to the call of the early organizers, for it is obvious that efforts to secure a relatively new market would have resulted in some benefit for the self-seeking individual. But this is not the whole picture. As I have emphasized, the need to establish social credit for markets of services involved more than the already difficult and complex task of guaranteeing to the public's satisfaction the competence and probity of the producers: it involved shaping the need of the consumers, channelling it toward the conception of service advocated by the regular profession. The production of new needs, or the direction of largely unrecognized needs toward new forms of fulfillment, is a civilizing function, to the extent that it does not obey first to the profit motive, but seeks first to improve the *quality* of life. It is in this sense that the professions' organization for the market exceeded the market-orientation: insofar as they *had* to promote the fulfillment of new functions, they contributed to what Spencer called the "augmentation of life"; because they could not secure the market without guaranteeing the high quality of their services, they had to maintain certain standards among the producers. In Tawney's words:

> [Professionals] may, as in the case of the successful doctor, grow rich; but *the meaning* of their profession, both for themselves and for the public, is not that they make money, but that *they make health, or safety, or knowledge, or good government, or good law.* . . . [Professions uphold] as the criterion of success the end for which the profession, whatever it may be, is carried on, and [subordinate] the inclination, appetites, and ambition of individuals to the rules of an organization which has as its object *to promote the performance of function.*[21]

Guaranteeing competence, as we know, was part of the process of rationalizing and standardizing the "production of producers." But even this rationalizing aspect contrasts, at least superficially, with capitalist functional rationalization measured in terms of costs and output: indeed, ideology and normative conceptions of quality are more *visibly* incorporated in the "production" of men than in the production of real commodities.

The anti-market components of profession become much more distinct if we consider the aspect of "augmentation of life." After the industrial revolution, in fact, the "civilizing function" of profession had to face directly the consequences of unplanned, "savage," capitalist industrialization. These consequences appeared in condensed form in the large industrial city, which was not only the abode of the industrial proletariat, but also that of most professionals. The efforts of a few professional leaders to promote the "performance of function" necessarily had to come to grips with the life conditions of the poor and the abuses of the classes with economic and political power. The mission of medicine was, in this respect, particularly clear. As one historian remarks,

> The need for sanitary reform emphasized the need for social reform in general. . . . Hence the liberal movements that developed in all Western nations between 1820 and 1848, in opposition to the reactionary governments of that period, were closely associated with the movement for sanitary reform. It was no accident, for instance, that such a medical master as Virchow sympathized with the Revolution of 1848; or that on the other hand, Friedrich Engels prepared his endictment of English society largely in terms of unnecessary disease and death.[22]

Before medicine's "bacteriological revolution," the public health movement had to rely more on statistical and mechanical solutions than on biological ones: lawyers and men with a taste for statistics, engineers and architects, public figures and social reformers, joined with physicians in the struggle for the sanitation of cities and the establishment of boards of public health and medical facilities. In America, at the turn of the century, the slum reform movement similarly pooled together the efforts of social reformers and various reform-oriented professionals.[23] In their own area, lawyers attempted to reform the judiciary by striving to influence the selection of judges. Teachers, in America, struggled to pressure local school boards in a direction which they viewed as progressive.[24] The spirit of "professional" probity and advancement of function penetrated the civil service in the wake of the various reform acts; small clusters of men planted this idea in the civil bureaucracies: the best example is perhaps that of the British factory inspectors, whose reports Marx praised so vigorously.[25] These various efforts, together with the "anti-market" practice of graduating fees according to the client's income may be seen as paternalistic efforts for the protection of society: especially in the case of medicine and psychiatry, they continued traditional and declining forms of community or state assistance to the poor and derelict. On the other hand, inserted as these efforts were in a changing social order, they foreshadow the contemporary notion of guaranteeing the social order through public welfare functions—including the tutelary paternalism and the differential quality of services that are essentially rendered to the poor.[26] This orientation should not be overrated: more recently, the powerful professions have had to be forced into social service while, in the past, most practitioners, caught in strenuous competition, remained indifferent to the potential for "augmenting life" inherent in their calling.

The professions' "civilizing function" coexists, by definition, with a market orientation and is fuscd with it. Nevertheless, many view the professions' "service ideal" as a detached and basically distinctive trait.[27] The "community of profession" collectively holds this ideal (partly because it needs to profess it publicly, in order to gain social credit and autonomy); the assumption is that, in subordinating its members to collective norms and to an internal system of reward and punishment which makes "virtue pay," the profession instills the service ideal in its practitioners. In the words of one author, "[It] demands real sacrifice from practitioners as an ideal and from time to time, in fact."[28] As Freidson has observed, however, it is illicit to jump from the verifiable attributes of occupational organizations (expressed in formal documents, by-laws, codes, curricula, formal definitions or malpractice, and the like) to the attitudes of individuals. These attitudes can only be determined empirically and Freidson remarks that there are no data about the proportion of professionals who do, in fact, manifestly follow a service ideal; nor do we know how intense this orientation is, or how predominant, relative to other professional orientations; finally, we do not know if the service ideal is more widespread and more intense, in general, among professionals than among other workers.[29]

We *know,* however, that of all broad occupational strata today, professionals report most often *high* satisfaction with their work.[30] As Wilensky has shown, more refined questions than "how satisfied are you with your present job?" and a subtler survey design reveal that, at times, "the difference between occupational groups within the same occupational stratum is greater than the difference between groups two strata apart."[31] Nevertheless, despite the great importance of particular work settings and the variations among various professional groups, all of them declare more often than other workers that they "would try to get into a similar type of work if they could start over again."[32] In the light of Wilensky's other data, this response cannot be unambiguously tied to the objective advantages of professional work over other kinds of occupations: according to Wilensky's measures of dissatisfaction, the highest proportion of "alienated" workers was to be found among highly paid engineers in an unsatisfactory firm; these same engineers, solo lawyers, and urban university professors exhibited the same proportions of "high attachment" to their work as the two lower white-collar groups. However, those professional categories with the highest proportion of respondents reporting indifference on all the items of the questionnaire (16 percent among solo lawyers and professors in two universities with religious affiliation) were still six percentage points below the non-professional categories with the smallest proportion of work-indifferent members (lower white-collar and upper blue-collar under thirty).[33]

This ambiguity suggests that the professionals' response may be reflecting different levels of ideology which cumulatively shape *their view* of their relations to their work. At one level, identification with their work reveals the influence of the general ideology's positive evaluation of professions: Wilensky's professional respondents "know" that their roles are among the most prestigious and desirable in the society. At another level, they reflect the effectiveness of the process of "production of producers": the self has become invested in the work role, at least to some extent. In fact, in Wilensky's measures of the "fit" between prized attributes of the self and dimensions of the work role, the professions taken as a whole show relatively more attachment and less indifference to their work than the non-professional categories: the difference in scores between professional and between lower white-collar categories is almost everywhere larger than that between white collar and upper blue-collar groups.

By general agreement, work-connected values are losing their nineteenth-century "sacred" cast in our society: the attitudes of individual professionals may be increasingly converging toward a middle zone of indifference to work: all the lower occupational categories (except the lowest, which are characterized by a more salient and vigorous rejection of their generally detestable work) preceded them in this movement toward passive adjustment. Nevertheless, the difference in measures of attachment and indifference suggests that professionals still tend to be clearly more "work-oriented" than other occupational groups. This work orientation includes what we may call an entrepreneurial dimension: it will presumably be stronger among "free" professionals and it must have been still stronger when the professions emerged in their modern form, at the time of the industrial countries' take-off and during the consolidation of their development. As Wilensky remarks: "wherever economic growth is sustained, societal values which acquire a sacred cast and which are favorable to economic growth will appear, both furthering and reflecting that growth."[34]

We are not concerned here with the role played by the Puritan ethic in bringing about the economic ethos of nineteenth-century capitalism. But it is important to distinguish the two dimensions which, in Weber's analysis, fuse to form the "specifically bourgois economic ethic": one is an entrepreneurial dimension; the other is the notion of calling or vocation. Together, they provide an ethical justification for capital accumulation and the maximization of pecuniary interests. Insofar as the professions' work orientation is based on this ethic, it reinforces their market orientation and not their anti-market components. The entrepreneurial orientation and the notion of calling are, however, analytically distinct: Weber kept them separate, as he remarked that Protestant asceticism had "legalized the exploitation of this specific willingness to work in that it *also* interpreted the employer's business activity as a calling."[35]

In itself, the notion of calling is the ethical base of the modern division of labor. Durkheim also had seen its importance: in an individualistic and atomized society, the notion of calling appeared as the necessary link between the "cult of the individual" and the collective needs, characterized by increasing economic interdependence. In Durkheim's idealistic language, "the categorical imperative of the moral conscience is assuming the following form: *Make yourself usefully fulfill a determinate function.*"[36] In his approach, only the fit between individual talents and work roles could generate organic solidarity. Essential to this fit was the free choice of a vocation: "as this specialization results from purely individual efforts, it has neither the fixity nor the rigidity which a long heredity alone can produce. These practices are very supple because they are very young. As it is the individual who engaged himself in them, he can disengage himself, and betake himself to new ones."[37]

The elements that explain Durkheim's interest in the professions also explain the work-orientation of professionals. Because professional roles are privileged, desirable, reserved to a minority, and today, accessible only after relatively prolonged and difficult training, those who choose them do so, most often, by an apparently free choice: a choice, that is, in which the individual seeks to maximize the fit between his talents or preferences and a work role. In our society, what Durkheim called abnormal forms of the division of labor—forced choices and anomic functional diversity—have never ceased to predominate; professionals, therefore, atypically embody occupational "normality": because their choice was relatively free and their work is relatively interesting and creative, they maintain alive the idea that work may have an *intrinsic* value. This orientation toward work is characteristic, in itself, of the Renaissance ideal of craftsmanship. In principle, we should expect professionals to place more intrinsic value in their work than most other occupational categories. To the extent that this is true, calling supersedes the entrepreneurial orientation. While the latter's work ethic may be the most vigorous, the values it places on work are extrinsic: whether the goal is profit or salvation, God or mammon, it is outside the occupational function itself.[38]

The two dimensions—entrepreneurial and vocational—are *analytically* distinct, but they appear fused in the early modern professions. As the conditions of professional work change, the entrepreneurial emphasis on independent employment may be replaced by mere economic instrumentalism. The vocational orientation, on the other hand, encompasses both an emphasis on self-realization and creative self-expression, and a concern with the field of the profession as a whole, that is, with the "advancement of function" singled out by Tawney. The fusion of vocational and entrepreneurial orientations generates tensions, both for the individual professional and for the profession as a whole. The general conditions of work and the ideology of the profession broadly define, in each case, the type of tension that will arise.

I have implied in the preceding paragraphs that the "ideal of service"—for which there is scant empirical evidence—translates at the individual level into a work ethic which places *intrinsic* value on work. Whatever else the service orientation is in a secularized society, its ethical and motivational base must include a sense of work as self-realization and a sense of duty to one's calling deeper than just compliance with a set of standards. C. Wright Mills, commenting on the passing of the craftsmanship ideal in today's occupational world, observed: "The sharp focus on money is part and parcel of the lack of intrinsic meaning that work has come to have."[39] This decline is associated with a variety of objective factors. In any case, it seems legitimate to expect that the loss of work's intrinsic value will result in relatively greater commercialization for the profession and greater instrumentalism for the individual professionals.

To recapitulate this discussion of the first source of "anti-market" ideological values: what Polanyi called "the self-protection of society" immediately evokes the professions' service ideal, which I have treated as an orientation toward the advancement of the profession's function and, at the individual level, as a work ethic based on a blend of calling and craftmanship ideals. The advancement of function—which Tawney called "the principle of purpose"—necessarily involved the professions with the consequences of savage industrialization in the competitive phase of capitalism. The intrinsic value of work stood in contrast to the kind of work that was becoming the norm for the industrial masses: the sale of their labor power was compulsory (insofar as it was the only alternative to starvation), and in the factories work was also becoming increasingly separated from skill or craft. To the extent that the professions incorporated the "principle of purpose" and elements of the ideal of craftsmanship, they possessed anti-market and anti-capitalist components. Their corporate exclusiveness contributed thereafter to maintaining these components.

The second ideological source on which the professions founded their claims to ethicality was a pre-industrial conception of social bonds. The appeal to communal ideals constitutes, in fact, another element of "social self-protection" in Polanyi's view. The European pre-industrial community, however, was deeply inegalitarian, while different but no less inegalitarian strains ran through the fabric of the democratic United States. The ideology of community contained, therefore, elements of legitimation of the class structure. These ideological legitimations were in the broader sense religions. In Hobsbawm's words, they were manifest in "the general social conviction that men had duties as well as rights, that virtue was not simply the equivalent of money, and the lower orders, though low, had a right to their modest lives in the station to which God had called them.''[40] This pre-industrial ideology carried over in the model of the gentleman, which was also important in the nineteenth-century United States. This model animated the professions' mobility project. It was incorporated into the prevailing conception of liberal education and passed, from there, into the professions' attempts at formalizing an economic ethic. In the words of one author, ''The new professional men brought one scale of values—the gentleman's—to bear upon the other—the tradesman's—and produced a specialized variety of business morality which came to be known as 'professional ethics' or 'etiquette.' ''[41]

Anti-market and anti-capitalist principles were incorporated in the professions' task of organizing for a market because they were elements which supported social credit and the public's belief in professional ethicality. Thus, at the core of the professional project, we find the fusion of antithetical ideological structures and a potential for permanent tension between ''civilizing function'' and market-orientation, between the ''protection of society'' and the securing of a market, between intrinsic and extrinsic values of work. In the analytical framework I proposed, the securing of a market was the minimum common denominator which bound all kinds of professionals to obeying their ''community's'' standards. Thus, the professions embodied both leveling and differentiating principles of social organization: while standardizing the ''production of producers'' and the conditions of entry, on the one hand, professionals sought, on the other, to attain by these means legitimate but unequal status positions. It is from the ideal-typical point of view of collective mobility that we must now envisage their project.

PART II

THE COLLECTIVE CONQUEST
OF STATUS

Chapter 6

THE COLLECTIVE MOBILITY PROJECT

I have argued that the structure of professions results from two processes: the process of organization for a market of services, and the process of collective mobility by which the early modern professions attached status and social standing to their transformed occupational roles. The two processes are distinct analytical constructs which can be "read" out of the same empirical material. In other words, they are different ways of organizing or giving meaning to a unitary historical process.

The process of organization for a market of services, which I have analyzed in the first part of this study, has theoretical precedence: for indeed, in order to use occupational roles for the conquest of social status, it was necessary first to build a solid base in the social division of labor. Without a relatively secure market, the new pattern of mobility inaugurated by the nineteenth-century professions would have been meaningless. Actually, all the devices mobilized for the construction of a professional market and the organization of the corresponding area of the social division of labor also served the professions' drive toward respectability and social standing. I have attempted to show in the last chapter that this relation was reciprocal: the success of the professional mobility project depended on the existence of a stable market; but also, in the process of securing a market, the professions variously incorporated ideological supports connected with "anti-market" structures of stratification. These pre-industrial structures provided both models of gentility toward which nineteenth century professional men aspired, and images which legitimized status inequality. Because these models evoked legitimizing notions of disinterestedness and noblesse oblige, they helped to guarantee on the market the professions' ethicality. Insofar as the professions relied on these guarantees, they reinforced the ideological persistence of "old" stratification structures.

The analysis of mobility which I am proposing now necessarily returns to elements of the structure of profession which have already been analzyed from the perspective of the market. The incorporation of ideological warrants derived from the pre-industrial system of stratification does not contradict my theoretical standpoint: the organization of modern professional markets implied, in principle, the *formal* emancipation of the old professions from their aristocratic or communal supports. In the same manner, we must consider now to what extent the persistence of old stratification structures and imagery modified what was specifically new in the mobility project of the professions. Before this, however, I must clarify the objectives of this collective project, which I have characterized vaguely as "gaining status through work."

In the first place, the professional project of social mobility is considered as a *collective* project, because only through a joint organizational effort could roles be created—or redefined—that would bring the desired social position to their occupants. This point connects the professional project with broader processes of social stratification at work in the "great transformation." Suffice it to note here that the aims of this collective mobility project are, ultimately, individualistic, although the project and its means are collective: it is through the upgrading of an occupation—with the attempts to control the individual members which this involves—that prestige is to be attached to the professional roles, and by extension, to their occupants.

Although the means used in this collective search for prestige are those used in the establishment of the professional market, they spell, here, a different end result: that is to say, the result envisaged from the point of view of collective mobility (and of expected individual benefits derived from prestige) is not intelligible from the market point of view. The sources of prestige which are tapped or incorporated as means of social mobility in the professional project can be schematically differentiated along three main dimensions:

1. In terms of their relation to the professional market: are they attached to structures relatively independent from the professional market or do they flow, instead, from an achieved market position?

In the formative period, the predominant means of the professional mobility project are independent, as yet, of the market. I shall indicate, in terms of an ideal-type, how the situation changes when the market is established and the profession is consolidated.

2. In terms of their modern or traditional character, implicitly and explicitly defined in the preceding chapters. This dimension distinguishes the old or *ancien régime* professionals, dependent on aristocratic sources of legitimation and elite sponsorship, from the professionals who are attempting to devise their own criteria or exclusion-inclusion on the basis of tested competence and tested mastery over a professionally defined body of knowledge. The state backing which the latter *also* seek is claimed, however, on the basis of superior competence and no longer on that of association with an elite.

3. In terms of the "autonomous" or "heteronomous" character of the means employed: "autonomous" are those means in the definition or formation of which the professional (or pre-professional) groups played a significant, if not major, role; "heteronomous" are means chiefly defined or formed by other social groups. This dimension overlaps with the preceding one ("traditional" and "modern" means) only in part.

According to these dimensions, a classification of means by which prestige is attached to an occupational role (together with the institutional or structural source in which the means are commonly located) can be attempted. A general analytical approach is implicit in such a classificatory device: when a set of means is not available at a given time in a specific society, this lack of access leads professional entrepreneurs to emphasize or to rely more exclusively upon another set of means.

The overschematic classification in Table 1 is proposed only as an ordering device.[1] It cannot be generalized without substantial modifications to professionalization processes which take place within an already defined institutional context (that is, contemporary professions spawned by the state and by corporate economic organizations). In particular, the variable and diffuse ideological mechanisms which recognize a profession's functions as "noble," "progressive," or "socially useful" cannot be located in any one cell; rather, ideology colors the effectiveness of every set of means available to a profession in its mobility project, because it ultimately determines the public trust and prestige which a profession "deserves." Nevertheless, this classificatory device distinguishes between various means by which prestige is attached to an occupational role. In other words, it ranks the typical means that can be mobilized if the members of an occupation are to be "normally" recognized as "gentlemen," as better educated than others in the occupational hierarchy, as more competent than their rivals in the same area of the social division

Table 1. MEANS OR SOURCES OF PROFESSIONAL PRESTIGE

I. INDEPENDENT OF THE PROFESSIONAL MARKET

	Autonomous Means	Heteronomous Means
"Traditional" Means	Aristocratic or liberal education. (Institutionally located in corporate bodies like the Inns of Court, Royal Colleges, academic bodies, or in "ancient" universities.)	Aristocratic or gentlemanly characteristics (noblesse oblige). (Structurally located in "aristocratic" or "old" elites.)
"Modern" Means	Systematic training and testing. (Institutionally located in professional schools and "modern" university.)	Registration, licensing. (Institutionally located in the state.)

II. DEPENDENT UPON AN ESTABLISHED PROFESSIONAL MARKET

Autonomous Means	Heteronomous Means
Cognitive exclusiveness. (Institutionally located in professional associations, "modern" university.)	Higher incomes and prestige than most other occupations. Connections with "extra-professional" power. (Institutionally located in the state, corporations, and university.)

of labor, as the sole legitimate providers of a valued service, as the sole keepers of a valued body of knowledge, as legitimate claimants to higher economic rewards, and the like.

This preliminary analysis has attempted to clarify the outlines of the social mobility project pursued by the old professions. The more extended analysis that follows will have a two-fold purpose: first, that of clarifying the connections of this new path of middle-class mobility with the system of stratification that takes shape during the "great transformation"; and second, that of defining the general patterns of individual motivation which may account for the collective character of the project.

Most contemporary studies of stratification depart from the classical sociological tradition in that they view stratification systems as hierarchies of ranks whose social units are individuals or families. Differential rewards or disadvantages accrue to these social units as a function of their rank, or their position with regard to the distribution of a valued attribute. The emphasis is on individuals (or families) and allocation mechanisms. The Marxist perspective emphasizes, instead, structural relations of inequality between collectivities which can become *real* groups and organize in order to act upon these structural relations. In any case, classes and not individuals are the proper units of analysis of the class system. Focusing on status, Weber also underscored that status derived from communities, however amorphous; an analysis of social prestige had to start, therefore, with collective units. In a somewhat similar vein, Stinchcombe starts by asking what kind of social units typically serve as guarantors of "credit ratings" in different societies and epochs; he calls "credit rating" a "particular kind of reputational measure of stratification which measures prestige at the crucial point where it is turned into the control over resources."[2] And he adds: "With modernization . . . [the] credit rating of the lineage as both a firm and a family becomes differentiated into a credit rating of nuclear families and a credit rating of special purpose organizations. . . . *Many of the important stratification phenomena in modern society have to do with the ranking of organizations.*"[3]

Now, although a profession as a whole is too loose and disparate a "community of fate" to be considered an organization proper, its raison d'être, from the point of view of stratification, is the *collective* credit rating which it passes on to its members and which is totally determined by the success of the profession's *organizational* efforts. This collective credit rating establishes, first, the relatively superior ranking and the command over resources of two organizations: the professional association and the professional school, which strive in effect to monopolize the function of guaranteeing the future performance of their members or students. This monopoly, I have argued earlier, gives *some* guarantee to the public about the behavior of individual members, but it also places the profession, as embodied in these two organizations, ahead of its competitors. From this point of view, loose occupational communities of independent producers of services are spurred to organize by the competition for prestige, a resource which they aim at converting into monopolistic power in their markets. The success of their efforts becomes visible when they collectively outrank (or eliminate) competitors and when they also obtain supervisory or controlling authority over related occupations.

In terms of an ideal-type, what was new in the professional project is that the typical professional organizations claimed the rank of sole distributors of credit ratings on a new basis—that of competence, as defined and measured by a system of testing, and later, by the professional school. Elite status was no longer claimed on the basis of identification with the extraneous stratification criteria of "aristocratic" elites, but in new organizational terms: elite status and even "gentility" were conferred by the position of the profession on an occupational ladder and measured, essentially, in terms of educational distance from other occupations. The new criteria of stratification inaugurated by the professions hinged, therefore, on the emergence of an educational system oriented toward the modern division of labor. In the same manner, we have seen that control of the market ultimately required the institutionalization and the control of a system for the standardized production of producers. The professions' potential for *both* market control and superior ranking largely depended, therefore, on the organization of an educational system along modern lines.

Until a profession is stably organized, the distinctive pattern of mobility is collective and consists in the organizational effort itself. *Individual* mobility still tends to follow the pattern of patronage or competitive entrepreneurship. An impressionistic indicator of organizational strength is the emergence of a professional association recognized as representative by the public authorities or by a significant sector of the public. Externally, this means that the professional association must be recognized by the state: for, indeed, given the new "objective" basis on which privileges are claimed, only the state has the appearance of neutrality necessary to guarantee the "objectively" superior competence of a category of professionals. Internally, the emergence of a professional organization as "representative spokesman" for the profession is possible only if the organization is not challenged by another one of equal credibility. This means, in turn, that the "representative" association should have succeeded in enlisting the support of all the relevant professional elites, or at least obtained their neutrality.

Because of the professional association's efforts to regulate competition, the entrepreneurial form of individual mobility begins to be considered disreputable at this point, and is seen as harmful to the collective effort. A much more significant indicator of organization, however, is the institutionalization of the passage from professional training to professional practice: it means that a large majority of the practitioners come from educational institutions accredited as the sole legitimate ones by the profession as a whole. When entry into the profession is thus tied to an organized system for the production of producers, the pattern of individual mobility typical of the organized profession approaches the pattern of career—that is, the characteristic mode of advancement of individuals in organizations. In Wilensky's words, "A career, viewed structurally, is a succession of related jobs, arranged in a hierarchy of prestige, through which persons move in an ordered, predictable sequence. Corollaries are that the job pattern is instituted (socially recognized and sanctioned within some social unit) and has some stability (the system is maintained over more than one generation of recruits)."[4]

Let us pull together the various elements of the argument up to this point. Whether the leaders of the profession project wanted to be ''like gentlemen'' or not is immaterial—although one may presume that the individual motivation to be as respected as the ''higher branches'' in England, or as one's best clients in the United States, must have been quite strong. What is important is that attributes of ''gentility'' and references to older legitimizations of privilege had to be incorporated as sources of social credit and guarantees of ethicality, *so long as the professions were not sufficiently organized to substitute their own organizational rankings,* based essentially on the control over a system for the production of producers.

The criterion of education and tested competence pertains to a model of stratification in which individual position is determined more by the cohesiveness and relative ranking of organized occupations than by lineage. The rise of the industrial bourgeoisie had already represented a step in the direction of ''organization-based'' mobility. As Stinchcombe remarks, in the nineteenth-century model of business entrepreneurship, ''the main way for an organizational leader to get ahead is to improve the position of his organization rather than to move up within it.''[5]

The rise of the ''learned'' bourgeoisie links individual mobility to education—an attribute which, in theory, is easier to come by than capital.[6] In the entrepreneurial pattern of mobility, the ''credit rating'' of a nuclear family and that of ''special-purpose organizations'' intersected in the family firm. The *consolidation* of the older professions, as well as the rise of newer ones, coincides with the ''organizational revolution,'' which extends bureaucratic administration to all sectors of economic and social life. In the mature professional pattern, the basic status of the nuclear family is conferred upon the head by an educational center, which is itself ranked with regard to other centers, and by the profession itself, ranked with regard to other occupations. Further advancement takes place, then, in a professional market in which the formal and informal organization of the profession are the chief determinants of individual career.[7] Moreover, with the decline of the free professional, both individual ''credit ratings'' and careers tend increasingly to depend on bureaucratic organizational frameworks.

It is possible to see, in this light, what binds the average (or even not so average) practitioner to the organized profession, once the latter is consolidated. Internally, consolidation means that cognitive exclusiveness is achieved (at least in relation to competitors) and that an educational system is institutionalized and relatively standardized. It should also mean that the various sectors of the profession—generalists, specialists, academics, researchers, eminent practitioners, regional groups and the like—have divided among themselves the power of governance and have reached the stage where a relatively stable coalition is possible. These various groups, moreover, are implicitly or explicitly ranked in a hierarchy of power and prestige which is intelligible to all, if not accepted by all. At this point, professional elites are clearly identifiable and so is the ranking of professional schools and organizations (or the ranking of organizations in which professionals work). The majority of the practitioners need not—and in fact do not—participate in the central professional associations, which are almost invariably controlled by well-entrenched elites.[8] Although there is evidence to suggest that involvement in professional associations, among other professional activities, helps advancement in organizational contexts not directly controlled by the profession, this allegiance is more important for the individual than for the professional collectivity.[9] Indeed, so long as the non-affiliated do not have the power to form an effective rival association, the formal affiliation of a majority of practitioners is not an indication of a profession's cohesiveness. Power within a profession lies in controlling education and career facilities, because in an organized profession the practitioners, almost without exception, must pass through the educational centers and through the organizations in which career unfolds. From the point of view of socialization into the profession and professional "cohesion," control over members is therefore a matter of structure much more than a matter of obedience to an association's code of ethics. It is clear also that this control is exercised to the extent and in the direction favored by a profession's organizational elites.[10]

At this stage, personal prestige is almost equivalent to organizational prestige: doctors are identified with their hospitals, lawyers, architects, and engineers with their firms, and every professional with his academic origins. Personal and organizational connections fuse in a new pattern of sponsorship: the average or the beginning professionals who aspire to a career must get into the "right" networks, that is, the networks leading to the top rungs of the organizational hierarchy. It is always the case that organizational elites, as Stinchcombe remarks, have a deeper involvement and a larger stake in the fate of the organization or organizations than "inferiors" or non-elites.[11] But, in the context of an organized profession, the latter are bound to the elites by a shared frame of reference and a common system of evaluation: there are, after all, relatively few other criteria of personal progress and professional excellence than those sanctioned by a profession's elites. A problem to which I shall return later is that of the various degrees and forms of marginality: for, indeed, to orient one's professional life outside the system of evaluation and rewards with which the elites are ideologically identified and which others endorse, at least tacitly, is to accept marginality by force or choice. It also involves the possibility of taking a critical stand, individually or as a group, implicitly or explicitly, toward the dominant organization of a profession.[12]

When a profession is organized, then, *the bonds between professional elites and non-elites are structurally supported by the overlap between individual mobility and organizational rankings:* in pursuing individual mobility, aspiring professionals reinforce the hierarchy of organizations upon which elites found their status and their privileges. But what explains the convergence of the most diverse individual motives toward the project of professional mobility in the formative or preconsolidation period?

A collective project always serves in some fashion the self-interest of the participants: if nothing else, because it shapes individual interests into an emergent form. If we consider individual motivation, however, it appears that the collectivity should be able to offer or promise somewhat higher—or more secure or more desirable—rewards than those attainable outside its bounds. Since the professions are projects of organization for a market at the same time that they are projects of collective mobility, economic rewards should be considered first: do the average rewards of the "regular" sectors of the profession compensate for the social control to which the "regular" members submit?

For this, let us take some illustrations from medicine before the bacteriological revolution: the economic rewards that doctors could expect varied greatly according to country and locality. Some of the main factors of variation have been discussed above: the size, stability, and socioeconomic status of the clientele; the personal reputation of the physician and that of the group or school to which he was connected; and the sponsorship of aristocratic elites, local notables, or public authorities.

By the mid-nineteenth century the modern or reformist professional elites in the cities were relatively affluent and well-established; this was true even in England, where their parity with the traditional elites was not officially sanctioned until the Medical Act of 1858.[13] Although the initial investment in training varied, the costs of establishment—that is, some source of income which could support the practitioner in a respectable standing and keep him from the temptations of purely commercial practices—must have operated as a sharp differential in a beginner's chances.[14] Younger and more marginal men appear to have found the going rough. The necessary respectability came from connections and independent income. Those who were lacking in both were particularly threatened by unqualified competition. This was all the more so since a rising tide of quackery claimed to fill the unwarranted promises that critical physicians were no longer willing to make. Exacerbated competition contributed to the public's suspicion that the profession was mercenary and selfish. This suspicion, furthermore, hampered the efforts to raise the uneven standards of training and curb quackery. The average practitioner was caught in a dilemma: if he should attempt to stabilize his income and demand payment, his clientele could respond by doubting his motives and ethicality. Not surprisingly, complaints about unpaid fees were frequent, even among successful practitioners. We can imagine how much harder it was to make a living for average physicians and for the younger men who had to compete with more established and older colleagues. In the United States, despite opposition by the American Medical Association and other societies, hard-pressed physicians often contracted for the annual medical care of a whole family for a very small sum.[15]

In the United States, besides, training standards were often abysmally low: "In his inaugural address at the University of Nashville, in 1829, President Lindsley declared that it was easier at the time in Tennessee to qualify for the practice of the law or medicine than to build a dray, or shoe a horse."[16] This situation aggravated the discredit with which even serious professionals had to contend. But even in countries like France and Germany, where medical training was among the very best available in the nineteenth century, quackery could not be effectively contained. Nor could the average member of the medical profession secure a comfortable income: thus "One half of the physicians of Berlin received, as late as 1895, an annual income of less than three thousand marks; and that of their colleagues in Vienna was even less than that amount."[17]

These examples from medicine support a logical proposition: the process of organization for market control has to be relatively advanced before a profession can offer its members substantial and secure enough *economic* rewards in exchange for its attempts to regulate professional behavior. Regulation of competition tends to favor the already established elites of the profession by freezing the market in a given configuration of advantages. Therefore, the motivation to respond to the efforts of the organizational leaders cannot be interpreted in "pure" economic or market terms, at least not until the organized sectors of the profession have attained a relatively high measure of control over the market. Because the double nature of the professional project fuses economic and status rewards, it is difficult to define theoretically the organizational stage at which it becomes *profitable* to join the "regular" profession and submit to its control. It follows that the model of motivation adequate to explain market behavior—a model which should logically be derived from that of classical economics—cannot account for the merging of individual motives into the collective project of profession.

We need to find a means of accounting for this convergence that goes beyond economic self-interest, while making allowances for it. As I have constantly emphasized, the professional project is an organizational project: it organizes the production of producers and the transaction of services for a market; it tends to privilege organizational units in the system of stratification; it works through, and culminates in, distinctive organizations—the professional school and the professional association. Today, professional roles tend to be organized or included into bureaucratic structures. A model of "bureaucratic motivation," which accounts for "the motivational significance of various structural features of bureaucracies,"[18] might therefore be more adequate than a market-oriented model of economic action for this later phase. Indeed, organized professions possess the structural means to incorporate and regulate individual ambition into *a career,* that is, an organized trajectory of individual advancement. In the formative period, however, we need to account for motivation in a stage of *transition* toward the organizational definition of career.

In terms of an ideal-type, a central characteristic of the modern professional project is that it emancipated profession from the warrants provided by the old system of stratification. From the point of view of the stratification system, this amounted to substituting new criteria of status and prestige for the old ones. As we know, the upgrading of an occupation into a profession, or the upgrading of a profession in terms of respectability and social credit, implies the articulation of principles of inclusion and exclusion. Which groups may be attracted or, conversely, threatened by such a project?

The first obvious answer is that the professional groups entrenched in the traditional system of stratification will oppose the new criteria of professional legitimacy. As we shall see in the illustrative case of England, their presence colors and conditions the mobility project of the reformers.

The second obvious answer is that the modern elites of a profession have nothing to lose and nothing to fear, since they are in a position to define the criteria of inclusion and exclusion. However, they are already reaping substantial rewards from their professional work. These rewards may seem suspect to potential followers: since profession is not only a category in an achievement-oriented occupational structure, but also a status category in a stratification system with ineradicable ascriptive features, its rewards can *always* be connected with particularistic and "usurped" advantages. Moreover, in a transitional period, the universalistic legitimations of these advantages are neither institutionalized nor visible enough to appear as the principal determinant of differential rewards. Therefore, suspicion of the modern elites who lead the organizational project may be strong among marginal potential followers.

For instance, in the first attempts to organize American civil engineers, this suspicion was predictably present in the desire to promote universalistic criteria of profession. It was difficult to organize scattered and often antagonistic practitioners, the most successful of which were almost necessarily connected with public authorities. In consequence, the *American Railroad Journal* recommended in the 1840s the "substitution of a professional society for governments as the agency controlling engineer training and selection." It also went on to list as "the grand obstacle to the advancement of the profession in the United States" the fact that, for many a successful engineer, "his political creed, and the number of votes he and his friends can command, would far outweigh the professional claims of a rival who might unite in himself the genius of all the engineers of the age."[19] Other writers proposed that younger engineers take the lead in professional organization, a fact which leads the historian Calhoun to this realistic observation: "There was a dissenting democratical element within the engineering profession, whose extent and significance it is hard to judge. . . . [However] the successful engineers against whose leadership it protested had the resources and prestige, if anybody did, to overcome the practical obstacles in the way of organization."[20]

These considerations may be extended: reformist or modern professional elites would naturally tend to take the leadership of the organizational effort; in fact, they did so.[21] Because of their elite position, their attempts at elevating the profession were obviously exclusive. To be qualified as modern, these attempts *must* have included an emphasis on serious training and on stricter testing of cognitive and technological proficiency. However, the elite status already achieved by the organizational leaders led them to also take into account more diffuse and ascriptive criteria of professionalism, such as those of gentlemanly standing and proper connections. The defense of universalistic and relatively more "objective" educational differentials appears, thus, as one shared ideological basis which non-elite professionals could use to challenge the internal stratification system of the emergent profession.

For professionals who feared exclusion or resented their own marginal status, vigilance against the built-in oligarchic and elitist tendencies of the organizational leaders may therefore have been one reason to join the movement. The non-elite professional groups most likely to be so oriented would be those who, like the younger civil engineers threatened by the depression of the 1840s, had autonomous reasons to organize and in some cases had independent counter-projects.[22] We may safely assume that non-elite professionals had more intense economic preoccupations than the organizational leaders. It is likely, therefore, that their economic insecurity oriented them toward bread-and-butter considerations. On the other hand, they were the most threatened by "unqualified" competition and needed to join the upgrading project in order to put social distance between themselves and their "unprofessional" competitors. Competition from "irregulars" appears, therefore, as perhaps the strongest incentive toward the bridging of differences between professional elites and non-elites. However, discrepancies too strong to be reconciled within the same organization would obviously lead to the emergence of rival professional associations. This, as we know, was the case before a modicum of cognitive unification was achieved.

These lines of cleavage—and especially those generated by a profession's internal stratification—appear and reappear throughout the process of professionalization. One factor of unity may be emphasized, however: regardless of the organizational conception to which they responded, only those practitioners who already could define themselves as professionals in the more stringent terms proposed by the organizational leaders would have a stake in the corporate defense and upgrading of an occupational category. Only they would have been attracted, in one fashion or another, by the autonomous organizations through which the professions were seeking to advance their goals of mobility and market control.

Now, which types of practitioners would either be threatened by the organizational project or find it irrelevant? One type is the practitioner with a purely commercial orientation and a moderately profitable practice; regulation of competition and restrictive codes of professional behavior would interfere, rather than help, his individual project. Another type is the solidly entrenched "local," protected by social and geographical isolation, and therefore indifferent to the professional redefinition which preoccupied those lacking these natural protections. Another yet is the less educated older professional, unless he could join with the others, and press for placing protective "grandfather clauses" among the principles of inclusion.

This discussion has attempted to clarify the diversity of motives among professional groups or professional types in a pre-consolidation period. It has not given us yet the model of motivation in a period of transition. The elements of an answer, however, have already been implicitly assembled; their point of convergence is the historical context of the first wave of professionalization.

Modern professions are a typical product of the "great transformation." They emerge, thus, as the age-old foundations of status are being destroyed by the twin processes of urbanization and industrialization. In an apparently limitless expansion, national markets are developing for commodities and for labor. An impoverished and brutally exploited industrial proletariat is replacing the peasantry at the bottom of the emerging social hierarchy. At the same time, the increasingly complex social division of labor opens new roles at the top of the ladder. Wrenched from its roots in household and community, work is becoming for the majority of men the principal determinant of social position and life chances. The units of the emerging stratification system, as I pointed out before, tend to become classes and occupation-centered organizations.

This view fits with the argument advanced by Kenneth Boulding about the "demand" for organizations: one of the predominant individual needs which organizations satisfy is the *need for status*. He writes: "Organization *formalizes* the status of an individual and hence makes him more secure in it. . . . By formalizing an individual's position . . . the status may be both improved and rendered more apparent; *uncertainty* of status is in itself a painful position for an individual to be in."[23] Although the supply side is even more important, the social effects of the industrial revolution shape the demand for status-giving organizations: "The demand for status is in part an attribute of self-consciousness. It is likely to increase with a rise in literacy and with a rise in democratic consciousness. . . . *It is in the rise of the market as a dominant instrument in the organization of society, and in the consequent disorganization of the status structure, that we may look for the reasons of a rising demand for status.*"[24] Professional markets had to be organized while, at the same time, new bases for status had to be created.

Applied to the professional project, Boulding's general argument reveals a powerful motivational base for the organizational effort: the organization of profession was more than simply a means for developing, in a relatively autonomous frame of reference, new criteria of status. It was also a means for conferring status by establishing social distance between the professionals and other groups: the as-yet socially unacceptable self-made men of the industrial bourgeoisie, in societies which maintained pre-industrial criteria of stratification; and the occupational categories which were losing their traditional status, such as craftsmen or independent farmers. Profession was, besides, a means for distinguishing oneself from the status-less proletariat into which whole sectors of the pre-industrial occupational hierarchy were being engulfed. Furthermore, the economic benefits to be expected, at least in the long run, from professional organization also contributed to guaranteeing status. Finally, if literacy and "democratic consciousness" are indeed related to status demands, it is logical to think that literate and reform-oriented professionals would have been among the most status-conscious sectors of the bourgeoisie.

One final point must be made in this connection. Among the *general* conditions under which people are motivated to found new organizations, two can be singled out as particularly relevant to the collective mobility project of the nineteenth-century professions. Under these conditions, (1) "[people] believe that the future will be such that the organization will continue to be effective enough to pay for the trouble of building it and for the resources invested"; and (2) "they or some social group with which they are strongly identified will receive some of the benefits of the better way of doing things."[25]

The second condition is fulfilled by a collective mobility project; I have explored above its roots in individual motives. As for the first, despite the disturbing appearance of cyclical economic crises, we may safely assume that in the second third of the nineteenth century optimism about the future was a sufficiently general state of mind among the middle classes and their professional sector to have animated a group of organizational leaders. Further reasons for buoyancy were, in England, the bourgeoisie's gains in political power and, in the United States, the exhilarating consciousness of nation-building. But above all, the "great transformation" set in motion a permanent revolutionary process which maximized some of the preconditions of professionalization.

The formidable effects of this unfinished transformation can only be alluded to: increasing standards of living, structural differentiation, industrial rationalization of work, the growing concentration of the means of production and decision-making in giant corporations and in a giant state apparatus, the corresponding growth of bureaucracy, the growing importance of science and technology, all contributed to the multiplication of skilled and high-level jobs.[26] As monopolistic capitalism super-

seded the competitive phase, new occupations developed in the shadow of bureaucratic organizations and they too aspired to increase their status. It is this contemporary wave of professionalization that is viewed as a collective mobility project in
the sociological literature. In E. C. Hughes' words:

> Work on the professions, as on other matters, reflects this: it is in part a study of social
> advancement (mobility). The advancement is of two kinds. The first is the rise of the
> individual by getting into an occupation of high prestige, or by achieving special suc-
> cess in his occupation. The second is the collective effort of an organized occupa-
> tion to improve its place and increase its power, in relation to others. That effort, in
> middle-class occupations, characteristically is directed to achieving professional
> status. For whatever else the word "profession" may mean, it is in modern English
> a symbol of high ranking among occupations.[27]

This view, however, tends to take for granted the ranking of occupations and the
process by which it was achieved. Until now, I have been concerned with a general
discussion of the specific structures and conceptions of mobility and status connected
with the rise of the modern professions. I want to explore now how pre-existing social structures helped or hindered the unfolding of the professions "modern"
potential. With emphasis on the ideal-typical, I shall consider two very different
modes of mobility: in Britain, I shall focus on the limits which the enduring cultural
influence of the gentry set on the professional project. In the United States, I shall
single out those structural features and processes which contribute to the thoroughly
modern foundations of social inequality. Because of this emphasis, my discussion
of the United States will necessarily deal with transformations still in process, and
will take us up to our own time. Before entering into the comparison of these two
ideal-typical cases, let us briefly recall the elements common to both professional
projects.

The form that the modern professions take after the industrial revolution is that
of corporate projects attempting, first of all, to organize "production" for a special
type of market and to gain in it quasi-monopolistic control. Given the singular nature of the "commodity" to be exchanged, the organization of production is concerned not with an inanimate product, but with the selection of producers or providers
of services. The end-point of this primary aspect of professional organization is,
therefore, the monopoly of relatively standardized education.

Secondly, in a world shaken by the "great transformation," the corporate project
of profession generates distinctive structural bases for status and new patterns of
social mobility. In their formative period, modern professions are, logically, transitional and mixed forms. While they still avail themselves, in varying degrees, of the
old status warrants, they put them to use in organizing their markets of services.
More typically, the professions' modern context contributes to define the relationships between the emerging occupational and social hierarchies. The prestige ranking attained by the professional collectivity is the first determinant of the members'
individual status in the society. Furthermore, in articulating new principles of exclusion and inclusion based on examinations and thus, ultimately on education, professions tend to subordinate individual status to the passage through organized
education.

In our century, growing bureaucratization and the "organizational revolution" increasingly model the pattern of individual advancement in the professions along the lines of bureaucratic career. However, the affinity between professions and bureaucracy—or, in other words, their common pertinence to the process of capitalist rationalization—was already apparent at the inception of the modern professional project. The new pattern of mobility opened by the professions depends, initially, on the uses of education. As Max Weber has shown, modern bureaucracy similarly works to make education into the intervening structure between social and occupational stratification.[28] As all forms of status, the "specific status developments" of both bureaucracy and profession tend to be monpolized.[29] Given the structural connections with allegedly "open" educational systems, this monopoly can claim universalistic ideological legitimations.

The double nature of the professional project intertwines market and status orientations, and both tend toward monopoly—monopoly of opportunities for income in a market of services, on the one hand, and monopoly of status in an emerging occupational hierarchy, on the other. The institutional locus in which both monopolizing tendencies converge is the educational system.

The analysis that follows will attempt to explore the complex mediations between stratification, education, and occupation that characterize the professional project in Britain and in the United States. In each case, the stage, and especially the pace, of economic development were certainly principal determinants of the differences. So were the alternative channels of mobility that existed in each case. So was each society's consciousness of its class structure: despite the cultural similarities and overlaps, each case illustrates, in Ralph Turner's words, a different "folk norm." He writes: "Within a formally open class system providing mass education, the organizing folk norm that defines the accepted mode of upward mobility is a crucial factor in shaping the school system, and may even be more crucial than the extent of upward mobility."

The British ideal type or normative model is one of controlled selection. In this process of *sponsored* mobility,"elite recruits are chosen by the established elite of their agents and elite status is *given* on the basis of some criterion of supposed merit. . . . Upward mobility is like entry into a private club, where each candidate must be 'sponsored' by one or more of the members." In the United States, the predominant model is that of *contest:* "a system in which elite status is the prize in an open contest and is taken by the aspirants' own efforts. While the 'contest' is governed by some rules of fair play, the contestants have wide latitude in the strategies they may employ."[30]

Professions, as we know, partake of both models, although in terms of an ideal-type, they endorse the ideology of contest mobility. In the tension between "folk norms," however, we can see the impact of the pre-existing class system upon the development of the market-oriented centers for the production of professional producers. The collective mobility project of professions sets limits to their market project and to its rationalizing ideology. It is chiefly in the educational system (or, more exactly, in its relations with the class structure and the labor market) that these limits become apparent.[31]

Chapter 7

USES AND LIMITATIONS
OF THE ARISTOCRATIC MODEL

The dual revolution—industrial and bourgeois-democratic—which transformed Western European societies and their offshoots in the nineteenth century is the historical matrix for most of classical sociology's concepts and ideas. Terms like "ascription" and "achievement," which we use so commonly today, not only evoke whole families of concepts at one end or the other of the *gemeinschaft-gesellschaft* typology; they also evoke the ideological climate in which the "great transformation" was perceived and conceptualized, the intersecting and conflicting currents of thought which provided the first binding links between concepts and the first efforts at comprehensive analysis. "Achievement," in this light, fits into a complex of ideas which was in large part shaped by the tradition of democratic liberalism. It is ideologically inseparable from the emphasis on the individual in a society dominated by the market. It evokes, also, the contractual theory of society with its foundations in the legal system, and the growing pre-eminence of economic determinants, based on the capitalist division of labor, in a changing system of social stratification. This word of caution is necessary to ward off the ready ideological implications of this analysis of collective mobility and to dispel any implication of evolutionism. It also serves to state a feeling of discomfort: for to focus on one single aspect of the "great transformation" is necessarily to be fragmentary and incomplete.

With these qualifications, we can now begin to characterize, as an ideal type, the professional project in nineteenth-century England. It challenged, as we know, well-established elites in the learned professions. In theory, therefore, England should offer a clear example of the reformist dimension in the professionalization movement: in their attack against corporate privileges, middle-class professional reformers were bound to accentuate the democratic and rationalizing potential of market-oriented professionalism. Moreover, the reformist spirit in the professions had been awakened by the broader movement for national reform; even during the years when the general spirit of reform had been quenched by patriotism and fear of the French Revolution, reformism in medicine and the law did not subside. Not only did professionals participate in the larger movement for political and social change; they often acted as its spokesmen, on behalf of classes to which they did not themselves belong.[1] The professional principles of competence and efficiency

were shaped in large part by the Benthamites' influence on the professional movement. Incorporated into the drive for administrative and educational reform in which
Benthamite and Dissenter influence was similarly prominent, these principles left
a deep mark on the state apparatus of the Victorian era.[2]

The specific aims of the professional project were, however, income security
and social respectability. These aims were sought in a context where aristocratic
status models and ideologies were available and never entirely defeated by the attacks
of the rising bourgeoisie against idle property and the system of patronage. The lingering social and political influence of the old ruling class set upon the project of
professional modernization limits that were both structural and ideological. I will
attempt to delineate them in this chapter.

The institutional persistence of ascription in the British system of social stratification is almost a commonplace in the sociological literature. Neil Smelser and
S. M. Lipset write, for instance:

> Great Britain constitutes a system intermediate between extreme individual mobility
> and extreme collective mobility. Individual mobility is emphasized, but individuals
> carry with them certain ascribed and semi-ascribed markings—accent, habits, man-
> ners, etc.—which reflect family and educational background and operate as important
> status symbols. Full mobility takes place only in the next generation, when mobile
> individuals can give their own children the appropriate cultivation and education.
> This case is intermediate because it is the family that moves collectively upward over
> two or more generations.[3]

The authors are ready to add that "the contrast between Britain and the United States
is a relative one." Their comments should attract our attention, however, to a distinctive paradox or peculiarity: it does not lie in the two-generation-or-more pattern of
mobility, but in the fact that Britain acquired an "open" class structure[4]—"open,"
that is, in the limited sense that it emphasizes individual mobility based on income,
occupation, and education—during the same historical period in which the elements
of status stratification were ritualized and therefore made explicit and visible to
the many.

The paradox disappears if we briefly recall Weber's concept of status stratification and then apply it to nineteenth-century Britain. Weber emphasized, as we know,
the monopolistic nature of status, based on the "specific, positive or negative, social
estimation of honor." He wrote:

> The development of status is essentially a question of stratification resting *on usurpa-
> tion*. Such usurpation is the normal origin of almost all status honor. But the road from
> this purely conventional situation to legal privilege, positive or negative, is easily
> traveled as soon as a certain stratification of the social order has in fact been "lived in"
> and has achieved stability by virtue of a stable distribution of economic power.[5]

The notion of usurpation can be traced back to the hereditary appropriation of political power by force in situations of conquest or in the struggle to establish domination.[6] But in a modern context, it refers exclusively to the conventional styles of
life which identify status groups and express their negative or positive social honor.
Usurpation refers, here, to the deliberate monopolization of status symbols and the
deliberate restriction of interaction with outsiders by which high-status groups set

themselves apart from others. It refers also to the fact that their superiority of status is seldom "spontaneously" granted or recognized by outsiders; on the contrary, we could say that it would not exist without monopoly: the "closing character" of status superiority spurs the outsiders to enter the circle by imitating the "higher" style of life.[7] These attempts by outsiders sanction the status superiority of the more prestigious group and constitute a status hierarchy.

A corollary of Weber's theory of status is that "all groups having interests in the status order react with special sharpness precisely against the pretensions of purely economic acquisition."[8] One of the major general consequences is that the development of a status order and its legitimization hinder the free development of the market, if nothing else, at least "for those goods which status groups directly withhold from free exchange by monopolization." And Weber adds, "From the contrariety between the status order and the purely economic order . . . it follows that . . . everywhere some status groups, and usually the most influential, consider almost any kind of overt participation in economic acquisition as absolutely stigmatizing."[9]

Now, the British aristocracy and gentry had faced, for many centuries, the expansion of the market and the transformation of the economy—though never, of course, on the revolutionary scale and pace attained after 1780. Economic growth and political pressure (including the major upheaval of Cromwell's interregnum and its aftermath) had multiplied, as well, the demands for acceptance into elite circles by wealthy merchants and business men who "were not gentlemen," either by birth or by education. *Legal* closure of the high-status group was not possible in eighteenth- and nineteenth-century England, except indirectly, in what concerned political rights and the privileges accorded to the Established Church and its members.[10] Nor was this distinctively English landed obligarchy willing to oppose the expansion of the market or the implantation of a new economic system for, at least in the first fifty years of industrialization, it profited too much from both.

Indeed, since the seventeenth century, the gentry had been alert in seizing opportunities for commercializing its agricultural output and for investing—not only in large-scale trade, but also in mining, manufacturing, and local commerce. The political and cultural continuity of the gentry rested in large part upon its solid base of economic power.[11] Its response to change had been extremely intelligent: rapidly securing position in an expanding market, the British landed class had protected its status monopoly by elaborating a conventional style of life and cultural symbols. This allowed them to co-opt on clearly stated terms those parvenus who were, anyhow, too rich to be rejected. The still powerful upper class was open enough to absorb without difficulty the minority of rich bourgeois who could buy their way across the main status barriers or "were in businesses which had acquired respectability through tradition."[12] The combination of this openness with the multiplication of pressures from below in a changing society explains both the high degree of "stylization of life" and the extent to which stylization was imitated, even beyond the sectors most likely to be co-opted.

As T. H. Marshall notes, the process of status stratification gained new vigor in the nineteenth century:

> When a section of society is threatened by invasion from below, as the English gentlemen were in varying degrees from the sixteenth century onwards, they protect themselves by constructing barriers out of those attributes and symbols of social differences which are most difficult to acquire. Conspicuous expenditure can be copied by those who get rich quick, but correct manners, the right accent, and the "old school tie" are esoteric mysteries and jealously guarded monopolies. And it was in the nineteenth century that these symbols gained their great ascendancy in English life.[13]

While the English gentleman was acquiring his Victorian characteristics at one end of the status stratification, other styles of life and characteristic cultural elaborations were also emerging behind each segregating social barrier. Particularly powerful, because it was supported by an idea of the social order that was ultimately triumphant, was the style of life and thought of the industrial bourgeoisie; it was especially distinctive where it was tied to dissenting religion and to the new industrial regions, like the North or the Midlands. Also, toward the end of the century, when standards of living had risen sufficiently to allow the elaboration of a style of life by the laboring poor, English working-class culture jelled into forms now considered traditional—but which were then distinctive cultural innovations.[14]

The elaboration of both positive and negative status symbols, carried by styles of life rooted in the class structure, appears as a cultural and social counterpoint to the rationalizing impact of the industrial revolution upon British society. Education was the obvious protective barrier for high status groups.[15] However, an upper class—even if it is as influential and as flexible as the British—cannot maintain total control over education in a rapidly industrializing society. With a focus on the role of professionals, we must examine the relations between the emergent system of national education and a status hierarchy shaped by the ideals and conventions of the old ruling class.

HIGHER AND LOWER BRANCHES

At the beginning of the nineteenth century, all intellectual callings were becoming increasingly respectable and respected. Only the clergy, medicine, and the law were, however, firmly established as "learned" professions. The first of the three older professions will not concern us directly: undoubtedly, the clergy was touched and transformed by the general movement toward moralization and competence in the performance of function. Undoubtedly too, as clerical offices became more clearly separate from the laity, this dependent profession gained a measure of autonomy from lay control. Many clergymen, especially in nonconformist churches, were active and often prominent reformers. The profession as a whole, however, did not have the same need for "objective" guarantees of competence as the market-oriented professions. Protected from competition within their church, clergymen did not depend for their income on the transaction of personal services on the market: the "living" which most of them enjoyed was a prerogative attached to their office and relatively independent of performance. The security afforded by the traditional corporations and the patronage system gave to the established elites in law and medicine something comparable to a "living." The situation was different for the lower class of practitioners, exposed to the full rigors of competition. The traditional division between "higher" and "lower" branches mirrored the social and political subordination of the rising bourgeoisie to the old ruling class. This division coincided in large part, though not entirely, with that between the elites and the rank and file of the profession. The biographer of Thomas Wakley, known as the "battling surgeon" for his advocacy of medical reform, describes the situation in 1815, when Wakley joined the ranks of the medical profession:

> Now and again, a man whose original conditions ought to have limited his aspirations would break through his trammels and become a leader, when in the ordinary course of events he should have remained a private; but this occurred infrequently. The almost invariable rule was that those who were specially picked out by circumstances quite independent of merit for promotion, received that promotion, less fortunate individuals remaining in the shadow of obscurity, whatever their claims to success.[16]

The story of professionalization is largely that of the aspirations of rank-and-file professionals, as interpreted and organized by their leaders.

The professional sectors were not quite as small as one may surmise. The first separate enumeration is that of the 1851 Census: in the better-defined secular professions we find at this date over 38,000 people, out of a population of almost eighteen million. This figure included 17,500 physicians and surgeons; 2,088 barristers; 11,684 solicitors; 1,486 architects; 4,086 surveyors; 853 engineers; 4,416 accountants; and 522 dentists.

Surgeons and solicitors, though still part of the "lower" branches, had some claims to social standing on the basis of their affiliation with the two ancient professions of medicine and the law. The "higher" branches, to which they were formally subordinate, were synonimous with the ancient chartered corporations, which had emerged in law and medicine when they slipped away from ecclesiastical jurisdiction. The 1851 figures gives an approximate idea of the respective numbers of barristers and solicitors. As for doctors, a prominent member of the Society of Apothecaries, writing in 1834, estimated that there had been about 12,000 practitioners in 1812–1813 and that their numbers had been continuously growing. In the 1830s, the Royal College of Physicians of London counted 113 fellows and 274 licentiates, while the Royal College of Surgeons of England, in existence only since 1800, had already more than 8,000 licentiates and approximately 200 fellows.[17]

Despite the different nature of the two ancient liberal professions and their different relations with the university, the sociological implications of the division into "higher" and "lower" branches were similar in both: the men who were co-opted by their social peers to the Inns of Court or to the fellowship of the two medical Colleges were few in number and monopolized substantial social and professional privileges. As a rule, they belonged to the upper class or, if exceptionally successful, made their way into it. The elites among these elites had often passed through one of the nine leading public schools and had gone from there to Oxford or Cambridge. In fact, for a long time, no physician could be admitted to the rank of Fellow of the Royal College if he was not a graduate from one of the two English universities or had not "incorporated" his degree by residence in one of them—this criterion tended to exclude all Dissenters, unless they came by way of Trinity College at Dublin and an "incorporated" degree, and also most people of modest means. To understand what these criteria of selection meant in professional terms, it is necessary to consider briefly the development of each profession.

In continental Europe, the development and the codification of the law had coincided with the multiplication of the universities in the fourteenth and fifteenth centuries. In Italy especially, but also in some French universities, the demand for lawyers and administrators led to notable developments in civil and canon law. In England, the civil courts had resisted the introduction of the Roman Code and created, instead, a native common law, considered much too coarse and plebeian to be a fit subject of university teaching.[18] Training in the law took place outside the university in collegiate residence halls which became the London Inns of Court. Since the fifteenth century, the Inns had monopolized the power to confer upon their members the right to plead in court. Attorneys, instead, had developed as legal agents and officers of various courts which were responsible for regulating them. Unlike the future barristers, they had never joined into a guild. They had, therefore, been defenseless in face of attempts to subordinate them to the bar:

> In the fifteenth century, though there was already a functional distinction, there was no complete professional separation, for there was nothing to prevent an attorney becoming a member of an Inn of Court and eventually being called to the Bar. In the sixteenth and seventeenth centuries, however, the Inns, aided by judges and actuated, it seems, by motives of pure exclusiveness, embarked upon the deliberate policy of refusing admission to attorneys.[19]

The policy of restricting the number of attorneys admitted to each court had failed to check, we are told, their "multitudes and misdemeanours." Restrictions produced, instead, a tremendous confusion, as an irregular class of legal practitioners—the solicitors—developed, from the fifteenth century on, out of their original situation as the legal servants of king and noblemen. In practice, attorneys and solicitors were treated as a single category by the Act of 1729—a direct response by Parliament to petitions against unqualified attorneys by local justices. The Act subjected the lower branch of the law to various mandatory regulations and to stiff penalties in case of infraction: clerks were theretofore to be articled for five years to an attorney who could not take more than two apprentices at a time; they had to be duly enrolled in the court where they intended to practice, and take their oath and be examined before admission by a judge. The Act did not do anything to prevent infractions, and implementation remained very lax. Nevertheless, it provided a base for the work of the first effective professional association, founded shortly thereafter by a small group of attorneys who practiced in London. The Society of Gentlemen Practicers in the Courts of Law and Equity was still a very small body, chiefly concerned with the defense of the profession's jurisdiction and acting as a watchdog on parliamentary regulations. It performed its task quite effectively against both the encroachments of the barristers and the monopolistic pretensions of the Scriveners Company of London.[20] More typical of the eighteenth than of the nineteenth century, the Society was only indirectly concerned with training as a means for establishing control over the profession and over its market. A second association, the Law Society, founded in 1825, was in fact the main protagonist of the professionalization movement in the lower branch of the law.

Despite the Law Society's efforts to provide legal instruction for articled clerks and its pioneering emphasis on compulsory examinations, legal education, in the words of Sir William Holdsworth, "was almost the last thing to be reformed" in the nineteenth century.[21] By the middle of the eighteenth century, legal education and examinations had become as perfunctory or nonexistent at Oxford and Cambridge as they were at the Inns of Court. The training of the English lawyer was narrow and purely practical—"a crabbed, barbarous study" as one lawyer put it. This, in turn, had led to the progressive deterioration of the available literature. Not until Blackstone started his Vinerian lectures at Oxford in 1753 was there in England anything approaching systematic training in the common law. Blackstone's appeal, however, was more speedily heeded in America, both before and after independence, than on his side of the Atlantic. Thus, despite its ancient origins, the English legal profession lacked an organic connection with the university at the beginning of the professionalization movement of the nineteenth century. In this respect, the situation of the law was comparable to that of the newer occupations which were also seeking professional standing: lacking a tradition of formal theoretical training, the reformist leaders had to struggle to institute one, as they set about to upgrade their profession by new criteria of competence.

The development of medicine had been different. It had always been considered a branch of higher learning. Medical organization and medical science had been particularly backward in England, especially if compared to late medieval and Renaissance Italy. The sixteenth-century revival of the Greek and Latin medical classics, however, gave medicine a place of honor in the predominantly philosophical and theological English universities. As for practice, the founding of the Royal College of Physicians of London in 1518 was a deliberate attempt to import foreign models for the regulation of the profession and the improvement of its art. Within its jurisdiction—seven miles around London—the College received powers of licensing like those formerly granted only to bishops, as well as powers of discipline over its members and of prosecution against unlicensed practitioners.

For the first two centuries of its existence, the College applied its powers vigorously, though not always successfully: its main targets were empirics, midwives, and physicians who practiced in London with licenses other than its own, and, most especially, the subordinate though competing companies of Barber-Surgeons and Apothecaries. By the mid-eighteenth century, however, the College had ceased to prosecute on its own either rivals or pretenders. In fact, the Galenic conformism which the College, as an examining body, had imposed upon its candidates had become an anachronism; the staunch conservatism of the College ruling oligarchies made it look anachronistic in non-intellectual spheres as well.

The College had always conceded a favored status to the Oxford and Cambridge graduates, whether doctors or bachelors; but it had never been willing to recognize their right to practice without further examination within its jurisdiction, despite the frequent protests of the university licentiates.[22] Access to the highest rank of Fellow was normally reserved to Oxford and Cambridge doctors. In the first decades of the nineteenth century, this privilege, had become a means to exclude the Scotch and foreign-trained doctors, who were perhaps deficient in the classics, but often better trained in practical medicine than the College Fellows. It was argued that the Scotch universities were not resident universities and that a Scotch degree, therefore, "was not evidence of character or of social education."[23]

The Royal College of London, besides, had shown little or no interest in extending its seal of approval to doctors outside its jurisdiction.[24] The Fellows' interest in the promotion and advancement of medicine appeared to have been a thing of the past already in the eighteenth century. "The physicians," observe Carr-Saunders and Wilson, "had long established themselves in the upper ranks of society, and when scientific inquiry lost its novelty, they joined in the ample life of the great houses where elegance and wit were pursued. . . . Social qualifications became the first requirement for membership, and it was held that the necessary 'morals and manners' could be learnt only at the universities."[25]

The exclusiveness of the Royal College of Physicians, so infuriating to its own licentiates, had had the obvious effect of multiplying the numbers of practitioners with other kinds of licenses or no license at all. The bulk of the respectable medical men were clustered, in fact, in the companies of surgeons and apothecaries, whose subordination to the chartered company of physicians had become merely nominal by the late eighteenth century.

The surgeons were the next lower step in the medical hierarchy. Before the sixteenth century, they had been considered substantially equal to the physicians. But as the physicians rose to the status of a learned profession, the surgeons sank into that of a trade, merged with the barbers' guild. This stigmatizing union was not broken until 1745, after surgery had entered a phase of rapid and remarkable progress. With the incorporation of their own college in 1800, the surgeons had obtained the right to give license to practice throughout England. Elite surgeons, such as Sir Astley Cooper of Guy's Hospital or his predecessor Henry Cline, were perhaps the most famous medical men in England. Their lectures in anatomy far exceeded in fame and attendance those of the Royal College of Physicians. Despite their justified reputation, these men perpetuated themselves at the head of the major London hospitals by patronage and nepotism:

> Hospital appointments with all their advantages, direct and indirect, honourable and pecuniary, were given to certain Fellows of the Royal College of Physicians of London, personal influence counting for much in the matter; examinerships and lectureships at the Royal College of Surgeons of England were given to certain hospital surgeons who were elected to the desirable appointments which qualified them for their professorial duties largely in consequence of their ability to pay big fees for their introductions to big men. The man who could not pay these fees or afford a university education was fated to remain in the rank and file of his profession.[26]

Below the surgeons were the much more modest apothecaries. Their Society had been authorized to hold qualifying examinations in the eighteenth century. Its fees were low and it jealously protected the members' monopoly of dispensing, while the two other corporations increasingly neglected to defend their membership against encroachments. For all practical purposes, the apothecaries represented the great majority of family practitioners. The Act which they obtained in 1815 increased their powers but left them as a medical order inferior to the licentiates of the two

Colleges or the university graduates. They had, for instance, no clear right to charge fees for their medical services above and beyond charges for the medicine they dispensed. The Apothecaries Act, however, had sanctioned their right to practice and to conduct examinations which fully qualified the aspirant for general practice. The candidates had to fulfill the requirements of a five-year apprenticeship, "together with a sufficient medical education and a good moral character."[27] The Society pioneered the first written examinations and helped bring about a system of practical medical training to prepare the candidates. From the beginning, medical education was understood as that dispensed by recognized medical schools or teaching hospitals. It became customary for the licentiates of the Society to take a second examination at the Royal College of Surgeons; in the 1830s, most of the College's licentiates were of this new breed of qualified general practitioners in both medicine and surgery.

From the ranks of these doctors undoubtedly came the followers of Thomas Wakley, the radical champion of medical reform, editor of *The Lancet* and spokesman for the profession's rank and file. Up to a point, they supported and defended him in his often bitter battles against the administration of the London hospitals and the oligarchy of the Royal College of Surgeons. But insofar as Wakley attacked all forms of traditional monopoly, many abandoned him.[28] In the chaotic situation of the early nineteenth century, with eighteen different licensing authorities in the United Kingdom, competition was bound to strengthen the defense of narrow-based monopolies. This fragmentation limited the modernizing impact of partial reforms and delayed the reconstruction of monopoly on broadened universalistic bases: the connection of qualifications and monopoly of practice with training that would be both specialized and systematic were still too tentative to overshadow the traditional advantages of the established professional elites.

The conventional life style and patterns of behavior of the gentry, acquired in the family or in the educational preserves of the old ruling class, had been the hallmark of the successful eighteenth-century professional. Wealth, which some of these men amassed, was not only a sign of professional excellence, but also a stepping stone toward social standing, which the purchase of an estate conferred more securely than a law firm or a medical practice.[29] For the bulk of the middle-class challengers in the nineteenth century, such narrow gates were closed. The bases of prestige had to be reconstructed in order to permit, at the same time, middle-class access to status and middle-class monopolization of its benefits. As the reform movement gained power and scope, it was bound to reach the hallowed halls of the elite universities. But the educational ideals embodied in these institutions—and perhaps even more clearly in the nine leading public schools than in Oxford or Cambridge—were not supplanted: revised and adapted to their new functions, the old conceptions left a deep mark on the national system of education that was organized during the nineteenth century.

Around 1800, the curriculum of Oxford and Cambridge included some developments in the direction of mathematical and scientific education. At Oxford, chairs had been endowed in anatomy, in clinical medicine, and in English law. To a certain extent this evolution was a response to the notion of a modern curriculum that had come forth from the Dissenting Academies in the previous century. Nevertheless, the chief concern and business of the two English universities was classical education and not "useful knowledge." Except for the clergy and higher-level teaching, the older professions were not directly served by the universities. The classics, however, served the professions in a different way: as the intellectual sanction which Oxford and Cambridge bestowed upon the gentry's hegemony, a classical education functioned as a gate-keeping mechanism for the most prestigious professional roles. Thomas Gaisford, who had gone to Oxford in 1800, put it clearly: "The advantages of a classical education," he declared, "are two-fold—it enables us to look down with contempt on those who have not shared its advantages, and also fits us for places of emolument, not only in this world, but in that which is to come."[30]

Education at Oxford and Cambridge was not only much more expensive than at the Scotch universities, at Trinity in Dublin, or on the continent; until reforms began in the 1850s, it was dominated by the Anglican Church and excluded Catholics and Dissenters.[31] The fact that students were recruited from narrow upper-class circles strengthened the symbolic link between the universities' classicism and the self-image of a class. Later in the century, the development of a wider network of public schools relied on this fusion between the reproduction of class and the content of education: the classical curriculum which they favored became the cornerstone of a gentlemanly upbringing and a sign of successful assimilation into an elite life style for the sons of the upper middle class.

The middle-class challenge in the first part of the nineteenth century relied on a different, instrumental conception of education. Examination was its obvious weapon. The traditional corporations used qualifying examinations, and by 1800 Oxford and Cambridge had begun to take their own testing seriously. The issue, therefore, was not examination per se, but its content and conduct. From the 1830s on, official committees, spurred by the reformers in the "lower" branches, began investigating the status of medical and legal qualifying systems. Despite their attempts to defend their privileges, the traditional corporations were no longer able to stem the tide.[32] Some of the arguments offered then against serious and mostly written examinations are worth quoting, for they illustrate the traditional conception of the making of a professional.

Reporting to the 1847 Select Committee for Medical Registration, one spokesman for the Royal College of Physicians praised "the great advantages which result to society from there being an order of men within the profession who have had an education with the members of the other learned professions; from a certain class of the medical profession having been educated with the gentry of the country and having thereby acquired a tone of feeling which is very beneficial to the profession as a whole."[33] Or, in 1854, arguing against the extension of examination to the barristers, the Treasurer of one of the Inns of Court appealed in these words to the principles of laissez-faire: "I do not think that Examination is really of any use. I think the advantage of dining in the Hall is associating together. . . . If he [the new barrister] is not qualified, he will get no business, and if he is qualified, he will get business." Another one added: "I think that anyone of liberal education and good character who has the opportunity of acquiring the knowledge requisite for a Barrister will do so, if he really means to practice as a Barrister."[34]

This reference to practical training—on a totally voluntary and a-systematic basis—reveals the confidence which these elites derived more from their social rank than from the corporate monopoly that was now being threatened. The guarantees which they thought they offered the public were based on social privileges with *pre-existed* the entry into practice. A classical education certified beforehand as gentlemen those who were going to acquire, however, casually, specialization by apprenticeship with one of their social peers. Thus ennobled, these gentlemen could grace professional life with the virtues of aristocratic disinterestedness. Their gentlemanly idea of profession, based on the respect and deference due to the traditional social hierarchy, is still present, though ambiguously transposed, in Adam Smith's statement about the market value of professional services:

> We trust our health to the physician; our fortune and sometimes our life and our reputation to the lawyer and attorney. Such confidence could not safely be reposed in people of a very low or mean condition. Their reward must be such, therefore, as may give them that rank in the society which so important a trust requires. The long time and great expense which must be laid out in their education, when combined with this circumstance, necessarily enhance still further the price of their labour.[35]

In Adam Smith's words, confidence in the professional and the price of his services are still associated with social rank, an "anti-market" principle, as much as with the length and cost of training. The statement, however, expresses the double project of the professional reformers: on the one hand, to make their education "pay" on the market; on the other, to make professional training and income, in and of themselves, synonymous with social status and respectability. The project, as we know, involved a conception of professional proficiency which established a direct link between training and market-oriented practice. We must determine now to what extent the educational principles of the old ruling class and the structures that sustained them were challenged by the new conceptions of the middle-class reformers.

THE DEFERENTIAL CHALLENGE

The breaking up of the old professional monopolies by the men of the "lower branches," the introduction of competitive examinations in the service of the state, and the conquest of professional status by relatively new or transformed occupations such as engineering, architecture and surveying, dentistry, accounting, and with more difficulty the arts, journalism, and schoolteaching, are three distinct aspects of the same process of collective mobility: that by which the British middle classes opened up the existing structure of opportunities and the paths of access to "social honor," without ever completely erasing the quite tangible advantages of the aristocratic upper stratum.

Commenting on the motives of the reformers, W. T. Reader somewhat cynically notes: "If the gentry wanted to hang on to political power, that in itself the middle classes did not very much object to, but what did annoy them was to find themselves shut out of the material rewards of power. They wanted some of the jobs for some of their boys, and they intended to break into the official world in the same way as they were breaking into the world of the professions, which also the gentry had been inclined to regard as preserves of their own."[36]

The private interests of middle-class families could not account, however, for the reshaping of British society that the nineteenth century achieved. Neither do the parliamentary reforms of 1832 and 1867 explain the gentry's adoption of the reformers' objectives. During the 1820s, Tory governments had liberalized custom duties and the internal labor market, as well as repealed the laws against Catholics and Dissenters.[37] In fact, as Harold Perkin points out: "The radical change produced by the Reform Act was from aristocratic rule by prescription to aristocratic rule by consent. It was not so much the actual existence of a large anti-aristocratic block vote which swayed the politicians, as the fear of creating one."[38]

As the industrial mode of production asserted itself, the general interest of the nation increasingly appeared to coincide with industry's requirements. The gentry and the middle-class radicals were united, besides, by a powerful common fear: the danger to private property evoked by Chartism—or more exactly, by the infusion of socialist ideals into the working class movement for universal suffrage. Compared to this threat, the middle class' attacks on the system of patronage and aristocratic misgovernment seemed reasonable indeed.

While economic interests moved the bulk of each class' armies into position, what shaped the battles was the striving for hegemony within each class—that is, the striving for an idealized and organizing image of itself and the social order that each class both consciously and unconsciously projected. To achieve hegemony meant to achieve more than economic and political power; it meant seizing the "moral and intellectual direction" of the historical process and being able to claim the allegiance of others besides the logical soldiers in each class camp.[39] For the middle class, which concerns us here, the struggle for hegemony involved, on the one hand, the disciplining of the working class, the subordination of the workers' original strivings to its own project. On the other hand, it involved converting the old ruling class not only to its programs, but to its principles of action, so that ultimately the aristocracy's lingering grasp on state power became more a division of labor between partners than a serious obstacle to middle-class progress.

In 1826, James Mill anticipated in these words the achievement of hegemony by the middle class:

> On the political and moral importance of this class, there can be but one opinion. It is the strength of the community. It contains, beyond all comparison, the greatest portion of the intelligence, industry, and wealth of the state. . . . The people of the class below are the instruments with which they work; and those of the class above, though they may be called their governors, and may really sometimes seem to rule them, are more often, more truly, more completely, under their control.[40]

The central principles of the middle-class vision derived from the idealization of capitalist entrepreneurship. Capital and active property, in the hands of the industrious and talented, necessarily evoked the motor principle of individual competition. This binomial stood as the social and moral opposite of the passive enjoyment of inherited property and the redistribution of its benefits through patronage, which in the eyes of the bourgeoisie characterized the gentry and its rule. Useful knowledge—the core of the Benthamites' ideas about education—corresponded to a social

order founded on capitalist production, in which competition imposed upon the capitalist an informed and constant vigilance for his best interests and an overall concern
with efficiency.

However, as articulated by professional men and especially by professional civil
servants, the principle of efficiency deviated from the entrepreneurial image of the
image of the social order and symbolized the differences that were to emerge in the
middle-class ranks. Dependent on the state for guaranteed monopoly as well as for
the broader reforms they were trying to achieve, professionals could not invoke the
hidden hand of the market to the same extent that the entrepreneurs could to justify
their goals and their actions. The production and the recognition of competence demanded deliberate action on the part of professional associations and on the part of the
state; it demanded, for one thing, the deliberate organization of a system of education
on which recruitment to desirable positions would ultimately depend. As Perkin
notes, the entrepreneurial vision reduced the state to minimal functions of arbitration
and policing, even though the purely negative content of the laissez-faire ideal was
denied in practice by the interventionist and increasingly centralized Victorian state.
"For the professional ideal, on the other hand, it was the positive aspects which were
important: selection of talent and expertise, efficiency and economy interpreted as
the effective solution of social problems and the abolition of waste arising from social
and administrative neglect, and the extension of government as and where necessary
to meet the social demands upon it."[41]

Despite its disjunction on the issue of state intervention, the middle class projected
a relatively unified ideology in its challenge to the moral and social order represented
by the aristocratic elites. Competition crowned the efforts of the ablest, reconciling
the best interests of individuals to those of the commonwealth. This invisible and
impartial judge tempered the mettle of which men were made, inculcating self-
respect and self-dependence, which patronage and the debilitating effects of personal
dependence could never teach. Therefore, to let merit be freely identified and rewarded by competition was as much a moral imperative as a social one. Thus spoke
Macaulay, defending in front of Commons the introduction of competitive examinations in the Indian Civil Service: "the intellectual test which is about to be established," he said, "will be found in practice to be the best moral test that could be
devised."[42]

The examination embodied principles that were dear to both sectors of the middle
class: as a symbol of competition, it appeared to open channels of upward social
mobility to the ablest and most industrious; as a test of competence, it matched merit
to function on the basis of expertise, defined and assessed by juries themselves composed of experts. Thus, while examination appeared to subject social position to an
impersonal test, analogous in this to the test of the market for the entrepreneur, it
also appeared to emancipate the expert from the sponsorship and the unqualified
judgment of outsiders.

Resistance was perhaps greater in the Civil Service, where patronage and the
prevalence of party considerations were institutionalized, than in the professions
which accepted, at least ritualistically, the principle of examination. Macaulay's
proposals were incorporated into the East India Company Charter of 1853, replacing
patronage altogether by examination. In response, Trinity College in Dublin quite

early offered specialized preparation for the Indian Civil Service tests; university graduates moved swiftly to the head of the new system's recruits.[43]

Despite the recommendations of the Northcote-Trevelyan Report of 1853, directly and deeply influenced by Macaulay and the I.C.S., reform was longer to come to the permanent Home Service.[44] Some objections to the Report were definitely inspired by the desire to defend a class prerogative: it was feared that "a lower tone of feeling would prevail" in a Service staffed by "picked clever young men from the lower ranks of society."[45] A more justifiable criticism was raised by those who thought the Service's salaries could not compete with the income that could be expected from the market professions and that only second-rate men would therefore be attracted. Another voice objected that scholarship did not make a good administrator. But a reality test came to silence public opposition and spur the reform movement on: the appalling disasters of the Crimean War added broad popular support to the pressure exercised by insiders. In 1855, the Civil Service Commission was established. Until the late 1870s, however, the various reform schemes fell short of the thorough reorganization envisaged by Northcote and Trevelyan. Though recruitment by qualifying examination was instituted, promotion perpetuated patronage. The examination, besides, shunned technical specialization, inspired as it was by the competitive academic standards that had been developing at Oxford and Cambridge since the first years of the century. As students or administrators, many elite civil servants had been associated with this renewal. Educators, on their side, had been among the most enthusiastic supporters of civil-service reform since the days of the Northcote-Trevelyan Report.[46] "One after another stressed the benefit which the change would render to educational standards, and to the cause of education throughout the country."[47]

The first civil service reforms, thus, tightened the bonds between elite educational institutions and the governing elite. In the 1850s, Oxford and Cambridge's new emphasis on serious testing had suggested a model to the small and closely knit group of elite reformers. In turn, the need to prepare upper-class students for the administration's examinations sustained the trend toward change in the elite public schools and universities.[48] The changing nature of the ineluctable tasks which the governing elite had to face at home and in the empire pressed for a further evolution of curricula at the two leading universities.

The endorsement of the examination system by the elite schools and by influential sectors of the governing elite gave to the competitive system a prestige it could not have acquired through the single efforts of the middle-class radicals. In 1862, for instance, the President of such a gentlemanly organization as the Royal Institute of British Architects remarked that "the fact of the system of Examination for offices in all the services under the Government having worked satisfactorily, seems to have led to a desire to introduce a similar system into the education of an Architect."[49] However, until practically the end of the century, the influence of Civil Service reform did little to institutionalize the new kind of practical learning that was the battle cry of middle-class professionalization movements.

Besides Oxford and Cambridge, England had at mid-century only two other universities and one college. The University of London started with the foundation, in 1826, of what was chiefly a medical school. In keeping with the prevalent influence of its Benthamite and Dissenting founders, it was the first university in England that did not administer a religious test to its students. The year after, the Anglicans responded by founding King's College: despite its religious exclusiveness, it aimed frankly at providing preparation for the professions.[50] In 1836, the two were joined by charter into the University of London. Both Durham, founded in 1837 under religious sponsorship, and the secular Owens College at Manchester, grown out of the early efforts of the local statistical society, had strong regional ties and clear scientific and technical vocations. With the addition of the Royal Colleges of Mines and of Chemistry and the Military Academy at Woolworth, this was practically the whole English apparatus for higher-level professional and scientific training.

The bulk of professional education was provided by apprenticeship, a form of training which clearly favored young men with a family connection in the professions or with a good deal of money to back them up: "For good class training, with all that that implied in the way of introductions and opportunities, as well as straightforward technical competence, it seems to have been unwise to budget for an outlay of less than £1000."[51]

To give an idea of how many families could have afforded first-class apprenticeships for their sons, in 1865–1866, out of roughly twenty-four million inhabitants in England and Wales, only 200,000 tax assessments were about £300 per year. Of these, 42,000 represented incomes between £1000 and £5,000; 7,500 were for very large incomes over £5,000.[52] Of course, cheaper training—and much lower-status and meager opportunities—could be had through second-rate apprenticeships, or in the new technical professions such as engineering in particular. Engineering offered relatively easy entry to ambitious lower-status boys, who could be articled quite cheaply or could study at night in one of the Mechanics Institutes. The results, however, judging by Britain's poor showing at the Paris Industrial Exhibit of 1867 and by the opinion of contemporaries such as Matthew Arnold, were quite below the average standards of engineering education on the continent.

Given the state of education, every advance in the professional drive for competitive examinations exacerbated the problem of training. It was beyond the resources of the majority of practitioners to go to Edinburgh or to the continent in search of medical or engineering education.

The narrow institutional base of higher-level training hindered standardization. For the professional reformers, unable on the whole to work through existing educational institutions, organization in voluntary associations was doubly necessary. In London at least, the efforts of the "old style" corporations of the lower branches rapidly met their limits: in medicine, the resistance of the higher branches aimed chiefly at maintaining the traditional distinction of ranks within the profession. The modernizing project of the Society of Apothecaries was thwarted, thus, by the physicians and surgeons' refusal to accept them as peers and was limited, as well, by the Society's location in London and by its own narrow conception of monopoly. Although the apothecaries were the first to apply compulsory written examinations in 1839–1840, professional reorganization came from other quarters.

Much of the vigor of the professional reform movement was to be found outside London, in the leadership of the regional societies which later merged or federated into national associations. Not surprisingly, the medical society which became in 1856 the British Medical Association was founded in Worcester as the Provincial Medical and Surgical Society in 1832. Sir George Clark describes it in these terms: "By about 1840 his [Dr. Charles Hastings', founder and first president] association had become the one important medical association of provincial England; his task in the eighteen-forties was to conquer London." Sir George estimates that a decade later, "the future of medicine and surgery in Great Britain was . . . to be decided in bargainings between the state and the profession. The profession had a dual organization, the corporations and the voluntary associations, one of which latter was now predominant among them."[53]

The British Medical Association actively campaigned for the Medical Act which was passed by Parliament in 1858. The Act set up a single national register for all practitioners who satisfied certain minimal standards of competence. Control over registration was in the hands of the General Medical Council, constituted by representatives of the state, of the old corporations, of the voluntary associations and of the universities, though not yet of the teaching hospitals.

> It was the first body set over any British profession in which there sat members appointed by the state to take part in the regular routine of these functions. Yet, although the state created it, it was not an instrument for carrying out the will of the state . . . The official nominees were in a small minority among the members. . . . Thus the first national measures to supersede the system of chartered liberties in the medical profession were unlike any other professional constitution in the British Isles . . . in not merely permitting but presupposing the existence of strong voluntary associations side by side with the official machine.[54]

The Act of 1858 was only a first step in professional reorganization: it did not institute uniform qualifications, as the B.M.A. had advocated. To the great displeasure of Thomas Wakley, it did not give direct representation to the majority of practitioners. It did little to reform and unify the programs of training. Yet, in Wakley's own words, it was "the commencement of a series of important changes," in which the B.M.A. was to play an increasingly central role.

The Law Society, though similar in type to the British Medical Association, did not achieve the same success. In 1836 it had petitioned the judges to substitute written examinations for informal interviews. By 1853 the examination for attorneys and solicitors had been consolidated, and the lectures provided by the Law Society in London had become a full-fledged course of training, with increasing emphasis on general academic background. Successive parliamentary inquiries forced the Inns of Court to establish compulsory written examinations in 1872. Five years later, the Law Society was given sole authority over its examinations, a privilege which achieved its emancipation from the formal tutelage of the Inns of Court. Yet the bar successfully resisted the radical idea of a legal university, open to all law students without distinctions. By the end of the nineteenth century the project was definitively shelved: the division between barristers and attorneys in the English system of law had become permanently institutionalized. In fact, the Law Society's failure to unify the profession was a failure more apparent than real: in the course of the attorneys' rise to professional status, the association had successfully repulsed the barristers' encroachments and established a division of labor on solid grounds. The attorneys, in fact, were more indispensable to the barristers as a referral system than the barristers were to them as pleaders.

For all the advances that professionalization had made by the nineteenth century, it had failed to build the bases of a unified and coherent educational system, which alone could standardize the production of professional producers and establish monopoly on universalistic and objective appearances. Part of the problem lay in the professionals' attitude toward the state. The professional reformers, whenever possible, had relied on state action to break the preserves of their traditional adversaries. Where their own autonomy was concerned, they shared, however, the general laissez-faire rejection of state interference. Moreover, a clear notion of the state's educational functions was generally lacking, or perhaps too controversial to be endorsed. Sir George Clark's notes, for instance, that "the reform of medical education was not understood to mean the provision of more or better instruction." Not even Oxford or Cambridge conceived that their essential business was teaching but " 'to find out, at stated seasons, in the most thorough manner possible, what a young man knows, without seeking to enquire how he knows it. Thus it was that from 1815 to 1858 parliament remodelled some medical examining bodies and created others, but neither endowed nor even investigated medical teaching which underwent great changes, but without interference from the state.''[56]

The banner of state education had been vigorously raised by the Benthamites, though chiefly in regard to elementary education for the working class. On the one hand, the Benthamites may have been too radical for the rank-and-file professional, as indicated by the disaffection of Thomas Wakley's medical following in the 1840s.[57] On the other hand, not the least effect of Benthamite agitation was to incite the gentry to self-reform. As Perkin comments: "in spite of the failure of the Benthamites and their allies to create alternative systems of education for the various classes capable of completely replacing those of the aristocracy and its Church, they were able to stimulate the latter to reform and extend the existing provision and to do so in accordance with the spirit of the entrepreneurial ideal.''[58]

Again, the Benthamite reformers did not immediately succeed in creating a system of new grammar schools adapted to middle-class needs. Yet, their methods, and especially the competition their private schools presented, spurred the aristocratic "public" schools to reform. As Raymond Williams writes:

> Attendances at the old schools, particularly at the leading nine, had begun to revive in the period 1790–1830, and in their different ways Butler at Shrewsbury, from 1798, and Arnold at Rugby, from 1824, had begun to change their character. Arnold's influence was not mainly on the curriculum, but on the reestablishment of social purpose, the education of Christian gentlemen. Butler's influence is perhaps even more significant, for his emphasis on examination-passing marks the beginning of a major trend.[59]

Most of the proprietary schools that the middle class had set up as alternatives to the gentry's boarding schools attained "public" school status in the second half of the nineteenth century. Their curricula had been different from those of the nine older institutions: less devoted to the classical foundation, more oriented toward mathematics, science, and modern languages. The best among them, however, rapidly achieved the integration with the two elite universities that characterized the reformed schools of the aristocracy. By the time of the Schools Inquiry Commission, in 1868, schools such as Marlborough and Cheltenham contributed more undergraduates to Oxford and Cambridge than all but four of the nine aristocratic ''public'' schools.[60] As Brian Simon observes, ''both old and new public schools became desirable educational institutions, increasingly well filled with sons of the affluent and respectable; as has often been said, they played a key part in bringing about that fusion between new industrialists and old aristocracy that gave birth to the Victorian upper middle class.''[61]

Logically, these schools functioned as one of the chief mechanisms for the reproduction of this class. ''As soon as it is possible to make a good boarding school work over a wide area,'' wrote Edward Thring, headmaster at Uppingham, in the early 1870s, ''only those who have time to stay five, six, seven years or more at it have a chance. This at once silently decides that none but the monied class can form the bulk of the school.''[62]

The best ''public'' schools established themselves in the mind of middle-class parents as a direct stepping-stone to the elite universities. Thus, while the upper middle class took a public school education as a birthright for its children, the ambition to secure such superior schooling became, in Thring's words, ''the fixed idea with every Englishman.'' This superiority was built into a system by the work of the school commissions of the 1850s and 1860s and by the Acts which implemented their recommendations: the ''public'' schools and their emulators took the top place in a three-tiered system of schooling strictly segregated by class; they constituted, in the words of G. Kitson Clark, ''the final stage of the consolidation of the caste . . . of a new type of aristocracy.''[63]

The working class was assigned, obviously, to a strictly elementary network of publicly financed schools, attendance at which caught up only slowly with that of Anglican or Catholic voluntary schools. The examination system—the results of which conditioned the payment of state grants—reinforced the quasi-military discipline of these schools, the methods of teaching by drill and learning by rote, the narrowness of subject matter.[64]

The class divisions which the schools mirrored and reproduced were explicit in the Taunton Commission report on endowed higher-level schools: three grades were strictly distinguished by leaving age (eighteen or nineteen; sixteen and fourteen), by the fees paid, and by the careers for which the pupils were prepared. Free places for poor or local boys were abolished and replaced by open scholarships for ''boys of real ability in whatever rank they may be found.''

From the first level sprang the system of ''public'' schools, which by 1900 served some 30,000 students.[65] The second grade was ''to educate the sons of smaller professionals and businessmen, large shopkeepers, and farmers for the professions, commerce, and industry and have a leaving age of sixteen, so as to prevent them from preparing for the university.''[66] From the publicly subsidized third grade came in the last decades of the nineteenth century the developments in higher-grade elementary education that were to threaten the rigid system of class education. Pro-

moted by elective and usually radical school boards, the higher grade schools were
not only a threat to endowed and religious schools; their low fees and their technical
and scientific vocation, which made them attractive to the middle class, blurred the
class division between elementary and secondary levels, while their centers for the
improvement of student-teachers put the teaching profession within reach of the
working class. These schools, so ardently defended in the ensuing battles by the trade
union movement and the National Union of Teachers, incarnated labor's aspiration
of a common secular school for all children. Their future was at the center of the
intense social and political struggles of the turn of the century; but the apparent success of the middle class demand for state-supported secondary education signaled,
in fact, their demise and the defeat of the working-class ideal. The Education Act
of 1902

> rigidly defined differences between elementary and secondary education. . . . In
> place of the higher grade schools . . . there was offered a competitive system of schol-
> arships to transfer children from one set of schools, with an early leaving age irre-
> vocably fixed, to a quite different system which alone offered the opportunity for
> advancement. . . . From now on the pressure for secondary education for all inevitably
> took the form of a continuing attempt to open up the grammar schools—now the only
> secondary schools—to the working class.[67]

Since secondary education was planned as something *qualitatively* different from
what the school boards had provided in their higher-grade science schools, the model
deliberately chosen was that of the existing "public" schools. The middle classes
had obtained, in fact, their own bowdlerized version of the elite's instruments for
establishing and maintaining social distance in the new system of inequality.

More directly concerned than other sectors of the middle class, professional men
were among the most vigorous supporters of state subsidies for education. True to
their class interests, however, and split within themselves—between those who had
access to the closed circle formed at the top by Oxford, Cambridge, and the "public"
schools, and those who did not—the average professionals could neither have envisaged nor supported radical educational reform.

In the early nineteenth century, their choicest clients as well as their arrogant
colleagues of the "higher branches" relayed the model of the gentleman to middle-
class professionals. Most of them belonged to a social world in which university
education was still, on the whole, a thing out of reach. Thus, before the "civic universities" developed from the 1880s on, their project of social mobility took distance from those still lower in the social hierarchy by means of traditional ideological
legitimations, adapted from aristocratic models. Contemptuous as the middle-class
professionals may have been of the idle and wasteful living of the elite, their claims
for status reveal a diffuse feeling of envy and emulation.[68] Their project, in a sense,
aimed as much at enlarging the ranks of those who could be eventually admitted to
the world of high status, as it aimed at creating an *independent* scale of prestige and
social standing.

In general, if a collective mobility project—directed in part against established
elites—acknowledges that its own distinctive values cease to be predominant at a
given point of the upward trajectory, the challenge itself contributes to legitimize
the stratification system. Insofar as these deferential challengers admitted a ceiling

to the scope of their group's upward mobility, an added incentive existed for protecting the group's advantages against challenges from below—that is, for seeking to reproduce "downwards" the stratification barrier which the professional middle class itself had to face. This barrier, besides, did not seem totally impenetrable.

When the school system took shape in the last decades of the century, the bridges that scholarships provided across its class levels confirmed the notion that the top rungs of the status hierarchy were accessible. The system, moreover, was an effective moat against the leveling aspirations which the middle class attributed, in part accurately, to the working class movement. As the upper middle class had ceased to advocate any change in the "public" schools in the late 1870s, so the bulk of the middle class considered itself basically satisfied with what it had achieved at the secondary level in the early years of our century. Its main target thereafter became the universities.[69]

THE PYRAMID OF PRESTIGE

When the Victorian state entered the field of education in response to the demands of its middle and upper middle class constituents, it respectfully interpreted their implicit directions for a revised system of status inequality. As Raymond Williams puts it, educational thought and planning were shaped on the whole by "the continued relegation of trade and industry to lower school classes, and the desire of successful industrialists that their sons should move into the now largely irrelevant class of gentry."[70]

It would be patently absurd, however, to think that a modern industrial state can structure its educational system in terms of the exceptional continuity of a class culture, when the class itself has lost its hegemony. Britain's head start as an industrial power had provided her capitalists with a secure shelter from competition. Protected from foreign rivals, constituted predominantly by small family firms, British industry in the first half of the nineteenth century lacked the incentive to give scientific and technical education a decisive push. Nor was the state inspired by nationalistic reasons to develop scientific research and scientific education and put them at the service of industrial technology. However, from the 1860s on, the state was forced to entertain increasing concerns, voiced first by some farsighted industrialists, about the backwardness of English technical and scientific education. The reports of the Royal Commissions on scientific and technical instruction, as well as the work of the National Association for the Promotion of Technical Education, were directly influenced by this grouping of industrialists and scientists. This work—and the industrialists' direct sponsorship—were in large part responsible for the development of provincial universities from the 1870s on. German industry was perceived as particularly threatening and its technological superiority was attributed in large part to Germany's scientific excellence and to her system of Technische Hochschulen.

The influence of this movement was limited, however, by Britain's development as an imperialist power. Especially after the depression that started in the 1870s, British capital sought higher profits overseas. Sheltered by Britain's dominant trading position with regard to the underdeveloped world, British industry, largely unaware of the dangers, continued on its road to technological obsolescence. As

Brian Simon observes, "This tendency towards the 'freezing' of technique had a clear educational significance. An integrated system of science and technology—of education and industry—on the German or Swiss model no longer seemed so urgent."[71] Imperialism, moreover, made London into a world financial center; the shortage of clerks was felt more acutely than that of technicians toward the end of the nineteenth century. The corrective that was emphasized was grammar school education. Technical and scientific education developed chiefly at the university level—that is to say, near the summit of a hierarchical system which excluded at an early age the bulk of working-class children.

The provincial colleges—seven of which had been founded in the decade 1871–1881—received their first state subsidies in 1889. In 1930, Abraham Flexner compared them to the American state universities, which had often been their avowed model. He considered the British development "an amazing achievement in a brief period" and commented, "It is obvious why the provincial universities could not have been born earlier: they had to wait upon the provision of secondary schools and the dissolution of the Anglican monopoly at Oxford, Cambridge, and in the sphere of politics."[72] But the Oxford and Cambridge model had not been dethroned.

In the 1860s a Government Select Committee had concluded that technological and scientific training would be of little use if provided to the lower classes, except "as enlarging the area from which the managers may be drawn." It added, however, that "all the witnesses . . . are convinced that a knowledge of the principles of science on the part of those who occupy the higher industrial ranks . . . would tend to promote industrial progress."[73]

The accuracy of the conviction matters less here than the fact that the "new kind of learning" fit into the class mold of the educational system. Oxford and Cambridge increasingly opened their curricula to the "new learning" while the civic universities, in Sir Eric Ashby's words, "mellowed" their strong utilitarian bias "by a respect and attachment to the ideals for which Oxford and Cambridge stood."[74] Since education was destined to the co-optable middle class, it should not be severed from the culture that was the hallmark of a gentleman. Couched in class terms, the incorporation of the gentlemanly model tacitly led the "redbrick" universities to accept a place at the base of "a 'pyramid of prestige' of institutions fixed in the hierarchy according to their distance from the pure model of the English university to which Oxford and Cambridge in practice most closely approximate."[75]

For whoever was rich enough to aspire to a gentlemanly style of life, the new institutions in London or in the provinces could not match the grace or the advantages of Oxford and Cambridge. This persistent preference of the upper middle class, which still provided a disproportionate number of professionals, maintained the pressure for academic reform on the two ancient universities. Paradoxically, the aristocratic mystique that surrounded them helped their transformation: with incomparably greater prestige than the other institutions of higher learning, with better power connections and larger means, Oxford and Cambridge could attract the best teachers and, as academic criteria of selection became increasingly important, the best students as well. These objective advantages allowed them to translate their earlier position as centers of elite reproduction and co-optation into twentieth-century educational superiority. Their graduates "were readily given chairs at the provincial universities where they became the most prestigeful and influential members of the staff. The difference in quality—real or imagined—between graduates of Oxford and Cambridge and those of other universities has been so great that vacancies in subjects not existing at the two ancient universities were preferably filled by their own graduates trained in related fields, rather than graduates of other universities possessing specialized training.''[76]

The new universities opened up middle-class access to higher education considerably.[77] Given the enlarged pool of educated potential recruits, many professions upgraded their entry requirements by adding general education as a preliminary. Thus, the ''redbrick'' universities contributed to the professionalization movement in two ways: by providing systematic general education to broad sectors of the middle class, and by taking up, in most cases, the tasks of specialized professional training which had heretofore been fulfilled by examination-oriented private schools or by apprenticeship. With few exceptions, professional associations relinquished their training functions. The new institutions provided an educational base for the newer professions as well as for the bulk of professionals in medicine and engineering. They did not succeed, however, in erasing the hierarchical cast of the educational system:

> Oxford and Cambridge were national universities connected with the national elites of politics, administration, business, and the liberal professions. The rest were provincial, all of them, including London, taking most of their students from their own region and training them in undergraduate professional schools for the newer technological and professional occupations created by industrialism, such as chemistry, electrical engineering, state grammar school teaching, and the scientific civil service.[78]

In the 1930s, it was apparent to an incisive observer such as Abraham Flexner that the persistence of a hierarchical order had greatly hindered the standardization of scientific and professional education. By comparison with Germany and the United States, England was far behind in the development of professional and graduate schools. Flexner remarked, in particular, that British laboratories and teaching hospitals were underendowed and that their overall structure was haphazard and weak.[79] The universities' response to the practical needs of their different class constituencies had been flexible, but it had also been a-systematic and fragmentary. The unchallenged Oxbridge model provided the other institutions with undeniable standards of excellence, at the same time that it limited their capacity for organizational innovation. As a consequence, the newer universities competed to approximate their model more than they competed for research facilities and specialized faculty in an open academic marketplace. From one point of view, the lack of competition may account for the fact that the British universities failed to ''create new disciplines or professions and did not develop research systematically.''[80]

From the point of view of the professionals themselves, the internalization of the invidious status barriers embodied in the two-tier academic structure is significant; it may partly explain that professionalism in contemporary Britain has not been as successful an antidote to the unionization and the class consciousness of educated workers as it is in the United States.[81]

The twentieth-century continuity of Britain's hierarchical system of higher education reflects the persistence of old forms of status stratification and legitimation, which had particular affinities with traditional conceptions of higher learning. The

two-tier academic structure expresses, thus, the interplay of status and class principles of stratification: it can be seen as the institutional response of a traditionally
cast, though flexible and open, ruling class to needs arising from the economy and
from the state apparatus. Combining co-optation with segregation, the academic
system reconciled the maintenance of "aristocratic" status and the vested interests
of the old ruling class with the emergent class structure of industrial capitalism.

The aristocratic aspirations of the British middle class are often proposed as an
explanation for the persistence of the gentry's cultural influence in education and
for the decline in entrepreneurial efficiency and innovation which became apparent
before the end of the nineteenth century.[82] Attitudes, granted that they exist, cannot
constitute a satisfactory explanation for a structural phenomenon. On the entrepreneurial side, the neglect of scientific and technical education was rooted in Britain's economic structure and unique pattern of industrialization. It was perpetuated
by the illusory shelter which the empire built around capitalist profits. The effect
was that during the nineteenth century and part of the twentieth, industry did not
command the development of higher education, leaving it relatively free to follow
its traditional model. Industry's demand for highly trained scientists, managers,
and technicians was not vigorous enough, or came too late to overturn the "pyramid
of prestige" which cast an aura of social inferiority upon the new disciplines and
the newer universities.

Paradoxically, since the advance of British industry turned into technological and
organizational conservatism in the last third of the nineteenth century, alternative
channels of mobility remained open for a long time to men who had not passed
through higher education.[83]

The fact that industry was relatively inhospitable to university graduates may have
contributed, on the other hand, to the sense of closing opportunities for high-status
occupations conveyed at the turn of the century by such spokesmen of the upper
middle class as the journalist Escott, who wrote:

> Though the exigencies of modern life . . . have multiplied professions in England,
> they have not multiplied them in such numbers as to provide sufficient occupation
> for the sons of English parents. . . . Of the young men who have gone through an
> academic course, without discredit but without lustre, the great majority become
> curates, or schoolmasters, or emigrants. The mere university degree, even when
> accompanied by moderate honors, is becoming a drug in the market.[84]

In fact, enrollments in higher education were lower in Britain than in other industrial
countries until after the Second World War; unlike Germany, France, Italy, and
even the United States, Britain did not have an "academic proletariat" during the
depression of the 1930s.[85]

Politics, and the Labour Party in particular, offered still another channel of individual mobility that did not pass through the university. More significant, even,
than the alternatives, was the insulation of different classes and systems of social
status from each other; until 1944, this insulation contributed to reduce the pressure
from below for opportunities in higher education.[86]

On the professional side, the reform movement of the nineteenth century ultimately contributed to preserve the norm of sponsored mobility and an ideology of
stratification that was at variance with the characteristic legitimations of market-

oriented professionalization. The logic of this movement leads, in effect, to the development of a nominally open, standardized, and competitive educational system, functioning to reproduce and legitimize social and occupational stratification. The British professional reformers failed to join a movement for full-fledged educational modernization, and did not press the typical organizational and ideological features of modern professionalism upon the higher levels of the school system. This was possible in part because sources of social prestige—which were heteronomous from the point of view of the professional mobility project—remained continuously available. The reformers within the older professions could gradually fit their original drive for status into the pre-existing structures and thus keep their distance, in turn, from less successful colleagues and less "gentle" professions.

The English case shows with clarity that the internal characteristics of professionalization and of the professional model are subordinate to broader social and economic structures. The elaboration of status criteria and the adjustments in the educational institutions were not incompatible responses to the social effects of industrialization. England's incipient decline, both as an industrial pioneer and as a world power, reinforced the "natural" tendency of status barriers to crystallize. The substitution of criteria of status founded on modern specialized training for those founded, however remotely, on "aristocratic" culture and style of life is not yet complete today. However, in the words of a British sociologist, "the rise of the university graduate in Britain since World War II is comparable to the rise of the gentry in the sixteenth century."[87]

The non-elite system of national education asserted itself after 1944; it performs its essential function in the reproduction and legitimation of class, supplying industry and administration not with gentlemen, but with specialized, classified, and graded manpower.

In turning next to the American case, I shall similarly look at the professional project from the point of view of the available organizational and ideological resources. The fact that the educational system in the United States is less hierarchical than in England, and that its higher levels appear as models of modernity to the rest of the capitalist world, does not mean, of course, that it is less central to the reproduction and legitimation of the class structure. The professions and higher education ultimately developed a closer relation to each other and to the economy in the United States than they did in England. This points to a difference in the ideological means mobilized by the educational system, and to a different articulation of the educational system with the larger social structure. It illuminates, in short, the different context in which professionalization evolved.

Chapter 8

PROFESSIONAL PRIVILEGE
IN A DEMOCRATIC SOCIETY

Professions came of age in America after the Civil War, a period in which economic, administrative, and political power were consolidated and centralized. In the period between 1870 and 1920, the establishment of national organizational nuclei served by vast bureaucracies was so distinctive that many authors, following Kenneth Boulding, refer to it as the "organizational revolution." They tend to see it as the rather paradoxical culmination of the "great transformation" which had begun half a century earlier under the auspices of laissez-faire.

Corinne Gilb observes, for instance, that "professional organizations came relatively late in the organizational revolution" and suggests that "to articulate and sustain the new and needed levels of professionalism, and to hold their own in a society whose various other members were increasingly organized, the professions, too, formed organizations."[1] It is true that neither in Europe nor in the United States did professional organizations attain their present form or create their present relationships with state power until this century.[2] The radical changes in the larger market had fundamental consequences for the structure of professions, old and new, as they strove to establish or maintain their own secondary markets of services. To these general consequences I shall return later. We can expect them to be more visible, widespread, and far-reaching in the United States than in other advanced capitalist countries. Indeed, in America's passage from local or regional to national organizations, *all* the central institutions were distinctively formed or transformed: the structure of the federal government, the corporate nuclei of industrial capitalism, the industrial trade unions, the educational system, and the professions bear little resemblance to the institutional forms which fulfilled their functions before this phase, in which the United States became the world's leading industrial power.[3]

It would be misleading, however, to assume that there was a total discontinuity between the early attempts at professionalization and the consolidated forms of mature and successful professionalism. The professional project can be identified by its related objectives of market monopoly and social status. These goals were pursued at different times by different groups of professional reformers, using the resources that were accessible in their specific environments. The "organizational revolution" did not so much alter the nature of the professional project as it altered the resources available for its fulfillment. As new strategies became possible, new kinds of professional men appeared to be the most likely or the most apt to articulate or follow such strategies; but their ways of understanding what they were doing do not necessarily imply a conscious break with the past.

In considering the professional project as an adaptive response to major changes initiated elsewhere in the society, Gilb detracts from its active and specific dimensions. Her view implicitly discounts the persistence of social structures, the stubbornness of vested interests, the unconscious rigidity of habits and ideology—that is, the difficulty of creating something new out of materials that are both new and old.

In some cases, the radical changes that affected American society after the Civil War were but the culmination of trends already discernible in the antebellum period. In the new historical context, the professional project was carried through by more effective means than in the past, but the old ways of securing economic and social advantages were neither easily defeated nor entirely abandoned. To ask what kinds of strategies were possible at each time, how effective they were and who could best discern and mobilize the necessary organizational resources, is the only way of assessing the continuity or discontinuity of a historical process.

THE COMMUNAL MATRIX OF PROFESSION

Oscar Handlin has observed that "practically nothing is known about the history of the professions in the United States . . . books about the bench and bar of a particular locality or accounts of a prominent lawyer or even analyses of changes in the conception of law only tangentially throw light upon the evolution of the organized structure of the legal profession. The deficiency is equally prominent in the case of teachers, physicians, ministers, and other groups."[4] Recent studies have begun to fill the gaps, at least for some professions.[5] Yet an attempt to draw generalizations from the American past seems doomed to failure at the outset by the characteristic—and constantly increasing—multiplicity of social matrices. From the beginning of the colony, centrifugal forces appeared to work against the permanence of transplanted institutions, not only at the level of the state, but at the much more meaningful level of small rural communities. Family, community, and church, merged together, were the foundation of a well-ordered, stable, and hierarchical society: but the strangeness of the new environment, the leveling effect of free and abundant land, the scarcity of labor, and the heterogeneity of religious denominations encouraged the emancipation of the young, the scattering into new settlements, the erosion of traditional forms of subordination. Thus "by the eighteenth century . . . bonded servitude, with its carefully calibrated degrees of dependency, was rapidly being eliminated, drained off at one end into freedoom and independent wage labor, and at the other into the new, debased status of chattel slavery."[6] In this setting, the old institution of apprenticeship, which had smoothly integrated family with community, rapidly tended to become a limited contract, from which masters obtained the much needed labor and servants obtained specific skills, but not much more, on their way to independence. The bases on which to found the binding restrictions and regulations of a guild system were absent: access to crafts and even to professions remained characteristically open in the new world.

The erosion of traditional institutions, on the other hand, provoked anxious fears "of a calamitous decline in the level of civilization," of what Cotton Mather would call a "creolean degeneracy."[7] In his brilliant interpretation of the past of American education, Bernard Baylin suggests that the perceived weakness of the family and of secular community institutions rapidly led the colonists to place great emphasis on formal education.[8] The church was the obvious recipient of the cultural role that family alone could not fulfill. For religious sects, deeply concerned with the deliberate creation and maintenance of group identity and social cohesion through the propagation of their faith, this was a fervently assumed mission. Through education, the Puritans sought to maintain uniformity, to remove the threat that dispersion and diversity posed to religious unity—and hence to morality and civilization. Their strenuous efforts to transfer cultural models (which had their most influential, though not their only source in New England) into the "wilderness" explains the characteristic scattering of educational efforts, the multiplication of denominational colleges in the nineteenth century. As Baylin observes, "such a uniformity could not be maintained beyond the early period of religious enthusiasm and past the boundaries of the original clustering settlements. There took place not an abandonment of the original high ideals, not a general regression of educational and intellectual standards, but a settling into regional patterns determined by the more ordinary material requirements of life."[9]

A different trend appeared with force in the eighteenth century: to give apprentices, but not only them, the basic nonvocational instruction which their masters had contracted to provide but were no longer giving, evening schools were started in great numbers. Together with the self-improvement efforts of urban craftsmen, typified by Benjamin Franklin's group, these schools symbolized the voluntary concern with education for social mobility, with useful knowledge which would fit youths or adults "for learning any business, calling, or profession."[10] In both cases, the support for the schools was local. In the eighteenth century, New England was the first region to compensate for the ever-insufficient private endowments of its schools by general taxation. But long-term profitable investments were everywhere hard to find, and all the solutions reinforced localism: everywhere, financing came again and again from direct community contributions which bound all levels of education to the external control of individual or community donors.[11]

Thus, the predominance of local interests and local conditions is, in itself, a general organizing dimension of the American past. Before and after independence, localism governed the adaptation and the creation of institutional models. The broad schemes for national institutions in education and in the economy that had been envisaged by the foremost revolutionary leaders did not take root: in the first two decades of the nineteenth century, the tissue of American society was made of scattered and largely autonomous communities, only loosely connected by the overarching political structures. Even at the level of the polity, the Jeffersonian ideal tended to present the state as an instrument that would destroy the artificial and inequitable laws of the colony and restore a free society to its spontaneity, ordered by natural law and protected against inequity by the limitless supply of land.[12] In the second third of the nineteenth century, economic development and the beginning of massive immigration began to place unbearable strains upon the structures of localism. The multiplied effects of diversity and mobility, which the narrow local institutions were no longer able to contain, revealed themselves as full-fledged threats to the passing traditional order.

In the long search for institutional solutions of national scope, nostalgia vested the relatively uniform and relatively insulated communities of the past with mythical virtues.[13] On this ideological background, the visible augmentation of social inequality acquired particular stridency. Yet by the time of the revolutionary war, class lines had been deep and clearly drawn even outside the slave-owning South. In all but the areas of subsistence farming and the recently settled frontier, the unequal distribution of wealth had led to the crystallization of status and of a recognized social hierarchy. At the top stood an "aristocracy" of great landowners and merchants, favored in the South by the existence of a large servile class, but no less visible in the small cities and in the more "democratic" North. Buttressed by intermarriage, this upper class had had enough permanence to generate distinctive patterns of monopolization of social privilege. The sale of loyalist estates after the revolution did not substantially change the position or the composition of this class.[14] It was an aristocracy open to wealth, into which a few men who started from the bottom found their way. Jackson Turner Main estimates it at roughly 10 percent of the white population: it was constituted, he says, by approximately "10 percent of the landowners, the same proportion of ministers and doctors, most lawyers, a few artisans, and not far from half of the merchants qualified as well-to-do or wealthy."[15]

Detailed regional studies, however, show more concentration of wealth than Main suggests, perhaps because the categories he lists were partially overlapping. Thus, Aubrey C. Land's study of the northern Chesapeake finds that the largest estates (those evaluated at £1000 or more) represented 1.6 percent of the total in the last decade of the seventeenth century, 2.2 percent in the second decade of the eighteenth, and 3.6 percent in 1730–1739. Her analysis of inventories and estate accounts of free men confirms the hypothesis that "the men of first fortune belonged functionally to a class whose success stemmed from entrepreneurial activities as much as, or even more than, from their direct operations as producers of tobacco. . . . They were at once planters, political leaders, and businessmen."[16] Chief among their non-agricultural activities were land speculation, moneylending, and trade—which included keeping country stores and acting as liaison agents between overseas buyers and the small tobacco planters. Investment in manufacturing, though less frequent, provided the best opportunities for profit. Land also finds that law practice brought to many lawyers an enviable income, "freed from direct dependence on returns from the annual tobacco fleet"; to the most enterprising, it also brought considerable opportunities for profitable land or business deals.[17]

The poorer categories were not entirely excluded from the general prosperity of the area in the first half of the eighteenth century: what may be considered a respectable rural middle class of modest means but stable incomes grew from 21.7 percent in the last decades of the seventeenth century to 35.7 percent in the 1730s. Below this stratum of middle estates (from £100 to 500) lay a bottom class of free men with estates of £100 or less. Extremely vulnerable to market fluctuations, natural calamities, or even high levels of taxation, these small planters lived at the level of subsistence. In the 1730s they represented still over half of the total distribution of estates, down from three-quarters in 1690–1699.[18]

Urban areas allegedly offered better opportunities and higher standards of living than the older agricultural regions. By 1790, only 5 percent of a population slightly larger than three million lived in agglomerations of 2500 or more inhabitants. None of the twenty-four towns exceeded 50,000.[19] Boston, for instance, had less than 20,000 and was growing at an annual rate of 1.68 percent (compared to 34.7 percent for the population as a whole) in the second half of the eighteenth century.[20] Migration into Boston began a dramatic increase after 1765, as population pressure on land grew in the surrounding countryside. Yet the largest group of migrants came from neighboring small towns; taken together with the high rate of departures from Boston, this movement attests to the paucity of opportunities in the urban areas.[21] "By 1790," reports Allan Kulikoff, "45 per cent of the taxpayers in town in 1780 had disappeared from tax lists. Some had died, the rest left town. . . . Those who moved out of Boston were the poorest and least successful members of the community . . . only 42 per cent of those without real estate (rents) in 1780 remained in town in 1790."[22]

If Boston may be taken as a representative example, economic inequality was great in the towns and did not abate after independence. While Main estimates that an income of £50 per year scarcely met the needs of a family that had to pay rent and buy all its food, Kulikoff's analysis of taxable wealth in Boston in 1790 finds that 29.8 percent of the taxpayers were assessed at 0 to £25.[23] Two middle groups, assessed at £25 to 100 and at £100 to 500, represented, respectively, 31.4 and 25.5 percent of all taxpayers. At the top, the 13.7 percent assessed at £500 or more held over 60 percent of taxable wealth. Comparison with previous decades reveals a growing concentration of wealth in the hands of the wealthiest and a decline in the relative position of the middle categories. At the very bottom, the untaxed population of poor and near poor was growing enough at the end of the eighteenth century, especially in the economic depression that followed independence, to alarm the city's notables.[24]

The wealthy elite at the top monopolized not only the public marks of social honor but also the important political offices of selectman, overseer of the poor, and state legislator. Lower-level civic positions were shared with the artisan middle class, while poorer artisans and laborers dominated in positions without political power, such as that of surveyor of the boards or sealer of leather, and especially in positions in the fire companies and the constabulary. Moderate economic gains in one's trade or in real estate were possible for over one-third of the economically active in late eighteenth-century Boston, while small-scale migration operated as a safety valve for the less fortunate.[25] In such an economic context, the symbolic participation in civic responsibilities open to the humbler citizens acted as an element of cohesion, ensuring to the "men of quality" the deferential respect of their social inferiors. In colonial days, says Arthur M. Schlesinger, "Men in every walk of life not only accepted the concept of a layered society but believed in its rightness. The clergy preached it; all classes practiced it."[26]

After 1776, the political ideology of the new republic further defused the rumbles of revolt that had appeared in riots and crowd actions before and during the revolution.[27] Action against the established order was action against the will of the sovereign, that is, the people. Despite local and sectional readjustments, democracy did not fundamentally alter the class structure of the settled communities. Thus, the eighteenth-century matrix from which professionals drew sustenance and support remained inegalitarian and hierarchical.

From the elites had come the impulse to import and adapt foreign institutional and social models. Both before and after the revolution, professionals were prominent in the ranks of this elite.[28] In architecture, in particular, some men rose to high standing out of the skilled crafts. Thus, in prerevolutionary Philadelphia, a few master carpenters and masons "achieved both reputation and fortune, moved in the same circles with the merchant princes, and were regarded by all as the founders of professions."[29] In the more established professions of law, medicine, and divinity, however, the highest marks of distinction appear to have gone to those with formal education. Because American colleges—and, *a fortiori,* European universities—were only accessible to the wealthy, this recognition indirectly sanctioned the preeminence of rank and social class. Of the nine colonial colleges, only one, William and Mary, was in the South. While most of their graduates destined themselves to the professions (and in particular to the clergy, at least until the 1750s), many did not. It is not clear whether higher education represented for the latter a natural accompaniment and preparation for their gentlemanly status or a means of upward social mobility.[30] In any case, the composition of the boards of trustees, the predominance in them of wealthy local notables and clergymen from the "aristocratic" denominations, allow one to conclude with Richard Hofstadter that "it was the aristocracy that was primarily concerned with the colonial colleges, the well-to-do class that gave the bulk of private support, and the ruling group that provided the trustees."[31]

As Benjamin Franklin rapidly found out when he tried to gain support for his Academy among Philadelphia's first citizens, "ornamental training" in the classics was more important to them than useful knowledge. Training that would enable a young man to make "a temperate, reasonable living" in a prosperous mercantile community was advocated from early on by middle-class parents, critical of what they saw as the aristocratic deviation of the Quaker schools.[32] Their eminently practical needs continued to be served by day and evening private schools even after the founding of the Philadelphia Academy in 1751. From the beginning, the Academy favored its Latin School to the detriment of the English School, whose enrollment rapidly declined. To Franklin's dismay, the Latin School "was taken under the wing of the College of Philadelphia, and served as a feeder to it."[33]

Yet for all their aristocratic orientation and their imitation of English models, the small colonial colleges had distinctive features, not the least of which was their lack of autonomy in the medieval tradition of the university. The governance by lay boards, in nonconformist communities where no denomination could claim real hegemony, steered them of necessity toward a nonsectarian course, which was held steady after 1750 by the active competition for students. In the eighteenth century, the most significant trend was secularization, visible "in the more commercial and less religious tone of newly founded colleges; in the rapidly rising number of college graduates who went into occupations other than the ministry; and in vital changes in the curriculum, notably the rise of scientific studies and the modification of theology to include freer philosophical speculation."[34] A more varied body of students, reflecting the influence of the Enlightenment and the political ferment of prerevolutionary decades, prodded college faculties and presidents to curricular changes and to at least an acknowledgment of the scientific work done by amateurs on the outside. Despite the traditional timidity of their faculties, the colleges appear to have bred a majority of the political debaters and leaders whose role was so central in the years of agitation before independence.

Some of these colonial colleges harbored the early attempts by university-trained medical elites to institutionalize professional education in America. Indeed, until the foundation of Pennsylvania Hospital in 1751, the only hospitals the colonies had were pest-houses for contagious diseases or poorhouses: "It was thus from necessity as well as from choice that American medical education developed in the eighteenth century from educational institutions, whereas at the same time English medical education was deriving increasingly from institutions concerned with patient care."[35]

By mid-eighteenth century, it had become common among the rich to send their sons abroad for a period of study and travel in Europe. The future members of the urban medical elites completed their education in local colleges and commenced their apprenticeship at home, with prominent masters who were often themselves immigrant European physicians or trained in Europe. Those who could afford it went then overseas to study, most frequently at Edinburgh and in the London hospitals.[36] Naturally enough, on returning to America, these elite physicians attempted to organize the rapidly growing numbers of American practitioners on European standards, as interpreted and represented by themselves. It was clear that the general characteristics of colonial society and the conditions of medical practice in America would not admit the distinctions of branch and function supported by the English guild structure. The distinction of superior training appeared therefore as the best means to sanction social and intellectual differences and to introduce order into the profession.

In Philadelphia, following the courses in anatomy and midwifery started by Dr. William Shippen, Jr., and the beginnings of clinical teaching at Pennsylvania Hospital, John Morgan used his prominent social position and his impressive European reputation to found the first American medical school and place it under the auspices of the College. Of the five members of the faculty, all were trained in Europe and all but one had Edinburgh degrees. The ambitious program which Morgan outlined in 1765 in his *Discourse upon the Institution of Medical Schools in America* envisaged for the American physician what amounted to graduate education.[37] The same high requirements for admission were adopted in 1768 by the second American medical school, that of King's College in New York. But these high standards of entry, demanding a college degree or evidence of equivalent education, could not be maintained in the period of dislocation and reorganization of the Anglican colleges that followed independence. The university-based medical schools provided, nevertheless, what was for the time high-quality didactic training. More important, Pennsylvania and King's, followed before the turn of the century by Harvard and Dartmouth and, soon after, by Yale and by the University of New York, provided indigenous institutional nuclei for the professional movement in medicine. Together with the development of a medical press, this educational base strengthened the social ties of the early medical elites and reinforced the movement of association.[38] The local medical societies, since they began taking their first firm steps in the 1760s, had pressed the state for licensing legislation. Soon after the revolution, they began seeking the direct power to examine and license medical practitioners.

During the eighteenth century, lawyers in the colonial centers appear to have moved more decisively toward self-regulation than the physicians. In the first century and a half of the colony, law had seldom been practiced full-time: "The few persons who acted as professional attorneys were at first mostly pettifoggers or minor court officers such as deputy sheriffs, clerks, and justices, who stirred up litigation for the sake of the petty court fees.[39] But the growing complexity of colonial life and government necessarily affected the volume and the sophistication of legal disputes. There was not only enough legal work to sustain full-time practitioners in both the bar and the bench; it was work complex enough to require knowledge of the English common law beyond what local custom had incorporated and used in previous decades. In the second half of the eighteenth century, it became increasingly frequent, especially among the wealthy Southern planters, to destine their sons to the bar and send them to the Inns of Court in London to secure admission. "Upon their return," says Alfred Z. Reed, "these constituted the social aristocracy of the profession."[40]

Although the legal profession in the colonies was as heterogeneous as medicine was, elites by social rank and training clearly dominated, as they did in medicine, the urban bars. In Virginia, for instance, "there was such elitism even within the bar that, by the time of the revolution, there was the framework of a divided legal profession on the English model."[41] Attorneys were, however, the most common type of lawyer and the elites of the profession strove to institutionalize a system of attorney apprenticeship with examination by the courts. Judges in parts of New England, the central colonies, and the South had allowed the country bars actual control upon admissions to membership. "The requirements they exacted for admission to their privileges were in some cases so severe as to justify the suspicion that they were more interested in fostering their own monopoly than in serving the state. The reaction against Federalist politicians was a factor in inducing the legislatures to sweep away the entire system."[42]

The revolution had a paradoxical effect upon the legal profession. While it disrupted and even shattered the upper bars—especially in the South, where they had been the most aristocratic—by forcing Tory lawyers into exile or retirement, it also raised the remaining elite to new heights. Called in great numbers to the bench and the government of the new republic, lawyers assumed the political and social prominence that led Alexis de Tocqueville to consider them the true aristocracy of America.[43] The Inns of Court could no longer provide American lawyers with a mark of distinction; however, with the rise of supreme courts in every state and in Washington, a graded bar—linking admission to the higher courts to years of apprenticeship and experience and, indirectly to the possession of a college degree—appears to have developed and spread in the North, as an indigenous mechanism of professional stratification.[44]

Independence bestowed important new functions upon legal elites that had been, at the same time, decimated by its aftermath; it is therefore logical to think that ordinary legal practice had to pass into the hands of lesser and humbler men. In the economic depression after 1776, lawyers, specializing as they did in debt collection, foreclosures, and land deals, became an obvious target of public revulsion. The majority of practitioners could not claim, to defend themselves against popular hostility, the deference accorded to gentlemanly status. Nor could many of them claim the superiority derived from formal education: the few professorships in law that emerged after independence in the colleges, or the famous private law schools, such as that of Judge Tapping Reeve at Litchfield, catered almost exclusively to the elites.[45] The latter, protected by their less visible kinds of practice, by political office and by social rank, weathered out the Jacksonian attacks against the legal profession in the sanctuary of informal urban "inner bars."

The imported professional models added a different kind of sanction to practitioners already stratified by wealth and social standing. But one should not exaggerate the effectiveness of these models. Even before the repeal of medical licensing laws and the weakening of apprenticeship requirements for attorneys in the 1830s, such legislation had been particularly difficult to enforce. In medicine, "while legislatures were willing to give licensing powers to medical societies, they were unwilling to enact laws which would have seriously deterred unlicensed practitioners."[46] Few medical societies had, for instance, the right to revoke the licenses they awarded, and the penalties for unlicensed practice were most often very small, if they existed at all.

The forms of professionalism that urban elites were attempting to introduce in the Eastern seaboard failed in the face of the dispersed and decentralized reality of the country, where most practitioners worked in rural areas, relatively insulated from the social control of their peers or betters. What I have called traditional means or sources of prestige for the professional project were thus, in America, either precarious or of limited scope.[47]

Autonomous traditional means—such as privileged professional corporations and hallowed upper-class schools with established monopolies over high culture—were nonexistent or weak. The prestige of the older colleges was little more than local. Even traditional professionals did not necessarily share in a systematic class socialization such as that provided in England by the public schools and the two elite universities.

Heteronomous sources of prestige, rooted in the existence and legitimacy of "old" elites, were themselves disunited and provincial. The elites shared to a certain extent general conceptions of gentlemanliness and common cultural traits. Geographical and social mobility, however, increased the diversity of the ruling class. With the passing of mercantilism and the demise of the hegemonic coalition of Southern planters and Northern merchants, this multiplicity was also reflected at the level of national politics.

Furthermore, in a newborn nation where the majority of the population remained rural until the second decade of our century, the difficulty of establishing modern status-giving institutions of national scope was compounded by the lack of adequate communication between the various sections of an immense and expanding territory. This perpetuated the import of some communal or purely local sources of professional prestige long after the appearance of modern centers for the production of professional producers.

The absence of a *national* aristocracy and of centralized warrants of traditional status has a paradoxical effect on the collective project of professionalization. Because the United States were "born bourgeois," the professional modernizers did not appear to be a sector of a rising class, as they did in nineteenth-century England, or a sector of a victorious class, as in revolutionary France. The appeal to merit and to a meritocratic ideology which underlies professional modernization acquires, in this context, an uncertain meaning: the invocation of merit based on superior training does not appear as one more element in the progressive ideology of bourgeois democracy. Rather, because the ideology of merit is not aimed at traditional preserves of the *ancien régime,* it comes into conflict with the ideology of egalitarian democracy and economic liberalism. The monopolistic tendency inherent in all projects of professional reform becomes all the more visible; meritocratic justifications are still too weak to legitimize closure of access. The absence of *central* traditional structures in the United States determined the characteristic fragmentation of the early professional project, while depriving it of the ideological unity that was inherent in the bourgeois challenge against corporate or aristocratic strongholds. In America, therefore, the ultimate success of professionalization as a collective assertion of status depended even more closely than elsewhere on the establishment of market control by modern means. This task, however, was itself attendant on the emergence and consolidation of national institutions and national frames of reference.

THE DISTENDED SOCIETY*

The entry of the United States into a period of extended and remarkably rapid economic growth coincides, roughly, with Jacksonian democracy—that is, the twelve years between 1829 and 1841 in which Andrew Jackson and his chosen successor Martin van Buren seized the presidency "from the remnant of the republican elite."[48] In the 1820s, the United States economy grew out of its colonial status— not because it was less dependent on foreign markets and foreign capital, but because growth now hinged on tasks of internal development and on the steady incorporation of new resources of land, labor, and capital. In the age of Jackson, the country experienced not only the wild boom of the 1830s but also the long depression of 1837–1845, which was the boom's ineluctable sequel. Beyond the exaggerations and distortions of both the boom and the slump, one may discern, as Marvin Meyers

*I borrow this term from Robert Wiebe in *The Search for Order.*

has suggested, the main features of sustained growth and of the coming economic order.[49]

"Reckless banking" was one of the main factors in the ups and downs of the economy. After Jackson, in 1832, vetoed the charter renewal of Nicholas Biddle's Second Bank of the United States, inflationary expansion of credit ran wild. In turn, the contraction that came after the first year of the crisis accelerated the downturn. Yet, considered together, Biddle's brilliant financial schemes and the expansionist inflation which followed the Bank war presaged the emergence of a modern credit system.[50]

In like manner, the frenzy of internal improvement of the 1830s did more than feed the boom and encourage deficit spending by many states. Canals, steamboats, and railroads, as determining factors of regional specialization and the emergent national divison of labor, accelerated and directed the movement of a growing population toward the West and to the cities. Finally, the transportation enterprises were focal points of technical and organizational innovation.[51]

Land speculation, to which much of the capital created by credit was directed, was not merely a "bubble." For all their recklessness, investments in urban real estate or Western public lands reflected the directions in which the country was really moving: in the decade 1830–1840, urban population grew at a rate of 63.7 percent, against a rate of 28.1 percent for the population as a whole. In 1830, there were 90 urban centers of 2,500 inhabitants or more, of which 23 had more than 10,000; only New York exceeded 100,000. In 1840, out of 131 urban centers, 37 had 10,000 inhabitants or more, while three cities were in the 100,000-plus category.[52] While major waves of immigration did not begin until the late 1840s, the rate of immigration in the 1830s showed a substantial increase over previous decades.[53] At the same time, the population of the North Central region more than doubled. By 1860, despite large scale European immigration, the population of the Eastern seaboard was down to 51 percent of the whole, from 97 percent at the turn of the century.[54] By 1840, although two-thirds of the labor force were still engaged in agriculture, the non-agricultural work force was expanding more rapidly than the agricultural. Mining, manufacturing, construction, and transport together employed 829,000 people—14.6 percent of the whole, but almost one-fifth of the *free* labor force.[55]

In sum, what was established in this period were the bases of the United States formidable domestic market, and the pivotal axes of their economic growth: interregional trade, linking the budding Northeastern manufactures to the Central foodbasket and to Southern cotton, and international trade, still dominated by cotton exports. This expanding intersectional trade fueled territorial expansion and induced the redistribution of population: migration into the Southwest and the North Central plains, indeed, appears to have followed the rising prices of, respectively, cotton and wheat.[56]

There are indications that social inequality was widening as the economy expanded. Census counts of wealth are not available before 1850. However, long-term trends derived from estimates and projections of the available evidence indicate "that inequality of wealth remained the same from 1800 to 1940 and then decreased a little, particularly among middle wealth groups. . . . A plutocratic elite emerged at the turn of the [nineteenth] century but it did not fundamentally alter the share of wealth held by the top 1 percent of persons. The main point is that there already was strong inequality in 1860, 1870, and earlier.''[57]

Projections back to 1810 permit to support the hypothesis of consistent wealth inequality throughout the nineteenth century.[58] With roughly similar distributions in a rapidly growing economy, the amount of wealth held by the very rich obviously becomes much greater and much more visible. The most significant changes concern the sectoral and regional concentration of the economic elite. In 1860, ''there were 4 million slaves valued at perhaps $4 billion or 15 to 20 percent of our national assets,'' writes Lee Soltow.[59] If slaves are considered as property—and, according to some estimates, even if they are not—Southerners appear to have constituted a disproportionately large section of the antebellum economic elite: ''Three of every five men were from the South in 1860 compared to one every five after the war. There were 70,000 Americans in 1860 with wealth of $40,000 or more, and 40,000 of that number lived in the South. There were 7,000 Americans ($N_x = 0.001$) with wealth of $111,000 or more, 4,500 of whom lived in the South.''[60] The Civil War brought to an abrupt end the privileged position of Southern planters. The destruction of slave property by emancipation reduced inequality among Southern *whites,* bringing it to Northern levels; Southern inequality was obviously much higher if blacks are counted in the population.[61]

Industrialization and urbanization, coupled with the large-scale influx of foreign-born immigrants, confirmed after the Civil War a trend that had been visible since the eighteenth century: the distribution of wealth became more unequal in cities than in rural areas. In 1870, the top 2 percent of adult men in urban areas owned 48 percent of urban wealth; in rural areas, the counterpart owned only 26 percent. Despite the apparently more egalitarian distribution of wealth among farmers, the bottom half of the curve was propertyless in both urban and rural areas: 40 percent of non-farmers owned 99 percent of urban wealth; the same percentage of farmers owned 95 percent of property in rural areas. In fact, the differences between urban and rural areas concerned only the rich and the well-to-do.[62]

Inequality in some rural areas must have been more visible before the destruction of the Southern slaveowning plutocracy and the Anti-Rent movement of the 1840s against the last quasi-feudal landlords of the Hudson Valley. But the growing commercialization and complexity of agriculture was creating elsewhere new lines of social differentiation: differential access to transportation and credit, and the differential impact of price fluctuations and soil erosion, were agents of stratification among the small wheat farmers of the North and West Central regions. More importantly, expensive mechanization (in a land where labor shortage was chronic) was widening the spectrum of rural inequality, as was the federal land policy, which encouraged speculative monopolization by large bidders. In agriculture as elsewhere, the number of wage-workers was growing outside the South throughout the period 1800–1860.[63]

In cities such as New York, the term ''millionaire''—applicable only to twenty-one rich men—was becoming fashionable in the early forties.[64] Tocqueville's prediction that a narrow and harsher ''aristocracy'' would be spawned by industry in democratic societies had become true by mid-century in the leading urban centers. Below that thin crust, caste and class lines were hardened as a consequence of large-scale immigration. Pauperism, which had been a not uncommon, though perhaps unobtrusive, feature of American cities before the 1830s, increased dramatically during the Jacksonian period, in large part as a consequence of protracted unemployment after 1837. Before the depression, inflation had kept real wages stagnant. The economic crisis smashed the incipient labor movement, composed chiefly of native artisan and skilled workers.

Obviously, there is nothing new in the hardening of structural inequalities that accompanies a period of rapid capitalist development. Nor is it surprising to find that caste lines based on race and ethnicity fuse with class domination and exacerbate the distance between social classes and status groups. But it is interesting that increasing—or, at least, increasingly visible—social inequality should coincide with the age of Jackson, hailed by contemporaries as well as recent historians as the Era of the Common Man and the Age of Egalitarianism.

This ideological interpretation appears to be founded on the democratization of the political process. The extension of suffrage to practically all white male citizens had been achieved, in almost every state, *before* large-scale immigration—that is, before the hardening of class and status lines and before the Protestant Crusade and the Nativist reaction. The extension of the franchise preceded the victory of Andrew Jackson, although it was completed during his presidency and was followed by other electoral changes of sweeping importance. Not that the nominating convention or the general ticket system actually gave "Tom, Dick, and Harry" access to political office and control over the nomination, election, and performance of their representatives; but these procedural changes laid the ground for the rise of a new kind of political party. For the first time, parties had to mobilize a large electorate in a new system, which made presidential elections into the cornerstone of American politics. "The political machine," says Marvin Meyers, "reached into every neighborhood, inducted ordinary citizens of all sorts into active service. Parties tended to become lively two-way channels of influence. Public opinion was heard with a new sensitivity and addressed with anxious respect. . . . As never before, the parties spoke directly, knowingly, to the interests and feelings of the public."[65]

The most significant dimension of Jacksonian democracy thus appears to be the rise of a political marketplace, dominated by a new brand of full-time politician, working within the apparatus of a party. The Jacksonians had an initial advantage in the new politics which they had largely contributed to create. Their skill and their success with the new methods and roles of electoral politics spurred their adversaries to rapid imitation. On both the Jacksonian and the Whig sides, "professional" politicians appear as the era's "true self-made men, moving freely up the ladder of their political society, ideally suited to command the great pragmatic party organizations of their time."[66]

The egalitarian and anti-aristocratic rhetoric of the age was by no means a Jacksonian prerogative.[67] The Democrats may have been quicker to seize its political potential, especially since egalitarianism responded to the sentiment of at least one sector, urban and radical, of their constituency. But despite the role played in Democratic politics by low-status New York ethnics and Loco Foco radicals, there is little evidence connecting party preferences to clearcut class differences.[68]

The historical context of the Jacksonian coalition is defined by rapid economic development, profound social dislocations, and objective democratization of electoral politics. In this larger framework, "the chief Jacksonian policies—opposition to special corporate charters, hostility toward paper money, suspicion of public enterprise and public debt—do not patently contribute to the needs of a distinctive class following."[69] But these policies correspond to an era of economic and territorial expansion placed under the sign of laissez faire.[70] Indeed, it is tempting to see the destruction of mercantilist restrictions upon the market and the emergence of a political marketplace under the ideology of democratic equality as the structural and the superstructural manifestations of the same historical process. Laissez faire is obviously the ideological zone where political and economic liberalism merge. In the age of Jackson, the faith in the progressive working of the market which appears to pervade all levels of society acquires moral and quasi-religious overtones: the hidden hand of the market is, indeed, the secular manifestation of the divine providence. This theme is explicitly sounded in the writings of the radical libertarian William Leggett: a government which recklessly interferes with nature, with "an overruling Providence," bears responsibility for the spreading social inequality and the injustice which rewards hard-working common people. The government of the Whigs and the Bank has fallen prey to the ambitions of "the consumers, the rich, the proud, the privileged";[71] to this narrow constituency, it grants special monopoly rights and, most specifically, chartered banking privileges. Monopolies negate at the same time free trade and equal rights; they cause "the extremes of wealth and poverty, so uniformly fatal to the liberties of mankind."[72] For Leggett, as for any good Jacksonian, the Monster Bank is the prime agent of destruction of a "natural," hence a harmonious, social order; it is the prime source of economic insecurity, of social dislocations and social changes alien to the American republic. The Bank must be relentlessly opposed "until every vestige of monopoly has disappeared from the land, and until banking—as most other occupations are now, and as all ought to be—is left open to the free competition of all who choose to enter into that pursuit."[73]

In typical Jacksonian fashion, Leggett is, in fact, seeking here a simple explanation for the passing of an idealized social order. Despite great differences in their articulation, less radical advocates of free trade than William Leggett sound a similar ideological theme: laissez faire, fused with democracy, is vested with a function of moral and social restoration.[74] Liberalism ideologically separates the impersonal, self-regulating market from society; but here the market is expected to return society to an original state of grace: stable, ordered, cohesive communities, which admit no special privilege, permit no alien aristocratic ambition. Untrammelled competition, paradoxically, will correct the ill effects of excessive fluidity in a society frantically engaged in economic expansion. This contradiction has its poignancy. As Marvin Meyers puts it, the Jacksonians selectively refuse to see that laissez faire leads, precisely, toward "the city, the factory, the complex market and credit economy," constantly producing fetters to its own working. The heart of the Jacksonian paradox lies, thus, in an impossible reconciliation.[75]

Paradox, indeed, may be the appropriate ideological characteristic of a transitional phase. The task before us now is to see how various professions experience and respond to the paradox and to the contradictory forces of the age: general economic growth and decline of particular areas; emergent national economy and local institutions; political egalitarianism and social inequality; old elites and new wealth; rejection of monopoly and need for expertise; defense of competition and recognition of the corporation as a legitimate economic unit; in short, free trade along with free development of the forces that undermine it.

THE PROFESSIONS IN A PHASE OF TRANSITION

Professional elites—in the traditional sense of gentlemen with a liberal education who got their specialized training through apprenticeship—were closely identified in America with the intellectual and patrician elites that presided over the life of the new nation in its first decades. This closeness logically included the professions in the deep-seated suspicion of monopolized privilege. Spokesmen for the incipient trade-union movement could thus declare, as Frederick Robinson in the early 1830s, "the capitalists, monopolists, judges, lawyers, doctors, and priests . . . know that the secret of their own power and wealth consists in the strictest concert of action. . . . Unions among themselves have always enabled the few to rule and ride the people."[76] Or, with clearer class consciousness: "The merchants may agree upon their prices; the lawyers upon their fees; the physicians upon their charges; the manufacturers upon the wages given to their operatives; but the *laborer* shall not consult his interest and fix the price of his toil and skill. If this be the *law,* it is unjust, oppressive, and wicked."[77]

With the working class still predominantly composed of craftsmen and aspiring small entrepreneurs, the attack upon inequality could easily be translated by the Jacksonian movement into a laissez faire demand for equal starting chances on the market. Opposition to the professions' entry requirements, on the other hand, would be particularly attractive to "upwardly mobile groups, including men who wanted access to professional standing on terms less stringent than had developed in the latter part of the eighteenth century."[78] The public appeared to support the leveling movement not only out of anti-aristocratic sentiment, but also out of mistrust and resentment of the power professionals derived from monopolized knowledge. In this fear, Richard Hofstadter has seen the first powerful manifestation of American anti-intellectualism. He writes: "[The Jacksonian movement's] distrust of expertise, its dislike for centralization, its desire to uproot the entrenched classes, and its doctrine that important functions were simple enough to be performed by anyone, amounted to a repudiation not only of the system of government by gentlemen which the nation had inherited from the eighteenth century, but also of the special value of the educated classes in civic life."[79]

Richard Shryock, the historian of medicine, holds a similar view. Americans, he says, proclaimed their right to "life, liberty, and quackery." In his view, "the masses seemed incapable of appreciating superior training in any profession and to the degree that they came into political power they were likely to lower training standards."[80] One by one, the states abrogated restrictions on unlicensed medical practice or repealed the legislation that medical societies had painstakingly obtained before the 1830s.[81]

Lawyers, in their role as agents of the wealthy, were an even more obvious target of popular suspicion than regular physicians—with whom, after all, few common people had much contact. "In 1800, fourteen out of nineteen jurisdictions required a definite period of apprenticeship. By 1840, it was required by not more than eleven out of thirty jurisdictions. By 1860, it was required in only nine out of thirty-nine jurisdictions."[82] In the 1840s and 1850s, New Hampshire, Maine, Wisconsin, and Indiana (the latter in its constitution) declared that law practice in all courts was open to any voter of "good moral character."[83] In this climate, local bars disbanded, and efforts to form new associations were doomed to failure.

Since the Great Revival of the 1790s, the public's espousal of "a warmer, more exciting, but less authoritative ministry" had likewise been challenging the pre-eminence of the traditionally educated clergy.[84]

In tune with the times, the principles of laissez faire and wide-open access were thus apparently extended to the narrow professional markets, leaving competition as the ultimate judge of skill. The roots and the consequences of this deregulation of professional practice are, however, complex and ambiguous enough to warrant cautious judgment. Equating the Jacksonian impact with straightforward "anti-intellectualism" seems more questionable than seeing in it the affirmation of a particular conception of education: instrumental and utilitarian, it was suited to the needs of an expanding territory, and also to the anti-aristocratic rhetoric of the age. Demands for free public education were a constant theme among the "common people" and a particularly strong concern of the Workingmen's parties. The popular conception of education was then, as it had been since the eighteenth century, a "non-intellectual" one, chiefly concerned with preparation for the business of making a living, but it was not necessarily opposed to schools as such.

As the country expanded westwards and as cities continued growing, proprietary schools appeared everywhere for instruction in medicine. Though they were predominantly didactic and often unabashedly commercial, they made some sort of medical education accessible to a large number of students, providing a focus for the crystallization of intellectual (or sectarian) tendencies among a population of otherwise scattered practitioners. The textbooks written by their faculties and the demonstration of therapies in their free clinics contributed to the standardization of practice, even though it was based chiefly on ineffective therapies and speculative theoretical systems.[85]

The pattern was different in the law: modeled on Judge Reeve's successful school, many private law schools appeared on the Eastern seaboard. But their mortality rate was heavy: by 1830 there were only six law schools in all the country, all but one—Judge Reeve's Litchfield—affiliated with colleges. The lack of success of the early private law school reflects the decline of admission requirements in the age of Jackson, but also, in part, the rise of a related market: that of good common law textbooks, which provided for ambitious students the needed complement to the traditional system of apprenticeship. Private, non-collegiate law schools did not multiply until the last decades of the century; by then legal education had available, in Harvard Law School, a leading model of reform.[86]

In medicine, most especially, competition for students among proliferating schools—or competition between school graduates and practitioners licensed by medical societies—tended to offset the common fight against empirics and to drive down educational standards everywhere. Thus "Harvard, where the standards were as high as anywhere about the time of the Civil War, awarded the medical doctor's degree to any candidate who could pass five out of nine oral examinations all taken on the same day."[87]

In a time of increasing social diversity, laissez faire in the professional markets multiplied the acceptable definitions of professional practice and professional services, diluting but not directly confronting the standards that had been set earlier by Eastern professional elites. The institutionalization of sectarianism in medicine and the lowering of educational standards in all established professions must have confirmed, in turn, the common man's belief that professional education and competence were not such that they could justify privileges and exclusiveness.

With a few exceptions, the multiplication of entry points into professional practice broke the ties that the professions—or, rather, their elites—had formed with the classical college. The latter, however, remained a center for the production of clergymen. Expansion and new settlements were thus accompanied by a proliferation of denominationally sponsored colleges. In a manner consonant with the themes of Jacksonian laissez faire, sectarian competition between the Protestant churches was inspired by the desire to maintain or reconstitute social homogeneity and cohesiveness. "The denominations," says Hofstadter, "not only desired to educate their ministers locally and inexpensively, but wished to keep their co-sectarians in colleges of their own, lest they be lured out of the fold."[88]

These colleges were, most often, little more than classic grammar schools—and not too good, either, at teaching the classical curriculum. But they bore the name of college and some times that of university, thus contributing to civic pride and to the boosting of real estate values. Since traveling costs were often more prohibitive than tuition, local colleges provided local boys with the means of getting a degree, if not always an education.[89] The inevitable devaluation of the college degree that ensued from this scattering of educational resources added to the ambiguity with which education was regarded—it was desired as a means of social distinction, but disparaged as impractical and aristocratic, at least as it was given in older colleges and in the more recent state "universities."[90]

Many currents thus converged, in the Jacksonian attack upon traditional professional elites and their standards, in the widespread sentiment that professions were imperfect and undeserving. There was, first, pressure for access from upwardly mobile men and an anti-aristocratic, instrumental conception of education; these two elements did not merge, as they did in England, into more stringent and modern standards of training and testing than those of the established elites. This lack is in part explained by a second factor: the expansion and diversification of American society, which facilitated the segmental proliferation of professional definitions. Territorial expansion demanded geographical dispersion of training facilities, while localism and the pluralism of elites suspended the need for standardization according to one central set of guidelines. There is, thirdly, democracy in politics and feelings, which opens up political ways of challenging elitist preserves, while asserting that reason and public opinion are the best legislators of professional competence, and indeed the only acceptable ones for a free and enlightened people. As Charles Rosenberg has remarked, "successful Americans no longer assumed without question the desirability of a stable graded society. No longer did maintaining the status of the learned professions play a part—a necessary part—in maintaining the stability of society itself."[91]

While economic development and societal "distension" corroded the traditional supports of every "old" profession, their effects were perhaps strongest on the profession that had been the most closely identified with community life—the Protestant clergy, of which the New England Congregationalists provide a clear traditional example.

The services of the ministry are not transacted on a market; for this reason, I have not included the clergy in my analysis of professional modernization. In the present context, however, the response of a section of the clergy to the decline of its traditional base illustrates one solution to the loss of professional status.

In New England, the institution of permanency or lifetime tenure had embodied the moral, social, and legal bonds between a pastor and his community. Permanency was central to the traditional conception of the ministry among the New Hampshire Congregationalists studied by Daniel Calhoun.[92] Since the eighteenth century, the entry of other denominations into New England had challenged the Congregationalist orthodoxy, while the ordained itinerant ministry of Methodists and Baptists came as an alternative to the declining institution of permanency. The continuous opening of new territory called for a recruitment effort which, in turn, increasingly brought to the fore the Methodist model of the clergyman, more responsible to the church at large than to a concrete and specific community. In fact, the move westward had a more dramatic and direct effect upon permanency than interdenominational competition or the new models for the ministry. The opening of the new agricultural areas of the Midwest signified, especially after the great improvements in transportation of the 1820s and 1830s, a general economic decay for rural New England. The supports for the traditional way of being a minister were simply cut from underneath the localist clergy of *all* denominations in most small towns. By the 1830s, the collapse of permanency in most of New England could be read in the shorter and shorter terms served by pastors, in the prevalence of "acting" over "settled" ministers, in the growing number of destitute parishes, decimated by migration, which could not support their ministry.

Calhoun's careful study shows that this collapse was accompanied by the slow growth of "a differentiated labor market among what had been a fairly homogeneous profession, a market within which . . . there existed routine channels for the movement of individuals from one segment to another."[93] By mid-century, a career line had emerged within the urban parishes and the central organization of the church: "Those who reached a large town church only toward the middle of their lives generally continued to operate in the large town circuit. But those who got to the large town circuit while they were still in their thirties stood a fair chance of moving on to public careers in city churches or in the religious bureaucracy.''[94] While small-town work was increasingly relegated to marginality, embryonic attempts to bend the organization of the church to a professionalized conception of the ministry emerged in urban and educational centers from the 1840s on. Separated from the laity, clergymen were to seek as a body, among themselves, new bases of professional status; while revivalists distinguished themselves from the laity by fiery preaching, the new breed of Congregationalist ministers would seek this distinction in a learned and autonomous elaboration of theology.[95]

Unlike doctors and lawyers, the New England Congregational clergy faced this period of disestablishment and transition within the protective framework of a central organization. Throughout the decline and the collapse of permanency, the continued existence of a central church allowed at least some ministers to envisage a solution for the profession's problems. This solution was bureaucratic in tendency: new careers emerged along the lines of a stratified labor market which coincided with the articulated hierarchy of the church. Toward the top of this hierarchy, leading ministers could then attempt to constitute themselves into a corporate body, distinguished and justified by its monopolistic control of esoteric theological knowledge.

If we turn, now, from the old profession of divinity to the new profession of engineering, we find that incipiently bureaucratic organizations also play a crucial role as sources of professional respectability and as matrices of career. The rise of the first engineering specialties—before the Civil War, only civil and mechanical engineering—coincides, in fact, with the emergence of large-scale enterprises concerned with public works and transportation in the first quarter of the nineteenth century.

Before that time, the best guarantees of competence a "technical deviser" could provide had been those of proprietorship and personal involvement in the risks of economic enterprise. The superior training of foreign engineers was recognized, when they happened to be available, as was the superiority of the few engineers trained at West Point or, after the 1820s, at Partridge Academy in Vermont. Native engineers, however, were chiefly trained on the job: "It was commonly expected that any large public works would become a 'school' for engineers,''[96] as did the railroads for mechanical engineers in the 1830s.

In the context of the largest economic organizations of the time, ownership could no longer function as a guarantee of competence. The warrant was sought in a merging of expertise with organizational rank, itself certified by the reputation and success of the organization's undertaking. At the beginning, expertise was not easily conceded by the project supervisors: "The construction of canals is an art within the complete attainment of ordinary capacities. All its rules have been fully explained by eminent engineers, who have written treatises on the subject,'' wrote two commissioners of the New York Canal System in 1816.[97] Hidden in this denial was the desire to promote Americans, rather than hiring more professional Europeans. But it is interesting to compare the commissioners' conception with the recommendations of their counterparts for the Susquehanna and Delaware Canal and Railroad Company in 1832. The latter explained: "In the selection of an Engineer, the Commissioners sought to obtain the services of a gentleman already advantageously known; uncompromising in the performance of his official duties, and in whose report, calculations, and estimates, an enlightened public and the moneyed interest might safely rely."[98]

From being an undifferentiated occupational category, whose respectability was subordinated to the ownership of capital, the civil engineers had become a distinct and respected professional group. While proprietorship used to be the best guarantee of technical competence, technical competence was now presented as a guarantee to proprietors.

On the basis of a gradually asserted competence, engineers moved into the structure of management and, finally, moved to translate their technical and managerial attributes into general social recognition. From 1839 on, in the midst of a depression in which over-investment in public works had played a major part, we find civil engineers concerned with organizing themselves on corporate bases in opposition to entrepreneurs and financiers. Despite the urgency of their economic plight, their efforts did not succeed in the 1840s; they were hindered, among other things, by geographical dispersion and the transiency of employment in the long recession. The first stable association of American civil engineers was not established until 1867, at a time when the opening of land-grant colleges and the emergence of modern universities was ushering in a new phase in the professionalization movement.

In the earlier phase, however, the engineer had completed his separation from the mechanics and engine drivers who, for some time, had appropriated his occupational name. As his technical knowledge became firmer, the engineer acquired a stepping-stone for scaling the ranks of management in the large projects where he was trained. As early as 1838, "superintendent" was, in the railroads, a salaried management position with technical prerequisites. Professional self-consciousness sprang from these ranks.[99] Also, the information which engineering cadres had acquired made them obvious choices for the role of commissioners. For the chief engineers, responsibility for inspections, repairs, and maintenance of the finished works led directly into stable administrative functions. Through the organization, the engineer—who had always had the function of representing the interests of capitalists and sponsors vis-à-vis contractors and craftsmen—found a path that led close to the owners' social status. This meaning was not lost upon contemporaries. Thus, in the 1830s, the Professor of Moral and Intellectual Philosophy and Political Economy at Union College could see in the factory a "perfect series of employments ascending, regularly, from the carding room to the throstle-frame, from the throstle-frame to the office of Superintendent, Engineer, or even Proprietor, each employment calling for greater intelligence and skill than the last, and each proportionately more lucrative and more respectable."[100]

This was largely a myth. For instance, the elite of mechanical engineers almost to the end of the nineteenth century was predominantly formed by gentlemanly owners of Eastern machine shops, not unresponsive to talent, but tending to recruit their apprentices primarily within their own high social class. This same elite, however, defended its prerogatives against the pretensions of engineering teachers and graduates, extolling the machine shop as a prototypical channel of upward social mobility.[101]

Civil engineers, on the other hand, had striven from early days for social recognition on the basis of a distinct professional status, ideally modeled on the "free" professions of medicine and the law. As Calhoun remarks, "for the civil engineer, even earlier and even more than for the mechanician, the Proprietor was increasingly a body politic or corporation."[102] This position marks the civil engineer as the first incarnation of the "organization man." His location in the largest economic enterprises of his time justifies Edwin Layton's general observation that "the scientifically trained, professional engineer has characteristically appeared on the technical scene at the point of transition from small to large organizations."[103]

In the emergence of the civil engineer, his particular links to the economic elite fuse with aspirations to a gentlemanly professional status; he thus appears to transfer some of the components of traditional professionalism into emergent bureaucratic organizations. With the increasing rationalization and depersonalization of management, the dependence of the engineer remains, but gradually loses the traditional aspect of assimilation into the high social status of the owners or sponsors. The paradox of the civil engineer in a transitional phase resides in his double function—technical and managerial; the managerial function ties him to the capitalists, at the same time that it opens for him a clear upward path which leads to social prestige through the organization. Dependent and upwardly mobile, the civil engineer stands perhaps as the first and clearest model of collective social ascension through a heteronomous organization.

Both engineering and the Congregational ministry were atypical among antebellum professions, since their members were mostly salaried, and not "free" professionals. They illustrate, however, a tendency at work in very different contexts: as communal supports wane, the social prestige of these professionals tends to be founded or reconstituted upon incipiently bureaucratic organizations. The ministry was losing its traditional identity, and found a bulwark of strength in an organization which it largely controlled and which gave it the means to continue recruiting, by providing different promises of career. Civil engineering, whose traditional identity was uncertain in the American context, gained the means of individual career and the means of collective social recognition through organizations which it did *not* control.

We must now turn briefly to the "free" professions of the law and medicine, to examine what trends emerge from their responses to the erosion of traditional community supports.

There can be no doubt that the lowering of admission standards to the bar in the Jacksonian 1830s made it considerably easier to achieve the status of attorney than it had been in the early years of the republic. Yet, as Alfred Z. Reed has noted, "the precise privilege that was widened . . . was the privilege of admission into this profession, not the immediate privilege of practicing law. There remained the institution of admitting courts with power to pass upon the noneducational qualifications that the applicant must still satisfy."[104]

On the one hand, the substance of the law was not ultimately determined by the bar, but by the legislature and the bench. This dependence of the bar upon external elements of arbitration and regulation prevented disagreements about the nature of the law and legal practice from crystallizing into sectarian divisions. On the other hand, judges could favor a certain kind of recruits to the bar and exclude others, thus maintaining a measure of homogeneity. The evidence is that they tended to do so. "Good moral character," indeed, could not be effectively proved within the narrow confines of a community, where the provision could be used to reject the occasional deviant. Beyond those confines, evaluation of character allowed for the relatively free play of social ostracism, which was first directed against the Irish lawyers and later, notoriously, against Jews, blacks, and women.[105] It is significant that despite the multiplication of legal functions and the decline of standards of admission, there were fewer lawyers at the end of the Jacksonian period than there were physicians or clergymen.[106] After admission to practice, the profession had other ways of enforcing conformity to standards. "For all the talk of Jacksonian democracy and for all the changes in formal rule," says Robert Stevens, "there seems little doubt that in major cities like Boston the leading members of the bar played a role, led a life, and enjoyed a status little different from that of their counterparts in 1800 or 1900."[107]

We shall presently see what new forces were operating in the definition of these urban legal elites. It appears, though, that social origins and formal education still qualified "the better class of applicants" to the bar: "by the simple device of professional ostracism, directed against those who insisted upon entering under the statute, a 'regular' or inner bar came into existence."[108]

The education of the "first-rate" applicants to the bar was a far cry from what it became after the 1870s under the influence of Langdell's Harvard Law School. Judge Story's law school at Harvard, or the New Haven private law school which Yale took under its wing, were little more than institutionalized and formalized apprenticeships, marked by an increasingly trade-oriented practicality. Students who were not admitted to the liberal arts college were often allowed into its law school. Under the pressure of competition for students, standards of entry were lowered and the aspirations to found legal training on general education in the classical curriculum were all but forgotten.[109]

Such standards of scholarship and training in the law as there were flourished around the higher courts. They were in evidence in the most settled parts of the frontier—for instance, in Ohio or at Transylvania University in Kentucky—as much as in the East.[110] The frontier admitted a greater variety of forms and styles of legal practice than the older cities of the seaboard. Yet even where itinerant courts remained predominant, this typical frontier institution generated informal regulations and a measure of discipline in the circuit bars.[111] Conviviality among the "gentlemen of the law" and a sense of fellowship which obviously excluded the socially unacceptable were powerful agents of conformity and cohesion. A rich social life revolved around the circuit court, accounting for the nostalgia with which lawyers recalled its days after it passed. In an open, public context, what singled out legal talent to a lawyer's peers and to his potential clients was not certified training but demonstration of forensic bravura, not unlike the fiery, romantic powers that revivalists were expected to manifest in their preaching.

The circuit system appears to have successfully performed the regulatory functions that more formal bar associations attempted to take over in later years.[112] In the circumstances surrounding the decline of the itinerant court we may discern, however, the need for different kinds of legal talent and the growing stratification of a settled bar.

The waning of the circuit bar was not merely a matter of changing styles in consolidated communities. Looking at Cumberland County in Tennessee, Calhoun finds that the circuit system, introduced in 1809, was already in decay by the 1820s. While legal practice in the stable court systems tended to be concentrated in the hands of a few lawyers, the itinerant bar provided an alternative and a way to reduce competition between practitioners. Lawyers were forced to "go on the circuit" by the internal stratification of the profession much more than by the meagerness of small-town legal practice: "Except in very small or very new counties, a fair amount of business was available in any one place; but the control that a few lawyers had over most of this business meant that the marginal and the middle-level practitioner had to scour widely to get enough for himself."[113]

Thus, for variable lapses of time, the circuit system appears to have functioned as a legal market complementary to that of the stable courts. As the volume of legal business increased, the circuit gradually lost this function. The internal stratification of the bar, manifested in earlier years by the differences of status and style between circuit and stable lawyers, took other forms. Stable partnerships and specialization became the principal factors of differentiation among lawyers in the central court systems. Partnerships allowed increased efficiency in handling legal business; at the same time, they were means for integrating out-of-town practitioners while preserving the leadership of local lawyers. From the 1820s on, the main line of specialization in Tennessee was debt collection. Lawyers of middling prestige appear to have replaced the complementary market and the relative security of the circuit courts by specialization in debt collection, which they advertised in newspapers as far east as Philadelphia. Elite practice, on the other hand, became increasingly characterized by "connections"—and, most significantly, by business retainers and out-of-court negotiations.[114] Debt collection came to symbolize the internal cleavage of which the circuit bar had once been a more colorful and personally gratifying expression.

Even before the Civil War and in a relatively "underdeveloped" frontier area, Calhoun's study uncovers the effects of a general trend that was shaping the evolution of legal practice: an external factor—namely, the increasingly diversified and novel legal needs of important business clients—was promoting the specialization and the stratification of the bar. Responding to this external impulse, elite lawyers tended to move away from litigation toward out-of-court negotiation and counseling. By mid-century, lawyers for the major economic interests—that is, for the public and private corporations, and in particular for the railroads—were beginning to replace the brilliant courtroom pleaders at the top of the emergent professional hierarchies.[115] As their clients' interests came to range wider and wider across the nation, so the regional scope of these lawyers' work broadened and so their regional specializations were coordinated. The role of this new legal elite was obviously far from being as prominent as it would become in the 1880s and after. Yet the characteristic privileged relationship between "big business" and the top echelons of the legal profession was already perceptible toward the end of the Jacksonian period.

At the other end of the profession's emerging hierarchy, routine work such as debt collection was increasingly sloughed off to rank-and-file lawyers. At the same time, there was a tendency for the courtroom to become the favorite arena of the non-established, for whom it still provided a means of gaining professional distinction and upward mobility. Secure in their largely commercial practices, elite urban lawyers no longer needed this public stage to swell their clienteles or establish their careers. Thus, at the New York Constitutional Convention in 1846, Calhoun finds some of these elite lawyers from the big city lending a hand to the leveling and decentralizing moves directed against the bar by a political coalition with nativist overtones. On the one hand, the professional status of the established urban lawyers would not suffer from the lowering of educational qualifications, since it did not depend on certified training but on the prestige and power of their clients. On the other hand, the number of lawyers was growing in the cities and centralized court systems provided an arena for the flamboyant eloquence of Irish upstarts and other potential competitors. Forgetting its own beginnings, the "inner bar" was now free to scorn spectacular demonstrations of forensic talent and to support a move for the decentralization of the judicial system.[116]

In this cursory examination, we have seen different types of external warrants of professionalism at work in the law: on the one hand, the traditional elements of social rank and community standing—fused, perhaps, with more uncertain standards related to training and competence—were recognized by the admitting courts and mediated, at least in the smaller communities, by informal mechanisms of social conformity. The hierarchy of the judicial system, we may assume, tended to reproduce the larger social hierarchy. On the other hand, as can be expected in a rapidly developing economy, the larger stratification system was changing under the impact of rising business interests; these factors of stratification were reflected in the incipient internal hierarchy of the legal profession. The emergent business corporation was drawing to itself new forms of legal talent, providing a structural support for a new type of legal elite, which had not yet moved to translate its de facto advantages into educational superiority.

The organizational resources which the law could derive from external factors—the judicial system and the growing importance of corporate business clients—were not available to medicine. The paucity and poverty of hospitals, as we know, had concentrated medicine's early organizational efforts on educational institutions. The proliferation of medical schools from the second decade of the nineteenth century on tended, in Abraham Flexner's words, to "tear from their moorings" the early, college-affiliated medical centers. As Flexner observed in his 1910 report, "the United States and Canada, have, in little more than a century, produced four hundred and fifty seven medical schools, many, of course, short-lived, and perhaps fifty still-born. One hundred and fifty five survive today."[117]

Even where they maintained university affiliation, these nineteenth-century schools were all proprietary enterprises, supported by student fees and serving their faculties well as sources of income (often very handsome) and referral networks. The initial investment could be very small. Hence, as Flexner later noted, a split among the faculty about the merits of a student or a new therapy was rarely fatal—it was likely, however, to lead to the foundation of one more school. The proliferation of medical schools in a "free medical market" was bound to reflect the growing sectarianism of the medical profession as well as the politicking and ambitions of professional leaders, even if they belonged to similar therapeutic and theoretical persuasions. This last aspect of medical dissension preceded, in fact, the legitimation of medical sects by various state legislatures in the second third of the nineteenth century.

In New York City, for instance, eminent physicians took turns in mobilizing support among the ranks of the county medical society and among the public authorities of the city and the state. These political maneuvers resulted, first, in breaking up Columbia's de facto monopoly of medical instruction by the incorporation of the College of Physicians and Surgeons in 1806. Eight years later, David Hosack capitalized on the resentment of those who were excluded from the College and felt threatened by the fact that the latter's degrees were equivalent to licenses. Hosack's successful strategy was to amalgamate Columbia and the College. His group argued, quite correctly, that medical education could not progress until New York City had one single medical school.[118] The argument for monopoly of training reflected the notion that unification and standardization of instruction is a prerequisite for corporate organization and professional control of a market of services. Yet, in the case of Hosack and his coterie, the strategy was premature: in the 1820s, the county society succeeded in forcing them out of the College.[119] As Joseph Kett remarks: "Teaching medicine was a profitable calling and a passport to an increased private practice. Control of the city's only medical school was too lucrative a prize for fair competition."[120]

Given the dynamics of exclusion and inclusion in a narrow professional market, one group could not muster sufficient technical and intellectual legitimacy to make monopolistic training acceptable; more importantly, no group in the profession could muster enough social power to extend the benefits of monopoly to the corporate body of the profession.

Calhoun has interpreted these political maneuvers as attempts to create substitutes for a nonexistent or uncertain pattern of career:

> Repeatedly, men seeking the advancement denied them within the communal profession tried to expand their chances by using the whole population of practitioners as a base on which to erect new, more elaborate, more formal, less personalistic institutions. Just as often, the narrower population of socially responsible practitioners worked to cut any new institutions back within the scope of community life. . . . Each level of dispute sloughed off new factions into the local medical population, creating new bases for quarreling.[121]

In circumstances of cognitive disunity, the shift toward more impersonal or more autonomous ways of professional self-definition was dangerous for the profession's collective fortunes: especially after the rise of homeopathy in the 1820s, the usual intra-professional jockeying for control of the existing or projected institutions fused with deep disagreements about therapy and theory. This became blatantly evident in the controversies over contagionism during the cholera epidemics of 1832 and 1849.[122] Educated urban physicians "still retained the patronage of the wealthy, the educated, and the respectable."[123] During the epidemic, however, their public disagreements added fuel to the attacks that medical sects with lower class followings— of which Thomsonianism was the most popular—had been conducting against the monopoly of "doctor-craft."

The case of New York City illustrates a more general conflict of interests between the two principal organizations of the young American medical profession: since most states recognized a diploma as a license to practice, the medical societies felt directly threatened by the schools. The practitioners whom the societies represented wanted to maintain licensing and apprenticeship as gatekeeping mechanisms, hoping to reduce the growing competition on the medical market. The societies, therefore, tended to attack the quality of teaching and training in the medical schools and to be, on the whole, more concerned about competition from school graduates than from untrained empirics. The schools, on the other hand, wanted to attract as many students as possible and to enlarge as much as possible the market for medical education. They could rightly point to the fact that their graduates were better trained and in more current medical matter than the average physician formed through apprenticeship. The conflict was resolved in favor of the schools: by 1830, according to William Rothstein, the prestige of a diploma far exceeded that of a medical society's license.[124] The inevitable consequence was a further deterioration of the medical societies' position, which accounts in great part for the general decline and abandonment of licensing laws in the 1830s and for the corollary of this process, namely, the institutionalization of sectarian medicine.

From the second decade of the nineteenth century on, the rise of patent medicines and of health sects—among which the most popular were Samuel Thomson's botanic medicine, Wooster Beach's eclecticism, and Sylvester Graham's vegetarianism— undoubtedly irritated the orthodox doctors and even put them on the defensive, but it did not directly challenge the status or the clienteles of the medical elites. What makes botanic medicine particularly interesting is the ardent adhesion of its leader to Jacksonian radicalism, an identification which perfected the fusion between Thomsonianism and democratic ideology.[125]

It was indeed easy to direct the Jacksonian denunciation of monopoly against the regular physicians' efforts to obtain legal privileges, even if it was a gross inaccuracy to identify the average licensed physician with the "aristocracy" or the "idle rich," as the Thomsonians invariably did. The Thomsonians saw the cause of botanic medicine "as intimately involved in a mighty reformation in which there was still much to be done to secure to the common man his rights in government as well as medicine."[126] Besides their attachment to democratic reforms, the Thomsonians, like most other medical sectarians, incorporated with questionable logic but compelling force "the themes of nature, providence, and nationalism."[127] By comparison with the savage therapies defended by orthodox medicine, the "natural" therapies— temperance, healthy diet, cleanliness, and herbal or natural medicines—were undeniably more attractive and at least as effective. Sectarian medicine's amalgam of democratic and romantic themes, its fusion of physical and moral prescriptions, and its belief in human perfectability established obvious affinities between the popular health cults and religious millennialism. But other sectors of the clergy, divested of their informal medical functions by the claims of professional medicine, also welcomed Thomson's emphatic assertion that every man should be his own physician.[128]

The defection of traditional, non-revivalist clergymen was seen as a betrayal by the regular profession of medicine. But despite these inroads in what the opponents of botanic medicine saw as their camp, Thomsonianism by itself does not appear to have carried much strength in the state legislatures; it needed other forces to heed its campaign for the repeal of licensing laws.[129] While Thomsonianism, with its mostly rural and lower-class following, must have made matters difficult for modest rural practitioners, it did not capture the wealthy urban bourgeoisies.

Things were different with homeopathy. The doctors who followed Samuel Hahnemann's system in America also incorporated, in much more sophisticated form than the Thomsonians, a romantic cult of nature's curative powers and supreme arbitration. In some areas, homeopathy succeeded Thomsonianism and appears to have inherited both its practitioners and its clienteles.[130] But the sociological differences between homeopaths and the earlier sectarian healers were most significant: homeopaths, in Europe as in America, were educated regular doctors who advocated a different kind of therapy and rapidly became fashionable among the upper classes. The character of their clientele, in turn, attracted to their ranks a ''genteel'' kind of practitioner, whom American regular physicians quickly dubbed a quack ''of the drawing-room.''

Given the state of pre-scientific medicine, the milder cures advocated by homeopathy had the great advantage of being harmless. More importantly, all healers, licensed or not, were equally ineffective; therefore, what chiefly made the reputation of the orthodox medical elites was their social position and formal education as well as the class of their clienteles. Homeopathy, therefore, broke the monopoly that regular medicine—or, more accurately, its urban elites—had had on these traditional warrants of professionalism.[131]

As homeopathy advanced and founded its own schools and societies in the 1830s and 1840s, the orthodox sect rallied against the challenge to its therapeutic practices. Homeopathy—which was often combined with eclecticism—was rapidly defined as the chief opponent of ''true'' medicine. In 1843 the Medical Society of Philadelphia opened the way by expelling all homeopathic doctors. In 1847, a group of New York regular physicians, unable to do the same in their county society, founded their own Academy of Medicine, from which homeopaths were excluded. In the same year, the American Medical Association was founded in Philadelphia as a voluntary society without licensing powers. What made it possible, according to Rothstein, was the unity wrought in the ranks of the regulars by the threat of homeopathic competition: medical school faculties, who wanted to get rid of their homeopathic rivals, formed an uneasy alliance with the practitioners who wanted to regulate the schools and rebuild medical societies. The A.M.A.'s Code of Ethics, adoption of which became a mandatory condition for membership in 1855, did not in itself define the homeopaths as ''irregulars.'' Yet, arguing that homeopathy was used as ''a trademark,'' the A.M.A. physicians succeeded for a time in ostracizing not only the homeopaths, but the students and the regular practitioners who had at any time associated with homeopaths or other irregulars.[132]

Inherent in professional codes of ethics is an effort to standardize professional behavior which, in the embattled situation of American regular medicine, was clearly aimed at solving the problem of competing commodities on the medical market. The growing number of healers, both ''regular'' and ''irregular,'' had indeed made competition very intense even in outlying rural areas.[133] The issue of standardization of fees loomed large for medical societies, as it had for their predecessors in the late eighteenth and early nineteenth centuries.[134] Competition made undercutting of fees a widespread practice, while the difficulty of collecting fees was undoubtedly ''the most commonly aired grievance of American physicians during the 1840s.''[135]

In a fragmented and harshly competitive market, economic survival was linked to the excessive number of practitioners. Regular physicians, moreover, faced the problem of enforcing discipline within their own ranks if they wanted to maintain their precarious distinctiveness. The supply of medical services had to be both reduced and standardized. With the licensing system in total decay, the only remedy was to force the schools to raise their standards for entry and graduation. The path chosen by the A.M.A. was thus to advocate unrealistic standards of preliminary education for medical school entrants or prospective apprentices, and to threaten with exclusion the schools or the masters that did not follow them. To adopt even much lower standards would have meant certain closure for lack of students for most medical schools.[136] The A.M.A.'s concern with standards reactivated the conflict between schools and apprenticeship in the newly founded medical society, despite the common opposition to homeopathy. The question of upgrading school standards also divided the elite from the rank and file of the profession.

Even before the founding of the A.M.A., important medical journals had supported the views expounded by Martyn Paine, a professor at the Medical College of New York City.[137] Paine argued that the unrealistic raising of standards, given the conditions of medical practice and general education in the United States, would turn away from any school, and into the ranks of empiricism, the hard-striving young men of modest financial means who constituted, in his view, the bulk of American physicians. Only two systems of medical education were possible in America: one that would preserve the decent, low-cost instruction offered by most schools, while admitting that an economic elite would be able to buy a superior education in a very few schools. The other system would raise requirements in all schools and thus reduce their number and the number of legitimate physicians. Because the need for medical services was real and widespread, it would be fulfilled by empirics or by apprenticed physicians, separated from the school graduates by an unbridgeable gap. Thus, as early as 1843, the problem of standardization of the medical practitioner—and hence of standard training—had been recognized as a central focus of organization and reform in American medicine and clearly linked to the issue of social access and exclusion. The A.M.A., however, which was not much more than another sect itself, did not have the social or intellectual power to advance uniformity. The conflict of interests in its constituency condemned it to weakness and ineffectiveness until its reorganization at the beginning of our century. At the local level, the voluntary medical societies were far more active than their national counterpart and served at least the purpose of identifying the orthodox physician to potential patients. Yet, the local societies were caught in the inescapable and seemingly insoluble dilemma of exclusiveness: ''Either they kept their membership requirements loose, in which case they could hardly claim to have purified their ranks, or they tightened requirements and lost any chance of presenting a unified front.''[138]

Especially after the Civil War, this dilemma resulted, in fact, in an increasing divergence of interests between the rank-and-file and the elites of the regular profession. While ''the younger, most active, and perhaps most ambitious members of the profession'' voiced their concern with competition and an overcrowded market at the A.M.A. meetings, the elite physicians sought to erect a clear separation between themselves and the bulk of their colleagues.[139] Small, select organizations connected with a medical school or a hospital provided them with a mechanism. In the early associations of this type, elite physicians pressured for conformity: taking the New York Academy of medicine as evidence, Calhoun argues that elite ''regulars'' deliberately strove for mediocrity, driving down intellectual originality and intellectual ambition as potentially disruptive forces. Impersonality and uniformity offered a respite from chaotic individualism in a fragmented profession.[140] Later, as we shall see, specialism began to emerge as a new trademark of the elite physician and as a new and dangerous form of competition for the average general practitioner.

Challenged by homeopathy on scientific grounds, orthodox medicine could not muster, in response, a demonstration or therapeutic superiority. Skepticism about the curative virtues of the traditional pharmacopeia was not limited to the public: in the 1850s, the most cosmopolitan sectors of the regular profession began to adopt the spirit of ''medical nihilism'' that was becoming prevalent in major European centers.[141] However, before the rise of bacteriology in the 1890s, orthodox medicine could not offer any substitute for ''heroic'' therapies. The bulk of the profession, its self-confidence undermined from within, rejected the discredit cast upon its technical tools. The emergent orientation toward scientific medicine was therefore an additional factor of disunity, which compounded the conflict of interests between elite and average practitioners and condemned the inclusive professional associations to ineffectiveness.

Thus in the two decades before the Civil War, medical societies lost their licensing powers and voluntary associations could not unify a structurally disunited profession. Competing medical schools multiplied the definition of the medical commodity and tended to drive all educational standards down. American hospitals were neither teaching hospitals nor centers of scientific research; yet by mid-century they were providing an organizational base for urban medical elites and, in some cases, a locus where sectarian differences could begin to be dissolved by clinical cooperation. But on the whole, the status of the medical profession had never been as low.[142]

In sum, the decline of traditional warrants and narrow-based monopolies in the profession of medicine was met by a variety of resources, all of them insufficient to check the disintegrating effects of free trade on the medical market. Medical associations, deprived of their licensing powers, were by themselves incapable of reorganizing the profession. Despite sectarian disunity, the medical school emerged as the major resource for professional organization. Where school and society succeeded in establishing a coalition, as in Massachusetts, proliferation was prevented: throughout this period, in fact, Harvard maintained its local monopoly of instruction.[143] Where the profession was too recent to have produced a recognizable hierarchy, as in the frontier state of Ohio, professional organization came from the state legislature, which retained control and limited the number of medical schools.[144] In most other situations, deliberate standardization of behavior and conformity with therapeutic and intellectual standards was sought by groups too small to have an overall effect on the profession, but prestigious enough to generate clusters of unified medical elites, based on the few vigorous institutions—schools or hospitals—that existed before our century. Paradoxically, however, the abandonment of licensing and the ease of access to a medical degree actually served to maintain the occupational identity of the profession, by conferring the title of doctor on a high proportion of medical practitioners.

Immediately after the end of the Civil War, the rise of the public health movement, which had earlier had to fight the sectarian excesses of the organized profession, began to enlist the efforts of urban physicians and to call for professionalism and expertise—both specific responses to the medical problems of the modern industrial city.[145] In the changed context of resources of the early twentieth century, these appeals contributed to the ideological legitimacy of medicine's successful reorganization.

The paradox of the Jacksonian period—political egalitarianism in a society where lines of stratification were hardening, despite the fluidity induced by economic development—appears to have been reflected in the situation of the major professions.

Economic development and the attendant social changes objectively undermined the professions' traditional communal supports, but the effect was uneven, and less significant than it would appear from the political attacks upon professional monopoly. Decentralization and geographical mobility across an expanding territory multiplied the possibilities of segmentation, reducing the impact of the political movement. The traditional professional elites of the Eastern seaboard had never succeeded in translating their local privileges into effective and extended monopolies, despite the legal advantages which they enjoyed before the 1830s. While *formal* guarantees of professional monopoly were abrogated during the Jacksonian period, informal social controls and bases of prestige could be maintained or reconstituted at the local level in both old and new communities.

Insofar as the choicest professional monopolies were based on grounds other than the manifest criteria of inclusion (formal education and licensing), the concessions to the common man did not establish open competition, except where it mattered less: the average and the marginal practitioners suffered from the exacerbated intensity of competition; but those professionals whom the upper classes identified as "their own kind" could maintain their advantages in the best sectors of the professional markets and rapidly move to monopolize new opportunities as they emerged. Thus, the enlargement of the professions brought about by the Jacksonian movement, and above all, by laissez-faire economic development, did not mean democratization.

On the contrary, if democratic encroachments were not always resisted by the established professionals, it was because the *internal stratification* of the professions was not threatened by them. Where the technical development of a profession allowed it, as in the law, specialization along technical lines followed and reinforced the lines of social stratification. In the professions as elsewhere, Jacksonian democracy attacked the forms, but not the substance, of inequality.

Although elite professional status and elite individual careers were protected by internal stratification, the increase in competition could not be entirely disregarded by the established professional elites. The power accorded to public opinion in the age of Jackson appears to have put a prize on *public* demonstrations of professional "competence": fiery preaching, courtroom bravura, "heroic" therapies on their popular substitutes, patent medicines and the ideologically attractive panaceas of the health sects—these were much more significant than anonymous certificates of formal training. To expand their secure but perhaps still narrow clienteles, even the established professional elites had to counter the flamboyance, the talent, or the fashionable appeal of their competitors. Moreover, in the urban centers, the increase in numbers and in social diversity of the professional population tended to destroy the diffuse, extra-professional bases for agreement and control. The resulting increase in dissension, unethical practices, and unseemly competitiveness in the free professions, most particularly medicine, posed a threat to the collective image of these occupations. Thus, both the concern about their position in an expanding market and the concern about collective status caused professional leaders to press toward conformity in their exclusive elite groups and associations. They lacked, however, the organizational and institutional means necessary for an effective standardization of professional practice; what they needed was a coherent and monopolistic system of training, which alone could produce a standardized definition of the professional producer and endow it with meritocratic legitimacy.

In England, the effort to establish superior competence on meritocratic claims characterized the movement of professional reform. In Jacksonian America, there were neither a visible "national" aristocracy nor central status-giving institutions such as the old English corporations or the two ancient universities. The traditional bases of professional prestige were local and scattered. This fact weakened, paradoxically, the import of meritocratic justifications of privilege. The ideology of merit clashed in America with the ideological egalitarianism of the political system. The universalistic and democratic content of the political ideology exposed, in fact, the potential for monopoly latent in the universalistic and rational appearances of expertise. In a sense, Jacksonian politics and ideology functioned as an alternative universalistic instrument for the breaking up of professional monopolies which had never been too tightly sealed. But popular democracy did not change the reality of the stratification system: in the small towns and in the narrow elite circles of the larger cities, the internal stratification of the professions continued to draw sustenance and legitimacy from the structures of social inequality, which in this period were beginning to acquire centers of national unification.

The "modern" professionalizing tendencies that did appear in this period—and by "modern" I mean tendencies which show continuity with and appear as a prelude to the consolidation of professional privileges in later years—were dependent upon emergent organizations. Free market competition, in professional markets as elsewhere, leads to centralization and concentration among the competing units. Bureaucratic organizations, legitimized by the authority of large-scale property, tended to undermine the free market: they supported the emergent hierarchy of the legal profession, and they established the identity of younger professions such as engineering or accountancy. Bureaucratization, however incipient, gave a framework of career to declining sectors of the traditional ministry. Medicine, on the other hand, lacked "heteronomous" supports and its own institutional framework was still too weak to function even as effectively as the church functioned for the clergy.

In sum, the undemocratic dimension of professional reform was more readily apparent in America than in societies with a clearly perceived aristocratic past. For meritocratic claims to function as effective ideological legitimations, new themes—such as an ethos of efficiency and the need to regulate anarchic competition—had to be accommodated by the dominant ideology. The social reorganization accomplished between the years 1870 and 1920 provided the structural support for this ideological shift. The rise of corporate capitalism transformed the larger market in which professions operate; it provided a new context of ideological and organizational resources for diverse professional projects.

Chapter 9

THE RISE OF CORPORATE CAPITALISM AND THE CONSOLIDATION OF PROFESSIONALISM

The classic, older professions sought to control their markets and to gain a privileged position in the occupational and social hierarchies. Modern professionalization is, thus, an attempt to translate one order of scarce resources into another: the possession of scarce knowledge and skills is, indeed, the principal basis on which modern professions claim social recognition and economic rewards. As used in the professional project, the notion of expertise incorporates contradictory principles. On the one hand, it embodies the rationalizing and universalistic legitimation of market monopoly, insofar as it is *standardized* expertise, accessible to all who care to be adequately trained and qualified. On the other hand, expertise is also used to claim superior rewards and to establish social distance from other occupational groups—a claim which is as much supported by the structural limitations on access to training as it is by the professions' deliberate efforts to achieve corporate exclusiveness.

The rise of modern educational systems brings an ideological resolution to the tension between universalistic principles and exclusive privilege embodied in the notion of expertise. Mass access to the lower echelons of the public school system allows the higher levels of the educational hierarchy to claim meritocratic legitimations for their selection of entrants. The inegalitarian uses of acquired expertise are thus concealed by the alleged universalism of the schools' criteria of selection.

The unification of training and research in the modern university is a particularly significant development. As graduate and professional schools emerged at the top of the educational hierarchy, the professions acquired not only an institutional basis on which to develop and standardize knowledge and technologies; they also received, in university training, a most powerful legitimation for their claims to cognitive and technical superiority and to social and economic benefits.

The rise of a new type of institution of higher education in the United States depended, in turn, on the massive availability of surplus capital, especially after the depression of 1893. While the university represents a major factor in the advance of professionalization, it is only one development in the twentieth-century maturation of industrial capitalism. Remarkable economic growth—interrupted, it is true, by numerous downturns and recessions before the cataclysm of 1929—is the background for the reorganization of American society after the Civil War. The growing importance of the great industrial corporations and the transformation of production under their influence; the motor role of new industries, especially mass-consumption industries, in our century; the centralization of power and decision-making in the political system; the emergence and consolidation of functional groups which speak directly to the state for their constituencies; growing governmental intervention in the economy, accelerated by the First World War and by the response to the Great Depression—these are some of the epochal developments that mark the waning of competitive capitalism.[1]

The transformation is accompanied by the predominance of a new type of capitalist firm and new modes of competition. Large productive units, characterized by high ratios of fixed capital per worker and high productivity, need to plan and regulate production, distribution, and employment in order to insure profits in expanding markets. Their new administrative structures emphasize expert decision-making as applied science and technology become increasingly integrated with production and with management.[2]

Associated with the expansion of the monopoly and state sectors of the economy, we find long-term trends toward the transformation of the occupational structure: the decline of small entrepreneurs and independent workers and the corollary bureaucratization of most work-settings are among the most significant. An expression of these developments is the steady increase of nonmanual occupations which service the public or private bureaucracies, create or handle new technologies, provide consumer services in the "affluent society," and fill the increasingly specialized slots of the division of labor.[3] From the last decades of the nineteenth century on, the growth of a public system of higher education attempted to respond to these new demands of the labor market.

To structural changes corresponds a shift in ideology toward new forms of legitimation of power. At the core, the emergent conception of authority appeals to the rationality of science—science as a method and as a world view, more than as a body of knowledge—and to the rationality of scientifically oriented experts who act in the bureaucratized institutions of the new social order.[4]

These long-term trends in structure and ideology are characteristic of the transition toward corporate capitalism. In the United States, they became discernible during the decades of national reorganization that culminated, politically, in the progressive movement and in the election of Woodrow Wilson in 1912. Progressivism is a generic name for a variety of political and intellectual responses to the waning of "a community-centered society" and to the inadequacy of old explanations of social cohesion and social change.[5] For one of the most perceptive students of the period, "the heart of progressivism was the ambition of the new middle class to fulfill its destiny by bureaucratic means."[6] However significant, this component was but one element in a movement characterized by its diversity. When progressivism became visible as a national force toward the turn of the century, it apparently unified a wide array of forces, some of them connected to movements which, in the previous decades, had attempted a "response to industrialism." Opposition to corporate business and agreement on the necessity of electoral reforms and administrative action create "the false picture of a revolt against a common enemy for a common purpose." . . . [But] the only unifying factor . . . is that each group was trying to cope with changes brought about by industrialism."[7] As Samuel Hays observes: "Almost every movement of the Progressive Era subscribed to the concept of the 'people' and believed that its demands sprang from them. But the 'people,' in fact, often opposed reforms . . . Support for change . . . stemmed from a more complex source than the 'people' and opposition to it came from a wider variety of groups than the corporation."[8]

It is impossible here to give even a cursory historical account of the complex decades that precede progressivism and to describe the Progressive Era itself, which in our century leads practically to the door of the New Deal.[9] I will focus, instead, on those features of it which best explain the new structural and ideological context of professionalization.

THE NEW CONTEXT OF PROFESSIONALIZATION

Some urban sectors of progressivism—in particular, those associated with the women's movement and the settlement movement—may have unwittingly transferred to the industrial city an individualistic fundamentalism of rural stamp.[10] But progressivism, in fact, symbolizes the point of no return for reform movements which had framed their protest in terms of the modes and values of a passing order. From there on, efficiency in the service of "moral uplift" becomes more and more the predominant theme, opening an area of reconciliation between leading sectors of progressivism and the large industrial corporation.

The emergence of a *national* ruling class was one of the core structural developments to which progressivism reacted and which, in turn, made possible the shift in dominant ideology. For many contemporary historians, the Progressive Era is, in fact, one act in the process by which this new and relatively coherent ruling class came to preside over the reorganization of both civil and political society.[11] In the Age of Jackson, a new kind of entrepreneur had "struggled to free business enterprise of the outmoded restrictions of special incorporation and banking laws and to end what was an overcentralized control of credit."[12] The rapid industrial expansion after the Civil War, the completion of the railroad network, and therefore the rise of national markets of commodities and labor, spawned a new breed of capitalists.[13] The downturns of the seventies and the eighties, capped by the major economic crisis of 1893, accelerated the merger movement and the drive for industrial rationalization in terms of efficiency and economies of scale. However, the strongest stimulus behind the rapid "combination movement" of the years 1897–1904 was not the desire for efficient production but the fear of anarchy and the risks of competition.[14] As the rising corporations expanded their capacity for self-financing, investment bankers also broadened their role. By the early 1890s the United States no longer needed to depend on foreign capital; finance capitalism emerged from the depression of the 1890s as the principal allocator of investment funds and an important coordinator of further growth. As investment bankers assumed a role of comparable importance to that of national political leaders and industrial magnates, a joint financial-industrial leadership came into being. Its rise both depended on and called forth a new, active role of the state.

Fearful of antibusiness regulation, business leaders had at first tried to prevent it by getting increasingly involved in politics. But the exacerbation of class conflict in the 1880s and the depression of the early 1890s showed to the most advanced sector of business that regulation and coordination of economic activity depended largely on "political capitalism"—that is, "the utilization of political outlets to attain conditions of stability, predictability, and security—to attain rationalization in the economy."[15] Government regulation was welcomed by the enlightened sectors of corporate business, so long as they could maintain a decisive influence over it. In the first decades of the twentieth century, organizations such as the National Civic Federation, while paving the road towards an entente with business unionism, influenced regulatory and legislative commissions, insuring that industry would be allowed a voice and a veto in the areas that concerned it.[16]

Adapting the system to the new needs of corporate capitalism required a close partnership between top-level economic leaders and the state. Political centralization, placing decision-making in the hands of "responsible" leaders, capable of reconciling sectional differences in a broad, "national" view, was thus an axis of the institutional order envisaged by at least some sectors of the national ruling class. In private as well as in public affairs, decision-making was to flow from the center to the periphery. Political leadership in the Progressive Era found the vision needed to unify the disjointed society under an ideology adapted to the phase of corporate capitalism.

Except in age and political experience, the Progressive Party cadres were not strikingly different from the Taft Republicans to whom they left the Grand Old Party in 1912. Both groups were overwhelmingly urban, upper middle class, Anglo-Saxon, Protestant, and highly educated: more than half of the Progressives were professional men, while 63 percent of the Old Guard Republicans had attended college.[17] The issue that divided them most clearly was the tactics of popular democracy: the Progressives endorsed the initiative, the referendum, the direct primary, and the recall of judicial decisions, which, to the Old Guard, spelled a threat to the Constitution and, more concretely, an attack upon the very structure of the party.

An analysis of municipal reform—a major battleground of the reformers after 1890—reveals, in fact, that "the ideology of democratization of decision-making was negative rather than positive. . . . It was used to destroy the political institutions of the lower and middle classes and the political power which those institutions gave rise to, rather than to provide a guide for alternative action."[18] Citywide elections—together with the promotion of strong mayors and the city manager form of executive—displaced the ward politician, close to his working-class and ethnic constituency. Municipal reform maximized instead the influence of "cosmopolitan" businessmen and professionals who could derive citywide recognition from their involvement with broad issues and their national connections.[19]

Hays observes an upward shift—analogous to that from the ward to the whole city—between township (or county) and the state level:

> The focal points of this transition were schools and roads. . . . In each case professionals with cosmopolitan rather than local perspectives were extremely influential

in shifting the scope of interest and level of decision-making. The state highway commission supplanted the township trustee in road affairs and the state superintendent in
public instruction became an increasingly influential figure. A similar upward shift in
decision-making took place between the state and federal government. The most dramatic aspect of this process was the change in regulatory legislation. . . . In each
case nationally organized businesses with markets and other interests beyond the confines of a single state actively promoted national regulation.[20]

A general process of political centralization thus appears to underlie the rhetoric
and the tactics of "direct democracy." The New England town-meeting was not, in
fact, the model of decision-making pursued by the reformers. Their inspiration came
from the efficient business enterprise: as one of the truly national institutions of the
period, the corporation, with its centralized control of functional components, provided a focal model for progressivism, for Teddy Roosevelt's New Nationalism
and, in general, for the new concept of the state.

Leaders in the established professions, and in the new applied specialties that were
emerging within the expanded structure of government and public services, actively
promoted rationalization on the corporate model. This new type of professional welcomed the corporate systems of decision-making "not only because of their scope
of coverage but because of their coercive potential. The professional sought to carry
standards of life generated by a few to the population at large. His task was to persuade the yet unconvinced."[21] For many of these men, the application of the corporate model to public affairs was a means of establishing the independence of their
professions from the private corporations and their "predatory wealth." The paradox
is only apparent. The new style of expert leadership which they sought to establish
could not exist without its corporate moorings; but the ubiquitous affirmation of the
expert in distinct corporate systems—an affirmation which sometimes led to open
conflict—reinforced scientific expertise as a transcendent principle and as a potential basis of professional autonomy.

The tendency appears clearly in the scientific management wing of mechanical
engineering and, most particularly, in the new concept of professionalism advocated by Morris Cooke, the favorite disciple of Frederick W. Taylor, the founder of
scientific management. Cooke, in fact, succeeded in steering the mechanical engineering profession toward reform, where Taylor himself had failed.[22] "The fundamental consideration in the work of an engineer—if he is ever to pull himself out of
his present status of being a hired servant—is that he shall make public interest the
master test of his work," wrote Cooke in 1921.[23]

As Director of Public Works for the city of Philadelphia from 1914 to 1919, Cooke
put the principle into practice and advanced the concept of the professional engineer
as expert leader in rational government. He used his battle against the utilities companies to denounce the engineering consultants associated with the companies' interests and to demonstrate the futility of a code of ethics in a professional association
controlled by business.

Although Cooke's influence was undoubtedly profound with the rank-and-file
of the profession, his faith in public service to solve the inherent subordination of
the engineer was not widely shared. Cooke's solution presupposed, indeed, that
the principles of scientific management would triumph and bring about "a mas-

sive restructuring of industrial bureaucracies and a reorganization of the utilities. If these things had come to pass, then Cooke's proposals would have made good sense."[24]

The corporate business leadership, while it was sympathetic to Taylor's rationalization and strict control of labor, was not about to share control of the enterprise with an independent group, no matter how expert and how scientific in its orientations. In the first decades of our century, scientific management, in fact, was more attuned to progressivism in public affairs than to the practical needs of big business, to whom Taylor had originally addressed his program. Reinhard Bendix has shown, however, that the social philosophy of scientific management—reinterpreted in the 1920s and 1930s and transformed by Elton Mayo's approach—was gradually incorporated by the top levels of corporate industry.[25] The intervening factor was the general shift in the dominant ideology which began with progressivism. As Samuel Haber convincingly argues in his study of Taylorism, scientific management provides a key to the emergent ideology of corporate capitalism.

Haber shows that Taylor's formulations integrated all the essential meanings that the core notion of efficiency took in the public mind of the time: the personal virtues of hard and disciplined work (and, therefore, the Yankee heritage and the Mugwump tradition); the "energy output-input ratio of a machine"; the relation between costs and profit in a commercial enterprise; and finally, social efficiency, that is, the "leadership of the competent" in a state of social harmony.[26]

For a time, the more simplistic and moralistic versions of the gospel of efficiency captured the popular imagination.[27] In the early part of the twentieth century, the language of efficiency appeared to unify the various reform campaigns into a "reform syncretism" centered on the new concept of the state: "Conservation, scientific management, and Americanization expressed cognate sentiments . . . the leaders of all three suggested measures which involved a rejection of laissez faire and the acceptance of social guidance and control."[28]

The impact of the ideology of efficiency was profound.[29] The most general and abstract dimension which it incorporates is the appeal to science—or, broadly speaking, to rational and systematized knowledge: science appears not only as the chief instrument for mastery and control over the physical and even the social environment, but also as the ultimate legitimation for practical choices and everyday courses of action. In this sense, scientific management and its popular versions accurately reflect—or anticipate—the transformation of the productive forces by the integration of applied science and technology at all levels of the production process.

In the concrete setting of industry, the ideology of scientific management expresses the demise of the self-made man or captain of industry as the central self-justifying myth of the capitalist class. The common submission of *both* workers and employers to the "objective" laws of science heralds, indeed, a later ideological development: that which sees in corporate capitalism and in the depersonalization of capitalist property a "managerial revolution" and the waning of class. As Haber observes of Brandeis' conception of industrial democracy: "Those aspects of management to which the laws of science did not as yet apply were to be subject to collective bargaining. Where science did apply, a union representative might serve as a watchdog to make sure that it was the laws of science and not class interest which was obeyed. *That the laws of science might serve class interest did not seem to be a possibility.*"[30]

In scientific management, science appears as the transcendent norm which will eliminate the arbitrariness of class power. In Taylor's own words: "The man at the head of the business under scientific management is governed by rules and laws which have been developed through hundreds of experiments *just as much as the workman is,* and the standards which have been developed are equitable."[31] Candidly emphasizing the *ideological* character of the transformation, Taylor adds: "In its essence scientific management involves a complete mental revolution on the part of the workingmen. . . . And it involves an equally complete mental revolution on the part of those on the management's side."[32]

At a more concrete level, scientific management is an expression of the core legitimation of mature capitalism: because technology and applied science promise a quasi-unlimited expansion of output and resources, they eliminate the cause for "zero-sum-game" conflict. Continuous economic growth and continuous increases in productivity are thus the mediators through which science resolves, or at least dilutes, class conflict.[33]

In the appeal to science, therefore, we find the overall cognitive and normative legitimation for the rise of the manager and the rise of the expert: ideologically, the "carriers of embodied science"—that is to say, trained and credentialed experts—are assigned a crucial and directive role, while the ideology also emancipates them from class allegiances and class interests.

In the context of the factory, scientific management projects the technocratic ambitions of the rising profession of engineering. But the contradictions and functions of the ideology are also revealed in this context. If, indeed, efficiency can be accurately and directly measured in the production of real commodities, this measurement is not unequivocal. As Haber points out, "Mechanical efficiency is an output-input ratio of matter or energy, whereas commercial efficiency is the relation between price and cost. Occasionally, these efficiencies are opposed."[34]

The glorification of technological ingenuity had justified, much before Taylor, the exalted position of the engineer, next to the master, in the hierarchical division of labor of the early factory system. It may be that this traditional belief concealed the essential subordination of the engineering profession from even such acute observers of the later industrial system as Thornstein Veblen.[35] But the practical engineers themselves, despite some misgivings, had less illusions about the ultimate determination of efficiency: "It was with a certain grimness that the engineers who seemed to believe that engineering could be practiced without regard to money values were condemned. 'These men may be ingenious inventors or designers, they may be great mathematicians, they may even be eminent as scientists, but they are not engineers,' " wrote the president of the Stevens Institute of Technology in 1907.[36]

The extension of notions of efficiency to organizations which produce only services or fictitious commodities maximizes the ideological implications. The extension discloses, first of all, an analogy between factory and society which symbolizes the bringing of the whole social order under the imperative creed of limitless economic growth. Efficiency in service industries cannot be gauged, however, by the direct mechanical measurement of input-output ratios of energy; its measurement is therefore necessarily reduced to cost-benefit evaluations. But when efficiency criteria are applied to the management of agencies outside the marketplace (such as the government, its administrative arms, nonprofit organizations such as schools, hospitals, philanthropies, and the like), evaluation of input and output becomes increasingly indirect. Above all, the attempt to measure efficiency in the production of services or fictitious commodities implies a necessary reduction of quality to quantity.[37] The tendency shows even with an apparently qualitative indicator of productivity or efficiency—that is, the proportion of "qualified" personnel at the various levels of an organization. The upgrading of qualifications is, indeed, equated with growing proportions of *credentialed* employees, with improvements in the personnel's average years of formal schooling or in the average scores obtained in a variety of aptitude tests.[38]

All these attempts to measure and increase efficiency in the production of services involve an extension of the role of the "experts." Scientific management ideologies attempted to bestow upon the engineer—and, later, upon the trained business administrator—the crown of the entrepreneur. In the same manner, the extension of the ideology of efficiency beyond the realm of real commodity production gave a decisive impetus to professionalizing occupations such as bureaucratic social workers, city planners, or school superintendents.

The possibility of claiming special "scientific" and organizational expertise comes to most of these occupations by virtue of their position in organizations which are increasingly bureaucratic. Centralization, hierarchical ordering, and delegation of administrative and managerial functions give those in planning or coordinating positions the possibility of defining the meaning of efficiency and the parameters for its measurement. Obviously, they do not perform this task of definition to their own disadvantage.

Two central structural changes underlie the ideological shift symbolized by scientific management and, in politics, by the Progressives: namely, the reorganization of production by the giant corporation and the quasi-simultaneous extension of state power and functions. Progressive reform took the corporate model of organization from the economy and transferred it to the polity, thus making political centralization concomitant to the centralization of economic production. It could be argued that the initial locus of bureaucratization in the United States is not the state, but large-scale industry.[39] From the Progressive Era on, bureaucratization advanced simultaneously in both political and civil society, providing a structural support for the diffusion of the ideology of efficiency.

The chief legitimizing principle of bureaucracy is, for Weber, its superior efficiency in the handling of large-scale problems. Bureaucracy appears to be the structural form under which the reorganization of commodity production by monopoly capital is "relayed" ideologically throughout the body social. In the particular historical development of the United States, central institutions of truly national scope were established almost contemporaneously in the economic and political spheres and, if we count the national universities, in the sphere of higher education as well. This parallel reorganization is reflected at the level of ideology in the unifying themes of efficiency, regulation, and expertise. It is during this phase of transition toward corporate capitalism that American professions consolidated their position in the occupational and social hierarchies. The success of professionalization movements in this phase therefore illuminates the organic relationship of professionalism—as an affirmation of expertise—with the two central structures of the new social order: namely, the large business corporation and the state.

In the light of the new ideology, the state acquires connotations of "objectivity" which are implicit in the appeal to science as an instrument of legitimation. The three main principles of progressive political reform, "non-partisanship, the strong executive, and the separation of politics from the administration"[40] all converge toward the notion of a transpolitical and ultimately technocratic state. Non-partisan, the state is severed from the visible class dimensions of political strife and debate. This "strong executive" administers, in fact, a social reality in which all interests can be reconciled by the magic of science applied to the limitless expansion of output. This emergent conception of the state foretells, thus, the not-so-unrealistic utopia of depoliticized conformity in a mass consumption society.

This "transpolitical," "efficient," and "strong" apparatus for administering the society of consensus is the logical support for expert advisers and administrators: "The scientific expert," writes Haber, "became the prototype of all administrators. . . . The expert's authority derived from his science, and the range of that authority often remained somewhat indefinite. For most progressives, the expert was to be neither on top nor on tap. He would do less than command but more than advise. He would surely count for something."[41]

The emergence of the modern university completes the institutional framework within which experts can become organically tied to the reformed apparatus of the state. The "Wisconsin idea" of the university hopefully proposes a symbiotic relationship between the new national institutions of higher learning and the transpolitical state. In this conception, the professional expert can achieve—at least ideologically—emancipation from "predatory wealth" and thus assert his altruistic autonomy. The connotations of classlessness attached by the ideology of scientific management to experts in private organizations are reinforced by the conception of a "neutral" state and by the rise of the national university.

With its emphasis on running the state as an industrial corporation, the ideology of efficiency resolves the particularly American conflict between the ideology of egalitarian democracy and the claims of expertise. Concretely, the notion of a transpolitical state run by "classless" experts reconciled the class interests of at least part of the Progressive leadership with the movement's clamor for democratic revival: "Efficiency provided a standpoint from which progressives who had declared their allegiance to democracy could resist the leveling tendencies of the principle of equality. They could advance reform and at the same time provide a safeguard to the 'college-bred.'"[42]

Progressivism combined the directive power of privately managed corporations with an appearance of neutral regulation. Regulatory legislation contributed in the long run to the legitimacy of the large business corporation: apparently under control, it could be regarded as one more responsible member of the industrial community. Responsible membership is implicitly defined as involving acceptance of two cardinal principles of the social order: the private appropriation of social surplus and the private direction of social production. But the appeal to science and to ''classless'' expertise appear to subordinate the new social system to objective and transcendent laws. Not surprisingly, the movements that shaped the emergent order could enlist the support and participation of cosmopolitan urban professionals: in a sense, these movements incorporated the characteristic fusion which professional ideology seeks to effect between the goal of monopolistic market control and antimarket themes of public service and social usefulness.

In sum, the emergence of a national ruling class and of a new system of social stratification in the period of transition toward monopoly capitalism is structurally supported by large organizations: in the private as well as in the public sector, organizations administered in the bureaucratic mode are the new foundations of power and property, as well as the generators of ''new middle-class'' occupations and careers. Their size and their mode of administration appear to insulate these large organizations from the direct influence of class interests. Guided—at least ideally— by principles of functional rationality and applied science, these apparently classless organizations transmute power into authority by invoking the legitimacy of expertise. Thus, the reorganization of American society after the Civil War not only established a new system of social stratification but also, logically, created a new set of ideological legitimations for inequality.

The corporation, the state, and the modern university—all three organized on the bureaucratic model—are the central status-giving institutions which the United States lacked in the age of laissez faire. A national educational system and, in particular, the national institutions of higher education, function in the new order as the central reproducers and legitimators of the class structure. Appeals to science and to limitless growth merge as a mainstay of the new dominant ideology. Mediated by organizations, the class structure of monopoly capitalism is ultimately legitimized as a functional emanation of the social division of labor and, therefore, as the mirror of differential abilities and motivations.[43]

The monopoly, state, and academic sectors (the academic sector being both the producer and the employer of credentialed experts) define the organizational contexts within which professions find new instruments for self-organization and self-assertion. Large-scale bureaucratic organizations transform, therefore, the social matrix of professionalization: they provide the climate of ideological legitimation for both old and new professions; they also provide models, sponsorship, equipment, and resources. Far from being in conflict with the model of profession, the ''bureaucratic phenomenon'' creates the structural context of successful professionalization. Outside of the central bureaucratic apparatus of the new social order lies professional marginality, in both the collective and the individual sense.[44]

GENERALIZATION OF THE PROFESSIONAL PROJECT; THE STRUCTURAL BACKGROUND

After the Civil War, the westward move, the massive rates of immigration and urbanization, together with economic growth and the long-term increase of agricultural and industrial productivity, brought about the gradual restructuring of the labor force. The principal changes are well-known: the first, the most significant, was the decline of agricultural employment. Agriculture remained the predominant field of employment until 1910, although it attracted a smaller and smaller proportion of all workers. From 53 percent of the whole in 1870, gainful workers in agriculture declined to 31 percent in 1910 and 27 percent in 1920; in this last year, employment in manufacturing and mechanical industries reached 30.3 percent of the labor force and began, in turn, its proportional decline. The second major trend is, therefore, the gradual decrease of workers engaged in the production of physical goods and the growing movement toward distribution—transportation, trade, and communications—as well as toward services of all kinds, after 1870.[45] The third most obvious change is the rise of the public sector, which overlaps in part the enormous increases in the clerical and professional occupations.[46]

In the rise of the cities, in the emergence of national labor markets and in the growing tendency toward concentrated employment in the large industrial corporation and in the state sector, it is possible to discern the structural bases of a national class system. Everyday reality, however, was different. Robert Wiebe remarks that even in the 1880s and 1890s,

> The concept of a middle class crumbled at the touch. Small business appeared and disappeared at a frightening rate. The so-called professions meant little as long as anyone with a bag of pills and bottle of syrup could pass for a doctor, a few books and a corrupt judge made a man a lawyer, and an unemployed literate qualified as a teacher. Nor did the growing number of clerks, salesmen, and secretaries of the city share much more than a common sense of drift as they fell into jobs that attached them to nothing in particular, beyond a salary, a set of clean clothes, and a hope that somehow they would rise in the world.[47]

In the rapidly growing urban centers, the massive presence of foreign-born whites exaggerated the estrangement from the city of a native population which, in 1890, was still predominantly rural and concentrated in small towns.[48] Americanization and the melting pot seemed hardly credible ideologies. The industrial proletariat was profoundly divided by the diversity of its origins and work situations. The relative concentration of foreign-born workers and, to a lesser extent, their children, in certain occupations and industries aggravated the fragmentation of the class. Unionization was minimal.[49] At the level of the community, ethnic and cultural issues were much more vital than the national questions addressed by the platforms and ideologies of the major political parties.[50]

A class system had to come out of these bits and pieces. At least some sections of the industrial proletariat had shown their capacity for cohesive action in the intense class struggles that followed the great railroad strike of 1877. During the 1880s and 1890s, the "threat from below" appears to have brought some reactive unity to the divided middle strata; it blurred, at least temporarily, the bitter divisions between old and new wealth: both to "gentlemanly reformers" and to urban middle strata, the arrogance of the plutocracy seemed decidedly preferable to the rise of the "uncivilized" masses. But in the early twentieth century the memories of Populism and of urban and industrial class struggle were attenuated, while the fear of Bolshevism had not yet taken hold: a change in attitude toward the working class and the urban poor was possible.

From the 1880s on, the social justice movement—in which women's organizations and settlement workers, besides the organized church, played an increasingly prominent role—had been outlining a new role for the educated urban strata. From the settlements, in particular, came a more radical approach to urban problems than the moral solutions of the Social Gospelers and other Protestant humanitarians. Focusing on the environmental roots of poverty and personal degradation, the new secular brand of urban reformers actively organized campaigns for protective labor legislation and minimum living standards. They were still inspired, however, by a Christian ideal of universal brotherhood and individual uplift. Although sympathetic to the broader demands of the labor movement, they refused to recognize the necessity of class conflict or to accept the reality of class struggle.[52]

A reform movement which appeared to confront the power of the new ruling class without denouncing the class system—a movement which, furthermore, implicitly gave a badge of moral superiority to middle class reformers with regard to *both* the "plutocracy" and the lower classes—could indeed attract a wide array of social forces. At the local level, progressivism appears to have been at least as much a movement of new aggressive business elites, represented by local chambers of commerce, as an expression of the bitterness of bypassed notables and old-fashioned entrepreneurs.[53] The constant rise in the cost of living was a possible unifying factor among otherwise disparate groups. Inflation affected, besides the working masses, "middle class and professional families . . . for their incomes were least responsive to general price changes."[54]

Another important factor is the very diversity and ambiguity of the progressive ideology: it projected, at one level, a quasi-Populist image but asserted more and more clearly as time went by the superiority of the competent and the role of the expert in efficient, "scientific" reform.

In fact, the central themes of progressivism—"moral uplift" for the masses, based on the formal expansion of political participation and on economic growth— are typical of an optimistic ideology, seeking the conciliation of irreconcilable interests. In a phase of transition, reformers who stressed individual effort and individual mobility could genuinely see more social fluidity and openness than the class system actually permitted. Espousing the promise of economic growth and efficient management, significant fractions of the intermediate class could promote, in the service of reform, the interests of the new industrial and financial magnates. For many reformers, the collusion may have been unwitting and their hopes of democratic reform sincere. As a hypothesis, I would argue that "new middle-class" reformers occupied, at best, ancillary positions with regard to the new ruling class. Yet their ideological convergence around the goals of rationalization and economic expansion was structurally based: there is evidence to suggest that the most significant fraction of the intermediate class—composed of professionals and managerial specialists with a "cosmopolitan" and national outlook—was rising and asserting itself in intimate connection with the central institutions of the new social order.

First among these was the bureaucratic apparatus of the state, including the system of public education.[55] The public sector was important not only as the fastest growing employer and as a privileged arena of action for the new "experts" in public affairs; public service and politics were also vehicles for the sense of identity and unity of the cosmpolitan sectors of the intermediate class. The emergent ideology assigned to the "transpolitical" state a central role of arbitration and social cohesion. The passage to corporate capitalism structurally required an expansion of the public sector. Consistent with these trends, the professional reformers addressed their demands for recognition and support to the state, as did the social reformers (who came frequently from the former group) in the fields of labor legislation, consumer protection, public health, school reform, and slum clearance. As the reform activists increased their leverage, their own self-assertion as experts tended to merge with their promotional efforts on behalf of the organizations where they worked.[56] In electoral as well as in social and professional reforms, the "expert" leaders defined the form that institutions, policies, or services were to take, reserving for themselves, at least in principle, the role at the helm.

In the dominant centers of the economy—the large business corporations—"new middle-class" occupations were more clearly subordinate to a heteronomous hierarchy than in the public sector. Yet, there too, new specializations or new articulations of the bureaucratic mode of organization spawned new claims to expertise.[57] Bureaucratization defined the typical pattern of middle-class career and a typical source of middle-class authority. For many professions, the corporation directly or indirectly provided a new context of organizational and ideological resources. The new approach to professionalization is typically illustrated by engineering, the largest of the new expert occupations called forth by large-scale industrialization.[58]

Edwin Layton observes that engineers, "like the progressives . . . saw themselves as a middle group between capital and labor."[59] This perception led them, on the one hand, to seek governmental recognition for their profession. At the Conservation Congress of 1908, the leaders of the four major engineering associations successfully proposed a series of resolutions, calling for the creation of a department of public works and "of a cabinet post for an engineer, thus according to the profession national recognition."[60] Engineers obviously welcomed the role that the predominant tendency within progressivism assigned to the expert: "Since engineering was the profession that applied scientific laws to practical problems, scientific solutions to social problems meant putting engineers in positions of leadership."[61]

But, on the other hand, engineers rejected the faith in democracy and the mistrust of the corporation that was voiced, at least rhetorically, by national progressivism. As corporation employees, the engineers could not oppose big business without renouncing the very base of power and social mobility of their profession: "where progressives favored regulation by government, engineers looked for reform coming from within the business community and through the agency of the engineer."[62]

What Layton calls the engineers' "obsessive concern for social status" fits with the image of an upwardly mobile group, largely drawn from a declining social category—small commercial or farm entrepreneurs—that was dependent on the large business corporation for its own advance.[63] By the end of World War I, this concern with status had fused with the conception of independent professionalism advocated at first by only a small elite. It had been, however, a contradictory conception: at the same time that engineering leaders attempted to exclude businessmen from their societies by raising the membership requirements, they continued to glorify the typical mobility path that led the corporate engineer from technical to managerial positions. Efficient management meant, moreover, that business would be run according to physical laws—embodied in technology—and to the "laws" of economics and social evolution—embodied in the corporation. Professionalism could thus be reconciled with business loyalty and with the public defense of corporate industry.

Not surprisingly, there was practically no opposition to this brand of professionalism until the 1920s. At this time, men such as Morris Cooke and his successors, moving away from elitist status concerns, sought to channel the economic discontent of average engineers into a direct relation with the state and into a broader technocratic conception of the engineer's social role. Engineering thus illustrates the alternative sources of support sought by a subordinate occupation in its professionalization efforts. In the context of the industrial corporation, professionalism was in large part a reaction to bureaucratic subordination; it nevertheless borrowed from the corporation a legitimizing ideology (scientifically based efficiency) and a model of individual advancement (promotion through the bureaucratic hierarchy). The public sector appeared, thus, as an independent or countervailing source of power and public recognition. Another such source was the modern university. The educational system was the third institutional area of major importance for the rising sectors of the intermediate class. The direct relevance of the national university to the success of professionalization justifies a brief account of its emergence on the American scene.

The decade of the 1880s marked a turning point in American higher education. Despite the high rate of population growth, enrollments had remained static since the Age of Jackson.[64] From 1885 on, attendance picked up steadily at the major colleges and universities. By the early 1890s, Edward Ross, returning from Berlin, could marvel at the "boom in educational lines": in the ten years from 1885 to 1895, the student bodies had grown by 20 percent at the private Eastern colleges and by 32 percent in the state universities.[65] Industrial and financial leaders may still have believed, like Andrew Carnegie, that bookish knowledge was "fatal to success" in business and that the "school of experience" was the best for American youth.[66] Yet, like Carnegie himself, they were insuring a steady flow of money for the institutions of higher learning or founding new private universities, like John D. Rockefeller at Chicago or Leland Stanford in California. Following on the promise of the 1862 Morrill Act, legislative funding was becoming a reality in the 1890s. The university had attained an unquestioned position among American institutions.

Lawrence Veysey suggests that one major underlying reason for this change was the concern of self-made men for the social status of their children. For the new and affluent America of the Midwest and the West, the college degree was acquiring a new meaning: not only because it was a distinction that could be achieved with relative ease, in imitation of the traditional Eastern elites; but also, more importantly, because it established social distance between an older and largely Anglo-Saxon immigration and the mass of newly arrived Central and Southern Europeans.[67] The function that middle-class aspirations increasingly assigned to the university had a powerful effect on its structure and later evolution. The emergent model of the American university, however, had been in gestation since the 1860s.

A first act in this process was the demise of the small sectarian college, which had proliferated in the Jacksonian period as the typical "unfree" unit in a "free market" of education. By 1860, says Hofstadter, financial insolvency was eliminating the more marginal of these institutions, while internal disorder was being resolved by a more secular turn and a more autonomous role of the faculties.[68] In both established Eastern colleges and outlying denominational schools, the proportional decline in the number of students preparing for the ministry reflected the advance of secularization.[69] The Jacksonian emphasis on "practicality" and, after 1840, the spread of didactic scientific instruction prefigured in a primitive way the educational models that were to compete after the Civil War.

The early conception of the college had relied on religion and, almost secondarily, on the classics, to emphasize strict "mental discipline." Its lingering effects may be traced in the rhetorical piety and conservative Christianity surprisingly voiced by presidents and demanded of faculties at new institutions like Johns Hopkins or the University of Chicago. Greatly transformed, the classical emphasis may have subsisted in the ideal of well-rounded cultivation of mind that came to be chiefly associated, in our century, with the private liberal arts college and with the Ivy League.[70] Yet, as an institutional model, "mental discipline" was on its way out by 1865.

In the decade that followed, the major trend of reform was undoubtedly utilitarian, in the sense of a voluntary adaptation by academic sectors to what they perceived to be the demands of "real life" in an industrial and democratic society.[71] What is generally seen as the typical American contribution to the modern university model derives from this tradition. If, as Veysey believes, unpopularity and public indifference explain the freedom of institutional experimentation enjoyed by the university until the 1890s, then we should consider the utilitarian model of reform as a deliberate effort to integrate the college into the mainstream of American life. Not surprisingly, the model found its chief advocates among the new faculty in the applied and social sciences and among administrators—especially the strong presidents who, in the manner of captains of industry, were fashioning the institutions of the future.[72]

The utilitarian desire for an "adaptation to reality" was concretely expressed in a number of "democratic" beliefs and programmatic changes. First of all, a broadened notion of "calling" contributed to dignify a great number of technical and specialized pursuits, which were henceforth able to claim a place in the American university, while the European institutions almost uniformly relegated them to vocational schools. The Morrill Acts—establishing land grants for colleges that would provide agricultural and mechanical instruction—deliberately promoted the vocational orientation of the university. This typical emphasis explains in part the wide diffusion of professionalization as a model for the collective improvement of social status. It also merges with the central role that the American university would come to play as an agency of individual social mobility, democratically dispensing its badges of status superiority to broad segments of the public.

The openness to multiple vocations is intimately linked, on the one hand, with the democratic belief in the equality of all fields of learning—a belief which guided the founding of Cornell in 1868, and directly inspired the elective curriculum.[73] On the other hand, vocational openness merges with the hope for a "classless" institution:

a university, that is, in which all students should be treated equally, and, going one step further, one that should admit all students regardless of sex, race, religion, and even previous educational attainments. As President Andrew Draper of Illinois declared in 1907: "The universities that would thrive must put away all exclusiveness and dedicate themselves to universal public service. They must not try to keep people out; they must help all who are worthy to get in."[74]

"Universal public service" meant, therefore, social and intellectual openness. In a developing country it also meant that the university was a logical center for the diffusion to the outside of all kinds of knowledge. In the 1890s, this last conception crystallized in the typically Midwestern movement of university extension. With the coming of progressivism, however, public service became a divisive issue, pitting a small minority of radical social scientists against equally utilitarian but more conservative presidents. While men like Richard Ely, Edward Bemis, and Edward Ross raised the issue of academic freedom in political and social terms at Wisconsin, Chicago, and Stanford, the college presidents tended to line up behind the progressive ideology of efficiency and expertise.[75] Few went as far in presenting the university as an apparatus of the state as President Charles K. Adams of Wisconsin, who declared in 1896: "The university is not a party separate from the State. . . . Its relations to the State are far more intimate and organic than those of a child to a parent; for a child has an individuality and rights apart from the will of the parent, while the University has no individuality and no rights apart from the will of the State."[76] Yet, the fading of the utility ideal into the general ideology of efficiency—strongly influenced by scientific management after 1910—accelerated the integration of the university with the central structures of corporate capitalism. The institutionalization of an alternative model—that which advocated the primacy of pure research—contributed to this institutional assimilation.

The conception of the university as a research institution was an adaptation to the American scene of what a large number of American scholars, scientists, and educators chose to see and admire in the German university.[77] The German influence was less a direct import than something mediated and radiated, after 1876, by Johns Hopkins, the first American graduate school. The Hopkins—and its even "purer" imitation, Clark University—failed to maintain themselves as pure graduate and research institutions; the main difficulty was financial, combined, at Clark, with opposition from the sponsors. The Hopkins had lost its leading role by the 1890s: the graduate schools at Harvard, Columbia, Chicago, and later Wisconsin were promoting a different and more viable version of what the Hopkins had started. Every university of some significance was beginning its own graduate program, in imitation of the leading national institutions. Yet the influence of the Hopkins had been enormous: small groups of its graduates had spread the spirit of scientific inquiry at other institutions, pressing "from below" for the advancement of the research function. Through the influence of the Flexner report of 1910, the Johns Hopkins medical school had become the unquestionable model of medical education. From the Hopkins had come the concept of the Ph.D. as a research degree and the decisive impulse for the emergence of a full-time and relatively well-paid academic profession. By 1893, says Veysey, "it could be said that some amount of graduate work was required to win a permanent appointment at nearly every prominent institution. At the turn of the century, the Ph.D. degree was usually mandatory."[78]

In a sense, it was contradictory that the makings of an academic career pattern should owe so much to the promotional efforts of "pure" researchers on behalf of research. Most of these men, indeed, shunned the utilitarians' concern with practical professions and vocational pursuits; most of them were only dimly aware of the fact that their conception of the university, to say nothing of their own livelihood, depended on the professionalization of teaching. The research function was institutionalized, however, by administrators who could not be, and almost never were, advocates of "pure" research. In their hands, evidence of original research became an important condition for hiring and promoting faculty, as well as a result that could be shown to legislators, or an enticement for powerful business donors, themselves increasingly interested in the application of science not only to industry but to a wide range of human problems.[79] From the phase of competing ideals emerged an eclectic institutional model in which two conceptions of research coexisted, separated by a blurred and imprecise boundary: the graduate school produced scholarly and scientific research as well as academic professionals for institutions of the same type or colleges of lower rank. Despite temptations to become more scholarly and academic, "the departments of commerce, the schools of engineering, the schools of business administration, tended to perfect the skills required by the industrial and business community. In this second view, research was a public service that originated in a client's need and ended in a client's satisfaction."[80]

The reconciliation of different ideals was facilitated by a feature which the German model, as understood in America, shared with the utilitarian emphasis on vocational training: this was their common insistence on specialization, which "scientific Americans, unlike most scientific Germans, identified . . . with the entire purpose of the university."[81]

From the 1890s on, the fact that the national university had become an integral part of the new social order manifested itself in the tendency toward increasing standardization of its basic features. Undoubtedly, regional and institutional differences persisted, fusing with differences in social environment, class image, and preferred educational orientation.[82] Around 1910, the differences between the Ivy League and the Big Ten or, more broadly, between private and public universities, had crystallized. Yet, for all the differences, institutional competition for place in the national hierarchy of higher education spurred imitation and increased uniformity. Reputation was concretely expressed in size: size of the student bodies, size and "completeness" of the faculty, size of the installations, size of the endowments. As Walter Metzger has put it, "in a vast society strewn across a vast continent," Big Education was bound to rise alongside Big Business, Big Government and, later, Big Labor.[83]

The increase in size promoted the alignment of the university with the bureaucratic managerial model taken chiefly from the industrial corporation. In the period 1880–1910, business leaders became almost everywhere the predominant group on university boards of trustees.[84] More directly important, the foundations that emerged in the first years of the twentieth century—in particular the Rockefeller Institute and the Carnegie Foundation for the Advancement of Teaching—played pivotal roles in the modernization of higher education and professional training along lines that replicated concentration and centralization in the economy. Critics such as Thornstein Veblen or John Jay Chapman bitterly denounced the subordination of higher learning to big business: "The men who stand for education and scholarship have the ideals of business men," declared Chapman in 1909. "The men who control Harvard today are very little else than business men, running a large department store which dispenses education to the millions. Their endeavor is to make it the *largest* establishment of the kind in America."[85]

Chapman exaggerated. Bureaucratization was largely an inevitable consequence of the increase in size, but it was also fostered by the desire for security of the average faculty member, who could not avail himself of the competitive advantages the academic marketplace was bringing to a minority of his colleagues.[86] On the other hand, the university appeared to offer to a rapidly growing number of teachers a refuge, and an alternative to the business world. Increase in numbers meant an increase in autonomy and independence, and business pressures for conformity responded in part to the new measure of power acquired by faculties.[87] The notion that the university was "different" persisted, despite the relative convergence of the institutional model with the corporation and the state apparatus.

This is not the place to assess what this convergence did to intellectual life, how much stifling of originality, repression of creative deviance, and sheer academic dullness resulted from standardization. As Veysey remarks, "the basic pattern of the university, as it clearly revealed itself soon after 1890, was that of a success-oriented enterprise whose less popular possibilities were deliberately blurred in the words and actions of its leading spokesmen. As more Americans began to accept the new institution, occasions for a measured appraisal of the move towards standardization grew fewer and fewer."[88] What matters here is the effect that the emergence of the national university had on the "cosmopolitan" sectors of the intermediate class and on the movement of professionalization.

To the elites of the new middle class, the university provided a common socialization, which preceded, in fact, their rise and assertion in the new social order. As Wiebe remarks, "since the emergence of the modern graduate school in the seventies, the best universities had been serving as outposts of professional self-consciousness, frankly preparing young men for professions that as yet did not exist."[89] The model of university that emerged in the nineties was characterized, among other things, by its openness to new fields of learning and to "professional training . . . in fields that had a genuine but still only potential and undeveloped scientific or scholarly content."[90] The early institutionalization of research careers merged, in America, with the pragmatic and utilitarian orientations imposed upon even the most traditional universities by outside financing; both factors helped the rapid development of applied sciences or "quasi-disciplines." The American university acquired, therefore, centralized and quasi-monopolistic power to sanction many different specialties as legitimate forms of knowledge and expertise.

More concretely, the links that professions, old and new, could establish with the university in time gave all of them an academic wing. Teachers in professional schools, relatively insulated from the pressures of the client or the marketplace, could promote a "purer" brand of professionalism than their practicing colleagues, while working at the same time to develop the cognitive and technical basis of their disciplines. It was in the academic sectors of medicine and, in particular, the law, that not only professionalism but also progressivism found their leading advocates. Since academics normally publish more than practitioners, the academics' views also tended to color the literature of reform and the literature of professionalization, projecting a misleading image of the mood and orientations of the professional rank-and-file. But, despite this discrepancy, the vocational openness of the American university reinforced the tendency toward professionalization. First, this was true because aspiring occupations or less "genteel" professions could realistically strive for university affiliation and hope to emulate the successful path followed by medicine and the law. Second, it was true because "academicization" rapidly increased the influence of university graduates in a field; and, simultaneously, because it gave academic professionals an increasing influence over growing numbers of professional aspirants.[91]

At the beginning of the twentieth century, only a minority of the professional and managerial middle class had passed through the university; but it was a particularly active, cohesive, and significant minority. Concerned with the present, while asserting their confidence in a future of which they had no total image, these men and women formed in the cities nuclei of "cosmopolitanism"—and from these sprang the cadres of modernization.[92] Journalists and editors of newspapers and periodicals played an important role in spreading and unifying their views.[93] Taking advantage of a system of communications which now physically integrated the country, these modern representatives of the intermediate class sought links in other cities and regions with peers of like mind. Indeed, their support for progressive reform carried on, at different levels of the society, the ordering function that state and corporation were performing at the center: the reformers' sectional organizing, as well as the modernization of local institutions which they undertook, were powerful forces of national integration, for they spread the central ideological themes of the new corporate order and established organizational relays between the local and national levels.

In the Progressive Era, sectors of the intermediate class whose self-definition and self-esteem were increasingly based on occupation, and increasingly oriented toward national frames of reference, acquired something akin to class consciousness. Professionalism was one expression of this consciousness.

The strategies of professionalization had been clear for a long time. National professional associations, and often training schools, had been in existence in dentistry, pharmacy, schoolteaching, and architecture since the 1840s and 1850s—that is, before the revival of organization efforts in the older professions toward the last decades of the century. What is interesting is the generalization of these strategies in the 1880s and 1890s, and their use by specialized occupations which in no way shared the market situation of the old "free" professions.

I have argued that the active and "cosmopolitan" sectors of the "new middle class" found both structural and ideological unity in national institutions. Higher education, politics, public service, and concentrated employment in the business corporation and in the state heightened the visibility of these groups. It is unlikely that urban professionals—either in established professions or in the emerging organizational specialties—would have taken the wealth of the Morgans, Vanderbilts, or Rockefellers as their parameter; but, instead, they compared themselves to each other. Income remained the one truly national and unifying criterion of status; yet in the new context of professionalism, income increasingly came to stand for the public recognition granted to special badges of competence—namely, the diplomas and licenses that universities and examination boards were dispensing to the most established professions.

Professions concerned with the administration of the business corporations—such as engineers, accountants, market analysts, and the like—emerged in subordinate markets, subsumed de jure or de facto under bureaucratic and hierarchical organizations. The *ideology* of independent practice, "fee-for-service" consultation, and professional autonomy (as a substitute for the former two) played an important role in the professionalization of these occupations. Yet market control—in the sense of an autonomous monopoly in the provision of expert services—was clearly beyond their reach. This was even more so in "public-service" occupations such as social work, school and college teaching, or school administration: these occupations do not *exchange* services at all with their users, but instead find themselves in situations of preestablished monopoly, entirely determined by the monopolistic expansion of the state into new functional areas.

Market organization and control was therefore a weak dimension of these "new style" professional projects. By the logic of my theoretical interpretation, then, *the dominant, and almost the unique, meaning of these professional movements was the conquest and assertion of social status.* The emergence of an occupation-and-education-centered middle class meant that comparisons tended to be made "upwards" rather than "downwards" by less prestigious or less fortunate occupations: the prizes won by medicine and the law (or by their elites) inspired others. As Wiebe observes, "the exceptional vitality of the new middle class derived in large measure from the very personal benefits its membership bestowed."[94] Not all sectors of the intermediate class could take these benefits for granted. This was the turning point, however, at which the material and moral benefits included in professional status became a "normal" part of the professions' image and of the expectations surrounding professional careers. Adopting—and adapting—the strategies of professionalization fruitfully used by medicine and the law, occupations in structurally different situations sought the rewards of professional status: prestige, as public recognition of collective worth; income, to be translated into respectable middle-class styles of life; and, to defend these rewards, monopolistic closure of access.

The quest for professional status spread as a typical concern of educated middle-class occupations, promising individual advancement through collective efforts. Bureaucratization and educational mobility extended this individualistic promise to the middle class as a whole and even beyond it, to the working class. Progressive reform, indeed, often assumed that the foundation for the moral and economic "uplift" of the masses, as well as for the Americanization of the immigrant, lay in some form of education. This emphasis on education as a social panacea reflects the per-

sistent strength of individualism, stated now in terms of maximizing individual abilities—and individual gains—through collective efforts. At another level, this belief
ideologically denies the effect of class and ethnic barriers, and thus plays a cohesive
role for the heterogeneous middle class itself: access to education, or rather the hope
of individual mobility through education, appears as one common characteristic
shared by large sectors of the intermediate class. At a time when middle strata, old
and new, were being clearly divided into "central" and "marginal" sectors by their
differential access to national centers of power and resources, they maintained certain
common elements of consciousness. A composite ideology, combining old and
new components of bourgeois and petty bourgeois status, old and new legitimations, contributed for a time to conceal the structural fractures within the intermediate
class.

In capitalist society, the central function of ideology is to conceal the existence
of class and the basic structure of exploitation. In the United States, the bourgeois
society par excellence, the concealment of class emphasizes individualism and individual solutions; it typically takes one sector of the intermediate class as exemplar
and as propagator.[95] In the Progressive Era, a new sector or stratum became the
focus of the ideology of classlessness, as a relay to the bypassed farmers and small
entrepreneurs: not coincidentally, this stratum found its main opportunities of advancement in apparently classless organizations, in an apparently neutral State, and
in apparently classless knowledge.

The "quantitative ethic" typical of a capitalist society both expresses and reinforces the role of money as the central indicator of success and social status. The
inflationary period that followed the depression of 1893 exacerbated the concern with
money among wage-earners and status-conscious middle strata. The low level of
emoluments constituted, thus, a major spur to organize, not only among industrial
workers or salaried occupations such as social work and schoolteaching, but for the
"learned professions" as well. The choice of professionalization over unionization
as a strategy of collective mobility, at least in this early phase, is of general significance: professionalism, indeed, makes an important contribution to the ideological
denial of structural inequality.

The tactics of organization adopted by would-be professionals are in many respects similar to those of the craft union. The overall strategy, however, reveals
the professionals' distinctive approach to social stratification. Discussing the contemporary differences between unionization and professionalization, two sociologists remark:

> Instead of engaging in a power contest between haves and have-nots, the [professional]
> association undertakes to protect and expand the knowledge base, enforce standards
> of learning, entry, and performance, and engage in similar activities designed to
> enhance the position of the practitioner while simultaneously purporting to protect
> the welfare of the public in the person of the client. Indeed, professional claims con-
> cerning the primacy of the public good over the practitioner's own private benefit
> might be viewed as a critical difference between the professionalizing and the unioniz-
> ing modes of mobility, were it not for the considerable evidence that the claims are
> watered down with rhetoric.[96]

The union perspective approaches the determination of the price of labor as a conflict between antagonistic and opposing class interests; this, indeed, is one of the dimensions of class consciousness. The institutionalization of business unionism depoliticizes this conflict approach and narrows it down to limited goals and limited institutional settings.[97] The ideological connotations, however, remain different from those involved in the professional project.[98] Appeals to the public interest can be used by unions as well as professional associations; business unionism can justify internal stratification by emphasizing collective identity and solidarity, as much as or more than professional organizations. On the job, however, goals *and* strategies focus exclusively on collective benefits, even if the union members may translate economic incentives into purely individualistic terms. When the ideology that links individual worth to individual "merit" expressed in "badges of competence" becomes *dominant*—when the dominated classes to some extent accept it, consciously and unconsciously—collective gains do not bring a sense of personal empowerment to the individual worker. If, in bourgeois ideology, "the consciousness of human worth is a consciousness *of self as individual, standing out from a mass who seem pretty much the same,*"[99] collective victories do not satisfy the individualistic compulsion to prove oneself "worthy" by one's own means.

As professionalizing occupations move to create and affirm collective worth, one of the incentives for participation, as well as one of the major goals of the movement, is to secure the supports for *individual* dignity and *individual* careers. Income and other indicators of status are important not only in themselves but also in comparison to the status indicators possessed by other social groups and individuals. Likewise, for most professionals, the coveted autonomy over the conditions and the technical content of work is *also* an element of qualitative distinction between professional work and subordinate or proletarian occupations. The expertise in terms of which all this is claimed is *also* a basis on which to exact deference and compliance in personal interaction. Individual differentiation, even though it must be attained within a collectivity and by collective means, is therefore a major promise of the professional project.

Moreover, although professionalization may be seen as "a power struggle, on a societal level," it is a struggle waged within the same class, against rival occupations, rather than across class lines.[100] The struggle on the societal level is largely an ideological battle for recognition, for only through social recognition can personal superiority be securely affirmed. Professionalization, as a movement for status advancement, *must* appeal to general values of the dominant ideology if it is to make its own values acceptable; unions, in their hours of glory, asserted the moral and functional superiority of the working class in terms that necessarily implied the rejection of the social hierarchy and basic values of capitalist society. The socialist movement explicitly asserted collective class identity in terms of the totality of a superior social order; but professions derive an ideology of neutrality from their generalized, "societal" appeal—that is, an ideology which implicitly stresses the classlessness of professionals and, explicitly, the service of the public as a whole.

It has been shown many times, however, that professions and professionalizing occupations address the "public as a whole" only in ideology: traditional professions sought sponsorship from the upper class, and emerging professions seek it today from particular groups in the legislative or executive branches of government. The claims of expertise and altruism made by professions do not have to be substantiated for an "undifferentiated mass," but for "segmental publics . . . such as clients utilizing services or colleagues employed in related tasks and fields, [who] are in a position to recognize the skills of the professional and grant the necessary autonomy."[101] Needless to say, these publics vary from each profession or segment of profession, and are themselves stratified in terms of class, race, gender, and culture.

Chapter 10

PATTERNS OF PROFESSIONAL INCORPORATION INTO THE NEW CLASS SYSTEM

Professionalization generally implies that status is chosen over class as a mode of approaching social reality and acting upon it. This choice is one of the principal roots of the professions' overall conformism with the social order, though by no means the only one. Going from the general background to specific examples, we must consider now how the "model" professions of medicine and the law sought to insert themselves in the upper rungs of the status system.

MEDICINE AND THE COHESIVENESS OF ECONOMIC INTEREST

In the age of laissez faire, American medicine had been particularly weak in organizational resources, by comparison with other professions. Incipiently bureaucratic organizations did not confer upon it the legitimacy of capitalist property, as they did for engineering and the commanding sectors of the law. Nor was medicine unified by an autonomous bureaucratic hierarchy, as were certain branches of the clergy. The elite of physicians—those connected with urban hospitals, public office, or the most reputable medical schools—led the attempts to unify the profession and raise its very low standards in the early part of the nineteenth century, as they did later. But the professional societies did not yet have sufficient power to enforce cognitive unification, which was indispensable in an extremely competitive market.

Thus the profession that would one day come to symbolize unparalleled professional power had, on the average, low standards, low status, low income, and low social credibility as late as the turn of the century. In 1896, "One doctor, writing in the *Pittsburgh Medical Review,* lamented that it was 'humiliating to make a comparison of the economic and social positions of our leading physicians and surgeons . . . with leading lawyers and other professional men.'"[1] While the official *Journal of the American Medical Association* declared in 1905 that "the standing and influence of the medical profession depend on the material success and financial independence of its members,''[2] the average annual income for a general practitioner was in those years between $750 and $1000.[3] What appears to have been more irking than the absolute level of income was the relative status it afforded to the average physician. A 1903 article in *Cosmopolitan* observed, for instance, that the income "of many a medical man who has spent years in acquiring a medical education is often less than that of an ordinary mechanic."[4] The average practitioner also looked toward his most favored colleagues, bitterly complaining about the unequal distribution of income and clienteles in the medical profession. From the 1860s on, the appearance of specialists and of specialty societies had preoccupied the ordinary physician. The A.M.A.'s code of ethics sternly discouraged advertising by specialists, yet by the 1880s there was a recognizable group of specialists in the larger cities: "Shrewd, practical, and often well-educated, these men took up specialties because of the easier work and the more constant hours. Such specialism, entered into from self-interest as much as [for] scientific reasons, posed a threat to general practice both in financial terms and in terms of relative social and professional standing."[5]

At the turn of the century, competition between generalists and specialists in an overcrowded field centered around the rising specialty of surgery. The technical and therapeutical progress in surgery was particularly threatening for a profession which had barely begun to incorporate scientific advances in its average daily practice.[6] In the absence of a formal system of referral and consultation, a purely financial substitute was developing: the practice of splitting fees between surgeons and the doctors who sent them patients spread after 1900, despite official condemnation.[7] While the practice acknowledged the growing division of labor within medicine, it could neither address the general problems of the relation between specialists and ordinary doctors nor solve the overriding and acute problem of competition for patients. The rapid development of hospital clinics and, after 1900, of outpatient departments affected both kinds of doctors and aggravated competition. The number of hospitals in America grew from less than 200 in 1873 to 4,359, with more than 421,000 beds in 1909. The major hospitals had begun to recognize specialties since the 1870s; by 1910, they were adopting a departmental organization. The development of hospitals added to the centrality and importance of the surgeons' role, while giving an increasingly important base of operations to affiliated doctors and "house staff." But it represented a grave threat for the nonaffiliated: as hospital standards improved, large numbers of middle-class patients began for the first time to seek hospital care, attracted, in particular, by the availability of specialty clinics. Outside doctors vociferously argued against this "abuse" which robbed them of paying patients; in many places, they demanded the introduction of a means test for both inmates and outpatients.[8] Their intention was to recapture the middle-class patients who were availing themselves of the cheaper and better medical services provided by modern public hospitals.

Parallel to the development of hospitals, the number of trained nurses had been growing rapidly since the 1870s. "Untrained" nurses and midwives were even more numerous.[9] To this, one should add the permanent competition that chiropractors, health cultists, and empirics offered from outside the regular profession. The average physician had, besides, another reason to worry: with better nutrition, sanitary reforms, public health campaigns, and, after the mid-nineties, the first antitoxins, death rates were steadily declining. The bulk of the profession tended to interpret its mediocre status and income as a sign that its services were becoming dispensable. In this fragmented situation, the "overcrowding" of the medical profession was a general concern shared, for different reasons, by all physicians.

As Abraham Flexner was to point out in 1910, the United States at the end of the nineteenth century had one of the highest doctor-to-population ratios in the world: while Germany had one doctor for 2000 inhabitants and one for 1000 in the large cities, the average ratio was one for 568 in America and one for 400 or less in the major urban centers.[10] Yet, before 1906, the production of doctors did not show any clear signs of abating. On the contrary, the therapeutic successes scored by surgery and bacteriology seemed to attract more and more students to a growing number of schools.[11] Yet, as most doctors understood, overcrowding went hand in hand with the growing stratification of schools and physicians.

In 1871, Harvard Medical School had begun to separate itself from the pack by instituting a mandatory, graded, three-year long course of study and written examinations; it soon followed these reforms by entry requirements which made it practically into a graduate school.[12] Harvard's example was followed, though slowly, by the best and richest schools in the 1870s and 1880s. At the same time, the leading schools were strengthening their ties with hospitals and improving clinical instruction. In 1893, this tendency found a model in the new Medical School of Johns Hopkins, planned around its own teaching hospital.

William Rothstein observes that "the best schools were able to raise their standards because they were not competing directly with the less prestigious ones."[13] Rising entry requirements and rising fees (or tuition) meant that only a socially exclusive body of students would be sought, admitted, and trained at the leading schools. The majority of the medical schools, on the other hand, followed the upgrading move only when forced by state licensing boards, as it began to happen in the nineties: serving lower middle class and working-class students in an increasingly competitive educational market, the average proprietary school could not possibly afford the full-time faculty, the expensive laboratory equipment, or the clinical facilities that were slowly becoming the ideal norm in the upper track. Thus, with the advance of scientific medicine, differences in medical training tended to become more and more closely associated with the class origins of the trainees.

The developments in the best schools brought twenty-two of them together as early as 1876 into the Association of American Medical Colleges. But, unable to enforce the three-year graded curriculum among its own members, the Association suspended its activities six years later; when it reappeared in the 1890s, with much greater strength and better representation, leadership in medical reform was firmly seated in the state medical societies and in the A.M.A. The societies addressed most of their efforts to the state licensing boards, coordinated since 1891 into a national organism. The strategy recommended by Flexner years later was already well delineated in the nineties. As Flexner was to declare, the state boards were "the instruments through which the reconstruction of medical education will be largely ef-

fected. . . . They should go beyond rejection of individuals and close unfit schools.''
For this task, however, it was indispensable that their membership be ''drawn from
the best elements of the profession including—not as now prohibiting—those engaged in teaching.''[14]

In the nineties, the ascendant of these ''best elements''—the largely Eastern elite
of well-trained specialists and full-time scientific faculties—was predominant in the
A.M.A. and growing throughout the country.[15] The isolation of the typical physician
of the 1860s—the private practitioner in a small town or rural area—had been increasingly reduced by the development of proprietary schools and especially by the
growth of county medical societies and medical journals. The *Journal of the A.M.A.*,
first published in 1883, provided a link for the minority who subscribed or read it;
numerous other periodicals, however, contributed to organize the profession and to
diffuse the advances of scientific medicine.[16]

The reorganization of the A.M.A. in 1901 and 1903 took notice of these changes:
the county society became the organizational nucleus of the profession. Membership was open by right to all ''reputable licensed physicians''; for all practical purposes, the invidious distinction between ''regular'' and homeopathic doctors was
being dropped, as it had increasingly been dropped by the physicians themselves.
The county societies and their members belonged automatically to their state society.
The state society sent delegates with voting rights to the legislative body of the
A.M.A. Membership in the national association was thus automatically granted to
all members of county societies, and only to them. After an initial period in which the
A.M.A. was weakened in membership and power by the reforms, its constituent parts
adjusted rapidly to the new, nonsectarian, and vertical organization. Specialists,
initially excluded because they did not normally join county societies, came back into
the fold, needing as they did the political base and the referrals provided by the mass
of general practitioners.[17] By 1910, the A.M.A. membership was over half of the
nation's physicians.

With this new organizational instrument, the elite of scientific doctors rapidly set
itself to the task of educational reform. In 1904 the A.M.A.'s committee on education became the permanent Council on Medical Education: ''Every member was a
researcher and all had appointments at medical schools which had either recently
adopted or were in the process of changing to the scientific model.''[18]

In 1906, the Council surveyed all the medical schools in the country, ranking them
according to diverse criteria: the performance of their graduates in state board examinations; their entry requirements and curriculum; their proprietary ''for profit''
status; and the presence or absence of instructional facilities—full-time faculty for
the preliminary scientific courses, laboratory, dispensary, hospital, library, museum,
and diverse equipment. The effects were immediate: rather than face publication
of the rankings, many commercial schools closed, and others consolidated or sought
university affiliation; homeopathic and eclectic schools were even more adversely
affected than the regular commercial schools. Between 1906 and 1910, the date of
the second inspection by Flexner, the total number of medical schools fell from 162
to 131, a net loss of about 20 percent. The unification of medicine was, therefore,
well advanced before the reform movement culminated in the Flexner report.[19] In

the latter's own words: "Nothing has perhaps done more to complete the discredit of commercialism than the fact that it has ceased to pay."[20] It was paying, in fact, to be a scientifically trained and up-to-date specialist.

From the cognitive and technical point of view, it could be said properly that "scientific medicine was not a triumph for any sect; it was the death of all sects."[21] But medical reform was more than the triumph of scientific medicine. From a larger perspective, it was marked by the same general principles that guided the general movement of reform in the nineties and in the first decades of the twentieth century: centralization, consolidation into larger units, efficient management by experts, and the inevitable accent on technology were visible in the reorganization of the A.M.A. as well as in the recommendations of the Flexner report.

While Flexner followed the lines laid out by the A.M.A.'s Council on Medical Education in 1906, he brought them to a drastic conclusion. As he declared, "the privileges of the medical school can no longer be open to casual strollers from the highway."[22] A preliminary requirement of two years of college was, in his view, indispensable. Medical education proper should consist of a four-year course, closely combined with clinical and laboratory instruction. The "normal and correct form" could only be a "complete school," based on the university and integrated with the latter's scientific departments. The 131 schools in the United States (155, counting Canada) should be cut down to the 31 which were well equipped to teach on modern scientific bases; following population criteria, they were to admit a greatly reduced number of students. The profession faced a twofold problem: to strengthen, on the one hand, the viable institutions and, on the other, "with all the force that law and public opinion can wield, to crush out the mercenary concerns that trade in ignorance and disease."[23]

Flexner's tone, however, was less frequently that of moral indignation than that of dispassionate prescription and rationality. In the language of economics, he concluded "[that] our methods of carrying on medical education have resulted in enormous overproduction at low level, and that, whatever the justification in the past, the present situation in town and country alike can be more effectively met by a reduced output of well trained men than by further inflation with an inferior product."[24] Building on precedent, the Flexner report made it eminently clear that medical reform was but one act in the larger process of rationalization of production which had arisen to meet the anarchy of competition and the excesses of laissez faire. With the decline of apprenticeship, the medical school had become the sole center for the production of physicians. The goal of educational reform was, thus, to standardize this production according to the new scientific norms.

Flexner's prescription—"fewer and better doctors"—became the rallying cry of the profession. Its different wings, however, had divergent goals. The scientific elite worried that American medicine, unless it reorganized teaching and practice, would be incapable of keeping up with the scientific standards of European medicine. Centralization of investment was indispensable to acquire modern equipment, permanent faculties, and research teams. Concentration was dictated by technological— and ultimately financial—imperatives, and also by the scarcity of competent researchers.[25] For these reasons, the scientific doctors had sought the support of the state and of the powerful foundations—such as the Rockefeller Institute, established in 1901 and interested in the modernization of medicine and research, and the Carnegie Foundation for the Advancement of Teaching, which was concerned with the reform of higher education as a whole and the "moralization" of the professions. It was, in fact, to the Carnegie Foundation (untainted by the Rockefeller name) that the A.M.A.'s Council addressed itself for its 1910 study of medical schools. The choice of Flexner, who was not a physician but an educator, and whose views had been formed chiefly at Johns Hopkins and in Germany, contributed to the study's air of impartiality and nonsectarianism. With the implicit leverage of the foundation's subsidy, Flexner obtained information that had never before been made available.

Much more than official sanction and punitive measures, foundation money brought about the implementation of Flexner's recommendations. The leading foundations clearly favored the Northeastern medical establishment: between 1911 and 1936, the Johns Hopkins Medical School got about $10 million of Rockefeller money and $2 from the Carnegie Corporation. Between 1910 and 1938, the nine leading foundations gave more than $154 million to medical schools, most of it going to the best private schools. The Rockefeller General Education Board gave slightly under $66 million to only nine schools.[26]

The large bulk of medical practitioners were neither entirely convinced of the merits of scientific medicine nor reassured by the scientific elite and its powerful allies. However, "they were even more concerned about what they perceived to be the depressed state of the profession, and thus most of them cooperated with the university-based physician in the effort to reform medicine and improve their condition."[27] The "qualitative" argument of the reform leaders—get better doctors—fused, therefore, with the "quantitative" and practical concerns of the rank-and-file—permit fewer doctors and provide more secure incomes. This fusion explains that a profession increasingly stratified by differential access to rewards and resources, and increasingly compartmentalized by specialization, could for a time act in unison behind its elite leadership. While blacks and women, as well as the lower middle class and the sons of workers, found themselves increasingly excluded from the reformed profession, the status of the average physician was considerably improved, as was his income, by the rapidly attained reduction in numbers.[28] The A.M.A. maintained its leadership and increased the institutional unification of the profession: in 1920, 60 percent of American doctors were members. The excellence of the leading schools and research centers put the United States ahead of Germany in medical discoveries in the decade immediately following the Flexner report.[29] The reform movement had indeed been an unparallelled success.

Yet, even as undergraduate medical education was being radically standardized, it was becoming insufficient. In 1913, the A.M.A.'s Council on Medical Education appointed the dean of Harvard's Graduate Medical School to chair a committee on graduate teaching: "This committee, a mere four years after the Flexner report, conceded the inadequacy of a four-year medical course in giving the student any more than the elementary fundamentals in medicine."[30] The problem of how to control graduate education—that is, the education of specialists—was becoming a central one in the profession. The A.M.A.'s Council, faithful to Flexner, favored university-based standardization. Specialist training, however, was centered in hospitals as, indeed, was the internship, which was rapidly becoming the necessary complement to basic training before the licensure. A few national centers, such as the Mayo Clinic, offered serious residencies for training in a specialty; these centers always were university-affiliated hospitals. But, on the large majority of hospitals, neither the A.M.A. nor the universities had much leverage.

In fact, a voluntary organization of specialists—the American College of Surgeons, formed in 1913—had swiftly moved to the leading position in the program of hospital standardization. The College, together with the specialist organizations in ophthalmology, offered an alternative qualification to the licensure or the university degree for specialists: voluntary examinations (or grandfather clauses) would lead the aspiring specialist to a certificate and to membership in a select professional body. The nucleus of the future specialty boards lay in this approach. Each physician, however, was sole master of deciding how much specialization or certification he needed or wanted to get. By 1920, says Rosemary Stevens, "neither the A.M.A., nor the American College of Surgeons, nor the National Board of Medical Examiners nor any other group, had a central, unifying role" with regard to specialist regulation.[31]

Professional endorsement by specialist boards or other groups spread in the 1920s. The specialists insisted that their certificates were not degrees, but marks of distinction which separated the more reputable specialists from the others, for the benefit of the public, as the licenses issued by the medical societies had done before the Jacksonian era. Yet "by attempting to influence hospital trustees only to appoint diplomates to hospital appointments, and by cutting off access to the major societies to those without the certificate, the specialist groups involved were on the way to creating the type of professionally controlled specialist monopoly which already existed in England and other parts of Europe."[32] These attempts correctly assessed the centrality of the hospital for modern medical practice and its potential as regulator and coordinator of medical services.[33]

The general practitioner, however, contemplated even the milder forms of specialist exclusiveness with dismay. For, indeed, if the basic instruction in general medicine was the same for all physicians, specialism relegated him to an unredeemably lower rank. Furthermore, Stevens points out that the general practitioner, by the late 1920s, was seldom "general," having given up major surgery and often obstetrics, otorhinolaryngology, and venereal diseases as well.[34] He was also directly threatened by the rise of the hospital, which often reserved its facilities to its own staff. He was seldom included in the cooperative group practices which spread after World War I.[35] In sum, the general practitioner—the small entrepreneur of medicine—was becoming increasingly marginal. The internal stratification of the profession was reemerging as a source of unresolved tensions.

Yet, something very important had been achieved through educational standardization: as Charles Reed declared in his A.M.A. presidential address of 1901, a new school of medicine had come into being, "the product of convergent influences and diverse antecedents."[36] The scientific basis of medicine and the scientific model of medical training anchored medical practice, for all its diverse and divergent patterns, to a valid cognitive system which appears to transcend human will or whim. In principle, every scientific doctor derived his expertise from the scientific method and founded his practice on universally valid techniques and results. This cognitive frame of reference guaranteed at least a modicum of unity and a partial principle of reconciliation, despite the divisive and contradictory forces emerging from professional practice.

Besides the unified intellectual basis which scientific medicine had attained, there were other factors which worked in favor of the unity of interests that had been contrived during the phase of educational reform, between 1904 and 1918. One factor was the numerical predominance of the generalists and part-time specialists, which lasted until the 1960s: it allowed them to play an inordinately important role in shaping the politics of organized medicine and thus reduced the effects of professional marginality.[37] Another factor was the increasing detachment from the problems of medical practice of the sector which concentrated on research and teaching. A third factor was the common opposition of most private practitioners, be they generalists or specialists, to compulsory health insurance and to anything which, in their eyes, would threaten private practice. Finally, there were the substantial economic benefits which artificial scarcity on the side of supply insured to most physicians, despite the notable differences of income between specialists, between specialists and generalists, and between geographic areas.[38]

In sum, the particular market structure of medicine enabled this profession to incorporate the interests of the large majority of general practitioners and blend them with the different interests of the reform leaders. The attainment of professional monopoly and of cognitive unification depended on this unique combination; the benefits of monopoly outlived the de facto breakdown of the alliance. The free enterprise ideology of the most retrograde sectors of the profession could be channeled by the leading specialist groups and the university or hospital-based elites toward the defense of corporate power: appealing to old liberal principles of legitimacy, the profession as a whole was able to resist governmental or public encroachments upon its power and to oppose, in general, those attempts to rationalize medical care which it could not directly control.

THE LEGAL PROFESSION, EPITOME OF SOCIAL STRATIFICATION

Medicine was unique in deriving intellectual unity and economic advantages for all its members through educational standardization and qualitative upgrading. Even today, internal problems of stratification, specialization, and marginality do not break up the organizational front of the profession. The common defense of monopolistic advantages in a seller's market and the scientific basis of professional expertise contribute to contain the divisive influences. In the law, the next largest of the market-oriented professions, professionalization replicated some of the features of the medical movement: elite practitioners with important corporate clienteles took the leading role in voluntary professional organizations. "It was these men," says Wiebe, "partly to honor themselves, partly to work for higher standards, who in the seventies began organizing city and state bar associations, capped in 1878 by the American Bar Association."[39] Their goal was to institute stricter standards of admission to the bar and to curb what they saw as unprofessional behavior. Law teachers in elite legal schools gave to the reform movement its necessary educational base. Yet elite practitioners and elite educators did not constitute, as in medicine, a unified leadership. Because these two wings of the legal profession needed each other to achieve their objectives, they reached temporary alliances; they did not merge, however, but remained distinct in style and goals and often bitterly opposed to each other.

Fears of overcrowding and complaints that the profession did not provide a decent livelihood ran rampant in the law, as they did in medicine before the 1920s; yet corporate economic defense could not be persuasively used as a unifying factor, for the types of legal practice were too divergent to admit even a common economic interest. Standardization of curriculum was attempted in the law, and the success of this move was not too far behind that of medicine; yet standardization could not be used as a weapon to run the poorer schools out of the field of legal education, nor did it provide a commonly accepted cognitive anchorage. This is in part explained by some general characteristics of the legal profession and of its cognitive base, which I will mention briefly, as a preliminary to the discussion of professionalization in the American case.

In the first place, the cleavages which divide the profession of law are a direct expression of its unique political functions. The judicial system is, of course, a branch of the state. The private practitioners of the law, with whom I will be chiefly concerned, are formally "officers of the court" and, in practice they are much more directly and intimately integrated with the functioning of the state apparatus (or, at least, its judiciary system) than any other professional experts. This special character obviously affects the cognitive basis of the profession. The high value placed on justice and on the maintenance of the social order in most societies gives to the law an appearance of transcendence; but the law is nevertheless a social product, visibly subject to change and open to interpretation, even where it is the most codified. Problems of interpretation of the law represent, in a sense, an institutionalized measure of cognitive dissensus. They constitute the core of professional practice and are ultimately resolved by public officials, be they judges or legislators. Political authority therefore permeates the cognitive base of the profession. As Talcott Parsons has noted, this immediately differentiates authority in the law from the presumption of certainty that surrounds scientific authority or the dogmatic pronouncements of "infallible" institutions such as, most conspicuously, the Catholic Church.[40]

Moreover, substantive conceptions of justice differ and often clash; they cannot always be directly identified with the interests of particular social groups or organizations, but their distribution is obviously not random: most social conflicts, latent or overt, revolve around issues of substantive justice. Conversely, when a system of law is relatively unified and generally accepted, conflict between individuals, groups, and organizations is routinely handled and absorbed by the judicial system. Formal rationalization of the law, in all its various forms, always tends to reduce the visible arbitrariness of adjudication and to relegate issues of substantive justice to an extralegal domain of social life.

Weber has shown the determinant influence of the form of political authority on legal rationalization. Although the process of legal rationalization differs in centralized bureaucratic states and in societies which emphasize indirect governmental regulation and contractual relationships, both bureaucratization and modernization on a laissez-faire model accelerate the formal rationalization of the law.[41] Different strata of jurists play, in each case, the central role: "Depending upon who are the leaders of a particular movement," says Weber, "the results favor either the prestige of 'science,' *i.e.* of the legal scholars or that of the practitioners."[42]

But in all cases, rationalization increases the power and prestige of an elite of jurists and adds to the appearance of autonomy and impartiality of the legal profession as a whole. The movement toward formal justice—that is, abstract and universalistic principles of legal adjudication—is supported, on one hand, by those who oppose authoritarian control in the name of freedom and individual rights and, on the other hand, "by those who wield the economic power at any given time and who are therefore interested in its unhampered operation."[43] In modern capitalist societies, legal formalization appears to establish an affinity of orientation between those who direct the economy according to principles of functional rationality and the class of lawmen. At the same time, the lawyers' emphasis on a procedural conception of justice tends to separate them from the substantive definitions implicitly held by other segments of the public.

Because the legal profession mediates the institutionalized resolution of conflict, its expertise and its livelihood directly depend on the stability and legitimacy of a given institutional and legal framework. In the wider sense of the word, the legal mind is therefore inherently conservative. As Tocqueville remarked, the predominance of customary law adds to this conservatism "a taste and a reverence for what is old . . . almost always united with a love of regular and lawful proceedings." The complexity of a legislation founded on precedent accentuated, for Tocqueville, the nonrational aspects of legal knowledge, while making the expertise of the lawyer more indispensable to the layman than in legal systems based on codified statutes:

> The absolute need of legal aid that is felt in England and in the United States, and the high opinion that is entertained of the ability of the legal profession, tend to separate it more and more from the people and to erect it into a distinct class. The French lawyer is simply a man extensively acquainted with the statutes of his country: but the English or American lawyer resembles the hyerophants of Egypt, for like them he is the sole interpreter of an occult science.[44]

This social and intellectual ascendancy explained the political role of lawyers in American society: the visible and invisible influence of this "aristocratic element" balanced "democratic instincts" with its own conservatism, shaping the whole of social and political life.[45]

Tocqueville attributed to the American legal profession a unity and prestige which only its elites enjoyed. Regardless of the system of law, it appears true that the democratic form of government, the extension of contractual relations, and the acceptance of litigation as a normal part of life increased the private demand for legal expertise and the emphasis placed on the partisan loyalty of counsel to client in American society. By comparison with other countries, these factors in part account for the predominance of private practitioners in the American legal profession.[46] Partisan legal expertise was, and still is, chiefly needed by the propertied classes and chiefly available to them. Closely involved in the defense of economic interests, the lawyer naturally became the subject of public opprobrium, especially in times of economic crisis.

In sum, the cognitive basis of the legal profession articulates "transcendent" values which are, in fact, backed by the force of the state. But despite its connection with a "transcendent" zone of the dominant ideology, this cognitive basis cannot appear to be as immune to class interests as, for instance, the scientific basis of medicine or engineering. This is precisely because the law in bourgeois democracies is made and changed as a result of institutionalized conflicts of interest, even if the class connotations and origins of these conflicts are not readily perceptible. It follows that the cognitive basis of the legal profession is only as "objective" as the state itself appears to be "neutral," that is to say, above *all* classes. As Weber has shown, "the formalism and the rule-bound and cool 'matter-of-factness' of bureaucratic administration" and "expertness" support rationalization in the law and increase its appearance of objectivity.[47]

It is therefore not coincidental that the American legal profession should have decisively moved toward professionalization in the Progressive Era. The bureaucratization of the state apparatus, the movements for civil service reform, and the articulation of legitimacy principles which emphasized the role of expertise all contributed to establish the state's "neutrality."[48] This, in turn, created a favorable ideological climate for the legal profession's assertion of neutrality and independence.

Parsons notes that the dependence of lawyers on political authority is balanced by their dependence on clients, and that both are checked by independent professional institutions.[49] It is true that most officers of the court, at least in civil law, do not directly depend on the state for their income; but the fact that their fees are paid by private parties makes them suspiciously dependent on their clientele. We need to examine here how each of these factors of professional "independence" from the state—clients, bar associations, and law schools—have evolved since the 1870s and what resources each has contributed to the professionalization movement.

The organic connection of the legal profession with the propertied class, and in particular with organizational clients, had been a source of internal differentiation and specialization in the profession since the days of Jackson. The rise and consolidation of a national economic elite placed more and more power in the hands of the lawyers' corporate clients. Parallel to the process of concentration and centralization of capital were changes in the mode of practice of the best business lawyers. The shift from litigation in court to counseling and negotiation was one of the most important changes. Today, this move away from the trial court affects to a certain extent all lawyers, depending on the size of their firm and on that of the city where they practice; the tendency can be observed even in criminal law, where plea bargaining now heavily predominates over jury trials.[50]

The preventive use of counsel became first visible in the largest business firms: after 1870, says James W. Hurst, the general counsel for the railroads became the paramount symbol of professional success.[51] The new type of lawyer did not limit himself to technical counseling. First of all, elite lawyers used their skills to articulate the legal framework needed by the new business system. To the corporate economy, lawyers contributed specific tools (such as the equipment trust certificate and the trust receipt), institutional models (such as the corporation), and patterns of action for adapting financial and price structures to a national market. By comparison, other areas of the law remained relatively undeveloped. Secondly, his mastery of largely uncharted fields and his clients' respect for his opinions gradually led the business lawyer into extralegal decision-making and economic planning. Railroad general counsel, followed by the counsel for investment bankers, inaugurated the role of the lawyer as corporate director; from the 1880s on, lawyers became a permanent fixture on corporate boards.

Following the needs of their business clients and the model they set, law firms themselves grew larger and, at the top, fewer. Partnerships had tended to replace solo practice since the 1820s, but the metropolitan firm with a large staff developed in our century.[52] The practice of these firms is as wide in geographic scope as their clients' business; their regional concentration, mainly in Wall Street and Chicago, was and remains extreme. Most of their work occurs out of court and is highly specialized. What had been only incipient trends toward specialization before the Civil War became in the 1870s and 1880s well-defined specialties in patents, industrial consolidations, real estate, insurance, taxation, and the like. Specialization accentuates today, as it did then, the fragmentation and disunity of the profession.

The rise of corporate clients was the major factor in the rise and affirmation of an elite of business lawyers. The expanding role of government and the growth of legislation affecting the corporation meant, in turn, that one major function of the legal elite became that of guiding their clients through regulations and of representing them before government through lobbying or negotiation. In sum, the elite of the profession provided services that were not strictly (and often not even remotely) legal services for a class of particularly powerful and wealthy clients. That this elite of lawyers should act as broker for the corporation in dealing with government compromised the image of the profession—not only directly, but also indirectly, because influence brokerage is bound to raise diffuse doubts about the "neutrality" of the state and therefore jeopardize the "objective" and universalistic appearance of the law.

Elite business lawyers, joined in some cases by prominent law teachers, led the movement of professional organization, starting in 1870 with the bar association of New York City, which was primarily aimed against the corruption of the Tweed city machine. Seventy-five lawyers, meeting at the fashionable resort of Saratoga in New York State, founded the American Bar Association eight years later. The avowed aim of these successful lawyers was to make the profession more respectable, and we shall see presently what this meant in their eyes. But the image of autonomous competence and impartiality sought by professionalization movements was bound to improve the corporate lawyers' own image, by strengthening their claim that they could maintain an independent position vis-à-vis their powerful clients.

The leading practitioners in the exclusive bar associations—a mere 1.3 percent of lawyers belonged to the A.B.A. in 1900, and not many over 9 percent in 1920— could not carry on the task of professionalization by themselves.[53] National law schools had developed since the Civil War, parallel to the development of corporate law practice.[54] From 1870 to 1895, the deanship of Christopher Langdell turned Harvard Law School into a model of legal education: the course of training was immediately lengthened from one and a half to two years, and then to three in 1899. Strict examinations were instituted on admission and during training. In 1896 an undergraduate degree became a requisite for entering the law school, a requirement which did not become effective until 1909 and did not begin to be followed by other leading law schools until 1916. The curriculum of Harvard Law School was revised in the Langdell period and made strictly professional; the hours of instruction increased but the number of subjects taught was drastically cut. Last but not least, Langdell developed the scientific approach to the law and the case method for teaching the new "science." In his eyes, law belonged in the university because it was a science, otherwise its teaching could well be left to apprenticeship. As Langdell declared, "all the available materials" of the science of law "are contained in printed books."[55] Its principles, more general than the law of each of the states, were to be found in the study of appellate court opinions. The "Socratic method" used in Harvard law classes aimed at discovering the core elements of the common law and the judicial deviations from these relatively few principles. In sum, the Harvard approach laid the basis for standardization of legal training.

By 1890, the case method penetrated Columbia University's law school, an encroachment which led to the resignation of its dean, Theodore Dwight, Langdell's rival in intellectual distinction. All the leading schools sooner or later adopted the case method. By 1900, "Langdell and [his successor, James Barr] Ames had seen the emergence of a remarkable uniformity in curricula" and we may add, in pedagogic approach.[56] The case method had severe limitations, which I cannot enter into here. As it evolved in different law schools, it admitted more and more the variety and complexity of the law, leading teachers to stress "the power of legal reasoning" more than the discovery of core "scientific" principles in the law. By the first decade of our century, with the modified case approach, "orthodoxy had finally been established" in the national law schools.[57] As Alfred Z. Reed prepared his 1921 report on legal education, the case method had extended far beyond this elite circle, to the proprietary law schools and even to the part-time night schools where, Reed believed, the students had neither sufficient previous training, nor time to prepare the cases, nor guidance from competent teachers. Deploring this pseudo-homogeneization, Reed remarked on the pattern it had followed: "One or two leading schools developed a curriculum which, in more or less modified form, is copied by other schools throughout the country. The bar examiners recognize this as orthodox, and build their own examinations upon it. Subsequently established schools can do nothing else than conform to this model."[58] By analogy with Flexner's recommendations for medicine, this should have been all to the good. Reed showed, however, why this standardization was neither practical nor even desirable in the law. But let us return for the moment to the elite law schools and examine what they contributed to legal professionalization, besides a model for the standardization of training.

In 1873, James B. Ames, without any experience in legal practice, was appointed assistant professor at Harvard Law School. As President Eliot of Harvard was to remark twenty years later, "it was an absolutely new departure in our country in the teaching of law."[59] A new vocation—academic law teaching—had, in fact, been created. At the turn of the century, no more than a quarter of law professors in the rapidly expanding field of legal education were full-time teachers.[60] They were, however, a most significant minority: they provided, in fact, a counter-elite to the professionalization movement. The old enmity between theorists and practitioners, each trying to shape the production of professionals according to its own educational conceptions, became more clearcut with the development of the Harvard approach and the growth of a new kind of professional consciousness among the teachers at national law schools.

Jerold Auerbach suggests that the double marginality of the academic lawyers—both within the profession and within the university, where they had "transacademic responsibilities not shared by their liberal arts colleagues"—may have inclined a large number of them to embrace the cause of Progressive reform: "It seems evident," he writes, "that the conjunction of two developments—the professionalization of law teaching and the nationalization of public issues within a reform setting—provided law teachers with their distinctive identity."[61] After 1910, says Hurst, original contributions to the field of public administration started coming forth, especially from the academic branch of the legal profession.[62] At the same time, a new image of the profession had been articulated by eminent law teachers: the success of a lawyer could not be measured by how much money he made; the real duty of the bar was toward the community; its real mission was public service, and the adaptation of the law to social reform. Louis Brandeis could see academic law teaching "as a fulcrum in efforts to improve the law and through it—society." Coherently with his position, he required to be "satisfied of the justness" of a client's case before accepting it.[63] Roscoe Pound, in turn, called for "a true sociological jurisprudence" which would found legal doctrine on "a scientific apprehension of the relations of law to society and of the needs and interest and opinions of society of today."[64]

The period from 1895 to 1915 was a formative one for the new profession of law teaching. Within it, ideological leadership was seized by the most vocal group, that is, the reformers who appointed themselves "keepers of the professional conscience," responsible for the proper socialization of the profession's best recruits and future leaders. Progressivism called these men into public service, and it insulated them from the compromising connections of the legal marketplace. Many law students and many lawyers welcomed these alternative careers "with a sense of release."[65]

This new sense of responsibility could not be entirely welcome to the elite of corporate lawyers who, since the nineties, had successfully challenged the constitutionality of the Federal income tax and vehemently opposed, among other things, the Progressive campaign for judicial recall, the first workmen's compensation act and, in 1916, the nomination of Brandeis to the Supreme Court.[66] In the first two decades of our century, this undercurrent of deep political disagreement increasingly colored the relationships between elite law teachers and elite practitioners both inside and outside professional organizations, complicating the divergent conceptions of professional upgrading which had become apparent since earlier years.

The A.B.A. had initiated the move for higher standards of admission to the bar in the early eighties, at a time when only a few jurisdictions prescribed a formal period of study, either in law office or in law school, before admission to the bar examination.[67] While the A.B.A. required only high school graduation of its members (until 1921), it consistently pressed for equivalence between office apprenticeship and law school training and for longer courses of instruction in the schools. Since the late seventies, furthermore, examination boards had replaced the state supreme courts as the gatekeepers of the bar. These boards were controlled by local or state bar associations, which fought for strong requirements, written examinations, and centralized boards. By 1917, the boards of bar examiners were centralized in thirty-seven out of forty-nine jurisdictions; thirty-six of the latter required a formal period of training; attendance at a law school, however, was not yet required in any state.[68]

During this time, the A.B.A. had entertained ambivalent relationships with the law schools: since the nineties, it had opposed them on the issue of "diploma privilege," which gave to the graduates of certain schools automatic accession to the bar.[69] And it had watched with great misgivings the increasing independence of its own creature, the Association of American Law Schools, organized in 1900 by the A.B.A. section on Legal Education, under the prodding of the law teachers' lobby. The A.A.L.S. soon asserted its educational elitism: after 1907, only schools with three-year programs were admitted as members; after 1912, only those with predominantly day programs; by 1916, barely 40 percent of all American law students were in A.A.L.S. schools. In 1914, feeling slighted by the A.B.A. and miffed by its uncooperative attitude, the A.A.L.S. started meeting separately; the two bodies did not come back together until 1920.[70] By then, World War I and its aftermath had placed the issue of qualifications for the bar in a clearer focus.

In the efforts to upgrade the profession, there had always been present a nativist and racist bias which could become quite explicit—as, for instance, in 1909, when the A.B.A. "approved a rule excluding aliens from the bar."[71] The fight for higher standards was aimed in principle against incompetence, crass commercialism, and unethical behavior; but it was clear in the language of the leaders of the bar that "the poorly-educated, the ill-prepared, and the morally weak candidates" meant chiefly those growing numbers of the metropolitan bars who were foreign-born, of foreign parentage, and, most pointedly, Jews.[72]

Before the war, small-town lawyers had opposed the professionalization movement, seeing it as another ploy of the corporation and its legal servants to "push them to the wall." This kind of lawyer, says Hofstadter, saw that "much of his work was taken from him by real-estate, trust and insurance companies, collection agencies and banks, which took upon themselves larger and larger amounts of what had once been entirely legal business."[73] After 1918, xenophobia, heightened by the patriotic fervor of the war years, reconciled the small-town lawyer of unreproach- ably Anglo-Saxon origins with the idea of professional upgrading.

Elite corporate lawyers, in turn, had gained in public stature from their unques- tioning cooperation with the war effort.[74] They were now in a better position to lead the attack on the "enemy within." In Auerbach's words, "patriotic nationalism, xenophobia, reinforced by postwar nativism and anti-radicalism, washed away the stain of social obloquy from corporation lawyers and transferred the taint to attor- neys from ethnic minority groups."[75] In a profession which is part of the state and traditionally serves as a stepping-stone into politics, higher educational standards could be used not only to restrict access to the bar by blacks, immigrants, Jews, and radicals but also to limit their political participation. The A.B.A. leaders were now ready to join the academics' battle; in 1920, furthermore, common opposition to Alfred Z. Reed's controversial report on legal training solidified their alliance against "the night law schools and the immigrants who crowded into them."[76]

This outcome of Reed's investigation was unintended and ironic. When the A.B.A. requested it from the Carnegie Foundation in 1913, it had hoped to emulate the impressive success of the Flexner report and to obtain the means for running the poorer schools out of legal education. Reed fully acknowledged that there was an obvious hierarchy among the law schools;[77] but, far from recommending the elimi- nation of the part-time schools, he urged the leaders of the profession to help them. His argument was cogent and clear: because the law was a public and eminently polit- ical profession, its doors could not be restrictively closed in a democracy. From that point of view, the night law schools were, indeed, coal to the fire under the American "melting pot" and a necessary democratic institution. But it was a fiction to main- tain that there was, or could be, a unitary bar: "Under the notion that there is such a thing as 'a' standard lawyer, radically different educational ideals are brought into conflict with one another, to their mutual injury; this in face of the fact that they pro- duce radically different types of practitioners. To begin with, the night schools are damaged by the obligation placed upon them to cover the same curriculum as the day schools."[78] The day schools, especially the leading ones, were understand- ably reluctant "to enter into what, from a scholarly point of view, is low-grade work." The answer was, in his eyes, to acknowledge realistically both the require- ments of science and the requirements of democracy, and to accept a differentiated bar: "If law school graduates enjoyed different privileges in the practice of the law, corresponding to the differences in educational effort between full-time and part- time work, the two types instead of rivaling could supplement one another."[79] In other words, Reed proposed to institutionalize what actually existed.

A.B.A. and A.A.L.S. leaders persisted, instead, in their efforts to drive the night schools out and to prevent their graduates from even taking the bar examination. After Reed's recommendations, they could add to their arguments the rhetoric of egalitarianism: for, indeed, what could be more odious to the American tradition than a divided bar, suggestive of the long-abolished English model? The democratic way to upgrade and dignify a profession was by homogeneization and standardization, as it had been similarly argued in medicine. A special committee, chaired by Elihu Root, had come out of the A.B.A.–A.A.L.S. joint meeting in 1920; it offered its recommendations one year later, at the Washington Conference on Legal Education, in the midst of the furor provoked by Reed's report.[80] The compromise that resulted established the undisputed educational leadership and controlling influence of the university schools: two years of college were to be required for admission to law school; the night school would be tolerated, provided that it offered a four-year program; the A.B.A.'s Council on Legal Education would have accrediting power with regard to the schools; all graduates should take the bar examination, but this privilege should henceforth be reserved to those who had attended law school. It was repeatedly argued during the proceedings that every energetic and perseverant young man could struggle his way through college and fulfill the A.B.A.'s requirements, with the clear implication that only the shiftless and lazy would not do so.[81]

The immediate results fell short of the A.B.A.'s intentions. The long-term outcome of the professionalization effort was, however, irreversible: the law school had become the center for the production of lawyers.[82] In the decisive year of 1921, the organized legal profession had, in fact, left to the highly accessible and highly stratified American educational system the task of reconciling the insoluble problem of internal stratification in the profession with the ideology of democratic egalitarianism.

Production and transmission of legal knowledge do not require the expenditures which, in medicine, justified the concentration and consolidation of training facilities. Also, practical experience is more important in legal teaching, especially in the Anglo-Saxon law, than it is in professions based on scientific paradigms: it was therefore hard to exclude practitioners and impose full-time faculties on the law schools.[83] Yet standardization of requirements continued apace, extending A.A.L.S. standards to "middle-grade schools," bringing new schools into the "national" category, and gradually driving out, in most places, the schools unaccredited by the A.B.A.–A.A.L.S.[84]

The apparent success of standardization does not make the profession any less fragmented: legal specialties are closely related to the status of a lawyer's clientele; both specialization and stratification appear to be associated with the prestige of a lawyer's school. These segments are separate and often impenetrable to each other.[85] Access to particular clienteles and to their particular legal problems is a condition for access to whole areas of legal knowledge; in consequence, "stratified" professional experience projects internal stratification (which closely replicates that of the society at large) upon the profession's cognitive basis, in a manner that no standardization of schools or requirements can modify. The field of recruitment is wide; but the educational system reproduces its hierarchical and heterogeneous character at every step.[86]

Today, a handful of large legal firms in Wall Street set the model throughout the country for the law firms that deal with corporate business.[87] These firms compete for the graduates from the top national law schools and in ordinary times, at least, they get their pick: the expanding forms of publicly supported legal aid may attract some of the most socially conscious graduates from this elite; service in one of these top national firms does not appear to hinder, however, access to high-level appointive office. It considerably helps, on the other hand, further careers in the big corporations' own legal departments or in other top-level corporate firms. Competition for the ''best men'' among these firms ''helps perpetuate an imbalance in the distribution of lawyers throughout the country, at the same time that this concentration of lawyers helps recruit and retain big business clients.''[88]

The quality of the law school attended is the best predictor of the type of practice a lawyer will have.[89] Because this is also the principal criterion of selection applied by the top-level law firms, they have since the Second World War let in some Catholic and Jewish graduates from the best and most exclusive law schools. In their selection of associates and partners, however, the top firms seek more secure methods of perpetuating the style which their powerful clients expect and trust in their lawyers: they apply, ordinarily, combined criteria of academic achievement, lineage, and personality.[90]

The composition of the lower rungs of the legal profession is a corollary of the class and status criteria applied in recruitment to the higher echelons. Solo practitioners predominate, representing still about 60 percent of all lawyers.[91] Typically, these independent practitioners appear to seek in a law career a substitute for the old entrepreneurial dream: the law is, indeed, one of the few ''independent'' avenues of social mobility which one can hope to follow without much initial capital or investment.

A study of solo lawyers, which compares them with their counterparts in large firms, finds that the former come predominantly from small entrepreneurial families, of Southern, Central, or Eastern European origins; most have studied in part-time schools. In metropolitan areas, these lawyers tend to constitute an ''ethnic bar,'' ''centered around ethnic legal associations, the local courts, and local politics, and . . . characterized by many mediocre performers competing for the same bread-and-butter cases.''[92]

Most solo lawyers—about 90 percent—tended to find in the law the ''orderly job pattern'' and the security they had presumably sought. But, in fact, the entrepreneurial dream of the ethnic solo lawyers did not take them very far: the different careers of solo and large firm lawyers appear, in fact, as the clear consequence of the segregated and stratified areas which the clientele's social position defines in legal practice. At the bottom—and even at the middle levels—of private legal practice, competition for clients is severe. In the thirties, when ''overcrowding'' became a matter of acute concern in the profession, a study found that the legal needs of the vast majority of the population are seldom, if ever, served. Not surprisingly, the experiments providing lower-cost legal services that started in the thirties met with resounding success.[93]

Competition and partisan loyalty to the client tend to generate the kind of violation of ethics that is publicly deplored by the organized profession. The stereotypes of the ''ambulance chaser'' and of the lawyer who espouses the unethical business practices of his clients contain no reference to the subtle or, at least, hidden violations of law and public interest that occur in corporate legal practice.[94] Where the volume of legal practice and the amount of fees are both substantial and secure, professional solidarity and at least the appearance of professional behavior are easier to maintain. At the top levels of the bar, traditional criteria of lineage and "style" are deliberately added to the brutal selectivity of the stratified educational system, keeping these choices preserves socially, ethnically, and politically homogeneous. "Overdiscrimination" by race, religion, and sex perpetuates the traditional mechanisms of professional exclusiveness, superimposing them on the meritocratic mystifications of the educational system.[95]

In conclusion, we may say that the two largest and oldest professions, medicine and the law, show two different resolutions of the internal stratification problem and two different modes of insertion into the class system. In each case, structure and function determined strategy: medicine found a principle for reconciling its internal cleavages because it was capable of spreading substantial economic benefits across its fragmented and stratified market. In return, the interests of the small medical "entrepreneurs" have to be respected, at least apparently, by the profession's elites. The law, lacking effective means for claiming the global solidarity of its membership, segregated from each other its most different areas of practice. In both cases, the average independent professional "entrepreneur" is relegated to a marginal position: power and influence flow, in these professions as in society at large, from the state, the corporation, and the national university.[96] These two powerful professions are among the most attractive to the stubborn believers in the receding bourgeois ideology of independence.[97] One of their accessory contributions to the dominant ideology may well be that of maintaining, without too much *actual* encouragement, the flickering flame of the entrepreneurial dream.

Chapter 11

PROFESSION AND BUREAUCRACY

The generalized tendency toward professionalization is commonly seen as one of the characteristic features of the occupational structure in advanced industrial societies. This tendency is part of a complex transformation which is typically seen to involve:

> (1) . . . decreasing occupational specialization with an increasing proportion of professionals and technicians in the labor force, (2) . . . a status-assignment system in which contribution in one's field is a major status criterion and gaining professional recognition an increasingly important mobility pattern, (3) . . . a system of power in which the professional is increasingly dominant, and (4) . . . a class structure in which there is decreasing class cleavage with class distinctions based upon access to education.[1]

This description is imbued with a questionable optimism about the evolution of work—that is, about the autonomy and responsibility actually attached to formally upgraded jobs—and about the social effects of mass education. However, its most general implications can hardly be questioned: the multiplication and apparent generalization of professional roles are related to deep changes in class structure and in ideology.

With oversimplification, two main tendencies can be made accountable for the structural changes in the stratification system: one is the tendency of the organic composition of capital to change, with the consequence that science and technology are ever more closely integrated with the productive process and labor is released from industrial production. The other tendency, related to the former but analytically distinct, is the diffusion of the bureaucratic mode of organization.

THE GROWTH OF ORGANIZATIONAL PROFESSIONS

The predominant role of applied science and technology generates new professions or, rather, new specialties, as well as new demands for the application of "old" knowledge and skills.[2] These skilled and highly specialized functions tend to emerge in the monopoly and in the state sectors of the economy, while the relatively autonomous evolution of basic research generates new fields and new disciplines that are essentially contained in the university.

The intimate relation of both new specialties and old professions with central organizations does not bring them, however, into the category of "organizational professions." Bureaucratic or large-scale organization appears to be a prerequisite for the varieties of engineering or chemistry, or for medical auxiliary specialists such as laboratory, anaesthetic, and radiology technicians; the appearance of these kinds of specialized occupations, however, can ultimately be explained in terms of the growing differentiation of knowledge and functions, even if they are contained by and inherently subordinate to large-scale heteronomous organizations.

All professions depend to a certain extent on large organizations and on the state—if nothing else, because all have a teaching arm. All professions are, today, bureaucratized to a greater or lesser extent. Organizational professions should not be seen, therefore, as sharply distinct from older and more independent professions, but as clearer manifestations of tendencies also contained within them.

Organizational professions proper are *generated* by heteronomous bureaucracies, and primarily by the expansion of the bureaucratic apparatus of the state. Given the difference between the state bureaucracy and the general phenomenon of bureaucratization, two categories can be analytically distinguished. The first category is generated by the concentration of administrative and managerial functions under corporate capitalism. Hospital administrators, "professional" business administrators, management analysts, school superintendents, college presidents and the like illustrate this type. Here, the claim of specialized or "professional" expertise for technobureaucratic functions which are unspecific and polyvalent does not aim at asserting independent professional status; rather, it borrows from the general ideology of professionalism to justify technobureaucratic power.[3] Significantly, subordinate professionals are included among the relevant publics to which this claim is addressed.

The second category derives directly from the expansion of the state's functions and attributions. Teaching at all levels, counseling of different types in public or semipublic agencies, social work, librarianship, city planning, and museum curatorship are essentially connected with education, welfare, and regulatory mechanisms "in the service of the public," even if these functions may be fulfilled by private institutions of charity or culture. For these aspiring occupations, the claim of expertise—sanctioned by external sources of credentialing—represents a possibility of acquiring countervailing power vis-à-vis the bureaucratic hierarchy of the organizations within which they are contained.

The two categories of organizational profession are therefore distinguished from one another by their different use of expertise. Another major kind of differentiation derives from the presence or absence of a client orientation. Different kinds of client orientation typically distinguish different professions and different *professional types* within the "public service" category. *Individual* careers within this category may lead to technobureaucratic positions: teachers may become principals and pass, from there, to positions in the district-wide administration; academics may become deans or even college presidents; social workers may become department heads in a welfare bureaucracy. The accessibility of technobureaucratic statuses in the hierarchy, combined with the differences or similarities in client orientation, define the legitimacy of administrative professionals vis-à-vis their rank-and-file professional subordinates. Conversely, these two factors also play an important part in determining the potential for conflict between the two professional categories in public-service bureaucracies.

Two organizational professions will provide illustrations for the brief discussion that follows. One of these—social work—is "purely" related to public service, at first in private philanthropies, now predominantly in state agencies. The other—school superintendency—is a mixed case. On the one hand, it is generated by the state's expanding functions; its members often took the leadership in promoting the monopoly of a given organizational form—the bureaucratized urban school system. Their professional advancement, on the other hand, appears less as a function of negotiated cognitive exclusiveness than as a function of their hierarchical position in a bureaucracy. For this reason, school superintendency exhibits technobureaucratic traits; it is astride of the two categories—"techno-bureaucratic" and "public service"—which obviously share many characteristics. In conclusion, I shall attempt to set out, by contrast, the "purer" traits of technobureaucratic "professions."

PROFESSIONAL USES OF EXPERTISE
IN HETERONOMOUS ORGANIZATIONS

The main instrument of professional advancement, much more than the profession of altruism, is the capacity to claim esoteric and identifiable skills—that is, to create and control a cognitive and technical basis. The claim of expertise aims at gaining social recognition and collective prestige which, in turn, are implicitly used by the individual to assert his authority and demand respect in the context of everyday transactions within specific role-sets.[4] "Regular" medicine claimed superior expertise—as did its rivals—when, in fact, there was little in its cognitive basis that was more effective, more scientific, or more identifiable than in competing "arts of healing." Thus, the observation is inaccurate: "In the recent history of professionalism, the organization push comes often before a solid technical and institutional base is formed; the professional association, for instance, typically precedes university-based training schools, and the whole effort seems more an opportunistic struggle for the rewards of monopoly than a natural history of professionalism."[5] In fact, professional associations emerged in the *older* professions before university training could have meant effective and specific instruction—before, that is, the successful movements for curricular reform in the second half of the nineteenth century. Moreover, the "rewards of monopoly" are an integral part of every professional project; to imply that they were not important in the "natural history" of professionalism" is to equate the latter with the ideological self-presentation of the older learned professions. I have argued instead that the cognitive basis is both an element of the structure of profession and one crucial resource which affects the outcome of professionalization as well as the choice of compensatory strategies. Their cognitive resources gave engineers a measure of independence, despite their close subordination to large-scale organizations and to the business cycle. The same capacity allegedly gave accountants the possibility of asserting their "neutrality" or "objectivity" on the model of the older learned professions and of gaining for the Certified Public Accountant a degree of professional emancipation from the large corporation.[6]

To command a cognitive basis is just as important for professions which do not move at all in a free market of services, but are circumscribed by the institutions in which they practice. Thus, if we disregard for one moment the significant differences in the status of their respective clienteles, social workers and university teachers can be considered to be in analogous structural situations: both function in institutional settings which guarantee, as it were, a demand for their services. Both receive their income (or the largest part of it) from the organization. Authority over the clients depends in both cases on organizational power as much as it depends on the power of expertise. But the university has a general monopoly over cognitive resources that can claim legitimate superiority in the society at large: this gives academics an obvious advantage in the assertion of autonomy and in the justification of their authority vis-à-vis "student-clients" and administrators.

According to its principal historian, the professionalization of social work hinged on the assertion of cognitive exclusiveness: "More than any other category of social workers, caseworkers believed that they had at least the beginnings of a scientific knowledge base as well as a specialized skill, technique, and function, which differentiated them from the layman or the volunteer."[7] As could be expected, caseworkers became the spokesmen and leaders for social work's aspirations to professional status. In the major cities, groups of practitioners moved toward the establishment of formal training programs that already existed. Even though social workers were not required to graduate from the new schools, these schools, "like the associations . . . helped shape social work as a profession in the image of casework, and at least provided an alternative mode of entry into the professional group—an alternative which social work leaders stressed as the swiftest, most direct, and most opportune channel of advance for those who chose social work as a career."[8] With this institutional basis for the standardized "production of producers," social-work leaders could then press for an upgrading of membership requirements in the American Association of Social Workers and use the Association of Professional Schools of Social Work to obtain further standardization.[9]

The assertion of cognitive exclusiveness was a distinctive and prototypical expression of the professionalization movement, but in social work the onset of this movement was not entirely autonomous: the first stirrings of professionalization came, in fact, from the reorganization of charitable societies along the lines of "scientific philanthropy." Thus, "The key word of this reorganization was efficiency; efficiency appeared to be the corollary of those techniques of functional specialization and centralized coordination and administration that characterized the business world."[10] The emergence of paid full-time social workers, as well as their subsequent quest for expertise, were originally the outcome of a largely heteronomous move toward the bureaucratization of welfare work. In pursuing their own strategies, however, the caseworkers helped to accelerate the transformation of welfare work from "voluntary service imbued with semi-religious sanctity" into a form of urban social control based on formalized methods and justified by professional expertise.

While the professionalism of social work was asserted—by means of association, training, and, ultimately, university affiliation—vis-à-vis welfare administrators and groups of colleagues, professionalization also involved the defense of the new forms of organized charity before public authorities and financial sponsors. This, in turn, presupposed a change in the ideological images and treatment of poverty.[11] "The unrelenting emphasis of the charity organization societies upon investigation and a full understanding of the facts surrounding each case evoked severe criticism from more sentimental and reform-minded contemporaries."[12] But it was, at the same time, the foundation of case work—the profession's nuclear skill. Similarly, the reorganization of philanthropic societies involved "an increasing interest in social agency administration and community-wide coordination."[13] This last feature, in turn, created new possibilities for professionalization along technobureaucratic channels.

In sum, the emergence of a subculture and of an identity on which a professionalization movement could be founded clearly revolved around the definition of a defensible cognitive basis. However, "the growing conviction among social workers in the early twentieth century that they possessed a skill to be acquired by formal education and experience" was a secondary or derived phenomenon.[14] The basis and the initial impulse for the movement were generated by *a redefinition of the organizational form which was to render the service*. The search for efficiency in mainly private philanthropic agencies led to bureaucratization. Thereafter, bureaucratization and professionalization efforts were conjugated. The bureaucratic tendency was prolonged and confirmed by the state's appropriation of the relief function. Not coincidentally, the professional goal of making entry dependent on formal education was considerably advanced in the 1930s—that is to say, at the time when the state's welfare function was finally institutionalized.[15]

In the case of school superintendency, bureaucratic origins similar to those of social work can be observed: the bureaucratization, here, affected the growing urban school systems. By the 1880s, according to Michael Katz, this process of bureaucratization was practically completed: "The process of bureaucratization within education," he writes, "was so thorough and so rapid because of the enthusiasm of the schoolmen themselves, who saw in the new organizational forms the opening up of careers and a partial solution to the problem of regulating behavior within the occupation."[16]

School superintendents also availed themselves of ideological resources similar to those utilized by caseworkers. The caseworker created a cognitive basis by generalizing empirical methods and experience and by incorporating knowledge and techniques from related fields (principally medicine, psychiatry, and sociology). School superintendents, *after bureaucratization had clearly differentiated them from teachers,* moved to create a distinctive program of training based on systematized experience and on methods borrowed from business and economics.[17] It then became possible for them to prove and legitimize expertise by the typical means of university courses of study and degrees.

The fortunes of the school superintendents' efforts "to seek security through professional 'expertness'" depended to a large extent on the introduction of scientific management ideologies in the bureaucratized school systems. While bureaucratization had defined for school superintendents roles with a measure of power attached to them, "scientific management" enabled them to use this power to define the substance of the sought-after efficiency. Echoing the aspirations of the school superintendents, Elwood Cubberley, one of the most influential educators in the United States, declared in 1915 before the National Educational Association: "The recent attempts to survey and measure school systems and to determine the efficiency of instruction along scientific lines have alike served to develop a scientific method for attacking administrative problems. . . . All of these developments point unmistakably in the direction of the evolution of a profession of school administration as distinct from the work of teaching on the one hand and politics on the other."[18]

Finding themselves under the fire of Progressive criticism, school superintendents and educators took the leadership of the movement to reorganize the schools along scientific management principles. In pushing this organizational reform, they were consolidating the power inherent in their own hierarchical position. "What they did," says Raymond Callahan, "was to use the business-industrial analogy to strengthen their position and defend themselves by arguing that, to operate the schools efficiently, they, the experts, needed to have authority comparable to that of a manager of a corporation."[19]

This case illustrates a dialectic between bureaucratic career patterns and claims of expertise which is different from that which prevailed in social work. In social work, new conceptions of philanthropy accelerated bureaucratization while being, at the same time, reinforced by it. One of bureaucratization's principal effects was the emergence of paid full-time caseworkers who soon found a basis for asserting expertise and pushing the volunteer out of the increasingly organized practice of public relief. Denying to the untrained volunteer anything but an auxiliary role was an obvious corollary of the collective drive for cognitive exclusiveness. Caseworkers appear to have directed this drive mainly against outsiders who were their direct competitors. Their aims were to define a *permanent* occupational role within a bureaucratic organization, to give it some expert status by creating more stringent criteria of access and to translate these status gains into economic rewards. In the same general category of state-related public services, schoolteachers offer an interesting parallel. Their case helps to set out the technobureaucratic component of school superintendency.

At least in the most developed states, school reform aiming at graded and coordinated school systems was well advanced before the Civil War. It continued apace in the 1870s and 1880s, impelled by the ever-growing number of children who had to be taken in charge by the public schools. The teachers' early efforts to upgrade their wages and their status included an ideological defense of both teachers and the schools: teachers self-consciously sought to displace the community's blame "for educational failure from the school to the home."[20] But the large bulk of teachers did not succeed in taking advantage of the reorganization: one major reason that the early school reform could be conducted at all, despite the constant scarcity of funds, was the availability of an abundant supply of cheap female labor. The reform based on the feminization of schoolteaching logically reserved the better-paid and higher-level positions in the system to males. Within the emergent school bureaucracies, male administrators were in a favorable position to capture most of the benefits of reform, while seeking the legitimation of expertise. Cubberley recognized the advantageous amalgamation of two principles of "superiority." In 1916, he recommended "a good college education" for the school superintendent, observing that "at least a year of graduate work is practically a necessity now." In addition, those men "of large grasp and ability . . . should go and obtain their Ph.D. degree" after a few years of experience. Teachers, on the other hand, did not need anything more than "a high school education and a two year normal school program for elementary teaching, and a college education for high school teaching."[21]

The advancement of schoolteaching as a profession paralleled the growth and expansion of its "higher branches"—namely, high schools in the first decades of this century. The movement received a decisive push from the Progressive interest in school reform and a new ideology of education. The Progressive Era, therefore, provided schoolteachers with a new basis on which to push professionalization along the path of expertise. However, because of the teachers' totally subordinate position in the bureaucratized school systems, more solidarity and cohesion were necessary than could be obtained through an as yet uncertain "science of pedagogy." This is undoubtedly one important reason why the collective advancement of schoolteaching as an aspiring occupation has always depended more closely on unions and unionist tactics than in almost any other "semi-profession."[22]

For both schoolteachers and social workers, the professional project was mediated by the bureaucratic organizations which, in fact, were the matrices of their occupational specializations. A protective institutional barrier is erected around occupations of this kind when the organization itself asserts its monopoly over a given functional area—over the formal education of children in the case of schools and, in particular, public schools; and over public relief in the case of philanthropic and welfare agencies. The professional project depends first on the organization; but within these general boundaries, particular categories of specialized workers upgrade their status by creating and claiming areas of expertise. Now, the forms in which expertise or technical competence are normally sought and asserted (through formal training, tested competence, and degrees) coincide, in theory, with the universalistic standards of bureaucracy. But these aspiring occupations look outside their bureaucratic contexts of practice for certification and training, as they also seek to control the content of training and its access. In so doing, they are, in fact, attempting to define autonomously the boundaries of a market of services which is subject to the overall control of a heteronomous organization.

Thus, on the one hand, bureaucratization stimulates claims of expertise: on the other hand, the quest of *externally sanctioned* expertise by aspiring professions tends to subtract from the discretionary power inherent in a bureaucratic hierarchy. In other words, as specialists generated by bureaucratic organizations seek to professionalize, they introduce into the career patterns of one organization checks that are administered by other organizations—namely, professional and graduate schools, professional associations, and, when licensing is attained, state boards. These checks are stronger in "autonomous professional organizations" such as hospitals, large law firms, clinics, and graduate schools (if we consider them as employers independent to some degree from the university administration); they are given more automatic recognition than in "heteronomous organizations" such as those that depend on the state's bureaucratic apparatus.[23] However, a contemporary research in a heteronomous organization—a social-work agency in a medium-sized city—also finds "some evidence to support the hypothesis that the less well trained supervisors gave differential treatment to their trained and untrained workers."[24] Supervisors who did not have formal degrees—that is to say, the proof of "externally sanctioned" expertise—exhibited some insecurity in their use of bureaucratic power: they hesitated to enforce their hierarchical superiority over subordinates who had at least as much training as they did.

The hierarchical distance between social workers and their supervisors was not so great that it could not be abridged by the workers' possession of an externally valued attribute such as a graduate degree. Schoolteachers, however, were subordinate to administrators who had themselves sought to expand and justify their bureaucratic power by claiming expertise and reaching for the university's legitimation. At the primary levels, the large pool of potential candidates and the relatively low educational requirements denied schoolteachers the kind of individualized countervailing power inherent in the possession of "superior" credentials. The need for collective bargaining and collective organization was, therefore, not diminished by the progressive raising of educational standards of entry.

It can be hypothesized that the structural predisposition toward collective bargaining power will be greater wherever an aspiring profession is subordinate to a hierarchy of authority, which itself includes categories with "superior" claims of expertise. The case of hospital nurses and hospital technicians appears to warrant the hypothesis: since no amount of externally sanctioned expertise can compensate for the subordination of auxiliary medical professions to the physician, unionization remains a choice at least as effective as further professionalization.

Now, the physicians' superiority over other occupational roles in the medical division of labor has been construed by Freidson as a central characteristic of profession.[25] Could not one assume, then, that the professional status of school superintendents flows logically from their possession of this essential quality—namely, their authority over an occupation which itself has professional aspirations? Built in such simplistic terms, a parallel between doctors and school superintendents would be totally misleading. The latter's authority over teachers—as well as their relative autonomy vis-à-vis elected school boards—do not depend on their possession of an "expert knowledge" but on the bureaucratization of the school systems. Turning the parallel around, it is almost more fitting to argue that the doctors did not secure their command over nurses and other auxiliary medical occupations until the large hospital—and especially the university teaching hospital—had become the institutional center of modern medicine. Up to a point, the physicians' relatively easy access to the top positions in the hospital's administrative hierarchy could be justified in terms of their superior knowledge of what the hospital was supposed to do. But the increasing bureaucratization of the hospital reduces the doctors' acceptability as top administrators; it generates, in fact, the specialized role of hospital administrator, which is a more precise structural counterpart of the school superintendent than the physician's role.

School superintendents sought to acquire the trappings of professionalism by associating their role with programs of training and college degrees. Their quest for externally sanctioned expertise did not typically aim at creating *individualized* countervailing powers within the school bureaucracy (except indirectly, as educated men command more respect in everyday interactions). Nor did it aim at excluding competitors from access to a set of specialized functions, for these were well-guarded by the patterns of promotion through bureaucratic hierarchies. The actual foundation of the superintendents' power hinged, in fact, on the promotion of an organizational form, bureaucracy, and of an organizational ideology, "scientific management." The public's general acceptance of the principle of rule by experts increased the superintendents' capacity to define the criteria of administrative efficiency: in this manner they could expand the measure of autonomous power inherent in their hierarchical position.

Like teachers and social workers, school superintendents function within heteronomous organizations: their autonomy, however, is limited by external constraints and conditions placed on the functioning of school systems, while the schoolteachers' autonomy is limited by the superintendency itself. The superintendents' effort to acquire valued attributes (graduate credentials) does not create the heteronomy of the teachers' role: it merely seeks to legitimize it in terms that are comprehensible to all. The superintendents relied on the same acceptable terms of credentialed expertise to justify the autonomy they were trying to establish vis-à-vis elective school boards.

To seek the symbols of professional expertise as legitimations for roles that are actually lodged in a bureaucratic hierarchy is typical of technobureaucratic professions. The "purer" case is that of the various specializations of business administration, spawned by the double process of concentration of administrative power and differentiation of functions at (relatively) high ranks. Other professions dependent on the big corporation, such as engineering and accountancy, are closer to the "public service organizational professions," in that externally sanctioned expertise represents, for them as for social workers, a potential of countervailing power within the organization.

However, none of the professions (or "professionalizing" specializations) connected with the administration of the corporation engages in organization-building efforts as part of a collective mobility project. Organizational professions such as schoolteaching and social work, as well as the mixed category of school superintendency, typically promote their own collective status by promoting the monopoly of a specific organizational form: bureaucratized school systems and "scientific philanthropy" thus derive much of their ideological legitimacy from collective efforts of their personnel. The corporation's ideological legitimacy is that of privately appropriated capital: it is grounded, therefore, in general dimensions of the dominant ideology. The technobureaucratic specializations which depend on the corporation share in these general ideological legitimations: the claim of expertise based on special knowledge neither modifies the patterns of career within the bureaucratic hierarchy nor adds to the organization's overall credibility. The difference may seem a pure matter of nuance. It becomes more perceptible, however, if the important dimension of client-orientation is taken into consideration.

CLIENT ORIENTATION, PUBLIC SERVICE, AND TECHNOBUREAUCRACY

In 1939, T. H. Marshall welcomed a trend which he thought was associated with the welfare state: "The professions," he wrote, "are being socialized and the social and public services are being professionalized. The professions are learning, not merely to recognize their obligations to society as a whole as well as those to individual clients, but also to break down the traditional isolation which separated them from one another. They are ready to work as a team."[26] In his view, the administrative professions were not only a most representative sector of the new middle class: they were also a natural reservoir of leadership for the intermediate classes, weaned by their form of employment from the competitive "motives and incentives which are reputed to make capitalism work." To this "socialized" professionalism, Marshall assigned the function of defining and working for "social efficiency, as distinct from both business efficiency and mechanical efficiency."[27]

We need not enter here into a discussion of the ideological conceptions that would inform this social efficiency. There is ample evidence that administrative professionals, as much as the others, often expect their clients to conform with the standards of the dominant culture, marked as they are by class inequality and racism. A frequent correlate of this bias is that professionals tend to conceive of their services as means of bringing nonconforming clients closer to these standards.[28] Despite his unwarranted optimism, T. H. Marshall is in fact suggesting that the new forms of public delivery of professional or paraprofessional services operate to free the ideal of service to the collectivity from the market pressures of the old professional model (though not from the pressures of collective status defense). From my point of view, organizational professions contributed at their inception to the definition of the form that the delivery of public services would take; and they may, in the same manner, redefine it. Such definition—or redefinition—of function must take into account the profession's actual or potential publics, as well as its subordinate and auxiliary occupations.[29]

Client participation aims at the direct involvement of the public. This can be a deliberate policy used by bureaucratic agencies to manipulate their clients. There is evidence, for instance, that citizen-participation policies on the part of urban renewal agencies have led "in most cases to the acknowledgment and approval of bureaucratic activities which may have benefited the urban renewal program's *cliental* group—central city businessmen—but not the program's *target*—the poor living in the central city."[30] Insofar as such policies involved the professional staff of the bureaucracy (in addition to technobureaucratic administrators), this would be an example of totally manipulative client-orientation.

Attempts to involve their clients on the part of bureaucratic organizations always need to be examined in their general political context.[31] However, organizational professions in the service of the public are directly and structurally tied to their clients. Therefore, redefinition of the organizational function and assertions of professional autonomy vis-à-vis the organizational hierarchy always touch upon the client orientation. This orientation may take various forms.

First, it may be *manipulative,* in a less conscious and more benign form than that suggested in the urban renewal case. Thus, in a marginal and recently emergent area of professionalization, child-care specialists are often compelled by federal regulations to incorporate the parents of their wards as auxiliaries. There is a tendency to maintain these auxiliaries in hierarchical subordination, while seeking among them and among other parents support for the professionalization efforts.[32]

Second, *indifference* to the client may be the norm in large bureaucratic contexts, or among professionals who do not define themselves as client-oriented. Doctors in bureaucratized health plans and large hospitals illustrate the first case. Academics— especially in elite institutions where "publish or perish" is the rule—are the most typical illustration of the second example. Professional indifference may be broken from the outside—by an organized movement of the clients themselves, or even by administrations bent on improving the "human aspect" or on increasing "teaching efficiency." Such external imposition may force the professional to analyze and re-examine his status and his function; or it may indeed change indifference into unqualified hostility to the client.[33]

Third, *hostility* toward the client may be the norm. This manifests itself, ordinarily, in interpersonal contacts: the professional demands deference and compliance, denies any active participation in the process to the client, and enforces maximum social distance. Such hostility appears to be common among professionals who are themselves subordinate, and therefore insecure of their status, when forced to deal with lower-class clienteles. In recent years, urban racial conflict has transformed this kind of interpersonal expression of hostility into overt political struggle. In the central cities, many sectors of professionalizing occupations and professions seek political strength and apply open political pressure to exclude minorities from participating in the definition of service organizations. This conflict was probably never illustrated more dramatically than in the New York City teachers' strike over decentralization and control of the schools.[34]

Fourth and finally, even in such extreme situations as these, some professionals side with their clients against their own colleagues. Crises need not be so acute for professionals to redefine the ideal of service as one which demands *partisanship.* What partisanship ideally means is *advocating* organizational change—and social change—in order to better serve the clients' needs; it means breaking down the barriers between professionals and laymen, at least enough for the client to express and define his need as he sees it; it means an attempt to seek and elicit the client's active comprehension and even his participation in the rendering of services; it means that professionals can neither expect nor demand trust from lower-class clients whom professions have systematically neglected or failed to respect; it means that this sort of trust must, in fact, be earned; it means, finally, attempting to organize the clients for collective action so that they can become their own advocates. In short, these forms of reprofessionalization, even if they may sometimes result in excesses of zeal which misread the clients' real needs, *challenge the division between professions and laity*. In revitalizing the notion of professional vocation or calling, advocacy throws considerable doubt on the compatibility of a profession's market orientation and status project with its service ideal.[35]

Members of public-service organizational professions have often been in the vanguard of these reprofessionalization efforts, together with public-spirited dissenters in the older professions. While the public service professionals can also provide conspicuous examples of the other types of client-orientation, the typical technobureaucratic professions cannot even be considered indifferent to their clients: *they simply do not have any autonomous orientation toward the clients, except indirectly*. The corporation which they serve mediates, in fact, the professionals' relation to the clients, as buyers or users of corporate services or products.

It is a distinctive characteristic of the technobureaurcratic ideology that it should make depoliticization of the citizenry into a major connotation of the "rule by experts." Ideological appeals to the safeguard of professional judgments and professional integrity can be used by all professions when they are threatened with client revolt or, more mildly, with client demands for some rights of review.[36] Technobureaucratic professions participate fully in this ideological practice. It is unthinkable, however, that professionals whose power *depends* on hierarchy and on the bureaucratic uses of secrecy should ever invite clients to share in this organizational power, if not for the manipulative purposes which I mentioned above.

The absence of client orientation can be construed as a characteristic dimension of technobureaucratic professionalism: its presence in different professional contexts alerts us, then, to the possible onset of other technobureaucratic characteristics. The fortunes of technobureaucratic professions depend on the heteronomous bureaucratic organizations for which they work. But the "professionalism" of business administrators, management analysts, and even engineers and accountants in the service of corporations, is not concerned with the organizational forms that mediate the production of professional services. Service to the public can hardly be considered a goal of the private corporation. Only a general crisis of legitimacy could seriously question the motives that govern profit-making in large private organizations. So long as this does not occur, neither the professionalization nor the reprofessionalization efforts of technobureaucratic specialties will typically include redefinitions of the organization which take clients' needs into account. At most, such redefinitions can preoccupy single professionals, in the privacy of a crisis of conscience.

It can be submitted that typical technobureaucratic professions incorporate, at best, only one dimension of true profession: namely, the possession of specialized skills. Their professionalization efforts do not mean, in my view, that big business and bureaucratic hierarchies might be transformed by the grace of altruistic service, or even by the professional devotion to work for work's *intrinsic* rewards. These efforts are best analyzed as an extension and an illustration of the ideological uses of expertise.

Professions and professionalizing occupations generated by heteronomous bureaucratic organizations can be situated along a continuum that goes from pure public-service expert roles to pure technobureaucratic roles. Today, however, all professions have some connection with bureaucratic organizations. These relationships constitute a most important dimension of the incorporation of professions into the structures of contemporary capitalism.

THE CONFLICT BETWEEN
PROFESSIONS AND BUREAUCRACY

Recent sociological analysis has considerably modified earlier approaches, which postulated an inherent conflict between the bureaucratic and the professional modes of work organization.[37] Two sets of assumptions underlied this perceived conflict: the one concerned an idealized notion of "free" profession, the other derived from having taken the Weberian model of bureaucracy as a totality. These premises led to an inescapable paradox, for indeed the contemporary increase in the proportion of professionals in the labor force is almost entirely constituted by professionals who work within large organizations or have organic work connections with them.[38] Skirting the paradox led to further unexamined analytical premises. For some authors, the general trend toward increasing professionalization appeared illusory, for it depended on bureaucracy—that is to say, the very force that was subverting the true structure of profession.[39] Another approach, not incompatible with the former, centered the assumed conflict between professional socialization and modal work experience at the level *of individuals:* as the carriers of the true norms and ideals of profession, individual professionals in bureaucratic work settings were bound to experience threats and contradictions.

In both cases, the conflict between the professional and the bureaucratic modes of authority and organization revolved around the ambiguous notion of professional autonomy: structurally, autonomy was implicitly equated with the largely mythical past of the "free" professions, in particular medicine and the law; this mythical condition was then contrasted with the structural realities of professional work under corporate capitalism. At the level of the individual, professional expectations of autonomy and professional frames of reference lead some analysts to predict socio-psychological tensions: they are seen to derive from the contradictions between the "personality" of the expert or professional, reinforced by his background and orientations, and that of the bureaucrat or manager.[40] These tensions derive, in the second place, from the contradictions between the self-regulation and peer control characteristic of professional work and the externalized controls of a bureaucratic hierarchy. In these contradictions lies the potential conflict between loyalty to the organization and loyalty to the professional community. Freidson and Rhea sum up in these words the assumptions beneath this postulate of conflict: "The consensus seems to be that [professional] workers require a kind of autonomy that is antithetical to Weber's model of rational-legal bureaucracy. . . . The proper way for such men to work is as members of a self-regulating 'company of equals'."[41]

One main current of empirical studies has contributed to demystifying the ideal connotations of profession and, therefore, their unwarranted extension to individual professionals. Research into *actual* processes of professional socialization, *actual* mechanisms of peer control, and actual professional practice has shown, among other things, the variety of motives that guide the choice of a professional career or careers; the reluctance to sanction one's colleagues, and the structural difficulties of doing so effectively; and the diverse "personalities" that emerge from professional training and the processes of educational stratification and self-selection which distribute graduates among different professional niches.[42]

With a different focus, other studies have questioned the second premise of the "inherent conflict" approach: reexamining the Weberian ideal type of bureaucracy, the systematic comparative study of organizations has shown, first of all, that "some of the components of the ideal type are relatively uncorrelated, while some are highly correlated."[43] Different *types* of bureaucracy can be distinguished: they exhibit some but not *all* the features of the Weberian mode. Particularly significant among these types are the "professional bureaucracies" or "autonomous professional organizations" which one author defines as "those in which professionals play the central role in the achievement of the primary organizational objectives."[44] The medical clinic, the graduate school, the large legal or accounting firm, large architectural offices, and research institutes, are typical examples: for the individual professionals on their staffs, these institutions become the locus of strains and conflicts that are different from those encountered in other types of bureaucracies. Furthermore, the analysis of the potential conflict between professionals and *heteronomous* organizations could be specified according to different dimensions of the bureaucratic mode and to different types of experts and expertise.[45]

The empirical studies which decompose the Weberian model into its constituent dimensions also tend to treat professionalism as a constellation of variables with attitudinal referents, some of which can be scaled. The evidence to which these studies arrive challenges the notion of a *global* conflict between professionalization and bureaucratization. Thus, Richard Hall finds a strong *positive* association between bureaucracy's reliance on technical competence in selection and advancement processes and *all* the dimensions of professionalism.[46] Hastings and Hinings' study of British accountants in large industrial organizations finds a similar congruence between the professionals' values of quantification and rationality, on one hand, and the organization's emphasis on "analyzing, planning, and controlling action" on the other.[47] These predictable findings indirectly confirm the largely common historical origins of both modes of work organization; they reinforce, that is, Stinchcombe's hypothesis that bureaucracy and professionalism are two subtypes of a larger category—that of rational administration.[48]

Richard Hall finds, moreover, that two other bureaucratic dimensions—hierarchy of authority and the presence of rules—have only weak negative relations with most professional variables, and *positive,* though weak, relations with the professional's sense of calling. In fact, only the professional feeling of autonomy shows a strong inverse relationship with all the dimensions of bureaucracy except technical competence. This leads him to the following conclusion:

> In some cases an equilibrium may exist between the levels of professionalization and bureaucratization in the sense that a particular level of professionalization may require a certain level of bureaucratization to maintain social control. Too little bureaucratization may lead to too many undefined operational areas if the profession itself has not developed operational standards for these areas. By the same token, conflict may ensue if the equilibrium is upset.[49]

The interdependence pointed out by Hall is coherent with the origins of organizational professions, which, as we have seen, emerge in symbiosis with the bureaucratization of their functions and work settings.

Most empirical studies of the postulated conflict between professions and bureaucracies stress, like Hall's, interdependence and specificity. A few findings should be briefly mentioned, as necessary evidence for a general assessment. A study of organizational professionals in social welfare agencies examines the relation between different dimensions of bureaucracy and *two* kinds of work satisfaction: the satisfaction of specific expectations about work, on the one hand, and, on the other, satisfaction with social relations on the job.[50] In this case, participation in decision-making appears to be the strongest determinant of specific work satisfaction, while the single best predictor of unsatisfactory work relations is the bureaucratic codification and enforcement of rules. The study implicitly suggests that the two dimensions of work satisfaction may compensate each other: since individual professionals presumably respond in terms of pre-existing expectations and career goals, they have different risks of dissatisfaction in the same bureaucratic work setting.

Several studies center on the professionals' previous socialization, thus implying that self-selection may be, among these relatively privileged workers, a major factor of adjustment to work. Studying the different orientations of engineers, lawyers, and professors in unequally bureaucratized work settings, Wilensky finds that "mixed types of orientation—mixtures, that is, of pure professionalism and careerism—are typical, consistent with the idea of the interpenetration of bureaucratic and professional cultures."[51] The findings that "bureaucracy is not a necessary bar to professional commitment," and that role orientation is more influenced by occupational training than by socialization on the job, lead Wilensky to deemphasize the threat to professionalism inherent in bureaucracies.

Consistent with Wilensky's results, G. A. Miller finds that Ph.D. scientists in aerospace industries are, on the one hand, relatively indifferent to the opportunities of participating in decision-making which so preoccupied the social workers; on the other hand they are, on the whole, less "alienated" by their work context than engineers or scientists with only M.A. or M.S. degrees.[52] Scientists with Ph.D.'s are concentrated in special units and receive a variety of advantages from the company. The detailed analysis suggests, however, that aerospace professionals respond to different elements of their work situation in the context of different personal motives. For the majority of professional personnel, "research freedom" and the opportunities of obtaining professional recognition outside the company matter more than bureaucratic variables such as the type of supervision or the presence of specific professional incentives. The study implies, on the other hand, that the higher alienation of engineers may be related to the frustration of their managerial aspirations, while scientists with lower degrees may be reacting, instead, to the fact that they have less research autonomy than their colleagues with Ph.D.'s. Earlier findings document, in fact, the lack of professional commitment of engineers and even of engineering graduate students, who lack a definite image of their professional tasks, see themselves in "any technical capacity," and characterize success in technobureaucratic terms, as "getting into management."[53]

In professions like engineering and accountancy, which depend on the large corporation and are often imbedded in it, the members frequently appear to have managerial or technobureaucratic career aspirations. The same should be true of the many professionalizing specialties—from information to sales—which emerge from the differentiation of functions in the corporate structure.[54] These "professionals" pose a different kind of problem for corporate management from those who take their discipline or their organized profession as a primary frame of reference—in industry, these are mostly synonymous with research scientists.

Encouragement of professional activities and professional incentives are not always conciliatory management responses to pressures *from professionals*: reversing the usual approach, a study of the professional ladder of advancement in large bureaucratic organizations finds that it also has another function. For professions and specialties with technobureaucratic aspirations or origins, professionalism may be imposed from above. Management, say the authors, "attempts to impose professionalism as a definition of success within the organization in order to maintain commitment on the part of those specialists who would ordinarily be considered failures for not having moved up into management. . . . It is not just a process of cooling out those who do not reach a goal, but an attempt to make alternative goals viable."[55]

For a large category of professionals whose concept of career is *inseparable* from technobureaucratic advancement, "professionalism" represents an ambiguous alternative: a "professional career" *within* the organization is *a sign of career immobility*. It can be perceived as such, or not. Professionals like engineers and accountants *already* have a stable status in the wider society: their credentials and degrees, guaranteed by professional institutions, in theory give them relative assurance of their "status continuity in a labor market."[56] What they expect to *gain* in the organizational context is, precisely, technobureaucratic power: the "professional ladder," however, provides neither control of resources nor participation in central decision-making.

On the other hand, specialists who find they cannot climb the ranks of management may assist management in the *creation* of "professionalism." Thus one company has created an elaborate "professional ladder" for its experienced salesmen, in an attempt "to create enough differences between these salesmen and the younger ones to reduce the stigma of failure to become a manager." Viewed from below, the attempt to professionalize a specialty is "one of the reactions to blocked mobility even among those already in management."[57] Higher up in the bureaucratic hierarchy, "professionalization" can be a strategy by successful technobureaucrats who seek to justify their power in terms of expertise. But at lower levels, or in the dual ladder system, "professionalism" may be an attempt *by management* to cool out, or to compensate for the blocked mobility *of individuals*.

The "dual ladder"—one example of multiple career lines—is one of the means by which organizations seek to incorporate their professional staff and to avoid the conflicts that could arise if the staff's technical competence and performance did not receive any rewards. As shown in one of the most studied cases of professionals in organizations, industry needs, precisely, the creativity of its research scientists.[58]

The organizational structure, therefore, reflects management's dilemma between the need to ensure the autonomy of its "discipline-oriented" professionals and the need to integrate their production into the structure of the industrial organization. While diverse "professional incentives" attempt to keep *individuals* satisfied, mechanisms of organizational segregation are used which allow a great deal of autonomy and informality to whole research departments. As Richard Hall notes: "The head of the department may be in conflict situations with the rest of the organization, but this is not necessarily passed down to the individual professionals, since the departmental organization may not vary much from that in a professional organization, as in the case of legal departments and law firms."[59]

Segregation mechanisms, however, may increase the other departments' resistance to utilizing research. Kornhauser identifies three main classes of mechanisms which attempt to deal with this type of resistance. (1) The "institutionalization of the teaching function," which "attempts to increase the authority of the scientists and experts." It is, I think, the only mechanism which attempts a *direct* reconciliation between two modes of authority—expertise and administrative power. The others tend to resolve the conflict at the level of individuals. Thus, (2) "the strategic deployment of scientists and engineers throughout an enterprise tends to reduce resistance to research resulting from conflicting perspectives on innovation"; it depends on "mobile individuals" to perform these integrative functions. (3) "Restrictions on the autonomy of research help to keep open channels of contact and communication and to increase the influence of the users of research on the research unit's activities and policies."[60] Like the second mechanism, the third one tends to displace some experts from staff to line functions (or from production to the organization and coordination of research): it reduces the scope of potential conflict by limiting it to the heads of research units or professional departments. These mechanisms also tend to multiply non-supervisory managerial roles, of which several studies find evidence in organizations with a high ratio of experts among their personnel.[61]

The emergence of intra-organizational "consultant patterns" is an interesting articulation of these adaptive mechanisms. One study of information specialists observes: "If high-status managers act as consultants to others over whom they do not have formal jurisdiction, situations in which low-status staff specialists attempt to give authoritative advice to high-status non-specialists are avoided. This new hierarchy modeled on the consultant pattern helps non-hierarchical forms of cooperation between divisional and departmental heads and the head of the information department."[62] The new structure, moreover, makes it unlikely that "high-status but non-specialist managers can make requests directly from low-status information specialists, [thus averting] another source of managerial-professional conflict."[63]

The consultant pattern incorporates and adapts a form of exchange of services—consultation—which is commonly practiced on a fee-for-service basis with outside experts. Together with the segregation mechanisms and the use of "semi-expert" administrators for the research departments, the consultant pattern shows that industries which use or produce knowledge are structurally compelled to incorporate or adapt organizational patterns typical of the university model and of the "organization of the labor market in higher education."[64]

This brief survey suggests a systematic approach to the potential sources of conflict between administrative hierarchies and professional staff. I have discussed earlier the significant variations of the typical orientation toward the client among organizational professions. If these variations are combined with the principal dimensions of personal work satisfaction, we obtain a typology of professionals in heteronomous organizations. (See Table 2.) I will outline it, as a first step in the discussion that follows. (It is assumed in all cases that professionals, by comparison with workers in other occupations, typically exhibit a high degree of interest and high expectations in relation to their work.)

Assuming that management in heteronomous organizations always faces the problem of integrating the professional staff (and in the last resort, disciplining it), while at the same time eliciting its adequate performance, we can advance some educated guesses on the potential elements of conflict in each case.

In cell A of Table 2, if we assume a minimal uniformity among public service organizations, the stage of professionalization reached by a particular group of specialists will determine different types of managerial responses. If the occupational specialty has *already* obtained external sanction for its claims of expertise (in the form of specific training and credentials administered by outside institutions), management's desire to elicit the "best" performance may be reflected—however

Table 2. TYPES OF PROFESSIONAL ORIENTATION IN HETERONOMOUS
ORGANIZATIONS

		Professional expectations emphasize	
		Participation in organizational decision making	Work autonomy vis-à-vis organizational bureaucracy
Professional practice presupposes	Positive Client orientation (dominant, manipulative, or partisan)	(A) Public-service, "new" professions (including "marginal" professions)	(B) From solo practice, which uses the organization as service, to advocacy (partisan involvement with clients). Academics with teaching emphasis may belong to this category
	Negative Client orientation (absent, indifferent)	(D) Technobureaucratic specialties and professions	(C) "Enclave" professions (scientists in industry or academics with research emphasis)

ideologically—in the preferential hiring of the personnel with the highest degrees or the best credentials. This would be the case for social workers and schoolteachers, among others: the possession of externally sanctioned expertise gives them, as we have seen, a measure of countervailing power with regard to supervision. It may also tend to push some of these public service professionals toward cell B. The accessibility of managerial roles, in turn, may move some of them toward cell D.

If, however, the specialists are only very marginally engaged on this path to professionalization, administrators will probably discourage (or at least not welcome) the efforts by a subordinate group to increase its potential for "legitimate" resistance to supervision. This appears to be the case in the emerging profession of child-care specialist.[65] For one thing, upgraded status is a good basis on which to demand a raise. Managerial opposition, in turn, may lead the marginal professionals to seek the active support of their clients and, thus, to move toward the varieties of advocacy in cell B.

In cell B, the technology, structure, and goals of a specific organization will determine to a large extent the orientations of management, and therefore determine the potential for conflict with the professional staff. Where the nature of the organization allows patterns of service delivery typical of solo practice, conflict may be centered around "red tape" interferences and the nonprofessional duties asked of the professional staff. For an individual, these conflicts can also emerge in *autonomous* organizations, where individual professionals may feel torn between their professional duties and the administrative or managerial tasks demanded of them.[66] If the tension between professional and nonprofessional duties is felt by most professionals most of the time, they are likely to invoke their clients' best interests against the demands of the organization itself. In the less established professions, where there is less insistence on professional dominance over the client, the clients may become actively and directly involved with the professionals' position (either in favor of it or against it). In the case of a potential alliance, the professionals' attitude can range from manipulation of the clients to advocacy, with varying degrees of each element in between. The force of administrative opposition depends on the degree of external support the administration itself may receive or expect from the public authorities or the public, and on the degree to which the professional staff is *replaceable*. Replaceability depends, in turn, on the profession's monopoly of access to practice, on the scarcity of supply, and on the professionals' security of tenure within the organization—that is to say, on the profession's *power*.

The more professional tasks involve the processing or transformation of things or symbols (rather than people), the more the relations with management will approximate those in cell C.[67] For this reason, academics "straddle the fence," depending on whether the organizational (or personal) emphasis is client-oriented (teaching) or not (research).

The situations in cells C and D are of the kind frequently analyzed by studies of professionals in industry. In cell C, management responds to the creativity-versus-integration dilemma with the array of strategies that have been discussed, most of which tend toward the two lines of authority—managerial or administrative, and professional—that are typical of large and autonomous professional organizations.

The passage from cell C to cell D is determined by the extent to which the profession or the individual professional have technobureaucratic aspirations of managerial mobility. The problems faced by the administrative hierarchy in cell D are closer to the problems posed by managerial and executive personnel than by a professional staff.

This rudimentary classification was centered on the individual professional and his typical orientations. To analyze the potential sources of conflict with the administrative hierarchy we need to clarify the determinants of management's orientations; this requires going beyond individuals and groups, into a comparative analysis of organizations. This can obviously not be attempted here, but we may briefly consider a particularly useful analytical framework: Charles Perrow's "technology-based" approach to organizations subordinates the content of specific relations of production to the mode of production—that is, the work that organizations do "in order to make some change in a raw material" which "may be a living being, human or otherwise, a symbol, or an inanimate object."[68]

Two aspects of technology, writ large, are particularly relevant to organizational *structure*, which is an "arrangement among people for getting work done." These aspects of technology suggest what kinds of organizations are structurally most dependent on autonomous performances by expert workers; they are, first "the number of exceptional cases encountered in the work" (which vary on a scale from high to low), and second, "the nature of the search process undertaken by the individual when exceptions occur." While all search processes are non-routine, "we can conceive of a scale from analyzable to unanalyzable problems" which call, respectively, on "logic" and "systematic and analytical" search procedures, or on "unanalyzed experience and intuition, chance or guesswork."[69]

With these two bivariate dimensions, a typology of both industrial and "people-changing" organizations can be constructed. Even where technology is the most standardized and routinized, experts may intervene at a given point of the productive process to formalize or devise technology, or to increase the knowledge of the raw material. Their integration into the on-going ocess of production, however, tends to null, since their typical interventions are one-time-only affairs. The less uniform or the less analyzable the raw material, the more regular and continuous will be the intervention of the expert or technician. The task structure corresponding to this technology should therefore allow him a high degree of *discretion*, or autonomous choice of means and autonomous judgments about the priority and interdependence of tasks. Discretion and power are the two components of *control*, which is itself one of the central dimensions of the task structure (the other is coordination, "which can be achieved through planning or feedback"). "Power" chooses autonomously among goals and strategies.

From a global point of view, Bendix had pointed out that "two antithetical principles . . . result from the division of labor" in bureaucratic enterprises:

> As organizations increase in size and complexity, efforts are made to routinize their operations by job classifications, product standardization, budgetary regulations, and other measures designed to simplify procedures and simultaneously increase central control. The tendency of these efforts is *to reduce the exercise of discretion by sub-*

ordinates. There is an equally important tendency in the opposite direction, however, for the use of standardized procedures which accompanies bureaucratization also leads to a lengthening of the chain of command and, hence, to *an increased subdivision and delegation of authority.* While an effort is made to centralize top decision-making along with this delegation of authority, it is probably inevitable that the discretionary exercise of authority increases at the intermediate levels.[70]

Perrow's approach to organizational theory locates the points at which the exercise of *discretion* by subordinates is *inevitable* (namely, in areas of high uncertainty where the "raw materials" or the technologies admit many exceptions and where, therefore, search processes—both analytical and intuitive—become indispensable). His distinction between power and discretion clarifies the difference between expert and managerial autonomy. Control of the discretionary areas can be pursued in two ways: it can be sought through the development of morale and organizational loyalty, the option favored by the "human relations" approach, or it can be entrusted to outside sources of socialization, which in our society tend to be professional institutions. *Professionalization, in other words, makes the use of discretion predictable.*[71] It relieves bureaucratic organizations of responsibility for devising their own mechanisms of control in the discretionary areas of work. There need be no basic conflict between the professional expectation of autonomy at work and large-scale bureaucratic organizations which create, by their technology, areas of discretion—unless, of course, professionals are more interested in *power* than in autonomy of technique. Power, in an organization, coincides with the higher autonomy of management.

Perrow's focus on endogenous variables and internal structure provides economical and general criteria for locating the organizations which should be the most capable of using and accommodating expert and professional staff workers. Historically, this capacity seems to have been highest in the industrial firms which we identify with the monopolistic sector. In his study of the fifty largest United States industrial corporations, Alfred Chandler, Jr., shows that the most dynamic and administratively flexible among them arrived independently at the same organizational innovation.[72] The *multidivisional structure*, he argues, was the organizational strategy by which these firms *had* to respond to the emergence of multiple markets. Their scale and their resources—both financial and administrative—appear to have been conditions for the successful establishment of the new structure, which in turn compensated for the disadvantages of scale. The financial and administrative capacity of these gigantic firms was necessary to support a structural adaptation which rested on internal diversification and on a measure of decentralization, expressed in the day-to-day operational autonomy of the various departments.

These dynamic industries, which were both the most flexible and the most capable of augmenting and institutionalizing flexibility in their time, logically depended on experts for their new managerial functions. Experts were needed to develop adequate information on both the "product environment" and the internal system of production; experts were needed to interpret this information and guide the policy-making instruments that were to act on it; experts were needed in research and development and in market research, which became, in these firms, integral parts of production and the main factors for increasing the adjustment between production and the market. The institutionalization of the division of labor between staff and line—which was also an achievement of the multidivisional strategy—shows that the industries which depended the most on experts were also the first to find structural means for integrating their educated manpower. It is legitimate to assume, therefore, that the decentralization and delegation of authority inherent in the multidivisional structure compelled the monopolistic corporations to rely on professionalism as a pre-existing means of limiting the potential abuse of discretion. Not surprisingly, these giant corporations were the most hospitable to the standardized professionals—that is, the university graduates who could safely be placed in discretionary, though subordinate and increasingly specialized, capacities.[73]

Whether the monopolistic market tendencies of the main industrial corporations led them, later, to internal problems of structural overcentralization and hardening of the organizational arteries is an empirical problem.[74] The point to be emphasized here is that, historically, *the core units of monopoly capital show strong structural affinities with experts,* on whom their management largely depends, *and with professionalism,* which tends to be substituted for bureaucratic control in the multidivisional structure. Dependent on experts, the giant corporations contributed to the diffusion of the general ideology of expertise and to its material sanction by the apparent efficiency which they brought to the production process. Internally, expertise is implicitly proposed as a legitimation for the hierarchical structure of authority of the modern organization; professionalism, in turn, functions as an internalized mechanism for the control of the subordinate expert.

BUREAUCRACY AND THE INTERNAL STRATIFICATION OF PROFESSIONS

In a bureaucratized world, professions can no longer be interpreted as inherently antibureaucratic. Both professions and bureaucracy belong to the same historical matrix: they consolidate in the early twentieth century as distinct but nevertheless complementary modes of work organization. The analysis conducted up to now has attempted to establish underlying structural affinities between profession and bureaucracy, affinities which go beyond the patterns of reconciliation and interdependence stressed by contemporary sociological studies.

In the United States, in particular, where traditional status-giving institutions had been fragmented or weak, the rise of large bureaucratic organizations in the private and public sectors toward the end of the nineteenth century constituted a new context of resources. Within it, professions old and new, established and aspiring, found new means of self-assertion. From its inception, the modern professional project had typically claimed market control, work autonomy, and status prerogatives on the basis of specialized training and scarce expertise. For a long time, however, the professions' claims were neither supported by obvious results nor attuned to the main structures of the dominant ideology. Gaining widespread legitimacy in the eyes of the public remained, therefore, a more difficult and improbable task than obtaining state sanction for market monopoly.

As capitalism moved into its monopolistic phase, however, the shift to a new dominant ideology accompanied the structural transformation of the economic, social, and political domains. Economic growth and productivity—due in large part to applied science—began to be felt at the level of the average standard of living; in this manner, they gave concrete support to the decisive affirmation of science as the predominant and undisputable system of cognitive and ideological validation. Expressed in the emergence of scientific management ideologies and in the notion of a transpolitical state, the shift in dominant ideology legitimized the status of the expert and exalted his role.

In itself, the reorganization of the systems of production and government not only generated new specialties which aspired to professional status; it also made possible, more broadly, the rise of a new system of social stratification. Professional aspirations were henceforth supported, and to a large extent shared, by expanding urban middle classes whose identity was founded on the educational system and on their occupation in modern and typically bureaucratized work settings.

Noting the fusion between professional and broader middle-class identities, one author observes: "Many features that are considered specific characteristics of the professions seem to be in fact aspects of upper class and upper middle class life and subculture. Thus, autonomy at work and many facets of professional ethics seem buttressed not only by professional norms and granted claims, but also by the class status of the practitioner, his social origin and the class position of his clients and other role partners."[75]

In the professions which typically render services to individuals, the state or non-profit organizations sponsor the service, acting as employers or "buyers"—otherwise, the cost of professional services tends to restrict them to the middle and upper middle classes. Since the upper middle classes increasingly depend on bureaucratic employment, it is plausible to assume that whatever changes this mode of employment effects in styles of life and expectations will be subtly relayed to "free" professionals through the influence of their clientele.[76]

Much more importantly, the majority of practitioners in all professions are connected with bureaucratic organizations as employees, as providers of services, as users of equipment or facilities, or as creditors—for this is, in a sense, the position of physician and other health professionals vis-à-vis federal and state medical aid plans. Moreover, all the professions which have successfully established their claims to expertise and their control over training and access are affiliated or connected with the university. Professional socialization begins, therefore, in a bureaucratized institution, whose specific patterns of work organization influence, outside its own bounds, the knowledge-producing and knowledge-using industries—that is to say, in practice, all of the economy, except for the most backward industries of the competitive sector.[77]

The university, as the main center for the "production of professional producers" is, in fact, the locus where both a bureaucratic notion of career and the traditional professional pattern of "fee for service" consultation coexist as models—the latter as an "entrepreneurial" option open alongside the otherwise bureaucratized academic career pattern. Beginning their own professional careers in this context, the apprentices undergo a peculiar process of socialization: they learn the tactics and absorb the ideology by which professionals in heteronomous bureaucratic organizations perpetuate professional autonomy or, perhaps more often, the professional illusion of autonomy.

Having discussed the common historical origins of professions and bureaucracy and emphasized the roots of most professions in the bureaucratized context of the modern university, I shall attempt to summarize the multiple relations of professions and bureaucracy in a synoptic form in Table 3. This synoptic description generates the proposition that the relations between professions and specific bureaucratic organizations are a most powerful determinant of stratification *among* professions and *within* professions.

First of all, distinctions between established and aspiring professions are based in large part on each profession's relationship with the university. The most developed and reputable professional schools in medicine, law, and engineering *added* to the prestige of the universities with which they affiliated during the "academic revolution." The relationship is inverted in the case of newer professions such as social work, librarianship, and city planning. However, even for the younger and less established professions, reaching the university means that they can develop their own distinctiveness: they are, indeed, under tacit command to develop their specific body of "theoretical knowledge" from a firm institutional base, which gives them academic control of a captive audience.

Second, at the societal level, the university operates as the most powerful preselector for the consulting professions—and whether or not the professions control the process of selection is immaterial. The various units in the system of higher education have themselves been relatively standardized and arranged in a recognized system of hierarchical prestige. This system operates as a switchboard to the world of work, but as a switchboard that would, at the same time, determine the distance and the speed of the trains. The trains are the different classes of colleges, universities, and professional schools at which the passengers arrive after having been filtered by a number of other switchboards. As shown by William Sewell, "Social selection is most vividly apparent in the transition from high school to college, but it is operative at every other transition point as well. Those who overcome the handicap of origin status or of sex at one level of the system find themselves again disadvantaged in moving on to the next level."[78]

The educational system as a whole, as well as the prestige hierarchy of colleges and universities, functions to guarantee the appropriate socialization of each cohort that is sent out into the world of work. Access to higher education and professional schools locates each cohort, as a whole, in the broader social hierarchy. The essential importance of attending the "best" schools for entry into professional life cannot be reduced to cognitive aspects, especially in those professions which have successfully standardized their basic training (and even their specialties). It appears, indeed, that the selection process bears little relation to later professional success, if one considers the purely individual level of grades and academic achievement.

Table 3. STRUCTURAL CONNECTIONS BETWEEN PROFESSIONS AND BUREAUCRATIC ORGANIZATIONS, BY TYPE OF PROFESSIONAL PRACTICE AND TYPE OF PROFESSIONAL EMPLOYMENT

	Type of Employment	Typical Client	Typical Connections with Bureaucracy	Plausible Effects on Profession
Consulting Professions	1. Solo practice	Individuals	Indirect (ideological climate, style of life)	Diffuse (not substantially different than effects on same socio-economic category).
			Buyer or user of services provided by bureaucratic organizations (hospitals, research institutes, libraries, universities, government agencies).	Stratifies professionals in terms of differential access to strategic resources.
	2. Autonomous professional organizations (medical partnerships, large law and CPA firms, large engineering and architectural offices)	(a) Individuals	As above	As above
		(b) Corporate & state bureaucracies	Direct: may be subordinate to powerful bureaucratic clients (corporate law firms, CPA firms, architectural offices working for state or federal government, etc.).	May compel professional organizations to greater internal differentiation and bureaucratization (corporate law firms, large engineering and architectural offices).
				Stratifies professionals and professional organizations in terms of major clients' power.

	3. Heterono-mous organi-zations (social-work agencies, schools)	(a) Direct contact with client	Formally subordinate; professional and bureaucratic modes of work organization are interdependent; the former are limited by bureaucratic regulations.	Typical problems of client-oriented professionals in bureaucracies.
	(scientists in industry)	(b) No direct contact with client	Incorporation: the whole bureaucratic structure takes into account the professional mode of work organization (segregation, professional incentives, etc.).	Tendency to "two lines of authority." Generation of technobureaucratic profes-sional ambitions; professionalism may appear as legitimation of blocked mobility or of technobureaucratic power. Stratifies individual careers (in both 3a and 3b); is affected also by the ranking of organizations.
Organiza-tional Professions	4. Heterono-mous organi-zations (man-agerial specialties)	Individuals or collectivities	Generated by bureaucracy. Subordination as (3) above	As (3) above
Academic Professions	5. Formally heterono-mous organi-zations (universities)	Individuals or collectivities (abstract publics); i.e. students or "scientific communities"	Formal subordination analogous to (3b) in work organization	Stratifies careers, also in terms of organiza-tions' rankings, as in (3) and in terms of access to strategic resources, as in (1)

Educational selection, however, has an *aggregate* effect on professional stratification: in terms of social connections, and especially in terms of ideology, elite schools socialize their graduates into an elite. The stratification of the training centers is obviously not independent from the broader structures of social inequality which, on the contrary, are *reproduced* by every level of the educational system.[79] As a study of engineers' career mobility indicates, "the combination of high grades and attendance at a highly selective school might be expected to eliminate or at least minimize the influence of ascriptive factors on post-college success, [but] it is apparent from these data that high selectivity does *not* mitigate the influence of social origins; rather, differential career success according to social origins is magnified in such settings."[80]

At the gates of the professional world, the professional minorities who control a field do not receive an undifferentiated mass of entrants, but a super-filtered, super-classified, specialized, and hierarchicized cohort. In the world of work, their connections with and dependence upon heteronomous bureaucratic organizations stratify the professions *internally* in terms of access to work-related resources, income, prestige, and vicarious power.

There are clear indications that this "externally produced" stratification affects the *cognitive* makeup of highly stratified professions. In the law, where a handful of firms dominates corporate legal business and selects the best talent, corporations have better legal protection than average private citizens; and not only that, but areas of the law unrelated to the corporate sector of the economy are relatively underdeveloped by comparison. External forces of stratification determine elite positions in most professions; indirectly, by the agency of these elites, these external factors affect the balance between indetermination and codification of professional skills. The large and autonomous professional firms bureaucratize, thereby tending to stress specialization and contributing to the routinization of techniques. They also appear to be pioneers in opening up new areas of practice: in accountancy, for instance, the "big eight" which dominate the field compensate for routinization by "moving into new areas of uncertainty" such as management analysis.[81]

At the level of individuals, we have seen that professionals, even if they are not directly employed by heteronomous bureaucracies, increasingly take their conception of career from the bureaucratic model: because this tends to be the predominant middle-class conception, because professionals assimilate it, however unconsciously, in the university setting, because they work within organizations that express individual advancement in terms of hierarchical steps. The bureaucratization of work-settings adds, furthermore, another important factor of internal stratification: the overspecialization of individual professionals in a given firm becomes a factor of "trained incapacity" that ties them to the firm and compels them to accept blocked mobility, by reducing their value on the broader professional labor market.[82]

Overspecialization of the individual is, in this sense, an element of proletarianization and it should not be confused with the differentiation and carving of new specialties out of a profession's common trunk.[83] These specialties are, in turn, themselves roughly ranked in terms of salience of the service, scarcity of the skill, length of training, and extrinsic factors such as the status of a specialty's majority of members or the status of its typical clientele (for instance, in Europe, a large proportion of women appears to lower the collective status of a medical specialty such as pediatrics).

It can be said that dependence upon heteronomous organizations stratifies the professions from the outside, pulling chosen professional institutions and chosen professionals toward the centers that control power and resources, while relegating others to marginality. *Bureaucratization,* however, can be an *internal* phenomenon which adds to the inequality between individuals, but it also tends to homogenize the terms of internal stratification: a hierarchical rank is clear and so, for the initiated, is the ranking of the organizations where they work, even though graduate schools, hospitals, and aerospace industries are not ranked by the same criteria.

The ranking of an organization among others of the same kind and the position of an individual within it (including his personal talent and "charisma") combine into a dialectic which determines in part the pattern of individual careers as well as the particular composition of professional elites. The terms of this dialectical interplay are typically different in different professions.[84] The more incorporated into heteronomous organizations a profession is, the more its members' prestige is determined by the organization: thus, the pattern of academic mobility—by "horizontal upward displacement" from campus to more prestigious campus—appears prima facie to replicate the pattern of the careers of executives in the private or public sector, or across both.

However, the individualization of organizational prestige is different in consulting or academic professions from what it is in technobureaucratic careers. The fact that achievements in the former are highly personalized seems to allow for an ideological blending of personal and organizational *prestige:* thus a professor may appear to carry with him some of the aura of Harvard as he moves to a state university, just as a physician "keeps" some of the prestige of Stanford Medical Center and transfers it to a lesser teaching hospital or to private practice. It is harder to think of a General Motors executive appropriating in this manner some of G.M.'s power and prestige, in addition to the hierarchical rank he has reached, before moving elsewhere: although the power and scope of the corporation he is leaving may guarantee a man's soundness and managerial capacity to other corporate employers, he does not confer any of the first corporation's power and prestige on the one he is joining. However, managerial achievements appear to be highly personalized if an executive enters the sphere of technocratic polyvalence, like Charles Wilson or Robert McNamara: the mark the man has left on the organization appears to effect, this time, an ideological blending of personal and organizational *power.*

In sum, to consider the relations between professions and heteronomous bureaucratic organizations implies, necessarily, an analysis of the professions' internal stratification. The preceding remarks are intended to suggest that the conception of professions as "communities" or as "companies of equals" which democratically exercise mutual supervision over deeply internalized common standards, is essentially an ideological conception.[85] Professional apprentices absorb this ideology during their socialization, together with other ideological components which justify internal stratification as a product of "natural" talent and trained skill. Like all power elites, the professional oligarchies which control each specialized field actually depend on ideology for their legitimacy. For less intangible means of power and control, these oligarchies largely depend on privileged connections with bureaucratic organizations.

As complementary modes of organizing and controlling work, both professions and bureaucracy rest on a certain measure of cognitive standardization, for both pretend to allocate people to work roles on the "rational" basis of "objectively" tested competence: "objectivity" requires that the content of such tests be specific, specified, and homogeneous, as well as accessible in principle to "all who would care to learn." In both cases, the determination of the criteria of competence is ultimately monopolized by professional or bureaucratic oligarchies. In both cases, the appeal to "objective" and universalistic legitimations is ideological: facts about the person which have nothing to do with competence intervene in bureaucratic as well as professional patterns of selection and career. There are, however, many important differences between the typical structure of bureaucracy and that of profession, and here I want to single out just one, which concerns the transfer of power or authority from organizations to individuals. Bureaucratic organizations—and their personnel—are separated *as a whole* from outsiders by the uses of bureaucratic secrecy and by impersonal organizational power. Vested in some roles, this organizational power becomes that of a real person only for as long as he or she occupies that role. There is a built-in limit to what can be done with it: were that power to be turned against the organization by the incumbent of the role, he would be fired as soon as discovered, thereby losing his position of power. The power that a bureaucratic structure is forced to let individuals manage cannot become a property of the person because it is not separable from the organization. The secret or "guilty" knowledge which individuals can accumulate through their roles in organizations is more transferable than power, because knowledge can be useful on the outside, provided that somebody is interested in the workings of a particular organization.[86] Now, professions are collectively separated from the laity by inaccessible or "tacit" knowledge as much as by testable and explicit expertise. Typically, professions maintain indeterminate and untestable cognitive areas in order to assert, collectively, the uniqueness of *individual* capacities. Collectively, they solicit trust in *individual* professionals and *individual* freedom from external controls, except for the ritual entry examinations administered by peers. The fact that the safeguards offered to the public in exchange for its trust—knowledge and internalized ethical norms—are inalienable from the person of the producer emphasizes the producer's individuality and illuminates the essential individualism of the professional ideology.

This individualism is, I believe, one of the powerful factors that make professions continue to appear, in the eyes of the public and of most social scientists, as the "anti-bureaucracy." It also explains in part why professions have been relatively successful in translating their "service ideal" into an ideological assertion of individual disinterestedness, and their indeterminate and tacit knowledge into an appearance of individual talent and "unique" interventions. These appearances allegedly distinguish professions from bureaucracies and professionals from business-men. As Talcott Parsons noted in his 1939 essay: "The fact that professions have reached a uniquely high level of development *in the same society* which is also characterized by a business economy, suggests that the contrast between business and professions, which has been mainly stated in terms of the problem of self-interest, is not the whole story."[87]

I have intended to make the story more complete. Various elements of the professional ideology have appeared in this analysis. It is time now to bring them together and attempt to define their structural bases, their origins, and their function.

Chapter 12

MONOPOLIES OF COMPETENCE AND BOURGEOIS IDEOLOGY

FROM HISTORICAL TO STRUCTURAL ANALYSIS

Looking backward from the phenomenon of profession as it appears in contemporary social life, I have attempted to trace its underlying unity in terms of the double movement by which it is historically constituted. The visible characteristics of the professional phenomenon—professional association, cognitive base, institutionalized training, licensing, work autonomy, colleague "control," code of ethics—have been considered from a double perspective: first, as structural elements of the *general* form of the professional project, and second, as specific resource elements, whose variable import is defined by different historical matrices.

As structural elements, these characteristics appear in various combinations in all the modern professions. As resources, however, they are qualitatively different in different historical contexts and therefore they vary in import or "useableness." In the nineteenth century, for instance, institutionalized training meant different things for the same professions in Britain and in the United States; the differences in meaning reflected larger differences in the whole structure of the social stratification system in each country, including the different ideological legitimations of inequality. A cognitive base, as the necessary premise of training, is necessary to every specific professional project, but in each project it had a different content; therefore, it occupied in each a different place among various strategic resources.

The history or "genealogy" of the elements that appear combined in the complex structure of profession can be traced across historical time spans and contemporary functional boundaries.[1] This has been done, for instance, in histories of professional schools or professional associations, or in histories of the cognitive corpus of various present-day professions (such as histories of legal thought, of architectural styles, of engineering techniques, of medical arts). I have focused my account on the complex mobilization and organization of these elements by different types of professional projects. It is time now to turn once again from historical diversity to the underlying structural processes and structural effects, which give a unified and broader meaning to this diversity.

As organizations of producers of relatively scarce and mostly intangible skills, modern professions first emerge from the personal ties of dependence characteristic of precapitalist social formations, and then organize, on the market model, various new or enlarged spheres of social activity. That is to say, ultimately, modern professions organize to exchange their services for *a price*. We have followed the diverse manifestations of this organizing project and underscored its inherent tendency toward monopoly.

From a broader analytical perspective, the professional project is part of a basic structural transformation—namely, the extension of exchange relations under capitalism to all areas of human activity. It is analytically useful to recall, very briefly, some of the well-known concepts by which Marx uncovers the essence of this process.

Marx's analysis of the *real* commodity form reveals, first, its dual nature: as *use-value*, a commodity's concrete utility is a function of the concrete needs that it can satisfy. Use-value only becomes a reality when the commodity "has found a resting place . . . [when] it falls out of the sphere of exchange *into that of consumption*."[2] That a commodity should be capable of satisfying the needs of some potential user is a necessary aspect of its twofold existence, and a sine qua non condition of *its exchange value*. As *exchange value*, or value, a commodity "at first sight, presents itself as a quantitative relation, as the proportion in which values in use of one sort are exchanged for those of another sort, a relation constantly changing with time and place."[3]

The institutionalization of exchange relations—which, obviously, presupposes some development of the social division of labor—establishes "the distinction . . . between the utility of an object for the purposes of consumption and its utility for the purposes of exchange."[4] The development and generalization of money, as the universal equivalent which expresses the quantitative relations between all circulating commodities, completes their "metamorphosis": "When they assume this money-shape, commodities strip off every trace of their natural use-value, and of the particular kind of labor to which they owe their creation, in order to transform themselves into the uniform, socially recognized incarnation of homogeneous human labor."[5] Indeed, in the labor theory of value, "the magnitude of the value of a commodity represents only the quantity of labor embodied in it."[6] Labor, the "value-creating substance," does not appear here as concrete labor, creating specific use-values, but under its abstract guise: it is *labor-time*, measured by its duration, which is itself a function of the average labor-power of society. "The labor-time socially necessary is that required to produce an article under the normal conditions of production, and with the average degree of skill and intensity prevalent at the time."[7]

Thus, the extension of market relations tends to generalize the double abstraction embodied in the commodity form: *value*, an abstract quantitative relation to the monetary equivalent, and *labor-time*, an abstract quantitative expression of the "average labor-power of society," expended for purposes of exchange.

Labor-power, the "value-creating substance," itself appears as a commodity on the market, inseparably from the appearance of capital: the appearance and the combination of these two structural elements signals "a new epoch in the history of social production." "The capitalist epoch," Marx writes, "is therefore characterized by this, that labor power takes in the eyes of the laborer himself the form of a commodity which is his property; his labor consequently becomes wage labor. On the other hand, it is only from this moment that the produce of labor universally becomes a commodity.''[8] Two central processes—relatively independent of each other and of variable historical form—constitute the "prehistory" of capitalism: first, the constitution of money-capital and its concentration in the hands of potential entrepreneurs; and second, the separation of the worker from the means of production. The second process is reflected in the juridico-political evolution which allows the individual worker to *sell* his labor—which makes him, that is, "the untrammelled owner of his capacity for labor, *i.e.* of his own person."[9]

In sum, the penetration of market relations into all areas of life is immensely accelerated and completed by capitalism. This character inseparably links the extension of market relations to the rise of a modern class system and to a juridico-political ideology which *ideologically* makes the isolated individual into the essential unit of the social and political orders.

This is the historical matrix within which professions organize the markets for their services. The advance in the social division of labor and the breakdown of personal ties of dependence, which are crucial in the rise of capitalism, are also preconditions for the formation of modern professions. The problem is, now, to relate the structure of profession to the particular nature of the commodities which professions produce and sell.

The term "fictitious commodity" is used by Karl Polanyi in reference to labor, land, and money—entities which are exchanged and organized into markets even though they do not correspond to the "empirical definition of a commodity": "The postulate that anything that is bought and sold must have been produced for sale," says Polanyi, "is emphatically untrue in regard to them."[10] A profound transformation in social structure and ideology is therefore necessary for such markets to arise. The change is deepest, and affects most directly the largest number of people, where labor is concerned. Since "labor" stands for wage-earning human beings, the mobilization and organization of labor in function of market requirements changes, therefore, the very structure of social life. Society, Polanyi asserts, becomes determined by the economic system.

The general process by which the commodity fiction extended to practically all forms of human labor affected professionals as well. The growth and diversification of the professional sector of the middle class changed the character of profession: in their efforts to secure a clientele or an income, the providers of these services became increasingly exposed to the constraints of capitalist competition in expanded markets. Today, insofar as most professionals sell their labor power to an employer, they represent but a special case within the general pattern of labor organization in capitalist societies. What complicates this specific instance is the process by which entry into professional labor markets is organized. Professional aspirants must acquire specific skills with a view to their sale. They normally acquire them through a relatively long process of training in monopolistic centers for the "production of producers." This training—or this passage—connects the sale of professional labor power with the educational system—that is to say, with the principal legitimator of social inequality in advanced industrial capitalism. This intimate connection disguises the stark characteristics of wage labor by covering it with all the structural and ideological advantages derived from status stratification and from the specific ideology of professionalism.

This ideology derives from the model of profession that emerged in the first wave of professionalization: founded on the importance of training and tested competence, this model, however, did not correspond to the generalized sale of labor power. The first modern professions—essentially medicine and the law—typically provided intangible goods under the form of services sold directly to consumers. In my analysis, I have emphasized the requirements imposed upon this project by the market orientation: the necessary homogenization of these intangible goods according to relatively universalistic standards could only be achieved at the level of training. The necessity to standardize training introduces into the model of profession a principle of equivalence between quality and quantity: excellence, it is implied, can be measured by "units of training" and by series of objective examinations. In our century, the generalization of bureaucratic patterns of recruitment reinforces the apparent equivalence between competence and length of training: while the use of IQ and other tests spreads at the lower and middle levels of the occupational hierarchy, expertise at the technical, professional and managerial levels tends to be equated with years of schooling and numbers of credentials.[11]

The differences that exist between the direct sale of professional services and the sale of professional labor power do not prevent the resort, in both situations, to a model of profession which corresponds only to the first. Before returning to the implications of this usage, I will attempt to state these differences with more structural precision, following the terms of Marx's analysis of the commodity form.

The labor which is standardized in the case of professional "commodities" is, first and above all, that which goes into training. Training—considered as the cooperative activity of instructors and students—appears indeed as the production of a marketable commodity, namely, the special skills of the professional producer. These skills can therefore be considered as exchange value created, in fact, before professional services are actually transacted between the provider and the user. Homogenized years of schooling and standardized credentials provide a "universal equivalent" into which these exchange values can be translated and by which they can be measured. The monopoly of instruction and credentialing appears, thus, as the structural condition for the creation of "professional exchange value."

The achievement of this monopoly of instruction depends on two related historical processes: the first is the process by which an organization of professional producers agrees upon a cognitive base and imposes a predominant definition of a professional commodity. The second is the rise and consolidation of national systems of education—the institutional infrastructure within which and by means of which such unified definitions of professional commodities can become predominant. In this sense, the creation of professional exchange value ultimately depends upon the state—or, more precisely, upon the state's monopolistic appropriation and organization of a social system of education and credentialing.

It is, however, inherently contradictory—as well as a departure from the strict commodity form—that the exchange value of professional skills should depend on cognitive and educational monopoly. This monopoly means that length of training can be arbitrarily determined. Taken together with the unquantifiable nature of intangible skills, the monopoly condition destroys the equivalence between length of professional training and a notion of the average labor time that is socially necessary for the production of a professional. Monopoly of training means, therefore, that the price of professional services is *not* the market expression of socially necessary length of training or average (educational) labor time.

Despite the distorting effects of monopoly, the production of special skills with a view to their sale creates exchange value. This value is vested in the individual. The social character of production is perhaps more visible in this case than in any other, for most education is subsidized by the state out of public funds; the products, however, are privately appropriated. Indeed, in the juridico-political framework of bourgeois society, the individual is the sole owner of his person and, therefore, of his socially produced special competences.[12] Professional training appears, therefore, as a lengthy process of production which, under special institutional conditions, creates exchange values and makes them the sole property of individuals. The *general* contradiction between the social nature of production and the private appropriation of its products is especially visible in the case of specialized training. We shall see later on how the ideology of profession addresses itself specifically to this contradiction.

In sum, the attempt to apply Marx's structural category of value to the "professional commodity" indicates, in this first phase of analysis, three things.

First, professional training creates or preserves value (by transmitting the skills of the instructor to the student) in the person of the apprentice professional. The professional himself appears, therefore, as the product of congealed or materialized labor, as "the use-value that has been produced for exchange." From this point of view, professional training is, in Marxist terms, *productive* labor.

Second, when professional skills are viewed as commodities under the aspect of exchange value, their distinctiveness appears to be lodged in the professional monopoly over training. From this point of view, the monopoly over training contains an inherent contradiction: it appears to be a central condition for the effective creation of "professional exchange value," and yet it tends to place the price of professional "commodities" outside the realm of market determination.

Third, through standardized and monopolized education, professional skills acquire *an appearance* of measurability and comparability in terms of years of schooling. Length of training and tested competence clearly appear as means to "objectify" professional skills, in the double sense that the skills acquire both a tangible, quantifiable expression *and* a "universalistic" legitimation. While both years of schooling and credentialing are related to the market value of specific professional services, the relation appears to be ideological: indeed, it functions more as an implicit justification for the price of the professional commodity and for the privileges associated with professional work, than as the actual quantitative translation of "average socially necessary labor time" into market value.

The first market-oriented phase of professionalization introduced a principle of objectification at the core of the professional commodity. Standards of value derived

from this principle tended to displace (though never entirely to replace) precapitalist standards based on narrow monopolies of status, on the social position of the
clientele, or on the personality and idiosyncratic biography of the professional. The
particular aspects of use-value in the professional commodities limited the scope
of this transformation.

Historically, the first professions to organize on a market basis were the classic
"personal" professions—most conspicuously, medicine and the law. The essential
feature of these profession's product is that *it tends to be immediately used or consumed (as advice or ministration) by the client or consumer*. This means that the
realization of use-value (its consumption) is immediate—that is, *independent of
capitalist relations of production*.

In terms of Marx's theory of exploitation, this implies that professional labor
sold on a market under the form of direct services—independently, that is, of capitalist relations of production—does not contribute to capitalist accumulation by producing surplus value. Since only labor which produces surplus value is *productive*,
professional services sold directly on a market are, strictly speaking, unproductive.[13]
"It is labor which is *not exchanged with capital, but directly with revenue,* that is
wages or profits (including, of course, the various categories of those who share
as co-partners in capitalist profit, such as interest and rent)."[14] Marx adds: "The
laborer himself can buy labor, that is commodities which are provided in the form of
services. . . . As buyer—that is a representative of money confronting commodity—the laborer is in absolutely the same category as the capitalist where the latter
appears only as buyer."[15] If we look at the "classic" personal professions from the
point of view of the use-value of their labor (historically organized into markets
during the nineteenth century and later on), their typical ideology appears to be
based on structural properties of the commodity or services they sell: any buyer can
acquire their "professional labor power" as a commodity for immediate consumption; and this kind of professional labor power does not enter *directly* into the process
of capitalist reproduction and accumulation.

The ideal of universal service to "all of mankind" appears, in fact, to reflect the
equalizing and democratizing effects of the market (equalizing if compared, for
instance, to aristocratic patronage which reserves professional labor power for the
use of an elite): unproductive labor can potentially be purchased and consumed by
all, whether they own capital or not. The claim of disinterestedness conceals, it is
true, the potential venality of the transaction of services; it does nevertheless reflect
the fact that this kind of professional labor remains outside (or removed from) the
capitalist mode of production. As unproductive labor, it is therefore different in
nature from the specific form that productive labor assumes under capitalism—that
is, the form of wage-labor "which, exchanged against the variable part of capital . . .
reproduces not only this part of capital (or the value of its own labor-power), but in
addition produces surplus-value for the capitalist."[16]

It can be noted, furthermore, that the unproductive character of the labor sold
by the personal professions not only bestows upon them an appearance of "classlessness" (because their services can, in principle, be universally used), but also
explains that close ties can be maintained with noncapitalist elites, at least in the

transitional phase (*i.e.* "the various categories of those who share as co-partners in the capitalist profit, such as interest and rent").

Let us consider now whether these structural connections between professional ideology and the sale of professional labor power can be extended beyond the personal professions. In the practice of the classic personal professions, the exchange of services typically tends to take place between the "free" professional and his individual client. The immediate realization of use-value—accessible, in theory, to everyone—appears to be a predominant characteristic of this kind of market transaction. Because professional labor is not, here, exchanged with capital and does not participate directly in the production of surplus value, it is, in strict terms, unproductive. The free professional escapes, therefore, capitalist exploitation. This point immediately suggests a corollary: if a professional works in the service of a capitalist firm, "*the same* kind of labor may be *productive* (that was) unproductive" in a "free" professional market. Marx writes: "If we may take an example from outside the sphere of production of material objects, a schoolmaster is a productive laborer, when, in addition to belaboring the heads of his scholars, he works like a horse to enrich the school proprietor. That the latter has laid out his capital in a teaching factory, instead of a sausage factory, does not alter the relation."[17] And he adds: "An actor for example, or even a clown, according to this definition, is a productive laborer if he works in the service of a capitalist (an entrepreneur) to whom he returns more labor than he receives from him in the form of wages."[18]

Professional labor which is performed for the benefit of a capitalist firm is therefore not structurally different from any other kind of labor which is subject to capitalist relations of production. From the point of view of exploitation, therefore, any kind of labor can become productive. From the point of view of capitalist accumulation—that is, the production and appropriation of surplus value—professional labor appears at first sight to have a relatively indirect connection with the actual production of commodities. Even the work of engineers consists typically of devising, planning, and supervising—tasks that are preliminary, parallel, or supraordinate in the physical process of production. This vague similarity among all the occupations generally regarded as professions merely indicates that the work in which these occupations engage is relatively removed from and "superior" to the manual work typically performed by the industrial proletariat. This general trait cannot compensate for the crucial differences between these occupations.

Engineers and other "technical devisers" emerged, typically, as salaried employees of either capitalist firms or public corporations in charge of building the infrastructure for economic growth. Accountants, as well as lawyers specialized in corporate affairs, typically reserve the use-value of their labor for capitalist clients, despite the appearances of professional "freedom." Furthermore, as changes in the organic composition of capital tend to bring about "the massive reintroduction of intellectual labor into the process of production," expert labor becomes an integral part of production.[19] Expertise is either drawn from occupations already dependent on the capitalist firm or tends to be qualified as "professional": the workers tend to seek professional status, or are granted "professional" privileges, for reasons internal to the organization.[20] Finally, the kinds of professional services delivered within the bureaucratic framework of the welfare state seem to be in an altogether different category.[21] *Salaried* experts or professionals share one characteristic: the products of their activity do not normally reach an *open* market. What engineers, accountants, employed architects, business administrators, social workers, teachers at all levels, and salaried physicians and lawyers all exchange for income on specific labor markets is their labor power and the skills inherent in their persons. The products of their activity, however, remain within the purchasing organization, where they are used directly by employers or by clients of the organization.

Two relatively independent dimensions seem to be involved in the determination of these differences: the degree to which an expert occupation is subordinated to capitalist relations of production, and the degree to which its relation to the production of surplus value is direct or indirect.[22] A classification of professional situations on this basis is attempted in Table 4.

One important point must be made: the farther one moves from the classic market situation of the "free" personal professions, the more purely ideological do the professional claims of disinterestedness and universality of service become. We have seen, indeed, that these claims, typical of the legitimizing ideology of profession, reflect the structural characteristics of unproductive labor and of a singular market situation. Such structural connections do not exist for professions which contribute to capitalist reproduction and accumulation more directly than do medicine or the law. Neither do the connections hold for salaried professionals—in par-

Table 4. RELATION OF PROFESSIONAL (OR EXPERT) SERVICES TO CAPITALIST PRODUCTION

Use-value of services	Services Exchanged for Capital	Services Exchanged for Revenue
Directly incorporated into production of surplus value	Expert services included within the corporation: professional and managerial (including freelance consulting)	Expert or professional services which contribute to the production of constant capital (in non-profit research and development)
Incorporated only indirectly (contribute to the reproduction of the labor force)	Contribute to the reproduction of the work force within the corporation or (rarely) in privately owned service firms (e.g., health professions, instruction of different kinds).	(a) Market situation: classic personal professions (b) Non-market situation: "welfare" professions in the service of the state
Not incorporated	Supervisory or controlling services	Services related to "law and order," containment, and ideological production (including "free" professions)

ticular, not for the organizational professions, either pure or technobureaucratic.

Insofar as the term "profession" incorporates the connotations of universal service and of an exchange of labor power radically different from that typical of capitalism, the very extension of the term beyond the classic professional situation of "free" and unproductive work is ideological. The sociological definitions which include these elements are, therefore, contributing to the ideological assimilation of structurally different kinds of labor. This ideological extension of the term "profession" applies to nonmarket and nonpersonal exchanges of skilled services the expectations and legitimations derived from the classic situation of unproductive professional labor. Historically, the force promoting both the ideological use and its ideological effects is *the status project* in which aspiring occupations are engaged.

Before turning to an analysis of the ideology of profession per se, I shall sum up the results of this attempt to apply Marx's structural categories to the "professional commodity." Table 5 presents the summary in diagrammatic form.

This tentative analysis has located the points of departure of the professional commodity from *real* commodities: the services that professions historically organized to sell are, in fact, skilled labor-power, the price of which tends to be justified in terms of expertise and length of training. The conditions of monopoly in which these skills are produced, however, invalidate the apparent equivalence between market price and special training. Finally, in the *practice* of many professions, use-value predominates over exchange value: this appears to be the structural foundation of the ideology of profession as it is formulated, first, by the classic personal professions which initiate the movement toward organization of their markets in the competitive phase of capitalism. The particular structure of the "commodity" exchanged on these markets indicates that the professional project of market organization is *not* a *direct* extension of capitalist relations of production: it represents, rather, an extension of exchange relations into new areas of life, as an effect of the generalized breakdown of the precapitalist *social* structure.

The origins of professions other than the classic ones (law, medicine, dentistry, and, with certain qualifications, architecture) are not typically found in "free" markets of services. And the practice of the classic professions themselves is changed by the rise of organizations. In general, professions do not consolidate their privileges until the "organizational revolution." What this term stands for is, in fact, the end of liberal capitalism. In the transition toward the monopolistic phase, the occupations which attain or aspire to the status of the classic professions, and which contribute to spread the latter's self-justifying ideology, do not typically depend on the extension of exchange relations; their origins are located, rather, in the transformation of the forces and relations of production in the capitalist enterprise, in the new functions of the capitalist state, and in the elaboration of new forms of the dominant ideology.

The radical differences between work situations which are usually regarded as professions suggest one line of thought: the market project of the classic personal profession represented a necessary but nevertheless provisional and temporary stage in the status project that is generally called "professionalization." Despite the apparent independence of the professional providers, these special markets required institutional guarantees which tied them closely to the state—in particular,

Table 5. PRODUCTION OF PROFESSIONAL COMMODITIES AND IDEOLOGICAL PRODUCTION

Principal characteristics	Professional services considered under the aspect of		
		Use-Value	
	Exchange Value	Market Situation (personal professions)	Non-Market Situation (organizational professions)
Main locus of production	Training centers	Practice	Practice
Product characteristics	Skilled labor power, inherent to the person of the professional; socially produced, privately appropriated.	Advice or ministration	Advice or ministration Research
Realization	Deferred to entry into labor market, after training	Immediate: product consumed as use-value (potentially accessible to all consumers)	Immediate: product consumed (or incorporated into other products) by specific clients or specific employers
Typical conditions of production	Monopoly of training and credentialing	Interpersonal exchange on a free market of services	Interpersonal services not purchased by client but provided by "welfare-state" institutions; technical or scientific products consumed or incorporated within organization

Table 5. (continued)

| | | Professional services considered under the aspect of | |
| | Exchange Value | Use-Value | |
Principal characteristics		Market Situation (personal professions)	Non-Market Situation (organizational professions)
Predominant appearance of product	Abstract, susceptible of being measured (quantitative expression: analogy between standardized education and homogenized labor-time)	Concrete, qualitative, related to client's needs, susceptible of differentiation in terms of status and style of life of clientele	Concrete, qualitative, either related to client or employer's needs or defined by bureaucratic regulations
Main ideological effect	False equivalence between credentials, length of training, and price of professional labor power	Universality of service, radical difference between professional mode of production and capitalist mode	Extension of the ideology of profession to structurally different kinds of work situation and conditions of production
General ideological premises	Individualism; skills as personal property	Individualism; equality among individual consumers or individual citizens	Ideology of expertise as the new foundation of inequality in the educational and occupational structure

to a state-controlled system of education and credentialing. The consolidation of large organizations in the private sector and the expansion of state functions signal, in our century, a general retreat from the "pure" market principle: in the large organizational units of the private or the public sector, greater predictability of operations tends to go hand in hand with the bureaucratization of functions and control.

In this phase, professionalization represents a collective attempt to protect and upgrade relatively specialized and differentiated activities: the privileges that are sought are justified by resorting to a model of profession which corresponds to the project and the practice of the market professions during the liberal phase of capitalism. In the first place, this ideological reference aims at legitimizing social inequality: it does so, on the one hand, by stressing the apparent fusion between educational and occupational hierarchies, and on the other, by tacitly assimilating the market professions' relative independence from the class structure and their ethical claims.

Secondly, one of the goals of professionalizing occupations—one of the privileges they pursue—is a measure of work autonomy. Autonomy in the organization of free markets of services went together with autonomy in determining the conditions of work in the first phase (or the first type) of professionalization. Such autonomy was obviously never conceded to the sellers of the typical labor-commodity, namely, the industrial proletariat. But it was not attained, either, by occupations which are often regarded as professions: the established clergy and the military, necessary though they were to the maintenance of the bourgeois state, *never* entered a market sphere. Nor did a "free" profession like engineering, directly relevant to capitalist production, attain the control over its own work which characterizes the classic market professions; the project of the "personal" professions was only a brief episode in the story of professionalization. This indicates that, today, the alleged conflict between bureaucracy and profession as modes of work organization is not so much a conflict between two different structures as it is a contrast between the structure of bureaucratic organizations and an ideology promoted by some of their members. The case of engineering suggests something else: that autonomy is more easily conceded when it concerns transactions between private persons than when it would impinge on the basic structure of decision-making in capitalist production.[23] For occupations which are encapsulated within (or dependent upon) large heteronomous organizations, the ideological appeal to the model of profession may represent an attempt to establish a last-ditch defense against subordination.

I have emphasized throughout this analysis that, today, the disparate occupational categories which we call "professions" are essentially brought together *by ideology*. It is an ideology used by the leaders of professionalization projects and shared by the members of various occupations. It is also shared and sustained by the whole society, not excluding its social scientists. We must examine, now, the affinities between the ideology of profession and the dominant ideology of bourgeois societies. First, I shall look briefly at the ideological trunk from which the professional branch derives. Second, I will consider what functions the ideology of profession performs within the social division of labor, with regard to the specific groups of workers who claim professional status. Finally, we must ask, however tentatively, what the ideology of profession contributes, today, to the dominant ideology.

GENERAL COMPONENTS OF
THE IDEOLOGY OF PROFESSION

During the nineteenth-century phase of professionalization, the emergent ideology of profession incorporated several traditional or precapitalist components which can be viewed as *residues*. We have discussed these elements at an earlier stage as "anti-market" principles.[24] Three of them are important here. The first is a work ethic derived from ideals of craftsmanship, which finds *intrinsic* value in work and is expressed in the notion of vocation or *calling*. This ethical notion is to be distinguished from the bourgeois entrepreneurial work ethic, in which work is a means toward capitalist accumulation, or in Weber's interpretation, a means toward salvation; in either case, the value of work is *extrinsic* to work itself. The second is the ideal of universal service; connected with the "protection of the social fabric" against the subversive effects of the market, it tends to respect and define, in the transitional phase, pre-industrial ideals of community bonds and community responsibility. In this sense, it incorporates precapitalist legitimations of social inequality, which are reflected in the model of gentlemanly disinterestedness. Third, its ideological status model appears as a secularized version of the feudal notion of noblesse oblige, which embodied the nobility's ideological aversion to commercial pursuits and its belief, anchored in a religious view of the social world, that high rank imposes duties as well as conferring rights.

These elements can now be linked with more precision to the structure of the "professional commodity." The visibility or predominance of "realized" use-value in the transaction of professional services emphasizes the concrete, qualitative aspects of the labor power expended; it appears, thus, as a direct support for the intrinsic value placed on work by the ideology of profession. The relative independence of the classic personal professions from capitalist production can be related, in turn, to the professions' particular affinity with status. Their detachment from the predominant relations of production gave the classic professions a measure of independence from the capitalist class structure and the possibility of maintaining social and ideological ties with precapitalist elites; the gentlemanly ideal, transferred by the nineteenth-century professions to their market project, is a manifestation of this apparent independence from class relations.

A short digression is necessary here to explore a particular aspect of the penetration of status into the nineteenth-century project of market organization. The market gives professional services *an appearance* of universality by leveling the differences between potential consumers; this equalization, however, is purely formal. The quantitative aspect of "professional exchange value" cannot equalize the qualitative differences inherent in use-values. The differential capacity to consume, determined by social inequality, mediates the quantitative and the qualitative aspects of market consumption. Specific styles of life which express "status honor" crystallize into modes and patterns of consumption.[25] Use-values, realized in consumption, are thus shaped and determined by status.

In fact, the use of professional services (including those most "universal" in kind, such as medical services or elementary education) was not extended to the mass public by extension of the market; these services were generalized, rather, by the extension of social-welfare functions. However, even after the development of the welfare state, professional services of a personal kind either continue to be reserved to those who are rich enough to pay, or they tend to be qualitatively different according to the clientele's capacity to pay. The socioeconomic status of the client not only influences the quality of the service, or the nature of the use-value, that a professional provides; it also influences the professional's *own* status and ranking, most especially in the personal professions.

The deployment of professional work within organizations, or in relation with them, substantially modifies the traditional threefold relation between status of the client, status of the professional, and quality of the product; it does not, however, entirely supersede it. One important sector of the services provided by the market professions is *luxury services*—that is, special use-values enjoyed by the rich and by the ruling class. Within the category of luxury services, some professional use-values are still almost exclusively reserved to the rich (architect-designed residences, for example), while some others, such as the private and speedy attention of eminent doctors, express the infinite variety of status gradations.

The permanence of these traditional effects of status is *residual;* and the reason for this may be found in the temporary nature of the professional project of market organization and in the structural differences between the classic personal professions and those professions of later and different origins. The status of all contemporary professions is typically based on organizations and is legitimized by the thoroughly modern ideology of expertise. The ranking of organizations is, today, the main determinant of professional status differentials. Of some rankings, only "the happy few" are aware; but I am interested in those intuitive prestige scales which are relatively public knowledge, in particular when they concern training institutions. The public ranking of organizations syncretizes intrinsic and extrinsic criteria of prestige: standards of professional and intellectual excellence merge with traditional forms of evaluation derived from the system of social stratification; the fame or the power of clienteles, the social origins of the student body, the style of life and social position of the graduates, are fused with the "objective" elements based on knowledgeable evaluations of expert performances. The public existence of such prestige rankings helps maintain the potency of traditional and ascribed determinants of status within the very strongholds of rational expertise.

Whatever its bases, the effects of prestige are clear: they *destandardize* the same values that the rationalizing effects of labor and commodity markets tend to homogenize and quantify. For professionals, the prestige of the training centers from where they come operates a first destandardization of degrees and skills. It blends with unmeasurable personal factors to stamp the individual producer with an aura of uniqueness. Status and personality effects, which are inseparable from the transaction of services, limit and counteract the ideological reduction to abstract and quantifiable value.

Despite the complexity and heterogeneity of its components, the ideology of profession cannot be considered independently of the dominant bourgeois ideology within which it is formed. At the center of the ideology of profession we find, necessarily, the general postulates of bourgeois ideology.

The notion that "the individual is essentially the proprietor of his own person and capacities, for which he owes nothing to society'' is a cornerstone of the bourgeois theory of democratic liberalism.[26] The model of society that emerges during the seventeenth-century crisis of the *ancien régime* is a market model, in which free individuals consent of their own will to the contrivances of political society in order to protect their own natural rights—and first and foremost, their right to property. In the foundations of liberal theory, the force that binds atomized individuals to each other is the market itself.[27]

A market society which is ideologically founded on the equal rights of free individuals but which equates freedom with possession involves an inescapable contradiction: it ''generates class differentials in effective rights and rationality, yet requires for its justification a postulate of equal natural rights and rationality.''[28] Thus, at the core of all liberal theories we find the impossibility of individual equality in a class society. Unable to achieve the impossible, ideology escapes the issue either by denying the centrality of class or by justifying it as part of the ''state of nature.'' The possessive market model created by liberal theory is described by its contradictory foundations: individualism, property, egalitarianism, *and class*.

The possessions appropriated by the professional consist, typically, of practical and theoretical knowledge, under the form of a special *competence*. This form of property has two distinctive characteristics: on the one hand, it is inseparable from mind and self; on the other, it constitutes a resource that cannot be depleted. Because it cannot be depleted, the form of property characteristic of the professional escapes the dictates of scarcity. Insofar as high prices on a market are a function of supply and demand, they can be attained in a market of competent services by acting either upon demand (which is difficult, as we know) or upon supply. Relatively scarce supply can be obtained in two principal ways, both of which are predicated upon monopoly of training and a restrictive definition of what constitutes competence: the first is the implicit or explicit refusal to produce as many competent providers of services as demand calls for; the second is by conspiracy, among the competent providers of services, to withhold these services from the market.

A professional conspiracy to withhold services, although not impossible in theory, would be highly improbable, however. Like all forms of personal property, ''cognitive property'' can be hoarded instead of being invested: only by its investment or application does cognitive property augment the available knowledge capital of a society or improve the lives of people who lack such knowledge. But historically, the class situation of the modernizing bourgeois professionals excluded the possibility of such hoarding: they not only *had* to make a living, they had to make it through a market for their services. Unlike the traditional professionals, they could not depend on their elite patrons (or on their family fortunes) for subsistence. The disintegration of precapitalist ties of dependence, as well as the limitations inherent in the ownership of land and capital, forced the professional fraction of the bourgeoisie to seek and ensure alternative means of subsistence on the market. This was the essential structural factor in the mobilization of their cognitive property. It was complemented by a traditional ideological one: men who claim to have better than average competence— especially where the competence concerns vital collective needs—would be *immoral* if they did not apply it in the service of the community. Thus, the dictates of the capitalist division of labor combine with the dictates of traditional moral law to mobilize the competence appropriated by the individual professional.

This aspect largely accounts for the "residual" persistence of a traditional ideal of service in the *contemporary* ideology of profession: the ideal of moral obligation to the collectivity is the main ideological response of profession to the contradiction between socially produced knowledge and its private appropriation. It appears, at the same time, as a justification and as a guarantee that such competence will, indeed, be "returned to society." Such an idealistic guarantee is not necessary, however, in a society where the large majority of people must sell their labor power in order to survive, and where special competences are sought with a view to their sale.

The ideal of service cannot solve the contradiction between the monopoly of training, which is the goal of professionalization projects, and the market situation, in which services are sold (in the classic personal professions) or skilled labor power is bought (in the case of salaried professionals). Monopoly of training can give a relatively high exchange value to the competence it produces, independently of the market; it allows, moreover, the creation of artificial scarcity, by means of which the theoretically inexhaustible knowledge resource becomes socially finite. The revelation that socially produced knowledge is privately monopolized (and artificially limited) challenges the egalitarian and democratic legitimations built into the dominant ideology. If, however, it can be convincingly established that the springs of knowledge flow for all who care to learn and are mentally capable of learning, the revelation is no longer as trenchant. The "natural" laws of the market do not suffice to justify the high exchange value of the special competences produced by monopolistic training centers. But if those centers appear to be open to all who "deserve" education, the individual appropriation of specially valued skills can be justified by another "natural" law: namely, the unequal distribution of "natural" intelligence and resolve, which maintains an inevitable selection process among individuals with equal rights and equal opportunities.

The generalization and apparent equalization of access to educational opportunities solve yet another ideological problem raised by professional monopolies of competence. The postulates of classical liberal theory were carried several steps further by nineteenth-century Utilitarianism, which was closely tied to the professional movements and to professionalism as an ideology.[29] All appeals to traditional moral law progressively disappeared from the Utilitarian model of society, as did the principle of an artificial identity of interests based on fear of the sovereign. As befits a society where generalized commodity production tends to subvert all organic bonds, the Utilitarians founded their view of the social order on the principle according to which individual "egoisms harmonise of themselves in a society which is in conformity with nature."[30] Seeking for their doctrines the status of science, they made even more abstract the abstract individual who was the unit of analysis of classical liberal theory. In the words of Elie Halévy, "the whole effort of the associationist psychology was to prove that egoism is the primitive motive of which all the affections of the soul are the successive complications."[31] This radical psychological reductionism accentuates the egalitarian dimension of liberal theory. It increases, therefore, the contradictions which egalitarianism generates in the dominant ideology. For, indeed, "according to the principle of the natural identity of interests, every individual is the infallible judge of his own interest, or is at least less fallible than anyone else, and can pursue it freely and without restraint."[32]

Can this position be reconciled with the professional's claim to be the best judge of his client's interest? Can it be reconciled with the reality of class society and class government, or with the principles of hierarchical voting admitted by the Utilitarians? The answer lies in education.

That individuals were not always the best judges of their own interests was proved by Malthus' theories. Therefore, the majority should be taught where their best interests lie: the state must intervene "not in order that the liberty of individuals may be limited, but in order that individuals may become free."[33] It is not difficult to see that the same reasoning applies, mutatis mutandi, to the state's intervention in favor of professional monopolies. In the most general case, however, the state's intervention, promoted and welcomed by the Utilitarians, consists precisely in organizing national systems of education. Embryonic in the first half of the nineteenth century, these systems tended more or less rapidly toward the "universal" stage of free and compulsory schooling. The intervention of the state in favor of "the greatest happiness of the greater number" solved the contradictions implicit in ideological egalitarianism: on the one hand, men are not all equally the best judges of their own interests, but they are all given, in theory, the means to become the best judges. On the other hand, the natural inequality of intelligence makes itself manifest in educational and occupational achievements. Elitism and elite rule can, therefore, be legitimized without renouncing the essential postulates of the egalitarian ideology: it is sufficient that the average person should appear to have stood at least a chance of proving his or her gifts.

In short, the apparent equalization of educational opportunity transforms the impact of ideological egalitarianism: from being a source of contradiction and potential demystification, the principle of *equality among atomized individuals* becomes a central source of legitimacy for the class system. For, indeed, "if all men start on some basis of equal potential ability, then the inequalities they experience in their lives are *not* arbitrary, they are the logical consequence of different personal drives to use those powers—in other words, social differences can now appear as questions of character, of moral resolve, will and competence."[34]

The liberal and Utilitarian construction of the individual as a "a natural unit of measurement in social science,"[35] and as the basic unit of the social order, appears to be the cornerstone of the new system of inequality. Because the intervention of the state as universal educator appears to reestablish equality of opportunity at the outstart, special categories of individuals who *monopolize* competence appear to have ipso facto proved their ability. They may, thus, *legitimately* claim special prerogatives, both juridical and social.[36]

More generally, individualism appears to be a central ideological *process,* which runs across the whole social structure, its meaning and import differently articulated and modulated at each level of the structure.[37] Its essential effect is to produce the "subjective illusion" by which the individual believes he acts as a free agent in identifying with the political and ideological structures of his society. Because actions, meanings, and words, appear to emanate solely from his subjectivity, the individual cannot grasp the shaping of his self by ideology, nor the relations between his free actions and thoughts and the social structure within which he is inserted. This subjective illusion, which can be seen as a characteristic effect of all ideology, is magnified by bourgeois individualism.[38] Because every person can be convinced that he or she is a free and responsible agent, endowed with equal rights, individualism appears as a crucial mechanism by which the ideology of the ruling class becomes dominant—that is, shared alike by the rulers and by the ruled and invested with the appearance of universality.

The particular relation that professionalism bears to individualism and to the subjective illusion deserves to be noted. Their special competence empowers professionals and experts to act in situations where laymen feel incompetent or baffled. In fact, the assumption by the public that the expert *is* competent creates a sort of pragmatic compulsion for the expert: to certify his worth in the eyes of the laity, he must act. Deferentially requested to intervene by his clients, the expert practitioner is compelled to do something; from this point of view, anything is better than nothing. As Freidson remarks: "Indeed, so impressed is he by the perplexity of his clients and by his apparent capacity to deal with those perplexities, that the practitioner comes to consider himself an expert not only in the problems he is trained to deal with but in all human problems."[39] Most particularly in the personal professions, the behavior of the expert asserts, ideologically, that a variety of ills—and, in particular, those that can most affect the person—have individual remedies. This reinforces the optimistic illusion of ideological individualism: personal problems of all kinds are purely private and admit, as such, individual and ad hoc solutions. In the predominant ideological way of addressing social issues and social relations experienced by individuals, therefore, structural causes, as well as collective action upon those causes, are relegated to a vaguely utopian realm. At the same time, the practitioner's "compulsion to act" reiterates to the layman that education confers superior powers upon the individual and superior mastery over physical and social environments. The social worth of the educated individual, his greater social productivity, and the value of his time are asserted in relative and hierarchical terms: in a fusion of practical ability and moral superiority, the expert appears to be freer and more of a person than most others. Himself a choice victim of the subjective illusion, he is also, by his very existence and actions, an effective propagator of bourgeois individualism. It is along this crucial dimension that the ideology of profession and the "possessive individualism" of expertise work to sustain the dominant ideology. We must attempt to discern the specific ways in which this is done.

PROFESSIONAL IDEOLOGY AND THE
SOCIAL CONTROL OF EDUCATED LABOR

The notion that organized professions are self-governing and self-disciplined communities of intellectual workers, bound by shared knowledge and shared norms, has a long tradition in sociology. Durkheim, for one, placed hopes for the regulation and moralization of economic life in a revived version of the medieval corporation.[40] The rules generated by professional "communities" have as their avowed object "to impose on the profession itself the obligation of maintaining the quality of the service, and to prevent its common purpose being frustrated through the undue influence of the motive of pecuniary gain upon the necessities or cupidity of the individual."[41] The service ideal and the intrinsic value placed on work are, as we know, the ethical foundations of these rules. So, at least, goes the more general justification, not of Durkheim's hopes alone, but of the public's trust. Community and ethicality are indissolubly related. In fact, profession is more often defined as *an occupation which tends to be colleague-oriented,* rather than client-oriented.

A curious paradox is involved here for occupations which claim to live by a service ideal, and yet tend to label as a quack any member "who stakes all upon his reputation with his clients—patients, students, 'cases'."[42] Indeed, the paradox, to be solved, requires the notion of an autonomous, voluntary, and organized community of peers: its standards of quality and probity embody the collective wisdom that ultimately protects the collectivity's livelihood—by keeping the product "good," they guarantee its saleability. In the classic personal professions, association and colleague control emerged in relation with market organization; they now appear to be warrants against the temptations of the market. Colleague control, furthermore, protects the public against its own undue or excessive influence on the professionals. I shall not examine here its questionable, and often questioned, efficacy. I want to ask, instead, what the normative system of profession means *for its members.* In order to grasp the *ideological* impact of notions such as "community of profession" or "company of equals" we must look, first, at the social reality to which they refer.

Throughout this study, we have encountered various forces that stratify the alleged community of profession. We paid particular attention to factors lodged in the organizations on which professions depend. The hierarchy of ranks available to professionals within bureaucratic organizations is an obvious determinant of differential standing for individuals. Less obvious and more important are the structural effects that the power and resources of organizations have on the internal hierarchy of professions. The power of the organizational client, the connections with the state, and the prestige of universities are external forces translated into dimensions of centrality and marginality *among* professions and *within* them. Insofar as a profession is itself an organization, however loose, its elites are, precisely, the connecting link with other elites in powerful organizations. Indeed, even medicine, the most powerful of the corporate occupations, does not wield a measure of independent power comparable to that of the industrial corporation or the state. Therefore, the general measures of success and power *within* a profession tend to flow, ultimately, from outside, from the central power structure of the society.[43]

Hierarchies of success measured by general societal criteria such as income, influence, and power tend to merge *within* a given profession with hierarchies of prestige measured in "peer esteem."[44] These internal prestige evaluations are diffused to the wider public, especially by the personal professions, but their origins and their use are primarily *internal.* It is *within* a profession or discipline that excellence tends to be transmuted into power and, vice versa, that power tends to be legitimized by fusing with excellence.

These two hierarchies—the one of power, with external origins and visible "to the outside," and the other of excellence and prestige, defined internally and translated into influence—*tend* to coincide. To the extent that they do not, the *internal* hierarchy becomes more esoteric, restricted to the initiated members of the profession or specialty. But in any case, *a profession is always defined by its elites:* the elites that wield internal power may not be the same that are visible to the outside, espeically when the media become the main agents of visibility; but it is always an elite that speaks to the relevant outsiders for the "whole profession," maintaining the image of a unified and solidary community, or projecting the achievements and identity of a specialty. Obviously, the more organized a profession is, the less its elites are challenged, and the more the profession will be identified by outsiders with its oligarchic spokesmen.

The question to pose now is: what factors maintain overall ideological solidarity *within* a profession? Certainly, no one would deny the proverbial professional hatreds and bickering. But is there something besides the binding force of economic interest that allows professionals low down in the internal hierarchy to consider themselves *professionals* and thus, at least minimally, the peers of the profession's elites?

A general starting point is the fact that a profession is by definition *organized*. As Stinchcombe remarks:

> Organizations are among the groups where the community of fate is shared *among unequals*. . . . In general, the fate of the organizational elite is more closely tied to the fate of the organization than is that of their "inferiors." . . . The more the subordinate's needs and wants are met by the organization, the more the superior controls the flow of these satisfactions, and the less the subordinate could meet these needs elsewhere, the less the upper classes have to court the subordinate's consent and compliance.[45]

The "courting of consent and compliance" occurs, in the professions, through initial recruitment and during training. Professional socialization aims, in fact, at the internalization of special social controls: it takes, that is, standards defined by the profession's elites and makes them part of each individual's subjectivity. Insofar as this socialization is successful, the elites will be in control not only of material rewards but also of the kind of esteem that counts—the esteem granted by a reference group of major importance for the individual. While esteem is, ultimately, easier and cheaper to dispense than power or income, it holds for the recipient something more than the promise of influence; it is intimately bound up with a sense of self, precisely because professions are *ideologically* constructed as occupations that one enters *by calling,* or at least by choice. As such, they appear to express an essential dimension of the self.

The less this is so, the more purely instrumental the choice becomes, and the less important the moral reward of colleague esteem appears in comparison with material rewards, which may or may not be controlled by colleagues. *The erosion of the ideological notion of calling tends, therefore, to undermine a powerful element of social control within a profession.* Obviously, the existence of alternative professional elites also diminishes the control over the self-esteem of "inferiors" exercised by any *one* of these elites, but it does not necessarily diminish the *overall* control of the profession over its members; the multiple elites may, indeed, share the same basic standards of "professionalism"—as is true, for example, of the various specialties within the field of medicine.

Alternative *standards* and alternative definitions of professional morality and worth do, in fact, loosen the grip that the tacit and explicit norms of a discipline or profession have on the self. This is the significance of dissenting groups or movements within a profession: while the entrenched elites always tend to rule them out as "unprofessional," these groups generate their own norms and solidarity. They may arise out of an effort to gain recognition for a new specialty, or out of full-fledged "paradigmatic battles," or out of the challenge to a profession's notion of its social function. The often profound impact of the student movements of the nineteen sixties was based, in large part, on the alternative sources of morality and solidarity they offered to professional apprentices. Despite the transiency of their personnel, student movements arise in situations that do bring people together: unlike schools and universities, many professional work situations maintain *isolation* among individuals. This is *one* of the important reasons why dissent within a profession tends to originate in its student wing.

But let us return to the average case of "successful" professionalization: the concrete reference group of the individual professional is more likely to be a specific group of colleagues than the profession at large. However, unless it is a dissenting group, it relays standards and norms which are compatible with those of the profession's elites. Compliance with these norms, we have said, is elicited by more than work-extrinsic material rewards. In fact, in almost all professions except perhaps medicine, the interest in material rewards is more likely to direct an individual outside his profession, to the centers of power where such rewards are more plentifully distributed. What *typically* binds a professional to his profession, and therefore to its elites, has to do *with the character of work itself.*

Many of the structural factors that tie an individual professional's self-esteem and sense of self to his work are common to all forms of work.[46] The fact that most professions generate a subculture is often presented as a characteristic element of these communities of workers.[47] It is obvious, however, that occupational subcultures are not confined to professions; in fact, they are particularly distinctive in relatively humble occupations, especially those that are geographically or socially isolated, such as seamen, lumberjacks, miners, railroaders, or circus and carnival people. *All* occupations which involve special skills and special worlds of work shape to some extent the worker's personality of self-presentation; initiation into techniques, languages or jargons, ways of dressing, and mannerisms, identify the individual with his occupation for himself and for outsiders.[48] The pleasure of "talking shop" is not restricted to the professions, nor is the anticipatory socialization which prepares an individual to look and act like people in his chosen field are supposed to. While the choice of a vocation reinforces the strength of anticipatory socialization, the result of *all* occupational socialization is the same; it tends to create conformity and to identify people with work roles, and also with the stereotypes of those roles that are held in the larger society. Occupational socialization, therefore, not only generates subcultural enclaves, marked by initiation and secrecy; it also reinforces the overall correspondence between the public's stereotyped expectations of people in special roles, and the aspect and behavior of the role players.

The particular strength of professional socialization is rooted in the length and the institutional character of training. A vocation is, by definition, something one follows full-time, and changes of vocation are psychologically as well as financially difficult in fields protected by monopoly of practice and lengthy training. The heavy investment of time, energy, and money that most professions require insures, for one thing, the stability of a recruit within the field. Unless the benefits are too low, or the costs too high, the investment already incurred reinforces commitment—by inertia, if nothing else.[49] This *stability*—which is distinctive in highly mobile societies—effects a particulary strong identification of the person with the role, both subjectively and for others; popular novels, films, and TV serials emphasize this permanence—you cannot *really* unfrock a priest, unmake a doctor, or disbar a lawyer. Occupational stability immediately evokes *career,* of which it is both a condition and an effect.

While biography is looking backward on one's life, an after-the-fact search for order and meaning, career is looking forward, with a sense of order to come, which depends crucially on the stability of institutions. Thus, career closely binds the projected self to organizations or to the professional institutions which insure "continuity in status in a labor market."[50] The expectation of career is therefore a powerful factor of conformity with the existing social order and a source of basic conservatism. Careers, Wilensky remarks,

> give continuity to the personal experience of the most able and skilled segments of the population—men who would otherwise produce a level of rebellion or withdrawal which would threaten the maintenance of the system. By holding out the prospect of continuous, predictable rewards, careers foster a willingness to train and achieve, to adopt a long view and defer immediate gratifications for the later pay-off. In Mannheim's phrase, they lead to the gradual creation of a "life plan."[51]

This life-plan is a privilege, enjoyed only by a minority within the labor force. Orderly careers, it has been emphasized, may well be one of the most significant expressions of inequality between different individuals and different categories of workers.[52]

Career expectations are an essential component of profession, to such an extent that asking what is happening to professionals today is almost equivalent to asking what is happening to their modal patterns of career. Stability and orderly progression through a work-life were the goals of the professionalization movement. Today, they make professions into prestigious and desirable occupations. Subjectively, career is a pattern of organization of the self. It epitomizes, therefore, the professional's self-involvement with his work as well as the legitimacy he confers to the elites—professional or organizational—on whom his future depends, both materially and psychologically.

For most recognized professions, an orderly career begins with training in professional schools or universities. The authoritative and authoritarian framework of relations between teachers and students is a fundamental element of institutionalized professional socialization. The hierarchy of excellence and prestige by means of which a profession legitimizes its internal stratification is produced in the university; professional recruits internalize it, first, in that context. The student's inevitable subordination and acceptance of his teachers' supervision are immediately and tacitly justified in terms of the teachers' greater expertise. The interrelations between the context of training and the contexts of practice are personalized; the teaching elites of a profession are often elite practitioners in the field. In any case, their personal sponsorship guarantees the proper socialization of the students to the professional world outside the school. As Freidson and Rhea remark: "Successful completion of a professional education is an objective measure of . . . technical and normative socialization, but its inadequacy seems to be implied by the characteristic tendency of professionals to rely on personal testimonials and recommendations."[53]

These personalized warrants do more than simply insure the adequate socialization of the new professional, guaranteeing that his "compliance and consent" will not be too difficult to obtain; they reinforce the control by an elite and the latter's legitimacy. Prestige filters down, from the "great men" in a field to those who study or work under them, through ideological mechanisms; the formation of cults and the vicarious enjoyment of the great man's prestige by his underlings are characteristic of the training situation, but they also extend to the world of work. They insure the new professional's willing and even happy acceptance of the hierarchical order of his profession and of the elite-defined ideology that underlies it. Vicariousness gives him, indeed, a sense of belonging to a society of peers, in which differential prestige can be ideologically redistributed.

Finally, the ideology of equality within a stratified profession depends crucially on the content and on the social meaning of training and expertise. The content of professional education is, in part, a function of its length. One author remarks:

> Practitioners are typically *overtrained*. . . . Admission to any skilled occupation is so hedged about with rules that the entrant must learn far more than he will typically apply in the course of his practice—with a consequent overlap in the abstract knowledge base of adjacent occupations. . . . A physician still knows much more than an electrician, although both may have the same ratio of used knowledge to learnt knowledge. . . . The social pressures within the major professions as well as in the larger society demand that *all* the available knowledge be mustered for crises, or at least be on call.[54]

It is almost impossible to distinguish the real from the ideological effects of this overtraining. First of all, there is no effective guarantee that the individual practitioners one deals with will, in fact, mobilize such comprehensive competences "in a crisis" for there is no guarantee that they have been keeping up with the advance of knowledge in their respective fields and that their training is not obsolete in all but a relatively narrow area of practice. Overtraining, however, aims at creating *complete* skills and at eliciting the layman's trust. Because of such overtraining, specialization is not seen by the public (or by the professional) as a narrowing down of competence, but as a deepening of knowledge, an *added* skill.

In most occupations, routinized specialties tend to become equivalent to the "dirty work" which professions delegate to ancillary occupations. Without a previous comprehensive training, specialization—even if it is not pure routine—tends to become both a factor in and an expression of subordination. The specialization of functions inherent in organizational roles gives to the incumbents a specialized knowledge which is fragmentary and rapidly exhausted. This kind of subordinate specialization ties an individual to a particular organization and a particular job, thus destroying the polyvalence of skill and its market value. For professionals too, it is a factor of potential proletarianization. On the contrary, specialization which is independently and autonomously acquired is a market asset.

There is another aspect to overtraining that occurs before specialization; it gives to the specialty, as noted, the character of an advance in esoteric knowlege which confers more power on the individual possessor of such knowledge. At the same time, overtraining appears to protect "the intelligence of the whole," the potential for understanding a whole field and its evolutionary dynamics. When the mechanization of labor robbed the skilled worker of his capacity to comprehend a whole process of production, his subordination to capital was, in fact, completed.[55] Insofar as increasingly specialized professionals maintain, through overtraining, the "intelligence of the whole," they escape the fate of most other specialized workers in our society. Overtraining appears, thus, as a specific attribute of *privileged* work, which confers special worth on its recipients and establishes a minimal parity between them; in a hierarchy of increasingly monopolized competences, all professionals have at least an initial share.

This share in monopolized knowledge brings them dividends of another kind; every profession, because of the monopoly of competence which it has or claims, "considers itself the proper body to set the terms in which some aspect of society, life, or nature is to be thought of."[56] Sharing in this general function of reality construction gives every professional a minimum of social authority. In this sense, "all professionals are priests; they interpret mysteries which affect the lives of those who do not understand."[57] Narrow specialization cannot achieve this mystical effect. For instance, the secret knowledge attached to certain roles within bureaucratic organizations seldom has general social significance; its specialized possessors do not contribute to defining and constructing for the public a usable segment of social reality. It is doubtful, therefore, that specialties whose functions are not really understood by any significant sector of the public, whose place on the "general cognitive map" is vaguely traced, can sustain the full ideology of profession.[58]

The visible professions which have a clear monopoly of competence—and not only a monopoly of practice—have *authority* over a kind of knowledge that is important for every man's life. The gap in competence between professionals and laymen, institutionalized by the monopolies of training and certification, ipso facto sets *every* professional apart: he belongs to a privileged society of "knowers," which the public tends to identify with its elite spokesmen. The "mysteries" interpreted by the individual professional have been named and partially revealed to the public before he comes in. It is a rare individual who can challenge by himself the whole image of a field and the social construction of an aspect of reality in which professional elites are particularly active and influential.

We began by asking what elements bind professionals to their work and maintain a sense of "community" and basic "equality" in stratified professions. Individualism and a sense of privilege and importance vis-à-vis the laity and other occupations emerged as general dimensions of professional consciousness. On the one hand, vocation, career, training, expertise, and authority are individualized attributes of *privileged work*. On the other hand, the unconscious (or conscious) comparisons with other kinds of work, made by professionals themselves and by the larger public, ultimately set professions out as communities of "superior" workers. These general elements of consciousness elicit "consent and compliance" from educated workers and underplay the realities of professional stratification. The minimal internal equality of professions is only relative and relational. The question is whether the ideological effects of professional consciousness can resist the forces which objectively undermine the privileges of professional work.

PROFESSIONAL PRIVILEGE
AND PROLETARIANIZATION

When the fields of action of the medieval guilds began to close, their expansion took capitalist forms: division of labor and specialization were accentuated locally and regionally, and the mastership became increasingly difficult to achieve. As Weber describes this process:

> From the fifteenth century on, strictly economic specifications were attached to the masterpiece . . . the requirement signified merely a compulsory period of work without remuneration to exclude persons without means. In addition to the requirement of the masterpiece, the masters who had achieved the position of price workers strove for a monopolistic position by prescribing a certain minimum capital for the prospective master. . . . With the closing of the guild was associated a tendency to hereditary appropriation of the position of master. . . . With this development the character of certain parts of medieval craft work as small capitalism is determined, and corresponding to this character *a permanent class of journeymen originates.*[59]

That parallel can guide us through the present situation. Let us for a moment assume that "mastership" can be equated with self-employment. The first observation is that the efforts at corporate closure of the most established professions have been successful, despite the fact that "universalistic" educational systems cannot limit apprenticeship as much or in the same way as the ancient guilds could.[60] William Kornhauser writes:

> The increase in the proportion of total professionals in the labor force hides the fact that *several major professions have declined in membership relative to the labor force*. With the exception of teachers, journalists, and clergymen, the main salaried professions increased more than ten times between 1900 and 1950, while the labor force only doubled and the total professions quadrupled. During the same period, *those professions in which many or most practitioners are self-employed increased less than the labor force in the case of lawyers, musicians, pharmacists, and physicians, or less than the total professions in the case of architects, artists, and dentists.*[61]

While the absolute numbers of self-employed professionals have obviously increased, their proportion in the total labor force has remained stable.[62] Moreover, self-employment constitutes a diminishing category *even* among the established professions: in the decade 1940–1950, only 5 percent of respondents in the established professions had managed to "move upward" into self-employment—a proportion identical to that in the other professional categories ("new," "semi-professional," "would-be," and "marginal"). Furthermore, self-employed professionals represented only 25 percent of all these professional categories taken together: but even in the *established* professions, the much higher proportion of self-employed persons (43 percent) was topped by the 45 percent who worked for private employers, and there were 12 percent who were paid by the government.[63]

Self-employed professionals had, in 1962, the highest median income of all occupational categories, although they represented less than 1.3 percent of the labor force.[64] Entry into this category shows a marked tendency toward occupational inheritance and self-recruitment.[65] In 1962, 14.5 percent of men in this category had fathers who *also* were self-employed professionals (an observed frequency 11.7 times greater than what would be expected on the assumption of independence, and by far the largest discrepancy of this kind registered in the table, which considers all occupational categories).[66] If the "mastership," in the sense of self-employment, is increasingly reserved to a minority of professionals (and to a hereditary minority, at that!), then the most significant difference among the majority of professionals is not whether they are self-employed or salaried workers, but *for whom* they work and *in what conditions*. These data only reiterate the well-known fact that professional status, even in the most exclusive categories, no longer insures the incumbent against the predominant relations of production in our society. The enduring attraction of such status must therefore be based on other kinds of privileges.

The closure of the "mastership" renders obsolete a traditional and still-cherished conception of the professional career: that "independence" can be achieved after apprenticeship. Professional lives either tend to be increasingly organized by bureaucratic career patterns, or they "progress"—in smaller, less bureaucratized professional firms—up to a point, beyond which almost nobody goes. In this latter situation, the arbitrariness and personalism of management are likely to be great; recognizing this, subordinate professional workers may organize to demand more bureaucratization, in the form of specified criteria of advancement and institutionalized and predictable promotions.[67] These attempts to stop the erosion of career hinge on "universalistic" bureaucratic standards which are—or should be—binding for *both* management and professional employees. These standards are, nevertheless, an expression of alienated work, of the employees' lack of control over their whole work setting. As such, they make manifest the general subordination of work to a preestablished division of labor, to a synthesis achieved at the top. Writing about the "malaise of technicians" in industry, an Italian political collective observes:

> One explanation of these difficulties, close to the technicans' heart, invokes the insufficient rationalization of the company—the persistence of archaic organizational forms, the inadequacy of channels of information, the manager's lack of training—in contrast with the superior organization of American firms. We argue that the technicians' malaise is rooted in the capitalist division of labor and that further rationalization will intensify rather than alleviate it. . . . Even where personal arbitrariness plays

> a restricted role, careers are dependent on two basic criteria: on one hand, social facility, adaptability, aggressiveness, talent for public contact, [and] on the other, conformity to the model by which the system operates, ability to innovate without altering pre-established plans, loyalty and "discretion" in relaying information to the top, and "legitimate" ambition.[68]

Technicians in large organizations may even appear to constitute a "new working class," precisely because of the specialization of their training and work, the threat of skill obsolescence, and the consequent greater subordination to management.[69] However, at the lower levels of the hierarchy, "professional" work in all fields (except *perhaps* medicine, scientific research, and academic work) exhibits the same trends to specialization and fragmentation.

The tendencies to proletarianization of educated labor have, potentially, great political consequences. The phenomenon has preoccupied the theorists of the "new working class," both in Europe and in the United States, especially since the events of May 1968 in France and 1968–1970 in Italy.[70] Describing conditions of increasing specialization, blocked mobility, skill obsolescence, and erosion of the market value of educated labor, these studies emphasize a double set of contradictions: between ideological expectations and work conditions, on the one hand; and between education and other areas of social experience, including work, on the other.

In his classic study of industrial work, Robert Blauner noted:

> Self-estranged workers are dissatisfied only when they have developed *needs* for control, initiative, and meaning in work. The average manual worker and many white-collar employees may be satisfied with fairly steady jobs which are largely instrumental and non-involving, because they have not the need for responsibility and self-expresison in work. . . . One factor which is most important in influencing a man's aspirations in the work process is education. The more education a person has received, the greater the need for control and creativity.[71]

Blauner's observations, however, no longer appear to accurately depict a new generation of workers.[72] The traditional legitimations of alienated labor are now in crisis, and they contradict the "search for self," however individualistic and alienated its forms, that is abroad in the general culture.

The growing importance of "educated labor," in both productive role and numbers, exacerbates the crisis and the contradictions: the amount of critical information available on society as a whole to an increasingly educated labor force contrasts with the narrow defintion of functions and rank in most work situations. For educated labor within large organizations, this broader contrast takes the form of a contradiction between the powerlessness and apathy which are the lot of the average citizen and the discretionary power granted to the worker, who is expected to exercise technical skills and theoretical intelligence, if only in limited functions. Managerial and technobureaucratic functions, moreover, are in sharp contrast with the tendency to overspecialization in many areas of technical and professional education. It can be said that "The technician, the employee, and the cadre have not been trained to be stupid, but to be intelligent: and this practical and theoretical intelligence cannot always be sufficiently controlled by the system, because the very kind of know-how that is demanded is already, in itself, contradictory."[73]

The political potential of this "new working class" is still undocumented by clear evidence, and is much too broad a subject to be considered here even speculatively; but we may suggest how the ideology of profession counteracts the structural contradictions of educated labor.[74]

First of all, a rough distinction should be made between those professionals or technicians who work for other experts in their field, and those who work in large heteronomous organizations. In the first case, the professional hierarchy, internalized and legitimized during training, will be ideologically most effective. In the second case, on the contrary, the different educational background of management may play a mystifying role: the subordinate "expert" may think, in fact, that many of his work problems would disappear "if only his superiors understood his work better (or were better trained)." We shall consider here only the general aspects that apply in both cases.

Blauner's study of industrial workers shows that the lack of control over the *immediate* work situation—in particular the rhythm and pace of work—is a fundamental determinant of their sense of powerlessness. Heteronomous control *of the worker's time* completes, under capitalism, the worker's expropriation from the means of production and from the "intelligence" of production. Now, the central characteristic of expert intellectual work is that it cannot be established from the outside *that a given result should be obtained in a given time*. This characteristic is tied to the experts' monopoly of knowledge, which makes it even more difficult for non-experts to "see" or to replicate the productive process in which experts actually engage. The secrecy and mystery which surround the creative process maximize the self-governance conceded to experts.

Thus the real and the ideological aspects of expert intellectual work combine to protect these privileged workers from the "tyranny of the clock." Even if their products and the organization of their work lives escape their control, they are *masters of their time;* this freedom extends from apparently trivial but nevertheless fundamental aspects of the work situation all the way to the *discretion* which they enjoy in the productive activity itself. Experts are not usually asked to punch time cards, they take their coffee breaks when they like, they arrange their work schedules and vacations with relative freedom, they have free access to telephones, and often have their own private lines and offices as well. In their work, they tend to have absolute discretion, even though their own decisions are inserted within the framework of goals and strategies chosen by others.

Many of the most visible symbols of occupational status among non-manual workers—private office, command over secretaries, reserved parking space, a waiting room, and the like—are "protecting" their time and their work, thus creating deferential respect for both. As Richard Sennett and Jonathan Cobb remark:

> Deference in American society has this at its root: a calculation that someone else's time is more valuable than your own, which seems to give the person the right to command your time in accordance with his needs. The most obvious example occurs in offices, where it seems right for secretaries to perform services for their superior, not because they respect him as self-sufficient or because they are awed by his abilities, but because the superior's work is considered more valuable than her typing, and so his time more valuable than hers.[75]

The symbols signify that some kinds of work and some kinds of people are worthier of respect than others. But the respect has real roots in the discretion and the freedom from immediate supervision that expert workers enjoy, no matter how limited their actual power.

We have seen earlier how management manipulates both the real and the symbolic dimensions of freedom at work and social prestige, in order to conceal the fact that "professional ladders" *do not* lead to increasing power and control in decision-making. Because it shapes the expectations of professionals, the ideology of profession contributes to the success of these strategies: it confuses, that is, discretion at the level of execution with real power and freedom of choice.

There is, first, the archetypical professional concern *with status*. In the newer professions, the creation, expression, and protection of special status tend to be the most central dimension of the professionalization project. *Relative* prestige and privilege, tacitly based on the invidious comparison with other occupations and other workers, influence, however unconsciously, a professional's assessment of a specific work situation.[76] Who he implicitly compares himself with is significant: it should be noted, in this respect, that the frequent *isolation* of professional departments and "enclave" professional workers in large organizations focuses comparisons on similar occupational categories. In theory, the very sense of ideological community fostered by professionalism should have the same effect, and keep comparisons from deflecting upward toward managerial ranks and their different kind of work and responsibilities.

The concern with status not only prevents *alliances* with other workers or with clients.[77] It also works as a preventive against the unity—and the unionization—of professional workers themselves. Unions are, in fact, an instrument of power of the working class, and as such are symbolic of a loss in general social status; for analogous reasons, even when there are unions, professionals are more reluctant than other workers to engage in militant tactics.[78] This ideological effect, in which concern with status can become a trap for subordinate professionals, is maximized by the second archetypical feature: professional *individualism* with all its facets.

Professional work conditions (and not only the general ideology) foster individualism. The professional's sense of power and authority flows not only from his actual command over special knowledge but also from his control over interpersonal situations. The first established professions—medicine, law, the ministry, and architecture—were typically concerned with the problems of individuals. Only indirectly did they define society as their client. Today, individualized service becomes an ideological remedy for the ills of a social situation, a screen for the social problems caused by the bureaucratic systems through which services are delivered—most notably in the medical and teaching professions.

The ideological insistence on individual aspects, the neglect of the whole, merges with specialization to confine the professional in an ideological conception of his role: the importance of narrow responsibilities is consciously and unconsciously emphasized, exaggerating the "dignity" of the functions. The dominant ideology attributes to professionals and experts special prestige as well as "moral and intellectual superiority": sharing in this ideology, professionals can easily mystify to themselves their actual power. Moreover, they are locked into conformity with the role society offers them to play—locked in by their vocational choice, by the particular mystique of each profession, and by their whole sense of social identity.

Finally, the technocratic *ideology* of science and objectivity excludes from the specialist's concern the social and political consequences of his acts. Nowhere is this truer than in the technical and scientific fields. Robert Merton notes that "engineers, not unlike scientists, come to be indoctrinated with an ethical sense of limited responsibilities."[79] As the technical auxiliaries of capitalist production, engineers, in particular, could never gain the power to define the social aims of technology, the overall purpose of their work. In this sense, they are a typical example of *powerless discretion.*

Scientists, engaged in the loftier and apparently more autonomous function of advancing knowledge for the whole of society, are similarly socialized into corporate irresponsibility, beyond the immediate and circumscribed area of their specific task. For the positivistic ideology on which most technical and scientific training tends to be based, "science and ethics are rigidly separated domains with distinct methodologies and subject matter. As a result, the purposes of science are shaped by the dominant class, while ethics is understood as personal, vague, and increasingly without foundation."[80] As "the citizen-self threatens to become submerged in the occupational self," the narrow conception of autonomous and responsible function becomes a support for the technocratic ideology and its premises of general privatization and depoliticization: "Paradoxically, the same ideology of the 'expert,' which gives the technician a certain autonomy within his or her own specialty, simultaneously prepares the technician to execute blindly the designs of others."[81]

In sum, the expert's and the professional's outlook on their work lives tend to be shaped, today, by individualism and narrow specialism. Thus, the "needs for control, initiative, and meaning in work" of which Blauner speaks tend to be defined, *by education itself,* in a way that is compatible with the requirements of production in advanced industrial capitalism. Flexibility, autonomy, and circumscribed responsibility are precisely the qualities expected from expert labor: as long as the protests of subordinate professional workers ask for more of these *individual* privileges, as long as that is the main purpose of their corporate associations, their potential disloyalty can easily be managed. Within the ideological constellation of contemporary professionalism, the ideology of expertise and of partial irresponsibility coexists with traditional components and with profession's own emphasis on individual career and individual solutions. With its persistent antibureaucratic appearances, the ideology of professionalism deflects the comprehensive and critical vision of society which is necessary to reassess the social functions of profession. In this sense, professionalism functions as a means for controlling large sectors of educated labor and for co-opting its elites.

FUNCTIONS OF THE IDEOLOGY OF PROFESSION; CONTRIBUTIONS TO THE DOMINANT IDEOLOGY

The perspective of the political radicalization of the intelligentsia has haunted bourgeois societies (and others as well) for at least as long as the "specter of Communism." The threat of communism was more potent and more total, but the threat of elite disaffection has often seemed a dangerous and perhaps likely prelude to it. Against this threat of disaffection, professionalization has functioned as an effective form of social and ideological control.

Speaking of the transition toward full-fledged capitalist production, Marx observed:

> Since handicraft skill is the foundation of manufacture, and since the mechanism of manufacture as a whole possesses no framework, apart from the laborers themselves, capital is constantly compelled to wrestle with the insubordination of the workmen. . . . [Machines] sweep away the handicraftsman's work as the regulating principle of social production. Thus, on the one hand, the technical reason for the lifelong annexation of the workman to a detail function is removed. On the other hand, the fetters that this same principle laid on the dominion of capital, fall away.[82]

The mechanization of production robbed the working class of its last hold on the means of production—its crafts and its skills. In the historical context of proletarianization, "the fetters that [the principle of craftsmanship] laid on the dominion of capital" became symbols of status superiority and instruments of division within the working class. At the other extreme of the occupational hierarchy, part of the traditions and ideals of craftsmanship were transposed into the ideology of profession by a sector of the bourgeoisie who did not primarily view themselves as workers.

As capitalism matured, the ideology of profession could be incorporated into generalized forms of social control, extended now to the growing class of nonmanual and "unproductive" workers. Dependence on capitalist relations of production and on bureaucracy is a generalized feature of work in the monopolistic phase of capitalism. The bureaucratization of work generates a "hierarchical image of society" and spreads some of the typical components of the ideology of profession to ever-increasing strata of the labor force. Compartmentalization and differentiation within the division of labor create (mainly bureaucratic) positions of relative privilege, which their incumbents strive to "dignify" and monopolize by claiming expertise and by professionalizing.

Ralf Dahrendorf calls this new middle class a Dienstklasse or "service class." He observes their concern with status and status symbols, in and out of work: "Status, for the service class, is not a static notion. Hierarchy always implies the possibility of promotion: social mobility and the service class belong inseparably together. . . . It is also of more general social significance that mobility within the ranks of public or private bureaucracies is *greatly facilitated by education*. Experience helps one move ahead to the next barrier, but this can as a rule be overcome only by formal education."[83] He adds: "Class involves a certain amount of class consciousness and political solidarity. . . . The members of the service class, however, are in Crozier's words, a 'classe sans conscience'. Instead of feeling cohesive, they all stand in a relation of individual competition to each other. Of course, not every bureaucrat competes with every other one. . . . But for the bureaucrat, *advancing his status is essentially an individual achievement*."[84] We can recognize in this description elements that the ideology of profession carried, from a traditional past and from the liberal phase of capitalism, into the division of labor of the monopolistic phase: individualism, expertise, and status-seeking. Adapted, reduced, transposed, and changing in content, these become central elements of the *dominant* ideology.

The ideology of the rising or ruling class is dominant precisely because it is *shared* by the dominated. Working through the "subjective illusion," it finds *material* existence in the institutions, relations, and symbols of social practice. Its origins are composite, reflecting styles of life and values other than those of the ruling class. Its essential function, however, is to reproduce the relations of production and the class structure by disguising their real nature and even their existence. In this sense, professionalization appears as an ideological counterpart of proletarianization. As the labor force tends to become totally subsumed under the formal relations of capitalist production, the real and the ideological privileges associated with "professionalism" legitimize the class structure by introducing status differentials, status aspirations, and status mobility at practically all levels of the occupational hierarchy.

The central legitimations of the new forms of inequality, which are their ideological foundations, are lodged in the educational system. In Louis Althusser's formulation: "At the outcome of a violent class struggle, both political and ideological, against the old ideological apparatus of the state [the Church], a new ideological apparatus has been placed in *dominant* position: in mature capitalist formations, *the dominant ideological apparatus of the state is the school.*"[85] The material and ideological importance of the educational system for both the consolidation of professions and the reproduction of the social order cannot be overemphasized. Education—arbitrarily *equated with years of formal schooling*—appears to be in our society a major determinant of occupation and of lifetime income.[86] Recent studies of income inequality invalidate the relation between differences in schools and in cognitive skill—measured chiefly by IQ tests—and earning power: they confirm, however, the statistically significant correlation between *years of schooling* and later income.[87] Whatever the merits of measuring cognitive development and ability by IQ tests, and whatever schools actually do to improve these scores, the undeniable fact remains that *schools do something for the social system,* something of fundamental importance. The findings indicate, in the first place, that "educational achievement is a more powerful predictor of earnings than ability, when ability is measured by IQ scores and class standing . . . *the credentials are more important determinants than naked ability,* or at least . . . than general educational development."[88]

The rise of a "credentialed society" cannot be adequately explained in terms of actual changes in the nature of work: "Overall, about 85 percent of the rise in educational attainment may be attributed to increased educational levels *within* occupations and only 15 percent to shifts in the occupational structure from occupations requiring less education to occupations requiring more. . . . Only at the extremes of the attainment distribution (that is, for college graduates and for persons with no education) was as much as one half the change in educational attainment attributable to shifts between occupations."[89] Because their data were too general, the authors were obliged to conclude, however, that "how much of the change reflects increased skill requirements . . . and how much is due to the availability of better-educated persons for the same jobs cannot finally be determined.''[90] It appears, indeed, that the growing supply of educated labor—which can itself be attributed in large part to the structural distortions of production and employment in late capitalism—determines the upgrading of the requirements for employment, perhaps as significantly as the changing *content* of most jobs.[91]

The general attitudes of management in private enterprise corroborate the *ideological* import of credentials. Practically without data to support their beliefs, managers tend to take "educational achievements . . . as evidence of self-discipline and potential for promotion. Moreover, trainability is presumed to correlate with educational achievement, as are productivity, personality—important in many jobs—and adaptability.''[92] Yet, even from the narrow point of view of managerial requirements, "data on the civilian occupations and personal attributes of large samples of American military personnel during both world wars provide strong circumstantial evidence that Americans of diverse educational achievements perform productive functions adequately and perhaps well *in all but a few professional occupations.*''[93]

There is evidence, therefore, that the hierarchy of "ability" established by formal schooling has unclear and uncertain correlates in social productivity, even if we accept the terms by which our society defines it. In America, "educational credentials have become the new property" for the large mass of the population.[94] This form of property is all the more difficult to challenge because it is less determined by inheritance than other forms and because its ideological fusion with the self is almost impossible to break apart and demystify. What are the overall ideological effects of the new structure of inequality?

The first effect is that the use of credentials as screening devices at all levels of the occupational hierarchy justifies the existence of a growing "industrial reserve army" and of a permanent surplus population. In Ivar Berg's words, "The most serious consequence of the educational upgrading of work opportunities is . . . the displacement of a significant population at the other end of the labor force, who must compete for jobs once held by people of modest educational achievement and with people whose educational achievements have gone up.''[95] The new form of property has the further merit (for the maintenance of the social system) of *immediately* justifying relegation or exclusion in terms that are highly compatible with the old liberal ideology of individual effort and rewarded hard work.

The new structure of inequality has a second effect. Because everybody has gone through some schooling—or, at the very least, believes that he or she should have gone—the ideological foundations of inequality are deep, intertwined with the roots of the subjective illusion: "If only I was smart enough, If I hadn't been too interested in making money fast, If I hadn't fooled around so much" read countless interviews with working-class people. Because they believe, at least in some way, "that working yourself up depends on the people, not on the chances you have" they blame themselves for not being something other than what they are.[96]

Moreover, the school teaches both implicitly and explicitly that different tasks and skills, no matter how important and exacting for the self, do not have the same social value, in the same way that different kinds of useful and honest work do not have the same dignity. As Sennett and Cobb put it, the child learns through experience in school not only that doing well in physics is better than playing the banjo but also that the "college-bound" are different, and *better,* no matter how much the tougher kids put them down. In the hierarchical and stratified school system, Althusser observes, "each mass that falls along the way is practically provided with the ideology fit for the role it must play in the class society," including "the role of the exploited (with all the 'professional,' 'moral,' 'civic,' and 'national' components of a highly developed apolitical conscience); the role of agent of exploitation . . . of agent of repression . . . or of professional ideologist."[97]

In our society, the reality of class and exploitation is deflected and concealed by the contradictions of a self that is shaped by class: ideology, indeed, transforms structure into personality. The hierarchy of competence is presented and lived, from early childhood on, as coincident with a *moral* hierarchy of intelligence, effort, dignity, and freedom. The first consequence is that challenging the structure of inequality requires, to a large extent, an ideological redefinition of the self: "We do not mean that the men and women we encountered were ignorant of the fact that class conditions limited their freedom" write Sennett and Cobb in their study of working-class Bostonians. "Rather, the use of badges of ability or of sacrifices is *to divert men from challenging the limits on their freedom by convincing them that they must first become legitimate, must achieve dignity on a class society's terms,* in order to have the right to challenge the terms themselves."[98] It is in this sense that ideology makes men and women put the burden of their "failures" on themselves first; it holds in front of them the possibility of purely personal and individual solutions, and thus prevents them from even conceiving that there may be collective and cooperative ways of challenging the very structure of social inequality.

Another consequence of the ideology of competence is the formation of an image of society that unconsciously fuses power with superior ability and superior development of the self. It is here that we must address another question: what is the direct and indirect role that professions and professionals play in generating and maintaining this ideology?

Historically, to found social privilege on education and tested ability was, if not an invention, at least the distinctive battle cry of the professionalization movement. We have seen how the professions obtained, with the organization of an educational system, the institutional and ideological structures on which to establish personal and collective mobility, and later, collective entrenchment. What is particularly significant in their role is that the superior badges of ability which they carry do not remain hidden within ruling-class circles or small intellectual coteries; they do not even remain circumscribed to the "magic circle" of elite universities: the professions carry the symbols of the new meritocratic ideology to the hospitals, to the public schools, to the factories, to the government agencies, to the everyday life of a majority of men, women, and children. Professionals do the helping, the judging, the advising. They have the jobs that seem useful, that could be helpful, that allow an expression of the self.

In Sennett and Cobb's interviews with working-class people, the persistent "attraction of the professions was divorced from the behavior of everyday professionals.'' They say: ''It is the position in which the doctor or university professor is placed *relative to other people* that makes these occupations seem so valuable.''[99] This everyday visibility of the professionals, tremendously increased by the welfare state and mass college education, has ideological consequences. During the Depression, they *seemed* to possess the only insurance against cataclysm.[100] Today, they seem to have, more importantly than income, a claim to dignity and respect. This claim appears *to be founded entirely on superior education.*

For most of the men and women who strive to improve themselves or their children, getting some education, even some college degree, is seldom the door to prestigious, ''socially productive,'' and ''free'' intellectual jobs. The educational ''property'' which they strive to acquire only brings them what seem like ''second-rate'' benefits, if one compares them to the ideal privileges of professional status. Yet, the first steps on the illusory road to high status can, and indeed are, taken: since 1957, more than 40 percent of the students who have completed the fifth grade have gone on to college. The prestige accorded year after year to the professions in occupational prestige scales reflects the ideological function which they perform simply by being visible: in our society, they keep ''open'' the road to freedom through *more* formal education, through *more* individual effort; they appear to be our last ideological frontier. The link they visibly establish between education and the labor market reinforces the ideological notion that there *is* such a link, and that rewards—both material and psychological—are, after all, *rationally* distributed to the ablest and the hard-striving.

Education, intelligence, persistent effort, and social usefulness appear to grant professionals dignity and the possibility of full human development. Professionals expect and demand deference in the nonpolitical circumstances of everyday life; they usually get it, most especially from working-class and lower-class clienteles. Is this because of their ability, because of their capacity to help a person in need, because of their credentials, or because of the symbols of their class and status position? It is impossible to say, and it does not really matter: the location of most professionals in middle- and upper-middle social strata infuses the lifestyle and the ethos of the dominant class with meritocratic and ethical legitimations. From the occupational and educational systems, the ideological effect spreads to the whole structure of social inequality.

The ideological apparatus of the school standardizes the general structures of the dominant ideology, in terms that reinforce the unequal distribution of knowledge. Respect for science, for knowledge, for the professionals' ''construction of reality,'' grows among masses of people who shall never see a university. This respect is *embodied* in a social hierarchy: it is not only respect for the man of superior knowledge, it is respect for those ''who know better'' *because their position of relative power proves that they do.* Personal experiences with the reality of class may contradict the belief in the untrammeled, ''objective'' play of meritocratic criteria. Yet the dominant ideology constantly restates this belief in every area of practice: in school, at work, in the media, in the doctor's office, in the courts, in the presentation of the class structure and in political life.

If bourgeois political ideology is characterized by democratic elitism—which, Peter Bachrach argues, makes democracy dependent "upon the ability of the gifted to command the deference of the many for the well-being of all"[101]—then professionalization helps diffuse this ideology in the civil society and reinforce its political usefulness. A dominant ideology which ties ability to the legitimation of monopolized competence and of the undemocratic uses of expertise is for professionalism both a foundation and a prison: for, indeed, even the purest and worthiest of professional behaviors cannot help legitimizing inequality and elitism by their factual demonstration that knowledge is beneficent power.

As power becomes equated with ability in everyday circumstances, the popular bases of a technocratic ideology are strengthened. A technocratic ideology, we know, regards democratic participation and political debate and accountability with impatience: superior ability and rational knowledge should not and cannot be hindered by an ignorant citizenry and nonrational political processes. As the masses unconsciously absorb technocratic visions of polity and society, those in power are progressively freer from having to prove special expertise and ability. The ideological relation is then reversed: power and privilege tend to become automatic warrants of superior competence.

As a heterogeneous category of the occupational structure, professionals are, in general, only agents of power. Consciously and unconsciously, they spread the technocratic legitimations of the new structures of domination and inequality, contributing to their ideological convergence with other beliefs, aspirations, and illusions. The individual freedom and control which professionals enjoy in and out of work is in part a mask: for themselves as well as for less privileged others, it helps to conceal collective powerlessness, subordination, and complicity.

Yet, experts and professionals do possess cognitive and technical competences which are important, if not always essential, for the social development of productive forces and the full satisfaction of human needs. By choice and socialization, they are often deeply involved with the intrinsic value of their callings. Dissatisfaction with the structural limitations of one's work and the social uses of one's productive activity need not remain a private crisis of conscience. The passage from purely personal problems to a collective evaluation of their causes begins to merge the personal and the political. Today, knowledge is acquired and produced within educational and occupational hierarchies which are, by their structure, inegalitarian, antidemocratic, and alienating. These structures achieve a fusion between the progressive content of special competences and the requirements of a system of domination. They serve, in this sense, as a principal support of the dominant ideology. To separate the progressive human meaning of one's work from the ideological functions inscribed in one's role is a task of personal salvation. This questioning has been attempted and it is taking place today, however silently, however timidly, in schools and in work places. Breaking with ideology, finding new norms for the social production of knowledge and the social uses of competence demands passion, vision, and hard work. This major historical task can only be sustained by a solidary collectivity, aware of its part and of its place in the overall struggle for human liberation. In a historical perspective, abandoning the "subjective illusion" and the seductions of bourgeois individualism becomes the premise of personal freedom.

We have followed different types of professions and different aspects of the professionalization movement in their "long march" through capitalist institutions: the free market of services, the labor market, the bureaucratic organization, the system of higher education. Much of the contemporary sociological work on the professions participates in and accepts their ideology. Much of the best empirical work tends to focus exclusively on the actual processes of interaction between professionals and laymen, especially in the classic personal professions, stressing the failure in communication of these asymmetric systems of interpersonal exchange.

I have tried to explore in this book the structural foundations of diverse professional practices, moving away from the predominance which everday life accords to individual and interactional dimensions. My central concerns have been these: the double movement which constituted, historically, the complex structure of profession; the structural resources mobilized by professionalization; and the ideology that professions help generate and which most professionals share. To view professions and professionalization in their historical matrix helps us to understand the inherent contradictions which limit and distort the human potential of professional work in our society. In this sense, sociological analysis can contribute to the practical redefinition of professional roles.

I would like to conclude by quoting the words of a political collective formed by professionals and technicians, for they suggest the bridge between theoretical analysis and social practice: "Role contestation originates with a refusal to view one's work as an isolated technical function and an insistence on seeing it as part of a larger social process. This *begins* as an act of individual defiance. . . . [But] the second phase of role contestation involves the development of new norms and new criteria which are alien to the capitalist logic."[102] The autonomy and the "intelligence of the whole" traditionally vested in professional work appear to be, now, uncertain privileges. To build or defend monopolies of competence and access does not protect these intrinsic qualities. For this, professional workers, in solidarity with all workers, must find the means of claiming and realizing the full human potential of all work.

Appendix

Appendix Table 1. *PROFESSIONAL ASSOCIATIONS OF NATIONAL SCOPE*

England		United States
	1897	Opticians
	1896	Nurses
Brit. Optical Association	1895	
Royal Brit. Nurses Ass'n	1887	Accountants
British Dental Ass'n		
Insti. of Chartered	1880	
Accountants		
	1878	Lawyers
Librarians Association	1877	
	1876	Librarians
	1874	Social workers
National Union Teachers	1870	
	1867	Civil engineers
	1863	Veterinarians
	1857	Teachers; Architects
Society of Engineers	1854	Pharmacists:
	1852	Civil engineers (N.Y.; fails to survive)
	1847	American Medical Ass'n
Royal College of Veterinary Surgeons	1844	
Pharmac. Society of Great Britain	1841	
	1840	Dentists
Royal Institute of British Architects	1834	
British Medical Ass'n	1832	
Law Society	1825	
Inst. of Civil Engineers	1818	

SOURCES: For England, Geoffrey Millerson, *The Qualifying Associations* (London, Routledge and Kegan Paul, 1964) pp. 246–258; for the United States, Harold L. Wilensky, "The Professionalization of Everyone?", *American Journal of Sociology*, 70 (1964): 137–158, p. 141, Table I.

Appendix Table 2. *POPULATION GROWTH DURING THE "GREAT TRANSFORMATION" (average growth rate, per thousand per year)*

Decades	England & Wales	Great Britain	Decades	United States	
				Total increase	Net migration rate
1701–11	2.7				
1711–21	0.3				
1721–31	−0.9				
1731–41	−0.3				
1741–51	3.6				
1751–61	7.0				
1761–71	7.3				
1771–81	6.8				
1781–91	9.5	9.0			
1791–1801	11.0	10.2	1790–1800	29.9	—
1801–11		13.7	1800–10	30.8	1.
1811–21		16.9	1810–20	28.4	.8
1821–31		15.2	1820–30	28.7	1.1
1831–41		13.4	1830–40	28.1	3.3
1841–51		12.5	1840–50	30.4	7.1
1851–61		11.1	1850–60	30.2	9.4
1861–71		12.7	1860–70	23.5	5.8
1871–81		13.9	1870–80	21.9	5.0
1881–91		11.2	1880–90	22.65	7.95
1891–1901		12.0	1890–1900	18.2	3.65
1901–11		10.3	1900–10	19.15	6.45
1911–21		4.6	1910–20	14.0	3.2

SOURCES: Phyllis Deane and W. A. Cole, *British Economic Growth: 1688–1959* (Cambridge: Cambridge Univ. Press, 1962), p. 288; Lance E. Davis et al., *American Economic Growth* (New York: Harper and Row, 1972), p. 123.

Appendix Table 3. *URBANIZATION AND INDUSTRIAL EMPLOYMENT DURING THE "GREAT TRANSFORMATION"*

A. Urbanization: Urban population (in Great Britain all principal towns including London, in U.S. all towns of 2500 or more) as percentage of total population

Great Britain		United States	
Year	Percent urban	Year	Percent urban
1801	18.82	1800	6.1
1851	33.02	1850	15.3
1891	44.44	1880	28.2
1921	57.32	1900	39.7
		1920	51.2

B. Industrialization: Distribution of the labor force as percentage of the total working population in selected years

	Great Britain					
	1801	*1831*	*1851*	*1871*	*1891*	*1911*
Agric.	35.9	24.6	21.7	15.1	10.5	8.3
Manuf., mining	29.7	40.8	42.9	43.1	43.9	46.4
All others	34.5	34.5	35.5	41.7	45.5	45.5
Total	100	100	100	100	100	100

	United States				
	1839–59	*1869–79*	*1889–99*	*1919–40*	*1950–55*
Agric.	56.9	51.9	41.5	21.5	10.5
Manuf., mining	14.1	20.7	21.8	24.7	24.4
All others	29.0	27.4	36.7	53.8	65.1
Total	100	100	100	100	100

SOURCES: Part A: B. R. Mitchell and Phyllis Deane, *Abstract of British Historical Statistics* (London: Cambridge Univ. Press, 1962), pp. 19 and 24–26; Lance E. Davis *et al.*, Economic Growth, p. 601. Part B: Deane and Cole, *British Economic Growth*, p. 142; Davis *et al.*, *Economic Growth*, p. 55.

Appendix Table 4. *GROWTH OF PER CAPITA PRODUCT IN LONG PERIODS; COEFFICIENT OF MULTIPLICATION IN A CENTURY (average centennial rates)*

Years	Great Britain	Years	United States
1700–80	1.2	1700–1840	1.4–1.7
1780–1881	3.5	1834–43 to 1894–1903	4.1
1855–59 to 1957–59	3.7	1894–1903 to 1957	5.2
		1834–43 to 1957	4.6

NOTE: The coefficient of multiplication gives a clear image of differences in growth rates: if the average annual growth rate had persisted for one hundred years, the value of the per capita GNP would have been as many times as large (as the coefficient of multiplication) compared to the value at the beginning of the period.

SOURCE: Lance E. Davis *et al., Economic Growth,* pp. 41ff.

Appendix Table 5. *EVOLUTION OF THE OCCUPATIONAL STRUCTURE UNITED STATES, 1900–1970*
(both sexes; in thousands & in percentages of total labor force)

	1900	1920	1940	1950	1960	1970
Managers, Officials, Proprietors, Farm Owners & Managers	7,460 25.6%	9,245 21.9%	9,132 17.7%	9,530 16.1%	10,400 15.5%	9,998 12.7%
Professional and Technical	1,234 4.3%	2,283 5.4%	3,379 7.5%	5,081 8.6%	7,475 11.1%	11,322 14.4%
Independent Professional & Technical	320 1.1%	420 1.0%	570 1.1%	654 1.1%	873 1.3%	1,200 1.5%
Professional & Technical Workers	910 3.1%	1,860 4.4%	3,310 6.4%	4,427 7.5%	6,602 9.9%	10,100 12.9%
Clerical & Sales Workers	2,184 7.5%	5,443 12.9%	8,432 16.3%	11,365 19.3%	14,184 21.2%	18,548 23.6%
Service Workers	2,626 9.1%	3,313 7.9%	6,069 11.8%	6,180 10.5%	8,349 12.5%	9,724 12.4%
Manual Workers	10,401 35.8%	16,974 40.2%	20,597 39.8%	24,266 41.1%	24,211 36.1%	27,452 34.9%
Craftsmen & Foremen	3,062 10.5%	5,482 13.0%	6,203 12.0%	8,350 14.2%	8,560 12.8%	10,027 12.8%
Operatives	3,720 12.8%	6,587 15.6%	9,518 18.4%	12,030 20.4%	11,986 17.9%	13,811 17.6%
Non-Farm Laborers	3,620 12.5%	4,905 11.6%	4,875 9.4%	3,885 6.6%	3,665 5.5%	3,614 4.6%
Farm Workers	5,125 17.7%	4,948 11.7%	3,632 7.0%	2,578 4.3%	2,057 3.1%	1,400 1.8%
TOTAL	29,030	42,206	51,742	58,999	66,681	78,408

SOURCES: U.S. Bureau of the Census, *Historical Statistics of the United States; Colonial Times to 1957,* Washington, D.C., 1960; U.S. Bureau of the Census, *Statistical Abstract of the United States: 1970,* 91st edition, Washington, D.C., 1970; Albert Szymanski, "Trends in the American Working Class," *Socialist Revolution,* 2 (1972):101–122.

Appendix Table 6. *GROWTH IN EMPLOYMENT OF PROFESSIONAL AND TECHNICAL WORKERS, 1960–1970*

Occupation	Number Employed 1970	Increase, 1960–1970 No.	Increase, 1960–1970 Percent
Total	11,140	3,670	49
Teachers	2,690	930	53
Elementary & Secondary School	2,310	710	44
College & University[a]	380	220	144
Natural Scientists	500	200	68
Chemists	140	40	39
Physicists	50	20	66
Mathematicians	70	40	123
Life Scientists	180	80	83
Other	70	30	87
Engineers	1,100	300	37
Health Workers	1,740	440	34
Physicians	310	60	24
Dentists	100	10	11
Professional Nurses	700	200	39
Technicians	260	120	86
Other	380	50	16
Social Scientists	130	70	128
Accountants and Auditors	490	180	57
Lawyers	280	80	37
All Others	4,210	1,470	54

[a]Full-time instructors only.

NOTE: Numbers are rounded to the nearest 10,000. However, percentages have been calculated on the bases of unrounded data, and may not add to total. In addition, about 6 percent of all scientists and engineers are full-time college teachers. Adjustments were not made to eliminate duplications.

SOURCE: Michael F. Crowley, "Professional Manpower: The Job Market Turnaround." *Monthly Labor Review*, October 1972, p. 12.

Appendix Table 7. *PROFESSIONALS IN THE ENGLISH OCCUPATIONAL STRUCTURE*

Year	Total working labor force (in thousands)	Professional occupations and subord. services (in thousands)	Professionals as percent of total
A. Based on 1911 Census Categories			
1841	6,908	162	2.3
1861	10,520	305	2.9
1881	12,739	457	3.6
1901	16,299	674	4.1
1921	19,355	856	4.4
B. Based on 1921 Census Categories			
1921	19,357	786	4.0
1931	21,055	933	4.4
1951	22,610	1,376	6.1

Source: Mitchell and Deane, *Abstract of British Historical Statistics,* pp. 60–61.

Notes

INTRODUCTION

1. For a classification of the attributes of profession, see Geoffrey Millerson, *The Qualifying Associations* (London: Routledge & Kegan Paul, 1964), p. 5; and M. L. Cogan, "Toward a Definition of Profession," *Harvard Educational Review,* 23 (1953): 33–50.

2. The focus on community and the functionalist perspective are well represented by William J. Goode, "Community within a Community; the Professions," *Amer. Soc. Rev.,* 22 (1957): 194–200; and Bernard Barber, "Some Problems in the Sociology of the Professions," *Daedalus* (Fall 1963): 669–688.

3. Such is the argument presented by Harold Wilensky in "The Professionalization of Everyone," *Amer. Jour. Soc.,* 70 (1964): 137–158.

4. Eliot Freidson, *Profession of Medicine* (New York: Dodd & Mead, 1970), p. 78. On the characteristics of professional training, see, for instance, William J. Goode, "The Theoretical Limits of Professionalization," in *The Semi-Professions,* Amitai Etzioni, ed., pp. 266–313 (New York: Free Press, 1963).

5. See Robert W. Hodge *et al.,* "Occupational Prestige in the United States: 1925–1963," in *Class, Status and Power,* Reinhard Bendix and S. M. Lipset, eds., pp. 322–334 (New York: Free Press, 1966).

6. See Eliot Freidson and Buford Rhea, "Processes of Control in a Company of Equals," in *Medical Men and their Work,* Eliot Freidson and Judith Lorber, eds., pp. 185–199 (Chicago: Aldine-Atherton, 1972).

7. See Eliot Freidson, "Client Control and Medical Practice," *Amer. Jour. Soc.,* 65 (1960): 374–382.

8. See David Solomon, "Ethnic and Class Differences among Hospitals as Contingencies in Medical Careers," in *Medical Men,* Freidson and Lorber, eds. (1972), pp. 163–173; and Dietrich Rueschmeyer, "Doctors and Lawyers: A Comment on the Theory of the Professions," in *Medical Men,* pp. 5–19.

9. See William Rothstein, *American Physicians in the Nineteenth Century* (Baltimore: Johns Hopkins Univ. Press, 1972).

10. Freidson, *Profession,* pp. 71–72.

11. *Ibid.,* p. 73.

12. *Ibid.*

13. The case of medicine in the People's Republic of China illustrates this point. First of all, the corpus of knowledge has been redefined according to social needs, with emphasis placed on prevention rather than on cure. Second, because specialization of functions has been broken down considerably within the medical team, the physician tends to lose at least some of his "inherent" superiority. Third, the effort to develop paramedical personnel—the famous "barefoot doctors"—substantially dilutes the physicians' monopoly of expertise. See Victor and Ruth Sidel, *Serve the People; Observations on Medicine in the People's Republic of China* (Boston: Beacon Press, 1973).

14. Talcott Parsons, "The Professions and Social Structure," in *Essays in Sociological Theory,* pp. 34–49 (New York: Free Press, 1954).

15. Parsons speaks, for example, of the legal profession occupying an "interstitial" position in the social structure; see Talcott Parsons, "A Sociologist Looks at the Legal Profession," in *Essays,* p. 375.

16. Karl Mannheim, *Ideology and Utopia* (New York: Harcourt, Brace and World, 1936), pp. 155–156.

17. Mannheim, *Ideology,* p. 156.

18. On the Marxist approach to ideology, see Karl Marx and Frederick Engels, *The German Ideology,* Parts I and II (New York: International Publishers, 1947); and Louis Althusser, "Idéologie et Appareils Idéologiques d'Etat," *La Pensée* (June 1970): 3–38.

19. For Gramsci's ideas on the intellectuals and hegemony, see Antonio Gramsci, *Prison Notebooks,* Quintin Hoare and Geoffrey Nowell Smith, eds. (New York: International Publishers, 1971).

20. For a clear statement of this view, see William J. Goode, "Encroachment, Charlatanism and the Emerging Profession: Psychology, Sociology and Medicine," *Am. Soc. Rev.;* 25 (1960): 902–914.

21. See Karl Polanyi, *The Great Transformation* (Boston: Beacon Press, 1957).

22. See Max Weber, "Class, Status, Party," in *From Max Weber,* Hans Gerth and C. W. Mills, eds., pp. 180–195, (New York: Oxford Univ. Press, 1954).

23. Frank Parkin, *Class Inequality and Political Order* (New York: Praeger, 1974), p. 24.

24. Parkin, *Class,* pp. 21–22.

25. Both the military and the clergy illuminate the problems faced by other "professions" within organizations and the uses of professionalism in this setting. I think, however, that the authority of the military does not depend on their special expertise, but on their control of the means of coercion. As for the clergy, I think that their influence, again, depends more on a factor other than theological or doctrinal competence—namely, on the public's religiosity. Nevertheless, the authority of professionals in secular callings also depends on the public's "faith"; therefore, the line is more blurred in the case of the clergy and the professions than it is in the case of the military.

26. For France, see Raymonde Moulin *et al., Les Architectes* (Paris: Calmann-Lévy, 1973); for a comparison of the German and American bars, see Dietrich Rueschmeyer, *Lawyers and their Society* (Cambridge, Mass.: Harvard Univ. Press, 1973); see Roderick McGrew, *Russia and the Cholera: 1823–1832* (Madison: Univ. of Wisconsin Press, 1965), on Russian medicine.

27. Blau and Duncan report that 37 percent of all professionals and 22 percent of self-employed professionals in the U.S.A. had fathers in manual occupations at the time of their study; see Peter Blau and Otis Dudley Duncan, *The American Occupational Structure* (New York: John Wiley & Sons, 1967), pp. 39, 496.

CHAPTER 1. THE HISTORICAL MATRIX OF MODERN PROFESSIONS

1. On the pre-industrial "professions" in England, see A. M. Carr-Saunders and P. A. Wilson, *The Professions* (Oxford: Clarendon Press, 1933), pp. 289–294.

2. Wilbert E. Moore, *The Professions: Roles and Rules* (New York: Russell Sage, 1970), p. 36.

3. See Carr-Saunders and Wilson, *The Professions;* Moore, *Roles and Rules,* chap. 2; Freidson, *Profession,* chap. 1; Henri Pirenne, "European Guilds," in *Man, Work and Society,* Sigmund Nosow and William H. Form, eds., pp. 160–169 (New York: Basic Books, 1962).

4. Martin S. Briggs, *The Architect in History* (Oxford: Clarendon Press, 1927), p. 35.

5. Bleeding and purging may have been related by "learned" physicians to speculative theories of pathology; as therapies, they were no more scientifically based than those derived from traditional lore. See Richard Shryock, *Medicine in American History* (Baltimore: Johns Hopkins Univ. Press, 1966), pp. 315–321.

6. For instance, in Beaumarchais' *The Barber of Seville,* Figaro typifies both the traditional master-servant relationship and the tensions that beset it in the passing of the old regime.

7. See Carr-Saunders and Wilson, *The Professions;* and W. J. Reader, *Professional Men* (London: Weidenfeld and Nicolson, 1966), chap. 2.

8. As Reader points out in relation to the clergy, the Dissenters were tolerated, not "established": "The social standing of any occupation was closely related to its position in the state." *Professional Men,* p. 15.

9. Freidson, *Profession,* p. 19.

10. Pirenne suggests that a similar succession of "innovative groups" characterizes the different stages of merchant capitalism; see Henri Pirenne, "Stages in the Social History of Capitalism," in *Class, Status, and Power,* Bendix and Lipset, eds., pp. 97–107.

11. On apprenticeship, see Philippe Aries, *Centuries of Childhood* (New York: Vintage, 1962), Part II; Bernard Baylin, *Education in the Forming of American Society* (New York: Vintage, 1960), pp. 17ff., and Reader, *Professional Men.*

12. See Baylin, *Education*, pp. 18–21.

13. For an interesting account of this passage, see William R. Johnson, "Education and Professional Life Styles; Law and Medicine in the Nineteenth Century," *History of Education Quarterly* (Summer 1974): 185–207.

14. Carr-Saunders and Wilson quote the following passage from Trollope's *The Vicar of Bullhampton:* Miss Marrable "always addressed an attorney by letter as Mister, raising up her eyebrows when appealed to on the matter and explaining that an attorney is not an esquire. She had an idea that the son of a gentleman, if he intended to maintain his rank as a gentleman, should earn his income as a clergyman, or as a barrister, or as a soldier, or as a sailor . . . She would not absolutely say that a physician was not a gentleman, or even a surgeon; but she would never allow physic the same absolute privilege which in her eyes belonged to law and the church." Carr-Saunders and Wilson, *The Professions*, p. 295, fn 1.

15. See Reader, *Professional Men*, chap. 1. For evidence on the still uncertain profession of architecture, see Briggs' discussion of architecture in France under Louis XIV and Louis XV and in eighteenth-century England. Briggs, *Architect*.

16. See Eric Hobsbawm, *The Age of Revolutions* (New York: Mentor, 1962), pp. 227–233.

17. Hobsbawm points out that both in business and in education, "without some resources, however minimal, it was difficult to get started on the highway to success." See Hobsbawm, *Revolutions,* pp. 227 and 232. The considerable differences between England, on the one hand, and France and Germany, on the other, cannot be reviewed here. Reforms "from above" in the Prussian bar attempted to reduce aristocratic influence, while accommodating the aspiring bourgeoisie into a new order of congealed status privileges. See Rueschmeyer, *Lawyers,* pp. 148–153, and Hans Rosenberg, *Bureaucracy, Aristocracy and Autocracy; the Prussian Experience, 1660–1815* (Cambridge, Mass.: Harvard Univ. Press, 1958), chap. 9.

18. Arthur Stinchcombe, "Social Structure and Organizations," in *Handbook of Organizations,* James G. March, ed. (New York: Rand McNally, 1965), chap. 4, pp. 153 and 160.

19. Stinchcombe, "Organizations," p. 153.

20. Hobsbawm, *Revolutions,* pp. 47–48.

21. See Polanyi, *Transformation,* chaps. 7 and 8; see also Reinhard Bendix, *Work and Authority in Industry* (New York: Harper and Row, 1956), pp. 94–99; and E. P. Thompson, *The Making of the English Working Class* (New York: Vintage, 1963).

22. Bendix, *Work,* p. 45.

23. Bendix, *Work,* p. 67.

24. Hobsbawm, *Revolutions,* p. 232.

25. *Historical Statistics of the U.S.; Colonial Times to 1957,* U.S. Dept. of Commerce, Bureau of the Census (Washington: U.S. Government Printing Office, 1960). The 1880 illiteracy rate for the total population older than ten was 17 percent; it was 9.4 percent for the total white population, 12 percent for foreign-born whites, and 70 percent for non-whites.

26. See Appendix Tables 2 to 4.

27. Hobsbawm, *Revolutions,* p. 353.

CHAPTER 2. THE CONSTITUTION OF PROFESSIONAL MARKETS

1. Polanyi, *Transformation,* p. 29.

2. Polanyi, *Transformation,* p. 130.

3. Everett C. Hughes, *The Sociological Eye,* 2 vols. (Chicago: Aldine-Atherton, 1971), vol. I, p. 364; italics mine.

4. Parsons, "Social Structure," p. 35.

5. See Marx's analysis in *The Grundrisse,* trans. and ed. by David McLellan (New York: Harper and Row, 1971), pp. 59–64.

6. Divinity is an exception, since the newer denominations may be considered as working on the wide market for religion which existed before the foundation of the later sects. However, the clergy does not sell its services, and for this reason it does not illuminate the relations between market and the stratification system which the professions were forming in the liberal phase of capitalism.

7. Daniel Calhoun, *Professional Lives in America; Structure and Aspirations, 1750–1850* (Cambridge, Mass.; Harvard Univ. Press, 1965), p. 55.

8. See Eric Hobsbawm, "The Crisis of the Seventeenth Century," *Past and Present*, 1 (1954), nos. 5 and 6; and Polanyi, *Transformation*, chaps. 9 and 10.

9. See Sir George Clark, *A History of the Royal College of Physicians of London*, 2 vols. (Oxford: clarendon Press, 1966), pp. 436ff and chap. 24.

10. See Sir William Holdsworth, *A History of English Law*, 12 vols. (London: Methuen, 1938), vol. 12, p. 53.

11. The first Medical Register appeared anonymously in 1779; the Law List began in 1839 and Crockford's Clerical Directory only in 1870. The early medical registers indicate that there was about one physician (counting all branches) for 2,000 inhabitants, and that London physicians were only about one sixth of the whole. See Clark, *Royal College*, pp. 601 and 603.

12. Blackstone's lectures in English law at Oxford in the 1750s were the first such lectures ever given at an English university. They failed to produce a switch to the systematic teaching of the law for another century. In medicine, the Royal College of Physicians obtained curricular reforms from Oxford and Cambridge, but the curriculum, as well as the College's own examinations, were still essentially centered on the Greek and Latin medical classics. Full academic recognition was not secured by physiology until 1883. In 1910, Flexner found the teaching of anatomy backward and routinized. Clinical medicine had not yet reached university status anywhere in England. See Abraham Flexner, *Medical Education in Europe* (New York: Carnegie Foundation for the Advancement of Teaching, Bull. no. 6, 1912).

13. See Abraham Flexner, *Medical Education in the United States and Canada* (New York: Carnegie Foundation, Bull. no. 4, 1910), p. 4, hereafter referred to as *Report;* Alfred Z. Reed, *Training for the Public Profession of the Law* (New York: Carnegie Foundation, Bull. no. 15, 1921), pp. 36ff; and William Rothstein, *American Physicians*, chap. 2.

14. Charles Warren, *A History of the American Bar* (Boston: Little, Brown, 1911), pp. 4ff; see also Louis B. Wright, *The First Gentlemen of Virginia; Intellectual Qualities of the Early Colonial Ruling Class* (Charlottesville, Va.: Univ. of Virginia Press, 1964).

15. See Rueschmeyer, *Lawyers*, pp. 154–160; and, of course, Alexis de Tocqueville, *Democracy in America*, 2 vols., Phillips Bradley, ed. (New York: Vintage and Alfred A. Knopf, 1945), vol. 1, pp. 281–290.

16. See Calhoun, *Lives*, chap. 4.

17. Polanyi, *Transformation*, p. 72 and fn 6.

18. On the notion of symbolic universe, see Peter Berger and Thomas Luckmann, *The Social Construction of Reality* (Garden City, N.Y.: Doubleday, Anchor Books, 1967).

19. The references to the medieval guilds are based on Pirenne, "Guilds" and Max Weber, *General Economic History* (New York: Collier Books, 1961), pp. 110–148.

20. For a development of this approach to educational systems, see Althusser, "Idéologie," and Gramsci, *Notebooks*.

21. Paradoxically, the economic success of the British bourgeoisie helped maintain aristocratic control over the machinery of the state and over central national institutions such as the ancient universities. See Chapter Seven and also two cogent presentations of the arguments about English exceptionalism: Perry Anderson, "Origins of the Present Crisis," in *Towards Socialism*, Perry Anderson and Robin Blackburn, eds. (London: Fontana, 1965); and E. P. Thompson, "The Peculiarities of the English," in *Socialist Register*, Ralph Miliband, ed. (London: Merlin, 1964).

22. On the notion of "organic intellectuals," see Gramsci, *Notebooks*.

CHAPTER 3. AN ANALYSIS OF MEDICINE'S PROFESSIONAL SUCCESS

1. For professional incomes in mid-century England, see Eric Hobsbawm, *Industry and Empire* (Baltimore: Penguin, 1969), pp. 156–157; and Reader, *Professional Men*, pp. 199–202. For the United States, see Daniel Calhoun, *The American Civil Engineer; Origins and Conflict* (Cambridge, Mass.: MIT Press, 1960), pp. 167–173; and Richard Shryock, *The Development of Modern Medicine* (New York: Alfred A. Knopf, 1947), p. 266; and Shryock, *Medicine*, pp. 158–159.

2. See Shryock, *Medicine*, p. 155.

3. See Flexner, *Report*, p. 7; and Rothstein, *American Physicians*, p. 93.

4. See Rothstein, *American Physicians*, p. 100.

5. On homeopathy in the United States, see Rothstein, *American Physicians*, chap. 6, and Joseph Kett, *The Formation of the American Medical Profession* (New Haven: Yale Univ. Press, 1968).

6. See Richard Shryock, "American Indifference to Basic Science during the Nineteenth Century," in *Medicine*, chap. 3.

7. Shryock, *Medicine*, p. 172.

8. Consider, for instance, the connotations of the following statement: "As patients grew richer, moreover, the practice of medicine became increasingly profitable. This had several consequences. First, a number of young men *with scientific interests* decided that the easiest way to support themselves would be to practice medicine. Second, the number of doctors in major cities became quite large, and medical societies sprang up."; Christopher Jencks and David Riesman, *The Academic Revolution* (Garden City, N.Y.: Doubleday, 1968), p. 213. Applied to the early nineteenth century, this observation gives the false idea that there was, from the beginning, a solid scientific core in American medicine. This retrospective projection is typical of most histories of medicine, American and European.

9. Not surprisingly, American "regular" physicians justified the exclusion of homeopaths from the A.M.A. *not* because they espoused an exclusive dogma but because they adopted "a distinctive title *as a trademark*." Rothstein, *American Physicians*, p. 172, italics mine.

10. Shryock mentions a study made toward the end of the nineteenth century, according to which 75 percent of American graduate physicians "turned within five years to nonmedical work, chiefly to secure a better income." Shryock, *Development*, p. 266. By 1910, when Flexner published his report on medical education, overcrowding was a major concern of the profession. Flexner expressed it candidly: "So enormous an overcrowding with low-grade material both relatively and absolutely decreases the number of well-trained men who can count on the profession for a livelihood." Flexner, *Report*, p. 14.

11. The influence of epidemics on attracting public attention to the state of medicine and to the lack of sanitation in the cities was obviously very great. See Charles E. Rosenberg, *The Cholera Years; the United States in 1832, 1849, and 1866* (Chicago: Univ. of Chicago Press, 1962).

12. Rothstein, *American Physicians*, p. 76.

13. Shryock reports that in 1858 some medical leaders in the societies advocated, as a measure against the schools, that the meaningless M.D. title be replaced, for the qualified physicians, by a title such as "Member, A.M.A." See Shryock, *Medicine*, p. 155. The exclusionary policies of the A.M.A. were chiefly directed against the most reputable of the rival schools, namely, homeopathy.

14. See Shryock, *Development*, pp. 267–269.

15. This blend is characteristic of the clinical mentality analyzed by Freidson, *Profession*, pp. 158–172. See also Parsons' penetrating comments, which also deal with the impossibility of organizing the sick into a collectivity; in Talcott Parsons, *The Social System* (Glencoe, Ill.: Free Press, 1951), chap. 10, pp. 477ff in particular.

16. On the benefits derived by doctors from the insulation of their work setting, see Freidson and Rhea, "Processes of Control"; on psychiatrists, see Rachel Kahn-Hut, "Confidentiality: Protection of the Professional," unpublished paper, San Francisco, 1972. Included in "Psychiatric Theory as Professional Ideology" (Ph.D. Dissertation, Brandeis University, 1974).

17. See the studies by Freidson, "Client Control" and *Profession;* and by Freidson and Rhea, "Processes of Control." See also Oswald Hall, "The Informal Organization of the Medical Profession," *Canad. Jour. of Eco. and Polit. Sci.*, 12 (1946): 30–44.

18. See note 17. In 1974, the California Medical Association was obliged to organize peer review boards, for fear of having them imposed "from above" with laymen included. In the same year, the A.M.A. threatened with expulsion the physicians who had collaborated with Ralph Nader's Consumer Advocates report on the medical profession in Prince George County, Maryland. The report made public the different fees charged by different doctors, their prescription preferences, etc. These examples show that the profession rejects lay control, not because it wants to police itself, but because, in fact, it does not.

19. Shryock, *Development*, p. 82.

20. Charles Reed's Presidential Address to the A.M.A. in 1901, quoted by Rothstein in *American Physicians*, p. 325.

21. Such was the case with the diphtheria antitoxin; while the profession was divided about its use, public health authorities dispensed it free to the poor in New York, Philadelphia, and California during

the epidemic of 1895. In Illinois, the State Health Department had it administered by its staff, while the physicians refused to use it; ultimately, the public health officers taught private physicians how to administer the immunization, since the public demanded it. See Rothstein, *American Physicians,* pp. 277–278.

22. This is not entirely true: in the U.S., for instance, public authorities refused to endorse the "regular" physicians wherever "irregulars" practiced in even modest numbers. In 33 of the 45 states which had licensing laws in 1900, non-regular physicians participated in the licensing process; they also sat on the public health boards in many large cities. See Rothstein, *American Physicians,* pp. 305ff.

23. See C. H. Haskins, *The Rise of the Universities* (Ithaca, N.Y.: Cornell Univ. Press, 1957 ed.)

24. See Shryock, *Development,* pp. 153ff, and *Medicine,* pp. 322ff.

25. Flexner in his *Report* deplored the state of American hospitals and argued that the only way out of this condition for American medicine was through university hospitals, in which physicians would be appointed from the school's faculty and not from the general population of practitioners.

26. This analysis is focused mainly on private engineers, for they illustrate the market situation of the profession more typically than army or navy engineers. Until the 1850s, only civil engineering had emerged in America as a distinct profession, probably because of its gentlemanly tradition, derived from affiliation with the corps of military engineers and from the overlap of functions with architecture. Calhoun suggests that if ever the profession of engineering shared the characteristics of the other "free" professions, it was before the Civil War, that is, before engineering became increasingly fragmented into specialties and dependent on large employers. My analysis is based chiefly on Daniel Calhoun, *Civil Engineer;* Monte Calvert, *The Mechanical Engineer in America; 1830–1910* (Baltimore: Johns Hopkins Univ. Press, 1967); Edwin T. Layton, Jr., *The Revolt of the Engineers* (Cleveland: Case Western Reserve Univ. Press, 1971); and on the sociological inquiry by Robert Perrucci and Joel E. Gerstl, *Profession without Community; Engineers in American Society* (New York: Random House, 1969).

27. Calhoun, *Civil Engineer,* p. 6.

28. Before the industrial revolution, the role of the civil engineer was not completely differentiated from that of the architect; architecture and military engineering overlapped in Europe. See Calhoun, *Civil Engineer,* chap. 1.

29. See Calvert, *Mechanical Engineer,* chap. 1.

30. *Ibid.,* p. 12ff.

31. *Ibid.,* p. 14.

32. For the status of apprenticeship in mechanical engineering, see Calvert, *Mechanical Engineer,* Table 2, p. 73, and also Calhoun, *Civil Engineer.*

33. On mechanics institutes and correspondence courses, see Calvert, *Mechanical Engineer,* pp. 36ff, 85, and 112.

34. Calvert emphasizes that even in civil engineering, independent consultations could not have involved more than one third of the profession by 1890. Calvert, *Mechanical Engineer,* p. 204.

35. See Calhoun, *Civil Engineer,* pp. 65–67.

36. Quoted by Calvert, *Mechanical Engineer,* p. 225.

37. On engineers in management, see Layton, *Revolt,* p. 13; and Perrucci and Gerstl, *Engineers,* pp. 132–137.

38. Calvert, *Mechanical Engineer,* p. 266 and pp. 265ff, for the engineering competence of the typical client.

39. Quoted by Calvert, *Mechanical Engineer,* p. 265.

40. An interesting illustration is the bias in favor of the public utilities companies shown by most engineering experts during the Progressive campaign against the utilities. As Director of Public Works in Philadelphia, Morris Cooke had a hard time finding an independent expert; this experience greatly reinforced his argument that the low social status of the engineer came from his association with "predatory wealth" and his refusal of public service. See Layton, *Revolt,* chap. 7.

41. Except for the chief engineers, the employment of engineers in the second third of the nineteenth century was unstable: at different times in the period from 1837 to 1844, "the total number of engineers on the five of those projects [various railroads and canal projects in the East and Midwest] for which an initial figure is available dropped from 116 to 3." Calhoun, *Civil Engineer,* p. 142.

42. Calhoun, *Civil Engineer,* p. 199.

43. Layton, *Revolt,* p. 6. See also his chaps. 3 and 10.

44. Shryock, *Medicine,* p. 171.

45. Layton, *Revolt,* p. 58.

46. Wilensky, "Professionalization," p. 148.

47. The adamant resistance of the courts and the legal practitioners to the practice of self-counsel, together with the competence demonstrated by "jailhouse lawyers" in recent trials, indirectly show the vulnerability of the legal profession to lay competition.

48. Thomas Kuhn, *The Structure of Scientific Revolutions* (Chicago: Univ. of Chicago Press, 1970 ed.), pp. 162–163, italics mine.

49. Obviously, I cannot do justice to the epistemological problems posed by Kuhn, nor to the empirical questions he raises for the sociology of science. For a sociological study which adds to Kuhn's analysis, see Diana Crane, *Invisible Colleges* (Chicago: Univ. of Chicago Press, 1972).

50. Kuhn, *Structure,* p. 164.

51. In Kuhn's analysis, the tendency to paradigmatic unification diffuses throughout a community of scientists the effects of paradigmatic crisis—that is, the experienced impossibility of resolving an *anomalous* problem within the confines of an insufficient paradigm. The resulting breakdown of consensus destroys the perception of scientific activity as a cumulative, progressive undertaking. Paradigmatic crises are ultimately resolved by reintegration around a new definition of scientific practice and scientific reality which can deal with the anomaly and reconstruct consensus.

52. Kuhn, *Structure,* pp. 23–24.

53. The quotation is from Freidson, *Profession,* p. 22.

54. Joseph Ben-David, *The Scientist's Role in Society* (Englewood Cliffs, N.J.: Prentice-Hall, 1971), p. 143.

55. See Rothstein, *American Physicians.*

56. Calvert, *Mechanical Engineering,* pp. 54–55.

57. Because of the predominance of practical interests in the profession, all sectors of the membership of the American Society of Mechanical Engineers were against adoption of the metric system (a ballot was sent to all members in 1903). Entrepreneurs opposed adoption by 5 to 1, teachers and junior engineers by 2 to 1, and draftsmen by less than that. See Calvert, *Mechanical Engineer,* pp. 178ff and the table of results from the ballot, p. 184.

58. Flexner, *Report,* p. 6. At the end of the nineteenth century, the U.S. had almost as many schools as there were in all the rest of the world, says Morris Fishbein, *A History of the American Medical Association: 1847–1947* (Philadelphia: Saunders, 1947), pp. 888–889.

59. See Rosenberg, *Cholera;* see also Calhoun, *Lives,* pp. 45–46.

60. Shryock, *Development,* p. 164.

61. *Ibid.,* pp. 190–191.

62. Freidson, *Profession,* p. 16.

63. *Ibid.,* p. xviii.

64. *Ibid.,* pp. 48ff.

65. On the delegation of "dirty work," see Hughes, *Sociological Eye,* pp. 345–346.

66. Freidson, *Profession,* p. 10.

67. A number of studies suggest that the surgeon should inspire as much mistrust as most plumbers. A Columbia study of 6,248 hysterectomies shows that 30 percent of the patients had no disease whatsoever. Despite (or because of?) the cost of medicine to the patient, the U.S. has twice as much surgery per capita as England. See Boston Women's Health Collective, *Our Bodies, Our Selves* (Boston: Private Printing, 1971), p. 125.

68. Freidson, *Profession,* p. xvii. For an analysis of the discretionary powers of the legal profession and its potential for social control, see Parsons, "Legal Profession."

69. Robert Bazell, "I am sorry, the Doctor is Busy Making Money," *New York Review of Books* (November 2, 1972), p. 41.

CHAPTER 4. STANDARDIZATION AND MARKET CONTROL

1. Starting with a different theoretical focus, Haroun Jamous and B. Peloille arrive at conclusions which reinforce my analysis of professionalization, both as a project of market organization and as an

attempt to increase collective social mobility. See Haroun Jamous and B. Peloille, "Changes in the French University-Hospital System," in *Professions and Professionalization,* J. A. Jackson, ed. (Cambridge: Cambridge Univ. Press, 1970), pp. 111–152. Quotation on p. 113.

2. Jamous and Peloille, "Changes," p. 112.

3. For an analysis of the genesis of guilds, their internal and external conflicts, and their disintegration under the advance of merchant capitalism, see Weber, *Economic History,* chaps. 9–13.

4. Jamous and Peloille, "Changes," pp. 139–142.

5. *Ibid.,* p. 120.

6. See Kuhn, *Structure,* and the reference to this thesis in my Chapter Three.

7. Jamous and Peloille, "Changes," pp. 139–140.

8. On this subject, nothing can be more illuminating than the Flexner report: the emerging hierarchy is recognized precisely as a function of the capacity which only few schools had of "appropriating" scientific teaching and research.

9. There are indications that this may be happening, for instance, in architecture (the pattern is classic in the medical field). As drafting becomes more standardized, there appears to be a growing reluctance to delegate it, as was generally done in the past, to fully trained junior architects, who also accept such tasks with reluctance. Concern can be noted in the professional journals with the problem of supplying the profession with architectural technicians more briefly and cheaply trained than the graduates of professional schools; it is emphasized that the two kinds of training should be kept thoroughly distinct. A similar concern with forming "second-class" professionals or, rather, technicians for jobs that have been standardized may be observed in most major professions. See "Who is going to sit at all those drafting boards?" *Progressive Architecture* (April 1973): 107–109.

10. On the emergence of specialties within the medical profession, see Rue Bucher, "Pathology: A Study of Social Movements within a Profession," in *Medical Men,* Freidson and Lorber, eds., pp. 113–127; Rue Bucher and Anselm Strauss, "Professions in Process," *Amer. Jour. Soc.,* 66 (1961): 325–334. For engineering, see Layton, *Revolt,* pp. 40ff. On scientific specialization, see Joseph Ben-David and Randall Collins, "Social Factors in the Origins of a New Science: the Case of Psychology," *Amer. Soc. Rev.,* 31 (1966): 451–465.

11. The evolution of the criteria for the attribution of talent can be illustrated by reference to the American legal profession. When apprenticeship was the dominant mode of professional socialization, the reputation of private practitioners (and also, therefore, their influence as teachers) was established on the demonstration of forensic bravura. The appointment to judicial office provided a different "demonstration effect," but the power of the role admitted a measure of forensic ability. Elective office may have introduced different criteria of ability, which carried over, later on, into private practice; but if a lawyer was inept in the courtroom, his electoral success in the past could not have helped him too much. As economic development and the growing size of economic units led to a large increase in the volume and importance of legal disputes, private legal practice moved to out-of-court negotiations. In such private circumstances, the badges of professional talent were intimately tied to the influence and power of the clientele. At the end of the nineteenth century, the formalization of legal training and the rise of university-based law schools once again instituted publicly *visible* criteria of talent, which merged with the reputation of the law school. Legal educators became a most influential sector of the profession, as they had always been in Germany, for instance, which had a long tradition of formal legal training. On the above, see Jerold S. Auerbach, "Enmity and Amity: Law Teachers and Practitioners, 1900–21," in *Perspectives in American History,* 5 (1971): 551–601. See also Calhoun, *Lives;* Johnson, "Life Styles"; and Rueschmeyer, *Lawyers.*

12. On the mediation of social rewards by specialized groups of colleagues in science, see Randall Collins, "Competition and Control in Science," *Sociology of Education,* 41 (1968): 123–140. Collins has an excellent discussion of the effects of competition on the contents of scientific activity.

13. See, for instance, Ernest Greenwood, "Attributes of a Profession," in *Professionalization,* Howard M. Vollmer and Donald L. Mills, eds. (Englewood Cliffs, N.J.: Prentice-Hall, 1966), pp. 10–19; see also Goode, "Community."

14. See Rothstein, *American Physicians,* pp. 65ff.

15. Calhoun, *Lives,* pp. 191–192.

16. *Ibid.,* chap. 2.

17. See Jencks and Riesman, *Academic*, pp. 205–206. The authors are led to suggest that "the primary role of the professional school may thus be socialization, not training" (p. 206).

18. For evidence on professional networks, see Hall, "Informal Organization," pp. 48–49, and Edwin Smigel, *The Wall Street Lawyer* (New York: Free Press, 1964).

19. Eliot Freidson, "The Impurity of Professional Authority," in *Institutions and the Person*, Howard Becker *et al.* (Chicago: Aldine, 1968), p. 29.

20. Clark Kerr, "The Balkanization of Labor Markets," in *Labor Mobility and Economic Opportunity*, E. Wight Bakke *et al.*, eds. (New York: MIT Press and John Wiley and Sons, 1954), p. 93.

21. Corinne Lathrop Gilb, *Hidden Hierarchies; The Professions and Government* (New York: Harper and Row, 1967), p. 109.

22. Goode, "Community," p. 196. On this point, see an economist's approach to the profession as a solution to "market failure" in Kenneth Arrow, "The Organization of Economic Activity: Issues Pertinent to the Choice of Market vs. Nonmarket Allocation," in *The Analysis and Evaluation of Public Expenditures*, Vol. 1, Joint Economic Committee, U.S. Congress (1969), pp. 47–64.

23. See, for instance, the functionalist approach, as represented at its best by Parsons, *Social System*, chap. 10; and Freidson's interactionist approach in *Profession*, Introduction and pp. 3–6.

24. For instance, Flexner recommended in 1910 that every entrant to a medical school should have at least a competent knowledge of physics, chemistry, and biology. Scientific training in these fields had been available for a long time, but it only became relevant for the average medical practitioner when the achievements of scientific medicine revolutionized medical practice. Or, again, the physical properties of iron and steel had been known for a long time before it became indispensable for trained architects to know them—that is, when steel construction became a normal part of architectural practice in the first decades of our century.

25. Familiarity with the classical buildings of Greece, Rome, and the Renaissance is considered to this day an essential ingredient of architectural training. This conception reflects the historical origins of the profession and the survival of traditional canons of architectural excellence. Also, in Germany, most particularly, the diffusion of Naturphilosophie after 1815 and until 1840 was connected to the revival of speculative systems in pathology. See Shryock, *Medicine*, p. 325. Positivism had undoubtedly encouraged the scientific development of medical research in the Paris school in the 1820s and after.

26. On the unemployment of professionals, see Walter Kotschnig, *Unemployment in the Learned Professions* (London: Oxford Univ. Press, 1937).

CHAPTER 5. MARKET AND ANTI-MARKET PRINCIPLES

1. On the apparent equivalence of exchange, see Karl Marx, *Capital*, 3 vols. (New York: International Publishers, 1967), Vol. 1, pp. 71–83.

2. Polanyi, *Transformation*, p. 132.

3. *Ibid.*

4. *Ibid.*, pp. 139–140, italics mine.

5. See Bendix, *Work*, chap. 2. Hegemony is used in the conception of Gramsci. See his *Notebooks*, and, in Italian, Antonio Gramsci, *Il Risorgimento* (Roma: Editori Riuniti, 1971).

6. The law administered coercion, of course, but not, in principle, for the advancement of its members' professional status.

7. See Emile Durkheim, *The Division of Labor in Society* (New York: Free Press, 1964), pp. 1–31.

8. Goode, "Community," p. 194.

9. The general proposition on political participation advanced by Alessandro Pizzorno, "Introduzione allo Studio della Partecipazione Politica," *Quaderni di Sociologia*, 15 (1966): 235–287, can be fruitfully applied to a historical study of the internal dynamics of professional associations. In Pizzorno's approach, one participates actively only among those with whom one feels a parity of conditions. Modern political parties, at their inception, are attempts to constitute *ideological* "areas of equality" which are conducive to political participation; as equality visibly declines, so does participation. Factional fights, reorganizations, schisms and even purges, as well as conflicts with the "outside," are seen by Pizzorno as processes which tend to reconstitute areas of equality, and hence may reactivate political participation.

10. Durkheim, *Division,* p. 25, fn 34 and p. 30.

11. See in this respect the illuminating analysis by Alain Touraine, *L'Evolution du Travail Ouvrier aux Usines Renault* (Paris: C.N.R.S., 1955), and *Sociologie de l'Action,* (Paris: Seuil, 1965), chap. 5.

12. Gilb observes that professional organizations came late in the "organizational revolution," as a response or a defensive reaction against the organization of other social groups. Her argument is applicable to the later professions, but it does not account for the formative years of the "classic" professions.

13. Gilb, *Hierarchies,* p. 45.

14. Parsons, "Social Structure," pp. 36ff.

15. Shryock points out that the therapeutic nihilism which preceded the "bacteriological revolution" brought about public discredit for regular medicine, despite the considerable advances which had been made before the 1890s in combating infant mortality and death in childbirth. To the public, it appeared "only as if that little which the patient had had been taken away," says Shryock of the popular reaction to growing medical skepticism. See Shryock, *Development,* pp. 249ff.

16. Freidson, *Profession,* p. 360.

17. Ben-David, *Scientist,* p. 134.

18. *Ibid.,* fn 46. In fact, the social thinkers or activists concerned with the professions, their functions, their ethicality, and their future, were often social reformers (or in sympathy with social reform)—the Webbs and R. H. Tawney in England; Flexner, Brandeis, and Roscoe Pound in the United States; and Durkheim in France.

19. Presumably, professions like engineering could have banked on the enthusiasm for technology that is often mentioned as a characteristic of the age (see Hobsbawm, *Industry,* p. 186); but it was a pragmatic enthusiasm, embodied in inventors' societies and mechanic institutes, most often "suspicious of anything in the nature of theoretical knowledge" (Reader, *Professional Men,* p. 70). Reader argues that this climate hindered rather than helped the professionalization efforts by engineers.

20. Barrington Kaye, *The Development of the Architectural Profession* (London: Allen and Unwin, 1960), p. 16.

21. R. H. Tawney, *The Acquisitive Society* (New York: Harcourt, Brace and World, 1948), pp. 94–95, italics mine.

22. Shryock, *Development,* p. 221.

23. For efforts in medicine, see Shryock, *Development,* chaps. 5, 12, 18, and 19. For the slum reform movement in the United States, see Allen F. Davis, *Spearheads for Reform* (New York: Oxford Univ. Press, 1967), and Roy Lubove, *The Progressives and the Slums* (Pittsburgh: Univ. of Pittsburgh Press, 1963); for schools, see Michael Katz, *The Irony of Early School Reform* (Boston: Beacon Press, 1968).

24. See Gilb, *Hierarchies,* pp. 38ff; and Katz, *Irony.*

25. Marx, *Capital,* Vol. 1, pp. 278–297.

26. On the rise of psychiatry in the institutional area left open by the withdrawal of community forms of assistance and penetrated by the state, see David J. Rothman, *The Discovery of the Asylum* (Boston: Little, Brown, 1971), and Andrew T. Scull, "From Madness to Mental Illness," *Arch. Europ. Sociol.* 16 (1975): 218–251.

27. For an interesting elaboration of the notion of "service," see Goode, "Limits."

28. Goode, "Limits," p. 278.

29. See Freidson, *Profession,* p. 81.

30. High job satisfaction was related as follows to occupational status among employed males in 1960 (percentage in each category who were *very* satisfied with their jobs): professional and technical, 42 percent; managerial and proprietary, 38 percent; clerical white-collar, 22 percent; sales white-collar, 24 percent; skilled blue-collar, 22 percent; semi-skilled blue-collar, 27 percent; unskilled blue-collar, 13 percent; farm, 22 percent. Quoted by Victor Vroom, *Work and Motivation* (New York: John Wiley and Sons, 1964), p. 131.

31. Harold Wilensky, "Varieties of Work Experience," in *Man in a World of Work,* Henry Borow, ed. (Boston: Houghton-Mifflin, 1964), pp. 125–154, pp. 143 and 146.

32. *Ibid.,* Table 1.

33. *Ibid.,* Table 3.

34. *Ibid.,* p. 148.

35. Max Weber, *The Protestant Ethic and the Spirit of Capitalism* (New York: Scribner, 1958), p. 178, italics mine.

36. Durkheim, *Division*, p. 43.

37. *Ibid.*, p. 331.

38. Reflecting the tension between entrepreneurial and vocational orientations, the American surgeon Harvey Cushing mused in 1933: "why [the doctor] should refrain from forcible collection of unpaid bills, why he does not patent some of his prescriptions, inventions, and discoveries and makes a fortune; why he should continue to counteract the spread of diseases he has painfully and at great educational expense learnt to diagnose and treat; why he should so strenuously oppose year after year the efforts of anti-vivisectionists and anti-vaccinationists with their Christian Science allies to cripple research . . . , knowing how [house] calls would increase did they have their way; and why at the same time he should continue to work longer hours for less pay during a shorter life of activity than most people, is an enigma to the hardheaded businessmen." Quoted by Shryock, *Development*, p. 418.

39. C. Wright Mills, *White Collar* (New York: Oxford Univ. Press, 1956), p. 230.

40. Hobsbawm, *Revolutions*, p. 237.

41. Reader, *Professional Men*, pp. 158–159.

CHAPTER 6. THE COLLECTIVE MOBILITY PROJECT

1. Apart from the deficiencies signaled in the text, the abstract character of the classification does violence to the historically specific genesis of the social structures that bound the professional project. For instance, the American model of the university was consolidated during a period of bureaucratic reorganization of productive and governing functions. Although both consulting and academic professionals have large areas of autonomy within the university, they do not control it. The university, therefore, cannot be adequately located at one or the other pole of the autonomy-heteronomy dimension. The same applies to the professional market, which depends upon the complex structural interrelations I analyzed above in the cases of medicine and engineering. The classification, moreover, does not apply to contemporary professionalizing occupations such as business management or city planning, whose professional markets are contained within organizational settings; therefore, the means for upgrading the occupation and attaching prestige to the role are located in a circumscribed, heteronomous and purely "modern" context. Finally, since a professional market is constituted by interlocking organizations, prestige flows from the whole structural complex—that is, from institutions that are controlled by professionals, as well as from others that are not. The institutional location is, therefore, extremely imprecise, since the complexity of the professional market does not readily lend itself to classification along a few dimensions.

2. Stinchcombe, "Organizations," p. 171.

3. *Ibid.*, p. 172, italics mine.

4. Harold Wilensky, "Work, Careers, and Social Integration," *International Social Science Jour.*, 12 (1960), p. 554.

5. Stinchcombe, "Organizations," p. 173.

6. Considering that the costs of a "good" and "recognized" education were higher than the costs of getting oneself up in business in the early part of the nineteenth century, the proposition that hierarchies based on education are more open than those based on money should not be generalized without caution. See Hobsbawm, *Revolutions*, pp. 231–233.

7. See, in this respect, Freidson, *Profession*, chap. 9, and Hall, "Informal Organization."

8. For a discussion of the American Medical Association's elites and the mechanisms by which they become entrenched, see Oliver Garceau, *The Political Life of the American Medical Association* (Cambridge, Mass.: Harvard Univ. Press, 1941); see also Auerbach, "Enmity," for the law; and Calvert, *Mechanical Engineer*, for the politics of the various engineering societies, in particular chaps. 6 and 11; and Layton, *Revolt*, chap. 4. For the proportions of practitioners who are members of the main professional association in their field, see Gilb, *Hierarchies*, pp. 119–127. The A.M.A. passed the 50 percent mark in 1912; 66.8 percent of American physicians were members in 1940. The proportion of lawyers who were members of the American Bar Association was 17.6 percent in 1940 and 46.2 percent in 1960. Some 42 percent of classroom teachers belonged to the National Education Association in 1960; 44.5 percent of architects were members of the American Institute of Architects in 1961.

9. Career patterns among a sample of engineering graduates indicate that "involvement in professional activities *precedes* movement into upper supervisory positions, suggesting the existence of a close

association between professional and societal success." See C. C. Perrucci and R. Perrucci, "Social Origins, Educational Contexts and Career Mobility," *Amer. Soc. Rev.*, 35 (1970), p. 453, fn.

10. See Freidson's discussion of elite control and its limitations in the profession of medicine: *Profession*, pp. 188–200.

11. As I suggested above, the organization of profession is based on the assumption of minimal equality among professionals; this adds a strong ideological bond to the organization, despite the very high degree of internal stratification. See Stinchcombe, "Organizations," p. 181.

12. Oswald Hall, "Types of Medical Careers," *Amer. Jour. Soc.*, 55 (1949): 243–253, proposes an interesting analysis of professional types: the successful specialists are most likely to be closely identified with a community's medical institutions. Their careers are based on formal and informal organizational networks. The individualist, although he may be financially very successful, is marginal to the professional establishment. The "friendly career" seems typical of a more old-fashioned kind of doctor, with strong personal loyalties to both his clientele and a small group of friendly colleagues—to one of whom he may transfer his practice upon retiring. Of these three types, the second and third are marginal; the third may generate a disposition to criticize the professional establishment. We may add a fourth type: the advocate, who is actively critical of the delivery of medical services and of the kind of practice with which the establishment is identified. The advocate tends to seek a base among reform groups in the community or among his clients, in which case he is very close to the "friendly career" type, with a more political connotation.

13. About 1850, it is estimated that a successful physician could make between £800 and £3,000 in London, compared to £500 to £1,500 in the provinces. The average earnings of GP's were estimated to hover around £500. Lawyers did not usually limit themselves to practicing law for an income. In 1850, "there were said to be eight barristers making £8,000, perhaps two dozen £5,000 and five £11,000." Between £500 and £1,200 a year was an ordinary income for junior barristers. A solicitor, if he lived by his profession alone, which few did, could make at most £2,000 a year. In general, "about £1,000 a year . . . evidently represented modest prosperity. There were plenty below and a reasonable chance of getting fairly well above, though, naturally, the very high incomes—say, from £5,000 up— were rare." (Reader, *Professional Men*, pp. 200—201.) In America before 1850, it appears that professionals of different categories commanded more or less the same annual income: $500 per year was, allegedly, the typical income of ordinary physicians. In 1835, as a comparison, the median salary of state governors was $2,000. (Calhoun, *Civil Engineer*, pp. 172 and 169ff.)

14. In England the costs of establishment were high: "What was required, in fact, for the young doctor, or lawyer, or architect, or any other professional man starting on his own, was some source of income to provide a couple of hundred pounds a year or so. Below that level, even in mid-Victorian England it was difficult to keep up sufficient appearance of gentility to attract clients." (Reader, *Professional Men*, p. 191.) For the beginnings of a surgeon, see S. Squire Sprigge, *The Life and Times of Thomas Wakley* (New York: Robert E. Krieger, 1974 ed.).

15. See Shryock, *Development*, p. 265. An unintended consequence of this practice may have been that of maintaining the habit of seeing a regular physician, and thus expressing some trust in the profession, even at times when it was in general disrepute.

16. Quoted by John S. Brubacher and Willis Rudy, *Higher Education in Transition* (New York: Harper and Row, 1968 ed.).

17. Shryock, *Development*, p. 266; see also pp. 251ff. Flexner analyzes extensively the distribution and economic situation of European physicians in his report on Europe. See Flexner, *Europe*, chap. 2.

18. Arthur L. Stinchcombe, "Innovation in Industrial Bureaucracies," unpublished ms. (1970), p. 4, chap. 5. Published under the title *Creating Efficient Industrial Management* (New York: Academic Press, 1974).

19. Quoted by Calhoun, *Civil Engineer*, pp. 187–188.

20. *Ibid.*, p. 189.

21. See, for instance, the analysis by Gilb, *Hierarchies*, pp. 30ff and by Layton, *Revolt*, especially chaps. 4, 5, and 7.

22. For examples of such counter-projects, see Bucher, "Pathology"; Calhoun, *Civil Engineer*, pp. 187–189; Calvert, *Mechanical Engineer*, chap. 14; Kaye, *Architectural Profession*, pp. 165ff; Jamous and Peloille, "Changes."

23. Kenneth Boulding, *The Organizational Revolution* (Chicago: Quadrangle, 1968 ed.), pp. 18–19.

24. Boulding, *Revolution,* p. 20, italics mine.

25. Stinchcombe, "Organizations," p. 146.

26. See Appendix Tables 5 and 6.

27. Hughes, *Sociological Eye,* p. 367.

28. See Weber, *From Max Weber,* pp. 240–242.

29. *Ibid.,* pp. 187–191.

30. Ralph Turner, "Sponsored and Contest Social Mobility," in *Class, Status and Power,* Bendix and Lispet, eds., pp. 449–458, quotations on p. 450.

31. As Weber suggests, status structures—and, in fact, the tendency of all stratification structures to create self-entrenching vested interests—put brakes on the rationalizing impact of bureaucracy, which itself generates new status barriers. See, in particular, *From Max Weber,* pp. 230–232.

CHAPTER 7. USES AND LIMITATIONS OF THE ARISTOCRATIC MODEL

1. See Harold Perkin, *The Origins of Modern English Society* (London: Routledge and Kegan Paul, 1969), pp. 252ff.

2. See Perkin, *Origins,* pp. 252–270, and in particular pp. 308–339.

3. Neil Smelser and Seymour M. Lipset, eds., *Social Structure and Mobility in Economic Development* (Chicago: Aldine, 1966), pp. 8–10.

4. One vivid statement on the "openness" of the class system is that by Schumpeter: "For the duration of its collective life, or the time during which its identity may be assumed, each class resembles a hotel or an omnibus, always full, but always of different people." Quoted by S. M. Lipset and Reinhard Bendix, in *Social Mobility in Industrial Society* (Berkeley: Univ. of California Press, 1959), p. 75.

5. Weber, *From Max Weber,* p. 188, italics mine.

6. See Max Weber, *Economy and Society,* 3 vols., Guenther Roth and Claus Wittich, eds. (Totowa, N.J.: Bedminster, 1968), Vol. 1, Part 1, chap. 4.

7. A hypothesis that Bendix and Lipset derive from Veblen is that "according to which a system of stratification is a fundamental source of mobility in and of itself. Apparently, there are imperatives which prompt men to resist and reject an inferior status and these persist regardless of the way in which any given society has legitimated inequality." Lipset and Bendix, *Social Mobility,* p. 63.

8. Weber, *From Max Weber,* pp. 192–193.

9. *Ibid.*

10. Until 1832, "the exercise of the least political rights was dependent on the ownership of landed property which was increasingly hard to come by for those who did not already own estates." Hobsbawm, *Industry,* p. 32.

11. On the dynamism of the British landed class, see Perkin, *Origins,* pp. 56–62 and 176–217. The author argues that the landed ruling class was, in fact, the chief promoter of *internal* free trade from the Restoration on. The breakdown of the ties of dependency was completed by what Carlyle later called "the abdication on the part of the governors"; the abandonment of paternalism by the landed oligarchy accelerated the formation of middle-class and working-class consciousness, and the articulation of their challenges to the old ruling class.

12. Hobsbawm, *Industry,* p. 83.

13. T. H. Marshall, *Class, Citizenship and Social Development* (Garden City, N.Y.: Doubleday Anchor, 1965), p. 206.

14. See Richard Hoggart, *The Uses of Literacy* (New York: Oxford Univ. Press, 1957), chaps. 4 and 5; Bryan Jackson, *Working Class Community* (New York: Praeger, 1971); Perkin, *Origins,* chaps. 7 and 8; E. P. Thompson, *The Making;* and Raymond Williams, *The Long Revolution* (New York: Harper and Row, 1961).

15. As Weber points out, the "awakening of charisma" and the imparting of expert training are two polar opposites in the area of educational goals, although they coexist in tension in many forms of education. In between, says Weber, we find "all those types which aim at cultivating the pupil for a conduct of life, whether it is of a mundane or a religious character. In either case, the life conduct is the conduct of a status group." *From Max Weber,* p. 426.

16. Sprigge, *Wakley,* p. 9.

17. Reader, *Professional Men,* p. 42.

18. Carr-Saunders and Wilson, *The Professions,* p. 308.

19. *Ibid.,* p. 40.

20. On the Act of 1729, see Holdsworth, *English Law,* pp. 53ff; and R. Robson, *The Attorney in Eighteenth Century England* (Cambridge: Cambridge Univ. Press, 1959), pp. 7–13; see also his pp. 25–30, on the conflict between the Society of Gentlemen Practisers and the Scriveners' Company.

21. This passage is based on the discussion by Holdsworth, *English Law,* pp. 78ff.

22. From the sixteenth century on, the physicians who had only foreign doctorates or had not completed seven years of residence at one of the English universities were excluded from the fellowship and taxed more heavily than Oxford or Cambridge graduates on acceding to candidacy or to the license (Clark, *Royal College,* pp. 134–135). On the conflictive relations between the Royal College and the two English universities, see Clark, *Royal College,* pp. 208–214, 507–510, 547–551, 565–569.

23. Clark, *Royal College,* p. 567.

24. In the first years of the nineteenth century, there were only 26 licentiates in the whole of England outside London. Only 18 "extra-licenses" more were granted from 1807 to 1815. Clark, *Royal College,* pp. 638–639.

25. Carr-Saunders and Wilson, *The Professions,* p. 71.

26. Sprigge, *Wakley,* p. 11.

27. See Clark, *Royal College,* pp. 649ff; and Sprigge, *Wakley,* pp. 12–13.

28. Indeed, when Wakley entered Parliament in 1835, the amendment of the Apothecaries Act had become a divisive issue among the Society's licentiates. Some desired an amendment that would raise the status of the English GP's and thus arm them against the invasion of Scotch doctors. Some thought that the best way to exclude the latter was by defending the Apothecaries' monopoly over dispensation of medicine in England and Wales. See Sprigge, *Wakley,* pp. 235ff.

29. An eighteenth-century pamphleteer pointed out that "poverty in any profession is but a bad sign of qualification and ability." (Quoted by David Glass, "Education and Social Change in Modern England," *Education, Economy and Society,* A. H. Halsey, Jean Floud, and C. A. Anderson, eds. (New York: Free Press, 1961), p. 396. On the upward mobility of professionals in the eighteenth century, see Robson, *Attorney,* pp. 134–135.

30. Quoted by W. H. G. Armytage, *Four Hundred Years of English Education* (Cambridge: Cambridge Univ. Press, 1970), p. 66.

31. The Royal Commission on the Universities of 1850–1852 was followed by Acts of Parliament which established executive commissions at Oxford and Cambridge. The latter made implementation of reforms much easier. The last religious tests were abolished in 1871.

32. For the findings of the Select Parliamentary committee on medical education of 1833 and the Royal College's response, see Clark, *Royal College,* pp. 683–692. In the legal profession, an 1834 commission recommended that a right of appeal be granted against the Benchers of the Inns of Court to those who had been refused membership. This reversed earlier judgments which favored the autonomous corporations. See Holdsworth, *English Law,* pp. 30–31.

33. Quoted by Carr-Saunders and Wilson, *The Professions,* p. 75.

34. Quoted by Reader, *Professional Men,* pp. 55–56.

35. Adam Smith, An Inquiry into the Nature and Causes of the Wealth of Nations (New York: Modern Library, 1937), p. 105.

36. Reader, *Professional Men,* p. 73.

37. On the limited effects of the 1832 Reform Act, see Perkin, *Origins,* pp. 238 and 313–316. I am indebted to his analysis of "The Struggle between the Ideals" for this section. See, in particular, chaps. 7 and 8.

38. Perkin, *Origins,* p. 315.

39. On the struggle for hegemony, see Gramsci, *Notebooks;* and, for England, see Bendix, *Work,* chap. 2 and *Nation-Building and Citizenship* (Berkeley: Univ. of California Press, 1975 ed.).

40. James Mill, in *Westminster Review,* 6 (1826), p. 254.

41. Perkin, *Origins,* p. 321.

42. Quoted by Armytage, *Four Hundred Years,* p. 121.

43. In the period 1855–1864, the competition for the Indian Civil Service attracted a large number of university graduates: 101 came from Oxford, 80 from Cambridge, 76 from Dublin, 27 from Edinburgh, and 58 from other universities; 79 did not come from a university. See Reader, *Professional Men,* pp. 93ff.

44. See Emmeline W. Cohen, *The Growth of the British Civil Service, 1780–1939* (Hamden, Conn.: Archon Books, 1965).

45. Quoted by Cohen, *Civil Service,* p. 107.

46. On the personal links of the reformers with Oxford and Cambridge, see Cohen, *Civil Service,* pp. 81–85.

47. *Ibid.,* pp. 107–108.

48. The establishment of a competitive entry examination at the Royal Military Academy of Woolwich in 1857 and at Sandhurst in 1871, added considerably to this pressure.

49. Quoted by Carr-Saunders and Wilson, *The Professions,* p. 314.

50. See Armytage, *Four Hundred Years,* pp. 103–104. In 1834, 347 out of 469 students at the University of London were medical, as was more than half of a comparable student body at King's.

51. Reader, *Professional Men,* p. 120.

52. Hobsbawm, *Industry,* p. 156.

53. Clark, *Royal College,* pp. 716 and 717.

54. *Ibid.,* pp. 728 and 730.

55. *Ibid.,* p. 614.

56. *Ibid.,* p. 615.

57. On this point, see *Ibid.,* pp. 715–717 and Sprigge, *Wakley,* chaps. 24 and 42.

58. Perkin, *Origins,* p. 294.

59. Williams, *Long Revolution,* p. 137. On the reform of the public schools, see also Armytage, *Four Hundred Years,* pp. 107–109; and Perkin, *Origins,* pp. 294–301. On the continuation of Thomas Arnold's pedagogical ideal by his son Matthew, and on the latter's attitude toward government, see Raymond Williams, *Culture and Society, 1780–1950* (Garden City, N.Y.: Doubleday Anchor, 1960), pp. 123–139.

60. On this process, see Brian Simon, *Studies in the History of Education; Education and the Labour Movement, 1870–1920* (London: Lawrence and Wishart, 1965), pp. 103–108. The means by which the middle-class schools gained national recognition from the 1850s on was a system of local examinations of their students, conducted by the universities. In the period 1850–1899, over 80 percent of Oxford and Cambridge students came from public schools; only 7 percent came from local grammar schools. Simon, *Studies,* p. 111.

61. *Ibid.,* p. 108. The evolution of the public school ethos from the moral and classical ideals incarnated in Thomas Arnold to a kind of "philistine athleticism" oriented to imperialist tasks need not concern us here. It is described by Simon, *Studies,* pp. 108–112 and analyzed at length by David Newsome, *Godliness and Good Learning* (London: Murray, 1961).

62. Quoted by Simon, *Studies,* p. 102.

63. G. Kitson Clark, *The Making of Victorian England* (London: Methuen, 1962), pp. 273–274.

64. On working class education, see Simon, *Studies,* pp. 121–162, and in particular, Mary Sturt, *The Education of the People* (London: Routledge and Kegan Paul, 1967).

65. Simon, *Studies,* pp. 97–98.

66. Perkin, *Origins,* p. 301.

67. Simon, *Studies,* p. 246. For this section, I have relied on his chapters 6 and 7 and on Sturt, *Education,* chaps. 18 and 19.

68. Carr-Saunders and Wilson observe that "the members of the first founded of these [professional societies] were very conscious that they had no social prestige and that their occupations were not "fit for gentlemen." Their declared objects nearly always included some reference to the raising of status. When application was made for a charter, it was generally submitted that incorporation in this manner would help to confer them the much desired prestige." *The Professions,* p. 302.

69. David Glass notes that "those sections of the middle class who sent their boys to boarding schools

sent 30.6 percent of their sons born between 1910 and 1929 to universities, as against 19 percent of the generation of boarding school boys born before 1910.'' The corresponding proportions, for boys who went to secondary grammar schools, were 11.4 percent and 9 percent. See Glass, ''Social Change,'' p. 401 and fn 51, p. 409.

70. Williams, *Long Revolution,* p. 143.

71. Simon, *Studies,* p. 67. See also Sir Eric Ashby, ''On Universities and the Scientific Revolution,'' in *Education, Economy and Society,* Halsey, Floud, and Anderson, eds., pp. 466–476; H. J. Habbakuk, *American and British Technology in the Nineteenth Century* (Cambridge: Cambridge Univ. Press, 1962); and Hobsbawm, *Industry,* pp. 185ff.

72. Abraham Flexner, *Universities: American, English, German* (New York: Oxford Univ. Press, 1968 ed.), p. 248.

73. Quoted by Ashby, ''On Universities,'' pp. 470–471.

74. Ashby, ''On Universities,'' pp. 473–474.

75. A. H. Halsey, ''British Universities,'' *Arch. Europ. Sociol.,* 3 (1962): 85–101, pp. 97–98.

76. Joseph Ben-David and Awraham Zloczower, ''Universities and Academic Systems in Modern Societies,'' *Arch. Europ. Sociol.,* 3 (1962): 45–84, p. 67.

77. The following table gives an idea of the frequency of students in total population at different times and for different countries (per each 10,000 inhabitants). The moderate increase in Britain's student population was chiefly carried by the ''red-brick'' universities. Halsey, ''Universities,'' gives data on the shift in subjects selected by the new student bodies.

	1913	1934	1948	1958	Increase in frequency 1913–34 (1913–100)	1934–58 (1934–100)
			(1947)			
Britain	6.8	11.3	16.3	18.8	165	165
USA	38.6	83.3	178.6	185.2	215	220
Belgium	11.2	13.6	24.9	49.5	120	365
France (Foreign st. excluded)	10.3	20.8	31.4	50.8	200	245
Germany	11.5	19.7	—	31.4	170	160
Switzerland (Foreign st. excluded)	10.3	18.7	26.4	42.4	290	145

SOURCE: Joseph Ben-David, ''The Growth of the Professions and the Class System,'' *Class, Status and Power,* Bendix and Lipset, eds., pp. 459–472, Table 4.

78. A. H. Halsey, ''The Changing Functions of Universities,'' in *Education, Economy and Society,* Halsey, Floud, and Anderson, eds., pp. 456–465, p. 461.

79. Flexner, *Universities,* pp. 280–281, 296–297. For his criticism of medical education in England, see *Europe.* For a critical account of the role played by Oxford and Cambridge in British intellectual life, see the brilliant analysis by Perry Anderson, ''Components of the National Culture,'' in *Student Power,* Robin Blackburn and Alexander Cockburn, eds. (Baltimore: Penguin, 1969), pp. 214–284.

80. Ben-David and Zloczower, ''Universities,'' p. 68.

81. On this point, see Kaye, *Architectural Profession,* and the interesting study of engineers by Kenneth Prandy, *Professional Employees* (London: Faber and Faber, 1965).

82. It is often suggested that the decline in entrepreneurial efficiency and innovation which became apparent before the end of the nineteenth century was due to the gentlemanly aspirations of the British businessman. Hobsbawm remarks that the public school ethos was never antagonistic to making money; it only discouraged scientific and technical vocations. Moreover, the average British businessman did not have access to the elite, nor was he interested in higher education—elitist or not—for either his sons or his staff. Even today, only 20 percent or so of the managers of middle-sized firms have attended a

university, and no more than 5 percent have attended one of the top public schools. The proportions must have been much lower among the owner-managers of the second half of the nineteenth century. See Hobsbawm, *Industry*, p. 185 and fn.

83. On social mobility in British industry, see data reported by Lipset and Bendix, *Social Mobility*, pp. 35ff. See also the data on the first employment of graduates in different fields in A. M. Carr-Saunders, D. Caradog-Jones, and C. A. Moser, *A Survey of Social Conditions in England and Wales* (Oxford: Clarendon Press, 1957), p. 83.

84. Quoted by Reader, *Professional Men*, pp. 183–185.

85. See Kotschnig, *Unemployment*, pp. 121–125.

86. See Glass, "Social Change," pp. 400 and 404.

87. Halsey, "Universities," p. 90.

CHAPTER 8. PROFESSIONAL PRIVILEGE IN A DEMOCRATIC SOCIETY

1. Gilb, *Hierarchies*, p. 17.

2. Gilb observes that "the greatest single spurt in the creation of new licensing boards in states across the country came between 1911–15" (*Hierarchies*, p. 38). What Gilb calls the "federalization" of professional organizations and the improvement in their management came also between 1901 and 1936.

3. The share of the United States in the manufacturing output of the world developed as follows (percentage of world output): 1870: 23.3 percent; 1881–1885: 28.6 percent (the largest share of all industrial nations); 1896–1900: 30.1 percent; 1906–1910: 35.3 percent; 1913: 35.8 percent; 1926–1929: 42.2 percent. Source: Douglass C. North, *Growth and Welfare in the American Past* (Englewood Cliffs, N.J.: Prentice-Hall, 1966), p. 28.

4. Oscar Handlin, Preface to Calhoun, *Lives*, vii.

5. Among recent histories of American professions are: Auerbach, "Enmity"; Calhoun, *Civil Engineer* and *Lives;* Calvert, *Mechanical Engineer;* Kett, *Formation;* Rothstein, American Physicians; Robert Stevens, "Two Cheers for 1870: the American Law School," *Perspectives in Amer. History*, 5 (1971); Rosemary Stevens, *American Medicine and the Public Interest* (New Haven: Yale Univ. Press, 1971).

6. Baylin, *Education*, p. 30.

7. Quoted in Baylin, *Education*, p. 74.

8. *Ibid.*, pp. 26–29.

9. *Ibid.*, p. 81.

10. See *ibid.*, pp. 32–36 and Bibliography.

11. *Ibid.*, pp. 43–44.

12. On the schemes for national construction of the revolutionary leaders, see Yehoshua Arieli, *Individualism and Nationalism in American Ideology* (Cambridge, Mass.: Harvard Univ. Press, 1964), Part I. For the Jeffersonian ideal in particular, see chaps. 7 and 8.

13. On the relation between nostalgia and anxiety, see Rothman, *Discovery*, and Robert H. Wiebe, *The Search for Order; 1877–1920* (New York: Hill and Wang, 1967).

14. See Allan Kulikoff, "The Progress of Inequality in Revolutionary Boston," in *Past Imperfect*, 2 vols., Blanche Wiesen Cook, Alice K. Harris, and Ronald Radosh, eds. (New York: Alfred A. Knopf, 1973), Vol. 1, pp. 106–128, see p. 109.

15. Jackson Turner Main, "The Nature of Class in Revolutionary America," in *Past Imperfect*, Vol. 1, pp. 70–78, p. 73.

16. Aubrey C. Land, "Economic Base and Social Structure: the Northern Chesapeake in the Eighteenth Century," *Past Imperfect*, Vol. 1, pp. 30–41, pp. 39 and 35.

17. *Ibid.*, pp. 38–39.

18. *Ibid.*, pp. 33 and 40.

19. Lance E. Davis, Richard A. Easterlin *et al.*, *American Economic Growth* (New York: Harper and Row, 1972), p. 131.

20. See Kulikoff, "Inequality," p. 115.

21. See *ibid.*, pp. 116–117. In 1791, 23 percent of the migrants arrived from foreign ports; 39.8 percent from nearby Massachusetts towns, and 31.4 percent from the surrounding agricultural areas.

22. *Ibid.*, p. 117.

23. Main, "The Nature of Class," p. 72, and Kulikoff, "Inequality," Table IIB, p. 110.

24. Kulikoff, "Inequality," pp. 111 and 119.

25. See *ibid.*, pp. 114–115 and 121–122.

26. Arthur M. Schlesinger, "The Aristocracy in Colonial America," in *Past Imperfect,* Vol. 1, pp. 10–23, p. 20.

27. See Pauline Maier, "Popular Uprisings and Civil Authority in Eighteenth Century America," in *Past Imperfect,* Vol. 1, pp. 42–64.

28. Kulikoff's analysis of Boston in 1790 finds that professionals, representing 4.1 percent of the work force, counted among the most prestigious groups and among the wealthiest occupations. Boston had 21 lawyers, 26 doctors, and 17 apothecaries. By mean assessed wealth, they ranked, respectively, second, third, and fourth after the richest category (merchants). See "Inequality," pp. 108 and 113.

29. Carl and Jessica Bridenbaugh, *Rebels and Gentlemen; Philadelphia in the Age of Franklin* (New York: Oxford Univ. Press, 1962), p. 180.

30. See a discussion of this point in Baylin, *Education,* pp. 90ff. On the decline of clerical undergraduates, see Richard Hofstadter and Walter P. Metzger, *The Development of Academic Freedom in the United States* (New York: Columbia Univ. Press, 1955), p. 192.

31. Hofstadter, in Hofstadter and Metzger, *Academic Freedom,* p. 149.

32. See Bridenbaugh, *Rebels,* pp. 30–69.

33. *Ibid.*, p. 45.

34. Hofstadter and Metzger, *Academic Freedom,* p. 186. See also pp. 185–208 for these developments.

35. Rosemary Stevens, *American Medicine,* pp. 18–19.

36. The Bridenbaughs report that in the years 1750–1776, at least 82 physicians and surgeons, associated with "some seven ocultists and dentists of reputable standing, and ten apothecaries, at the least, practiced in Philadelphia. More than half had studied in Europe and at least twenty had European degrees." Bridenbaugh, *Rebels,* pp. 275–276. See also Rosemary Stevens, *American Medicine,* pp. 15–16, fn 11.

37. On Morgan's plans, see Bridenbaugh, *Rebels,* pp. 283–289.

38. On the medical press in Philadelphia, see *ibid.*, p. 291.

39. Warren, *American Bar,* pp. 4ff.

40. Reed, *Training,* p. 36. Some 60 Americans had been admitted to the Inns of Court before 1760, 115 between 1760 and 1776, and another 61 between 1776 and 1815. See Robert Stevens, "Two Cheers," p. 411, fn 18.

41. Robert Stevens, "Two Cheers," p. 408.

42. Reed, *Training,* p. 38.

43. Tocqueville, *Democracy,* Vol. 1, pp. 281–290.

44. See Reed, *Training,* pp. 81–82.

45. On early education for the law, see *ibid.*, pp. 120–142.

46. Rothstein, *American Physicians,* p. 76.

47. See Chapter Six.

48. Marvin Meyers, *The Jacksonian Persuasion; Politics and Belief* (Stanford: Stanford Univ. Press, 1957), p. 101. For per capita economic growth in this period, see Davis *et al., Economic Growth,* pp. 41 and 34.

49. See Meyers, *Jacksonian Persuasion,* pp. 115ff.

50. See *ibid.*, pp. 108ff.

51. On investment in canals and railroads, see Davis *et al., Economic Growth,* pp. 482 and 496.

52. *Ibid.*, pp. 601 and 123; *Hist. Stat. of the U.S.,* A–181–94.

53. The following are net migration rates (per thousand, per year) for the period 1800–1920 (from Davis *et al., Economic Growth,* p. 123):

1800–1810	1.0	1830–1840	3.3	1860–1870	5.8	1890–1900	3.6
1810–1820	.8	1840–1850	7.1	1870–1880	5.0	1900–1910	6.4
1820–1830	1.1	1850–1860	9.4	1880–1890	7.9	1910–1920	3.2

54. See Davis *et al., Economic Growth*, p. 129.
55. *Ibid.*, see pp. 27, 186, 187.
56. See North, *Growth*, pp. 79–81.
57. Lee Soltow, *Men and Wealth in the United States, 1850–70* (New Haven: Yale Univ. Press, 1975), p. 123.
58. See Robert E. Gallman, "Trends in the Size Distribution of Wealth in the Nineteenth Century," in *Six Papers on the Size Distribution of Wealth and Income*, Lee Soltow, ed. (New York: National Bureau of Economic Research, 1969) pp. 1–30, see Table 1, p. 6.
59. Lee Soltow, Comment to Gallman, "Trends," p. 25.
60. Lee Soltow, *Men and Wealth*, p. 101.
61. Soltow (*Men and Wealth*, p. 103) gives the following inequality coefficients (G=0, perfect equality; G=1, perfect inequality) for the distribution of total estate among adult males in 1860–1870:

	1860 *Free males*	1870 *Whites*	1870 *All adult males*
U.S.	.832	.814	.833
North	.813	.810	.816
South	.845	.818	.866

62. See Soltow, *Men and Wealth*, pp. 107–108. Inequality coefficients are .886 for non-farmers and .765 for farmers, compared to .833 for all men older than 20.
63. The proportions of each occupational status varied as follows during the period 1800–1860 and beyond:

	1800	1860	1910	1957
Self-employed	57%	37%	22%	14%
Slaves	31	23	—	—
Wage-earners	12	40	78	86
Total labor force	100	100	100	100

SOURCE: Stanley Lebergott, "The Pattern of Employment since 1800," in *American Economic History*, Seymour E. Harris, ed. (New York: McGraw Hill, 1961) pp. 282–310.

64. See Douglas Miller, *Jacksonian Aristocracy* (New York: Oxford Univ. Press, 1967), p. 122.
65. Meyers, *Jacksonian Persuasion*, pp. 7–8. See also Richard P. McCormick, *The Second American Party System; Party Formation in the Jacksonian Era* (Chapel Hill, N.C.: Univ. of North Carolina Press, 1966).
66. Edward Pessen, *Jacksonian America* (Homewood, Ill.: Dorsey Press, 1969), p. 210. The rise of full-time politicians in intimate relation with the new national party machines is, undoubtedly, the most salient advance of professionalization in this period, if we understand it to mean the acquisition of certain attributes, such as the full-time specialization of function. But politicians, to paraphrase Weber, belong in "a house of power," as military men do, though in a different sense. They do not transact their services for income on a market (at least, they are not supposed to), but "exchange" them for votes on a political market-place. They are not subject, therefore, to a theory of professionalization that starts with an analysis of professional markets.
67. In the 1840 election, the Whigs ran General Harrison's campaign under the symbols of the Log Cabin and the Common Man, attacking Van Buren for his aristocratic origins and tastes.
68. The thesis that the Democrats represented a coalition of Eastern workingmen, small farmers from the West and the South, and urban radicals, is advanced by Arthur Schlesinger, Jr., *The Age of Jackson* (Boston: Little, Brown, 1945). Recent studies find, however, that the Democratic leadership was essentially similar to the Whig in status and political outlook, though their wealth may have been more recent (see Pessen, *Jacksonian America*). The electorate of all classes divided its support more or less equally between the two parties. Marginal regional variations are not consistent with mechanical class analysis. One historian suggests that the pragmatic essence of Jacksonian politics was precisely what could hold together a coalition of declining farmers and "rising men," so long as both groups were interested in

opposing the same kind of privileges. See Michael A. Lebowitz, ''The Jacksonians: Paradox Lost?'' in *Towards a New Past,* Barton J. Bernstein, ed. (New York: Random House, 1967), pp. 65–89. See also the pathbreaking study by Lee Benson, *The Concept of Jacksonian Democracy: New York as a Test Case* (Princeton, N.J.: Princeton Univ. Press, 1961).

70. See the brilliant interpretation by William A. Williams, *The Contours of American History* (New York: World Publ. Co., 1961), pp. 225–283.

71. Quoted by Meyers, *Jacksonian Persuasion,* p. 199. See his chap. 9 for an analysis of Leggett's radicialism.

72. Quoted by Meyers, *Jacksonian Persuasion,* p. 193.

73. *Ibid.,* p. 196.

74. See *Ibid.,* chaps. 10 and 11 in particular.

75. *Ibid.,* pp. 204–205.

76. Quoted by Lebowitz, ''Paradox Lost?'' p. 76.

77. *Ibid.,* p. 76.

78. Calhoun, *Lives,* p. 188.

79. Richard Hofstadter, *Anti-Intellectualism in American Life* (New York: Vintage, 1962), pp. 155–156.

80. Shryock, *Development,* p. 262.

81. The District of Columbia, Massachusetts, Maine, and Connecticut lifted restrictions on unlicensed medical practice in 1838; from 1826 to 1851, eight states repealed medical legislation or penalties for unlicensed practice, while five others exempted sectarians from existing legislation. In 1845, at least eight states had no medical standards whatsoever. See Stevens, *American Medicine,* p. 27.

82. Stevens, ''Two Cheers,'' p. 417.

83. *Ibid.,* p. 418.

84. Calhoun, *Lives,* p. 188.

85. Rothstein gives the following data to show the proliferation of medical schools before the Civil War (the first figure represents the number of medical schools in the United States; the figure in parenthesis represents the number of medical schools in New England, New York, and Philadelphia): 1770: 2 (2); 1790: 3 (3); 1810: 6 (5); 1830: 22 (14); 1840: 30 (16); 1850: 42 (17); 1860: 47 (16). Rothstein, *American Physicians,* Table V-1, p. 93.

86. On legal education before the Civil War, see James W. Hurst, *The Growth of American Law: The Lawmakers* (Boston: Little, Brown, 1950), pp. 258ff; Reed, *Training,* pp. 132–133 and Tables, pp. 444–445; Stevens, ''Two Cheers,'' pp. 415–416.

87. Brubacher and Rudy, *Higher Education,* p. 206.

88. Hofstadter and Metzger, *Academic Freedom,* p. 214.

89. See *ibid.,* pp. 212–216 and 222–230.

90. President Philip Lindsley of the University of Nashville, faced with the proliferation of small colleges competing with his university (more than thirty sprang up in less than 25 years), commented: ''Our people, at first, oppose all distinctions whatever as odious and aristocratical; and then, presently, seek with avidity such as remain accessible. At first they denounce colleges; and then choose to have a college in every district or county, or for every sect and party—and to boast of a college education, and to sport with high sounding literary titles—as if these imparted sense or wisdom or knowledge.'' Quoted by Hofstadter and Metzger, *Academic Freedom,* p. 212.

91. Rosenberg, *Cholera,* p. 160.

92. See Calhoun, *Lives,* chap. 4.

93. *Ibid.,* p. 155.

94. *Ibid.,* pp. 156–157.

95. *Ibid.,* pp. 170ff.

96. Calhoun, *Civil Engineer,* p. 48. See pp. 14–15 on foreign engineers in the first public works projects.

97. Quoted by Calhoun, *Civil Engineer,* p. 27.

98. *Ibid.,* p. 67.

99. See Calvert, *Mechanical Engineer*, pp. 14ff.

100. Quoted by Calhoun, *Civil Engineer*, p. 198.

101. See Calvert, *Mechanical Engineer*, pp. 12–14, 277, and chap. 8.

102. Calhoun, *Civil Engineer*, p. 199.

103. Layton, *Revolt*, p. 2.

104. Reed, *Training*, p. 88.

105. See Hurst, *Lawmakers*, pp. 283ff and, for the later period, Auerbach, "Enmity."

106. In 1850, there were 23,939 lawyers for 40,765 physicians and 26,842 clergymen; that is, respectively, 103, 176, and 116 for every 100,000 inhabitants. (Reed, *Training*, p. 442.)

107. Stevens, "Two Cheers," p. 421.

108. Reed, *Training*, p. 90. "Beginning 1859," says Reed, "power to inquire into the educational qualifications of the applicants was restored to the courts in Maine, Wisconsin, and New Hampshire." *Training*, p. 90, fn 3.

109. See *ibid.*, pp. 133ff, pp. 142–150 on Judge Story's Harvard Law School. See p. 153 for the total number of law schools and students enrolled during this period.

110. See Stevens, "Two Cheers," pp. 419–420 and fn 58.

111. This account is based on Johnson, "Professional Life Styles," and also on Calhoun, *Lives*, chap. 3.

112. On the difficulty of establishing bar associations where the circuit remained in existence for a long time, as in Wisconsin, see Johnson, "Professional Life Styles," p. 200.

113. Calhoun, *Lives*, p. 71.

114. See *ibid.*, pp. 78ff, in particular pp. 82–83.

115. On this evolution, see Hurst, *Lawmakers*, chap. 13.

116. See Calhoun, *Lives*, pp. 180ff, in particular 180–182.

117. Flexner, *Report*, p. 6.

118. See Calhoun, *Lives*, p. 33, and Kett, *Formation*, pp. 38ff.

119. See Kett's account in *Formation*, pp. 39–43.

120. *Ibid.*, p. 43.

121. Calhoun, *Lives*, p. 57.

122. See *ibid.*, pp. 45–46, and, in particular, Rosenberg, *Cholera*, pp. 65–81 and 163–164.

123. Rosenberg, *Cholera*, p. 72.

124. On the conflict between medical societies and medical schools, see Kett, *Formation*, pp. 43–46; and Rothstein, *American Physicians*, chap. 6, and pp. 99–100.

125. This account of sectarianism is based on Kett, *Formation*, chap. 4; and Rothstein, *American Physicians*, chap. 7. See also Rosenberg, *Cholera*, chaps. 9 and 12.

126. Kett, *Formation*, p. 108.

127. *Ibid.*, p. 123.

128. See Kett, *Formation*, pp. 127–130; and Rosenberg, *Cholera*, pp. 158–159.

129. Nor would the Thomsonians' attack on the exclusive medical fraternity of Philadelphia and New York, Kappa Lambda, have succeeded without the support of regular physicians who resented the pre-eminence and the positions held by Kappa Lambda members. See Kett, *Formation*, pp. 115–116.

130. See *ibid.*, p. 139. On homeopathy, see Calhoun, *Lives*, chap. 2; Kett, *Formation*, chap. 5; Rosenberg, *Cholera*, especially chap. 12; see, in particular, Rothstein, *American Physicians*, chap. 8, which I have mainly followed here.

131. See Johnson, "Professional Life Styles," pp. 195ff. In the 1860s, the Homeopathic Medical Society of New York charged that "devotees of their system paid half of the city's taxes and constituted at least 50 percent of its educated population." (Rosenberg, *Cholera*, p. 224.)

132. See Rothstein, *American Physicians*, pp. 171ff.

133. On competition, see Rothstein, *American Physicians*, pp. 108ff; Schryock writes: "By 1860 there was one practitioner for every 572 persons in the population as a whole. The ratio was apparently higher in rural than in urban areas." (Shryock, *Medicine*, pp. 155–156.)

134. See *ibid.*, pp. 158–161.

135. *Ibid.*, p. 149.

136. On the impact of the A.M.A. standards, see Rothstein, *American Physicians,* pp. 118ff. Rothstein estimates that in 1850 no more than 4 percent of the population of 23-year-old males (this was the median age of entrants in one medical school) had two or more years of secondary school education. The A.M.A. required subjects that were taught only in secondary schools.

137. See Rothstein, *American Physicians,* pp. 109ff.

138. Kett, *Formation,* p. 177.

139. See Rothstein, *American Physicians,* chap. 10; the quotation is from Rothstein, p. 202.

140. See Calhoun, *Lives,* pp. 52–55 and 58.

141. On "medical nihilism," see Rosenberg, *Cholera,* p. 223; Rothstein, *American Physicians,* chap. 9; Shryock, *Medicine,* p. 327.

142. On the status of the medical profession before the Civil War, see Rosenberg, *Cholera,* pp. 154–157; Shryock, *Development,* chap. 13.

143. See Kett, *Formation,* pp. 70–79 and 94.

144. In Ohio, however, the short-term results of state control were perhaps worse than those of a free market: the brilliant physician Daniel Drake, ousted by his rivals from the state medical college in the 1830s, was prevented by the legislature to found a competing medical school which would have been undoubtedly better than the official one. See Kett, *Formation,* pp. 19–20 and 79–94.

145. On the public health movement, see George Rosen, *A History of Public Health* (New York: Schumann, 1958); and Rosenberg, *Cholera,* chap. 12.

CHAPTER 9. THE RISE OF CORPORATE CAPITALISM AND THE CONSOLIDATION OF PROFESSIONALISM

1. For an account of this passage in the Marxist tradition, see Paul Baran and Paul M. Sweezy, *Monopoly Capital* (New York: Monthly Review Press, 1968). For a different, non-Marxist approach to structural changes in contemporary capitalism, see John K. Galbraith, *The New Industrial State* (New York: Signet, 1967).

2. For a historical account of the formation of these firms, see Alfred D. Chandler, Jr., *Strategy and Structure,* (Cambridge, Mass.: MIT Press, 1962). For productivity trends in the American economy, see Davis *et al., Economic Growth,* pp. 33–54 and 205–211.

3. See Appendix Table 5.

4. See Jürgen Habermas, "Technology and Science as 'Ideology'," in *Toward a Rational Society,* pp. 81–122 (Boston: Beacon Press, 1971); see also Magali Sarfatti-Larson, "Notes on Technocracy: Some Problems of Theory, Ideology and Power," *Berkeley Journal of Sociology,* 17 (1972–1973): 1–34.

5. The expression is Robert Wiebe's, *Search,* p. 133.

6. Wiebe, *Search,* p. 166.

7. Samuel P. Hays, *The Response to Industrialism: 1885–1914,* (Chicago: Univ. of Chicago Press, 1957), p. 142.

8. Hays, *Response,* p. 143.

9. On Progressivism, see Thomas C. Cochran and William Miller, *The Age of Enterprise* (New York: Harper and Row, 1961); Hays, *Response;* Richard Hofstadter, *The Age of Reform* (New York: Vintage, 1955); Gabriel Kolko, *The Triumph of Conservatism* (New York: Free Press, 1963); James Weinstein, *The Corporate Ideal in the Liberal State: 1900–1918* (Boston: Beacon Press, 1968); Wiebe, *Search,* and his extensive annotated bibliography.

10. See Hays' discussion in *Response,* chap. 4. See also Davis, *Spearheads.*

11. See, in particular, Kolko, *Triumph;* Weinstein, *Corporate Ideal;* and Williams, *Contours.*

12. Weinstein, *Corporate Ideal,* p. xii.

13. On the railroads, see Robert W. Fogel, *Railroads in American Economic Growth* (Baltimore: johns Hopkins Univ. Press, 1964).

14. Hofstadter points out that "almost three-quarters of the trusts and almost six-sevenths of the capital in trusts" came into existence in the short period 1898–1904 (Hofstadter, *Reform*, p. 169). The following table documents the consolidation process:

Giant Consolidations and Market Control (1894–1904)

Percent of industry controlled	Consolidations & parent company		Firm disap- pearances		Capitalization in million U.S.$	
	N	% of total	N	% of total	Value	% of total
42.5–62.5	21	6.7	291	9.7	613,5	10.3
62.5–82.5	24	7.7	529	17.6	2130,6	35.7
82.5 & over	16	5.1	343	11.4	998,0	16.7
"Large"	25	8.0	302	10.0	455,5	7.6
Total	86	27.5	1,465	48.7	4197,6	70.3

SOURCE: Louis M. Hacker, *The Course of American Growth and Development* (New York: John Wiley & Sons, 1970), p. 248. It is interesting to read the above data together with the following series (from Hacker, *Course*, p. 275):

Growth in Real GNP and Productivity (1889–1929)

Average Annual Percentual Rates of Change

Period	Real net national productivity	Total factor input	Total factor productivity
1889–99	4.5	2.9	1.5
1899–1909	4.3	3.1	1.1
1909–19	3.8	2.3	1.5
1919–29	3.1	1.6	1.4

15. Kolko, *Triumph*, p. 3.

16. See Weinstein, *Corporate Ideal*, for an analysis of the National Civic Federation.

17. On the Progressive leadership, see Alfred D. Chandler, Jr., "The Origins of Progressive Leadership," in *The Letters of Theodore Roosevelt*, Elting E. Morrisson, ed. (Cambridge, Mass.: Harvard Univ. Press, 1951–1954), VIII, Appendix III, pp. 1462–1464; Samuel P. Hays, "The Politics of Reform in Municipal Government in the Progressive Era," *Pacific Northwest Quart.*, 55 (1964): 157–169; George Mowry, *The California Progressives* (Berkeley: Univ. of California Press, 1951); Norman Wilensky, *Conservatives in the Progressive Era: The Taft Republicans of 1912*, (Gainesville, Fla.: Univ. of Florida Press, 1965), chap. 3.

18. Hays, "Politics of Reform," p. 168.

19. See *ibid.*

20. Samuel P. Hays, "Political Parties and the Community-Society Continuum," in *The American Party Systems*, William N. Chambers and Walter Dean Burnham (New York: Oxford Univ. Press, 1967), p. 171.

21. *Ibid.*, p. 170.

22. Calvert suggests that Taylorism may be seen as an attempt to create a new role for the old entrepreneurial elite, as the machine shop was displaced by modern industry. The American Society of Mechanical Engineers welcomed, at first, the favorable publicity that management engineering was creating for the profession. But scientific management, in fact, was wedded to bureaucratization and rationalization of production; it would only have precipitated the death of the machine shop, which Taylor himself loved so well. When Taylor assumed the presidency of A.S.M.E. in 1906, the reforms he attempted were bitterly resisted by the membership, and not only by the old-style entrepreneurs, who had already lost control of the

association to the elite of corporate engineers. See Calvert, *Mechanical Engineer,* pp. 235–243, and Layton, *Revolt,* chaps. 6 and 7.

23. Quoted by Layton, *Revolt,* p. 159.

24. *Ibid.,* p. 172.

25. See Bendix, *Work,* chap. 5.

26. Samuel Haber, *Efficiency and Uplift* (Chicago: Univ. of Chicago Press, 1964), pp. ix and x.

27. Brandeis' appeal for efficiency in the Eastern Rate case of 1910–1911 appears to have triggered in the press—and with the public—a real "efficiency craze," which had "both its explicitly moral and its apparently technical aspects." (Haber, *Efficiency,* p. 55.)

28. *Ibid.,* p. 62.

29. The ideology of efficiency is quite clear in Flexner's *Report.* Scientific management ideas were also influential on the management of universities, see Lawrence R. Veysey, *The Emergence of the American University* (Chicago: Univ. of Chicago Press, 1965), p. 353.

30. Haber, *Efficiency,* p. 96, italics mine.

31. Quoted by Bendix, *Work,* p. 278, italics mine.

32. Quoted by *ibid.,* p. 276.

33. Taylor thought that scientific management would result in such increases in productivity that large increases in both wages and profits would become possible; see quotation from Taylor in Bendix, *Work,* p. 276. Productivity played the same role in Herbert Croly's thought, which influenced Roosevelt. See Hays, *Response,* pp. 88ff.

34. Haber, *Efficiency,* p. 11.

35. See Thornstein Veblen, *The Engineers and the Price System* (New York: Harcourt, Brace and World, 1963 ed.).

36. Haber, *Efficiency,* p. 12.

37. Education illustrates the difficulty of assessing productivity in the services, both in terms of input factors (an attempt now almost abandoned) and of output factors, in which last case "output" may be measured either through numbers of pupils-hours of teaching per day, or by the students' achievement on standardized tests. The implications of the reduction of quality to quantity are evident. On the difficulties of measuring productivity in education, see Mark Blaugh, *An Introduction to the Economics of Education* (Baltimore: Penguin, 1970), chaps. 6, 7, 9.

38. The attempt to find "objective" standards for the selection of personnel is obviously not limited to service organizations or service workers. It was, in fact, pioneered by vocational psychologists in the Army during World War I, and continued by industrial psychologists, despite the initial reservations of management. See Bendix, *Work,* pp. 291–293.

39. Weber commented that the United States in the first decades of the twentieth century still bore "the character of a polity which, at least in the technical sense, is not fully bureaucratized." *From Max Weber,* p. 211. See pp. 209–211.

40. Haber, *Efficiency,* p. 101.

41. *Ibid.,* pp. 104–105.

42. *Ibid.,* p. 116.

43. The article by Kingsley Davis and Wilbert E. Moore, "Some Principles of Stratification," in *Class, Status and Power,* Bendix and Lipset, eds., pp. 47–53, is still one of the most coherent expositions of this ideological view, presented as social science.

44. Peter Drucker observes: "Knowledge opportunities exist primarily in large organizations. Although the shift to knowledge work has made possible large modern organizations, it is the emergence of these organizations—business enterprises, government agency, large university, research laboratory, hospital—that in turn has created the job opportunities for the knowledge worker. . . . The knowledge opportunities of yesterday were largely for independent professionals working on their own. Today's knowledge opportunities are largely for people working within an organization as members of a team or by themselves." Peter Drucker, *The Age of Discontinuity* (New York: Harper and Row, 1968), pp. 274–275.

45. The broad changes in the occupational structure appear clearly in the following table:

Percent distribution of gainful workers, older than 10 years,
by broad occupational categories

Category	1870	1900	1910	1920	1930
Physical goods	74.9	65.4	62.7	60.5	50.8
Transport, communications, trade	11.0	17.3	16.8	17.3	20.4
Clerical Occupations	0.6	2.5	4.6	7.3	8.2
Professional service	2.6	4.1	4.6	5.1	6.7
Public service[a]	0.7	1.0	1.2	1.7	1.8
Domestic & personal services	9.7	9.7	10.1	8.0	10.1
Total gainful workers	100.0	100.0	100.0	100.0	100.0

[a]Not elsewhere classified: omits, therefore, professionals, and, in particular, the large body of public-school teachers; clerical assistants; postal workers; and personnel employed in the construction and maintenance of roads, streets, sewers, and bridges, in government printing offices, in navy yards, etc.

SOURCE: Alba M. Edwards, *Population: Comparative Occupational Statistics for the United States,* *1870–1940* (Washington: U.S. Government Printing Office, 1943), p. 101.

46. As explained in note 45, the available figures for public service do not adequately reflect the enormous growth of the sector; the few categories covered by the census definition (public protection, armed forces, custodial personnel, public officials, and personnel involved at all levels in public works) show, nevertheless, the largest percentage increase of all occupational categories in the period 1870–1930. Here are some percentage increases for selected occupational categories:

Year	Total pop.	All gainful workers	All prof. workers	Teachers Profess.	Public service	Clerical workers
1870 ⎱	. . .	. . .	. . .	. . .	. . .	. . .
1880 ⎰	30.1	39.1	63.6		52.4	70.3
1890	24.8	30.7	62.2	252	72.7	56.3
1900	21.4	27.9	30.2		40.6	36.7
1910	21.0	31.3	40.6		47.6	43.7
				152		
1920	14.9	9.0	23.9		39.1	80.8
1930	16.1	17.3	46.4		35.8	29.7
1930 ⎱						
1870 ⎰	218.4	290.5	781.3	787	1631.3	1127.7

SOURCE: H. Dewey Anderson and Percy E. Davidson, *Occupational Trends in the United States* (Stanford Univ. Press, 1940).

47. Wiebe, *Search,* pp. 13–14.

48. Only 8 percent of the native white stock lived in cities of 100,000 or more, compared to 33 percent of the foreign-born; 58 percent of the latter were urban. See Davis *et al., Economic Growth,* pp. 135–136.

49. For the relative concentration of immigrants and their descendants in different occupational categories, see Edward P. Hutchinson, *Immigrants and their Children,* 1850–1950 (New York: John Wiley and Sons, 1956). The percentage of the work force that unionized varied as follows: 1880, .3 percent; 1890, 1.4 percent; 1900, 2.7 percent; 1910, 5.6 percent; 1920, 12.1 percent. From 7.4 percent in 1930, the proportion of unionized workers jumped to 16.6 percent in 1935 and then attained its present level (22 to 25 percent) in 1945. See Davis *et al., Economic Growth,* p. 220.

50. See Hays, "Political Parties."

51. In the 1870s, the new industrialists had sometimes found it difficult to enlist local support among elected officials, "old" elites, and even law enforcement agencies against their laborers. See Herbert Gutman, "Class, Status and Community Power in Nineteenth-Century American Industrial Cities; Paterson, N.J.: A Case Study," in *Past Imperfect,* vol. 2, pp. 10–25, Cook *et al.,* eds. For the different reaction in the 1880s and early 1890s, see Wiebe, *Search,* pp. 84–110.

52. See Davis, *Spearheads,* and Lubove, *Progressives.*

53. Extrapolating from the political visibility of the "gentlemanly" elites, Hofstadter offers a general explanation of Progressivism as a reaction to "status deprivation" (Hofstadter, *Reform*). The evidence available is often contradictory: the characteristics of the progressives at the state and national levels are not substantially different from those of the Old Guard Republicans; their characteristics appear to be reversed, moreover, at the precinct and local levels. See Hays, "Politics of Reform," and "Political Parties," pp. 163–164.

54. Haber, *Efficiency,* p. 21. The cost of living rose about 35 percent in the years 1897–1913 (Hofstadter, *Reform,* p. 168).

55. For data on the growth of government expenditures, see Davis *et al., Economic Growth,* pp. 653 and 661. For expenditures on education, see p. 651. In the period 1900–1930, the number of elementary schoolteachers increased by 63 percent, that of secondary schoolteachers by 671 percent, and that of college professors by 388 percent. The number of teachers in professional schools proper increased by 96 percent. See Anderson and Davidson, *Trends,* pp. 497 and 503.

56. In social work, this tendency deepened the gap between settlement workers, acting "from below" and social work professionals, who were asserting themselves as experts on the basis of the casework method and individual therapy in bureaucratized institutions of health and charity. See Davis, *Spearheads;* Roy Lubove, *The Professional Altruist* (Cambridge, Mass.: Harvard Univ. Press, 1965); and Chapter Ten here.

57. For instance, accountants and auditors are included by the census in the category "clerical occupations." The occupation (including "bookkeepers and cashiers") increased by 1407 percent in the period 1870–1930. See Anderson and Davidson, *Trends,* p. 584. The financial group in the occupations included under trade also grew very rapidly (by 126.9 percent in the period 1910–1930). See pp. 436 and 440.

58. In 1930, the category "technical engineers" was second largest (7.7 percent) to that of "teachers and professors" (38.4 percent) among professional and technical workers. The category had increased from 7,374 (or 2.2 percent of all professional workers) in 1870 to 226,249 in 1930. The percentage increases in the number of engineers and other technical or professional workers typically employed by industry are among the highest of all occupational categories:

	1870–1900	1900–1930	1870–1930
Technical engineers	486%	423%	2968%
Chemists, assayers, metallurgists	1046	432	5997
Designers, draftsmen	1373	442	7888

At the end of the period, 26.5 percent of all engineers were still in private practice, teaching, and research. The percentages employed by the public sector (12.2 percent) and other industries were growing: building and road construction employed 15.7 percent of all engineers; telephone and telegraph, non-bituminous mining, electric light and power plants, electrical machinery, and iron and steel machinery other than railways employed about 6 percent each. See Anderson and Davidson, *Trends,* pp. 497 and 549.

59. Layton, *Revolt,* p. 64. I follow his account in this section, in particular his chaps. 3 and 4.

60. *Ibid.,* p. 63.

61. *Ibid.,* p. 66.

62. *Ibid.,* p. 67.

63. In 1924 the Society for the Promotion of Engineering Education surveyed a representative cross-section of engineering freshmen: the parents of 42.5 percent of the sample were owners or proprietors of businesses, most of them small commercial or agricultural units. Another 28.2 percent were employed

in executive or supervisory positions; 5.6 percent were engineers or teachers; and 13 percent were skilled workers. Only 13 percent of the fathers had a college degree; 61.3 percent lived in rural areas or towns under 25,000. Quoted by Layton, *Revolt*, p. 9.

64. Attendance at twenty of the oldest and leading colleges rose 3.5 percent during the 1870s, while population grew by 23 percent. Veysey, *Emergence*, pp. 4–5.

65. Brubacher and Rudy, *Higher Education*, p. 161. Ross is quoted by Veysey, *Emergence*, p. 263.

66. Quoted by Veysey, *Emergence*, pp. 13–14. See also his pp. 266ff.

67. See *ibid.*, pp. 265–266.

68. See Hofstadter and Metzger, *Academic Freedom*, chap. 6.

69. Separate theological schools developed after 1865. By that date, ministerial candidates had dropped to one-fifth of the student body in sectarian colleges, from one-third in 1840. At Harvard, Yale, and Princeton, they declined from one in three in 1830 to one in thirteen in 1876. Hofstadter and Metzger, *Academic Freedom*, p. 350.

70. See Jencks and Riesman, *Academic Revolution*, chap. 6, on the "bifurcation of higher education."

71. In this discussion, I follow mainly Veysey, *Emergence*, especially Part I.

72. On the role of presidents, see Veysey's discussion of Harvard and Cornell, pp. 81–98 and of Western Universities, pp. 100–109. See also pp. 17–18, 61–62, and 360–380 on the new breed of administrators. See, as well, Hofstadter and Metzger, *Academic Freedom*, pp. 233ff and 305ff; and Jencks and Reisman, *Academic Revolution*, pp. 25–26.

73. The elective system was the chief reform that Charles W. Eliot had in mind when he began his forty-year reign at Harvard in 1869. Electives gave a decisive impulse to curricular expansion and to the influence of professional schools on undergraduate curricula. The elective system reached its peak around 1903; after that, it increasingly appeared to be incompatible with the maintenance of quality in heterogeneous and highly stratified urban environments. See Veysey, *Emergence*, pp. 81–100 and 118–119. See also Brubacher and Rudy, *Higher Education*, pp. 112ff; and Hofstadter and Metzger, *Academic Freedom*, pp. 360 and 397.

74. Quoted by Veysey, *Emergence*, p. 64.

75. On their cases, see Hofstadter and Metzger, *Academic Freedom*, pp. 425–451.

76. Quoted by Veysey, *Emergence*, p. 104.

77. The movement of American students to German universities became important in the 1870s and 1880s. Numbers peaked in 1895–1896, with 517 Americans officially matriculated at German institutions. Veysey, *Emergence*, p. 128.

78. *Ibid.*, p. 176.

79. For instance, President Eliot at Harvard "could solicit money on the frank promise that the scientific laboratories it would build would directly benefit the company making the donation." Veysey, *Emergence*, pp. 348–349.

80. Hofstadter and Metzger, *Academic Freedom*, pp. 381–382.

81. Veysey, *Emergence*, p. 127.

82. For the interplay of these factors and the major types of institutions at the end of the nineteenth century, see *ibid.*, pp. 283ff.

83. Hofstadter and Metzger, *Academic Freedom*, p. 454.

84. Their rise was parallel to the decline of clergymen. At 15 private institutions, the proportion of clergymen on the board of trustees declined as follows: 1860–1861, 39.1 percent; 1900–1901, 23 percent; 1930–1931, 7.2 percent. At Harvard, 7 trustees out of 36 were clergymen in 1874–1875, against only one in 1894–1895. Hofstadter and Metzger, *Academic Freedom*, p. 352.

85. Quoted by Veysey, *Emergence*, p. 346.

86. See Hofstadter and Metzger, chap. 9, in particular pp. 454ff. See also Richard Shryock, "The Academic Profession in the United States," *Bulletin of the American Association of University Professors*, 38 (1952):32–70.

87. For the increase in the numbers of college professors, see Anderson and Davidson, *Trends*, pp. 502–503 and note 55 above.

88. Veysey, *Emergence*, p. 439. See his penetrating comments on pp. 428–438.

89. Wiebe, *Search*, p. 121.

90. Ben-David, *Scientist*, p. 165. See his discussion of the American model of university, pp. 142ff; and Ben-David and Zloczower, "Universities."

91. The percentage of students in the corresponding age groups increased as follows in the United States:

Academic Year	Students as % of 18–21 yrs. old	Students as % of 18–24 yrs. old
1869–70	1.68	1.14
1889–90	3.04	1.78
1909–10	5.12	2.89
1929–30	12.42	7.20
1949–50	29.58	16.50
1959–60	34.86	20.49

From Daniel Bell, *The Coming of Postindustrial Society* (New York: Basic Books, 1973), p. 219.

92. Stinchcombe offers the following definition of cosmopolitanism: "First, cosmopolitans are likely to regard the social world as orderly and predictable, capable of being understood and manipulated. Second, they are likely to collect information about the world outside their interpersonal experience by entering into written communication about it. . . . Third, we will expect their orientation toward their immediate interpersonal environment . . . to be affected by their attachments to temporally and spatially distant considerations. . . . In general, cosmopolitans' actions will be oriented to an orderly system above their personal expertise; they will find out about that order through written communication; and the constraints of action in that order will reduce their responsiveness to concrete interpersonal milieux." Arthur L. Stinchcombe, "Political Socialization in the Latin American Middle Class," *Harvard Educ. Rev.*, 38 (1968), p. 512.

93. The Progressives included over 20 percent newspaper editors and journalists (Wilensky, *Conservatives*, chap. 3). From 1900 to 1929, the circulation of newspapers and periodicals grew considerably: the percentage increase for the aggregate circulation of all newspapers, including those in foreign language, was 184.2 percent for the period; the total circulation of periodiacls grew by 129.0 percent, and the *number* of news and opinion periodicals increased by 417.5 percent. See Anderson and Davidson, *Trends*, pp. 523–524.

94. Wiebe, *Search*, p. 113.

95. The intermediate class actually does function as a sociological "relay," and is relatively permeable. Although, actually, upward mobility rates do not differ substantially in most industrialized countries for the movement from "manual into non-manual," the United States has a relatively higher rate of access to elite categories for sons of working-class or "manual" fathers. See S. M. Miller, "Comparative Social Mobility," in *Structured Social Inequality*, Celia S. Heller, ed.(New York: Macmillan, 1969), pp. 325–340.

96. Marie R. Haug and Marvin B. Sussman, "Professionalization and Unionism," in *Professions in Contemporary Society*, Special Issue of *American Behavioral Scientist*, 14 (1971), pp. 525–540. See also the penetrating analysis by Jean-Michel Chapoulie, "Sur l'analyse sociologique des groupes professionnels," *Revue Franç. de Sociol.*, 14 (1973): 86–114.

97. It should be recalled that scientific management, by insisting on the common goal of productivity, instituted an objective that appeared to transcend class conflict. At its 1925 convention, the A. F. of L. endorsed the goal of increased productivity, as the condition for achieving its demands (personal communication by James O'Connor).

98. For an enlightening empirical study of factors affecting the choice between unionism and professionalization among employed engineers and scientists, see Prandy, *Professional Employees*.

99. Richard Sennett and Jonathan Cobb, *The Hidden Injuries of Class* (New York: Vintage, 1973), p. 65, italics mine.

100. Haug and Sussman, "Professionalization," p. 527.

101. Marie R. Haug and Marvin B. Sussman, "Professional Autonomy and the Revolt of the Client," *Social Problems*, 17: (1969): 153–161.

CHAPTER 10. PATTERNS OF PROFESSIONAL INCORPORATION INTO THE NEW CLASS SYSTEM

1. Quoted by Gerald E. Markowitz and David K. Rosner, "Doctors in Crisis: A Study of the Use of Medical Reform to Establish Modern Professional Elitism in Medicine," *American Quarterly*, 25 (1973), p. 87.

2. Quoted by *ibid.*, p. 88.

3. See Howard Berliner, "A Larger Perspective on the Flexner Report," March 1975, unpublished ms.

4. Quoted by Markowitz and Rosner, "Doctors," p. 88.

5. Rosemary Stevens, *American Medicine*, p. 49. On specialty societies before 1900 and on the A.M.A. attitude toward specialism, see her pp. 44–49; and Rothstein, *American Physicians*, pp. 207–214.

6. Rothstein points out that bacteriology contributed nothing to therapeutics until the diphtheria antitoxin became available in 1894 (*American Physicians*, pp. 272–278). In the meanwhile, surgery had incorporated anesthesia and was rapidly accepting asepsis and antisepsis: abdominal and pelvic surgery could be frequently and relatively safely attempted. The death rate from these operations fell from 40 percent in 1880–1890 to below 5 percent in 1900. By 1880, the numbers of full-time surgeons who could make a handsome living in their specialized practice were growing rapidly. See Stevens, *American Medicine*, pp. 49–50.

7. The A.M.A. amended its code of ethics in 1912 to condemn fee splitting and all forms of surreptitious financial agreements between doctors.

8. See Stevens, *American Medicine*, pp. 47–52 and p. 74, note 42: outpatient clinics numbered about 150 in 1900; by 1925, there were more than 5,000.

9. Edwards, *Occupational Statistics*, gives the following figures for nurses (see pp. 111–112):

	1870	1900	1910	1930
Trained nurses	1,204	11,804	82,327	249,189
Untrained nurses and midwives	11,365	109,150	133,043	157,009

10. Flexner, *Report*, p. 14.

11. The number of medical schools grew from 100 in 1880 to 160 in 1903, an increase of 60 percent. The average number of students per school increased from 118 to 173 (and the total number of medical students from 11,826 to 27,615). See Rothstein, *American Physicians*, p. 291.

12. See Rothstein, *American Physicians*, pp. 285–297. Harvard followed Michigan in placing its medical faculty on a salaried basis. This radical move by universities to regain control over proprietary medical schools was followed, but slowly: by Yale in 1880, and by Pennsylvania in 1896. In 1898, when the University of Vermont assumed full control over its College of Medicine, the decision was termed "revolutionary." See Stevens, *American Medicine*, pp. 41–42.

13. Rothstein, *American Physicians*, p. 282.

14. Flexner, *Report*, pp. 169, 171.

15. In the period 1897–1912, of the 16 presidents of the A.M.A., 11 had foreign training (9 in Germany); none had a purely private practice. See Berliner, "A Larger Perspective," p. 8.

16. In 1900, the A.M.A. counted only 8,400 members, out of a population of more than 100,000 regular physicians. The circulation of the *Journal* was estimated at 17,000. In 1898 there were, moreover, at least 275 medical periodicals, most of them monthly. For the development of the medical literature in the nineteenth century, see Stevens, *American Medicine*, p. 35 and p. 29, note 36.

17. See Rothstein, *American Physicians*, pp. 318–323.

18. Berliner, "A Larger Perspective," p. 9.

19. See Rothstein, *American Physicians*, pp. 294–297 and Tables XV–1, p. 287, and XV–3, p. 294.

20. Flexner, *Report*, p. 11.

21. Rothstein, *American Physicians*, p. 325.

22. Flexner, *Report*, p. 22.

23. *Ibid.*, p. 89. His guidelines "for reconstruction" are in chap. 9.

24. *Ibid.*, p. 16.

25. An indication of this scarcity is that the Rockefeller Institute awarded only $12,000 in 1901 and only $14,450 in 1902 of the $20,000 per annum available for scientific research. The Institute later decided to build its own centralized research "plant" with full-time personnel, importing foreign scientists for many of its specialized sections. See Berliner, "A Larger Perspective," p. 6.

26. See *ibid.*, p. 19; and Stevens, *American Medicine*, p. 69.

27. Markowitz and Rosner, "Doctors," p. 87.

28. The number of black doctors tripled from 1890 to 1910; after that date, "the flow was stemmed." (Stevens, *American Medicine*, p. 71.) From 1880 to 1904, 4.3 percent of M.D. degrees were granted to women. Of ten women's colleges in 1904, only 3 survived in 1910. Despite women's attendance at coed medical schools, the proportion of women graduates dropped to 3.2 percent in 1912. See Markowitz and Rosner, "Doctors," p. 97.

29. See Ben-David, *Scientist*, Table 2, p. 189.

30. See Stevens, *American Medicine*, p. 123. See pp. 85–97 on the American College of Surgeons; pp. 98–114 on the rise of ophtalmology and the first specialty board, and in general chaps. 6, 7, and 8. Stevens points out that in 1915, as the standardization of undergraduate education was being launched, only 23 percent of that year's graduates would be GP's; 36 percent would develop a specialist interest, and 41 percent would be full-time specialists (p. 116).

31. Stevens, *American Medicine*, p. 151.

32. *Ibid.*, pp. 160–161.

33. By 1929, 7 physicians out of 10 were in some way connected to a hospital. Stevens, *American Medicine*, p. 145, note 35.

34. See Stevens, *American Medicine*, p. 147.

35. On group practice, see Stevens, *American Medicine*, pp. 141–142 and p. 163 for the reaction of GP's and other physicians to the hospital practice of "closed staff."

36. Quoted by Rothstein, *American Physicians*, p. 325.

37. On the politics of organized medicine, see Garceau, *Political Life;* W. A. Glaser, "Doctors and Politics," *Amer. Jour. Soc.*, 66 (1960): 230–245, and "Socialized Medicine in Practice," in *Medical Men*, Freidson and Lorber, eds., pp. 65–81; Health P.A.C., *The American Health Empire* (New York: Vintage, 1971); Elton Rayack, *Professional Power and American Medicine and Economics of the A.M.A.* (Cleveland: World, 1967); and Stevens, *American Medicine*, especially Part V.

38. The 1935 Dodd Report, entitled "Economic Aspects of the Practice of Medicine in California," showed the following income distribution:

Income Category	Percent of California Physicians, 1933			1929 Labor force excl. farmers
	All Phys.	GPs	Full special.	
Net Loss	1.8	1.9	1.4	
Less than $1000 per yr	13.5	18.3	9.3	44%
$1000–2999	38.8	44.2	31.4	
$3000–5000	23.2	21.2	27.5	3.2%
Over $5000	22.1	14.4	30.4	2.4%

SOURCE: Anderson and Davidson, *Trends*, p. 538.

39. Wiebe, *Search,* p. 117.

40. Parsons, "Legal Profession," p. 376.

41. See *Max Weber on Law in Economy and Society,* Max Rheinstein, ed. (New York: Simon and Schuster, 1954), especially chap. 7 to chap. 11. See also William M. Evan, "Introduction," in *Law and Sociology,* William M. Evan, ed. (New York: Free Press, 1962), pp. 1–11.

42. *Max Weber on Law,* p. 314.

43. *Ibid.,* p. 229. Weber remarks that, in England, the bourgeois strata "have generally tended to be intensely interested in a rational procedural system," as the best suited to capitalist interests when a "dual judicial policy" (formalistic adjudication for the upper class, "class justice" against the poor and power-less) cannot be maintained. See pp. 230–231.

44. Tocqueville, *Democracy,* p. 287.

45. Tocqueville's observations about the political role of American lawyers were obviously correct: the percentage of lawyers in the U.S. Senate has varied from 55 to 75 percent in recent decades. (Between 1790 and 1930, the average was around 65 percent.) It has varied from 50 to 65 percent in the House. "Nearly two-thirds of all Presidents and a higher proportion, at least in recent decades, of Vice-Presidents and Cabi-net members came from the bar, and so did nearly every other state governor between 1870 and 1950." (Rueschmeyer, *Lawyers,* pp. 71ff; see also Mills, *White Collar,* p. 127.)

46. See Rueschmeyer, *Lawyers,* especially pp. 7–9 and 158–166. He gives the following percentage distribution for the major subgroups of the bar in the U.S. and in Germany (Table 1, p. 32):

	U.S., 1960	*Germany, 1961*
Lawyers in private practice	76%	22–23%
Lawyers in judicial office	3%	20–21%
Lawyers in govmt. service (incl. prosecuting attorneys)	10%	30–33%
Lawyers in private employment	10%	22–30%
Total members of the bar	252,385	57–59,000

47. See Weber, *From Max Weber,* pp. 216–221.

48. On civil service reform, see Frank M. Stewart, *History of the National Civil Service Reform League* (Austin: Univ. of Texas Press, 1921).

49. Parsons, "Legal Profession," p. 374.

50. See Jerome E. Carlin, *Lawyers' Ethics* (New York: Russell Sage, 1966), pp. 16, 26, 190; and Rueschmeyer, *Lawyers,* p. 38 and his note 34 on p. 203. On plea bargaining in criminal courts, see the excellent analysis by Abraham Blumberg, "The Practice of Law as a Confidence Game," *Law and Society Rev.,* 1 (1967): 15–39.

51. Hurst, *Lawmakers,* p. 297ff. I have relied in this section on his chap. 13.

52. As an example, the New York firm of Strong and Cadwalader had, in 1878, 2 partners, 4 employees in its legal staff, and 4 nonlegal employees. In 1913, there were 8 partners, 15 employed lawyers, and 20 "support" staff; in 1938, the number of employees was 44 legal and 85 nonlegal, for 13 partners. The Cravath firm had 3 partners and 6 associate lawyers in 1906; in 1940, it had 22 partners, 72 associate lawyers and 150 clerical employees. (Hurst, *Lawmakers,* pp. 306ff.) In 1967, firms with 11 or more part-ners were only 1.9 percent of the total number of legal firms (Rueschmeyer, *Lawyers,* Table 2, p. 42).

53. See Stevens, "Two Cheers," p. 456.

54. On the development of legal education, see Stevens, "Two Cheers," pp. 425ff; and Reed, *Train-ing,* especially chaps. 28, 32, and 33 and Appendix II. On Harvard Law School, see Stevens, "Two Cheers," pp. 430–449 and Reed, *Training,* chaps. 29 and 30, which I have followed here.

55. Quoted by Stevens, "Two Cheers," p. 436, note 50. See his pp. 435ff on the case method.

56. Stevens, "Two Cheers," p. 432.

57. Stevens, "Two Cheers," p. 441. See pp. 441ff for the doubts and criticisms raised by the case method. For Reed's criticisms, see *Training,* chap. 25 and pp. 381–385.

58. Reed, *Training*, p. 50.

59. Quoted by Auerbach, "Enmity," p. 551.

60. See Auerbach, "Enmity," p. 553. The number of law schools started increasing in the 1860s and especially in the 1890s, when the proprietary law school began to replace apprenticeship. While the number of lawyers increased by less than 85 percent in the period 1870–1900, the number of school-trained lawyers increased by 169 percent (Auerbach, "Enmity," p. 573.) When Reed published his report in 1921, the number of national elite law schools had increased from 2 in 1900 to 31; 24 such schools had 4,778 students in 1916. See Reed, *Training*, pp. 448–49.

61. Auerbach, "Enmity," p. 556. See his excellent analysis of Progressivism among law school teachers, pp. 553–562.

62. Hurst, *Lawmakers,* p. 337.

63. Quoted by Auerbach, "Enmity," p. 558. On Brandeis, and the profession's attitudes toward him, see Hurst, *Lawmakers*, pp. 371ff.

64. Quoted by Auerbach, "Enmity," p. 553.

65. See Hofstadter, *Reform*, pp. 156–164.

66. See Hurst, pp. 358–364 and 371ff. The American Liberty League, representing an elite of corporate lawyers and their clients, battled in the 1930s to declare the economic powers of Congress unconstitutional. See also Arnold M. Paul, *Conservative Crisis and the Rule of Law: Attitudes of Bar and Bench, 1887–1895* (Ithaca, N.Y.: Cornell Univ. Press, 1960).

67. See Stevens, "Two Cheers," pp. 454ff.

68. See Reed, *Training,* pp. 101–103 and 90–91.

69. On "diploma privilege," see Reed, *Training,* chaps. 21 and 22.

70. On the relations between the A.B.A. and the A.A.L.S. see, in particular, Auerbach, "Enmity," especially pp. 564ff. See also Stevens, "Two Cheers," pp. 459ff.

71. Auerbach, "Enmity," p. 585. I rely here on his analysis, pp. 574ff.

72. *Ibid.,* p. 585. The number of lawyers of foreign origin increased on the average twice as rapidly as the total number of lawyers in 1900–1920. See *ibid.,* pp. 574–575.

73. Hofstadter, *Reform,* p. 159. On overcrowding in the legal profession, see Hurst, *Lawmakers,* pp. 314ff. See also, for the 1930s, the A.B.A.'s Special Committee Report, *The Economics of the Legal Profession* (Chicago: 1938).

74. On the law profession in the war years, see Auerbach, "Enmity," pp. 582–584.

75. *Ibid.,* p. 600.

76. *Ibid.,* p. 588.

77. Reed's report distinguished four classes of schools: those in which work could be completed in less than 3 years part-time or full-time study, and which gave a first degree (16 schools, or 11 percent of the total); the national law schools, with high entrance requirements and a 7-year course of study, full-time and university-affiliated (31 schools or 21 percent of the total); schools with low entrance requirements and a full-time 3-year course (40 schools or 29 percent of the total); part-time proprietary schools with a 3-year course (55 schools or 39 percent of the total). In addition to these 142 law schools, Reed lists, in an appendix, 142 short-course night schools. See Reed, *Training,* pp. 414–416.

78. *Ibid.,* p. 57. See also his splendid summary, pp. 406–416.

79. *Ibid.,* p. 57.

80. On the political alignments and arguments at this important meeting, see Auerbach, "Enmity," pp. 591–599.

81. Jencks and Riesman (*Academic Revolution,* Table III, p. 77 and p. 96) point out that the children of fathers with less than eight years of formal education had about 8 chances in 100 of entering college in 1915–25, compared to 14 in 100 thirty years later. The children of fathers who had entered college had, respectively, 47 chances in 100 and 78 in 100. According to the census figures, only 5 percent of those born between 1895 and 1899 finished college.

82. In 1927, 32 jurisdictions out of 49 had no formal requirements for prelegal studies, 11 required a high school diploma or equivalent, 6 required two years of college or equivalent. By 1931, 17 states required two years of prelegal college studies and 33 at least three years of legal study (in either law of-

fice or law school). In 1938, only 8 states did not require prelegal college training. In 1947, all the states but Arkansas, Georgia, Mississippi, and Louisiana required at least 2 years of college before legal training. Delaware, Kansas, and Pennsylvania required graduation from college. The last stage of professionalization—that is, admitting to bar exams only those who had graduated from A.B.A. approved law schools—was well under way. After 1958, only in California did enrollments at 15 unapproved law schools continue growing; only 30 such schools existed in 14 jurisdictions. (Stevens, "Two Cheers," pp. 496–510).

83. On the resistance to continuing A.A.L.S. standardization efforts and pressure for full-time legal faculties, see Stevens, "Two Cheers," pp. 499ff. See his pp. 493–511 on the use of library standards by A.B.A. and A.A.L.S. to deny accreditation to law schools.

84. For an account of standardization after World War II, see Stevens, "Two Cheers," pp. 505ff.

85. See Rueschmeyer, *Lawyers,* pp. 113–114. On specialization, see his pp. 44–59. Smigel notes that the lawyers in large firms and the small solo practitioners—the top and the bottom of the metropolitan bar—hold each other in contempt, balanced, at the top, by an outright ignorance of the solo practitioner's existence. See Smigel, *Wall Street,* p. 173. On the relation between lawyers' ethics and the status of their clients, see Carlin, *Ethics.*

86. By comparison with Germany in the 1950s, where only 2 percent of persons trained in the law had working-class fathers, the proportion among American private practitioners was 20 percent. See Rueschmeyer, *Lawyers,* Table 13, p. 100.

87. See Smigel, *Wall Street,* pp. 171–190.

88. *Ibid.,* p. 342.

89. See Jack Ladinsky, "Careers of Lawyers, Law Practice and Legal Institutions," *Amer. Soc. Rev.,* 27 (1963): 47–54.

90. See Smigel, *Wall Street,* pp. 97–110.

91. Albert P. Blaustein and Charles D. Porter, *The American Lawyer* (Chicago: Univ. of Chicago Press, 1954), p. 8.

92. Ladinsky, "Careers," p. 54. Some 72 percent of the solo lawyers came from small entrepreneur families, while only 40 percent did in the control group of lawyers in large firms. Only 14 percent of the solo practitioners had attended elite law schools, versus 73 percent of the firm lawyers. Also, 57 percent of the solo lawyers had taken all or part of their training on a part-time basis. Firm lawyers were predominantly "WASP" (69 percent were Protestant, 74.5 percent of Northern European ancestry; 90 percent were third-generation Americans); by predictable contrast, solo lawyers were 69 percent Catholic, Jewish, or Greek Orthodox; 59 percent were first or second generation Americans and 68 percent were of Central, Eastern, or Southern European ancestry. (Ladinsky, "Careers," tables on pp. 48–49).

93. In 1930, 93 cities with more than 100,000 inhabitants had 29 percent of the American population and 48 percent of the population of American lawyers. The 1934 Yale study on who uses lawyers found that of 73 percent of U.S. families, receiving 56 percent of the national income, only 1.5 percent consulted a lawyer during the year. Experiments in lower cost legal services were started in Philadelphia (neighborhood legal offices), in Chicago (referral services of the local bar association), and in New York. Neither the study of unassisted legal needs nor the experiments in cheaper legal assistance were initiated by the organized bar, although the A.B.A. endorsed the latter in 1946. See Hurst, *Lawmakers,* pp. 314ff.

94. See Carlin, *Ethics,* pp. 51ff and 69ff.

95. During the reform of medicine, some eminent physicians expressed a conception of "professional respectability" not too distant from that prevalent among leading law practitioners. "In his presidential address to the A.M.A. in 1903, Dr. Billings talked with disdain of 'these sundown institutions' which were organized for evening instruction. He was disturbed that they enabled 'the clerk, the streetcar conductor, the janitor and others employed during the day to earn a degree,' " Markowitz and Rosner, "Doctors," p. 95. Medicine, however, appears to rely predominantly on the selection operated by the educational system and the informal networks it generates. See Oswald Hall, "Informal Organization," as well as his "Types" and "The Stages of a Medical Career," *Amer. Jour. Soc.* 53 (1948): 327–336.

96. Yet in the law, at least, this does not mean that the practice of the solo practitioner is not bureaucratized: Blumberg's analysis of criminal lawyers and public defenders shows that their allegiances,

frames of reference, and priorities lie with the court organization and its requirements, not with the client. Blumberg, "Practice of Law."

97. "Excellent" prestige ratings were granted to physicians by 67 percent of the sample in 1947 and by 71 percent in 1963 (the rank of physicians was second in both years). Lawyers received "excellent" ratings from 44 percent in 1947 and 53 percent in 1963; their rank was eleventh in the last year but they were fifth among the professions ranked (after doctors, scientists, college professors, and chemists). The poorly educated respondents were more generous with their ratings than the better educated. See Hodge *et al.*, "Occupational Prestige." A Gallup poll conducted in 1973 among adults under 30 showed that 25 percent chose medicine as their preferred occupation (that which they would recommend the most to a young man), 20 percent chose the law, 14 percent chose "engineer-builder," and another 14 percent "professor-teacher" (*San Francisco Chronicle*, Dec. 3, 1973, p. 18).

CHAPTER 11. PROFESSION AND BUREAUCRACY

1. William Faunce and Donald A. Clellan, "Professionalization and Stratification Patterns in an Industrial Community," *Amer. Jour. Soc.*, 72 (1967): 341–350.

2. Parsons links the two processes—integration of science into production and bureaucratization—by the force of technological determinism: "Technological advance," he writes, "almost always leads to increasingly elaborate division of labor and the concomitant requirement of increasingly elaborate organization." (Parsons, *The Social System*, p. 507). I cannot discuss here the assumption that technological advance requires a form of organization that can only be imagined as bureaucratic in our society. An excellent analysis of the epistemological assumptions behind this view may be found in Alvin Gouldner, "Metaphysical Pathos and the Theory of Bureaucracy," *Amer. Polit. Sci. Rev.*, 49 (1955): 496–507.

3. On the subject of technocracy, see Sarfatti-Larson, "Notes" and attached bibliography.

4. For empirical observations, see Sherri Cavan, "Aristocratic Workers," in *Academics on the Line,"* Arlene K. Daniels and Rachel Kahn-Hut, eds. (San Francisco: Jossey-Bass, 1970); Hughes, *Sociological Eye*, pp. 311–315; and James L. Walsh and Ray H. Elling, "Professionalization and the Poor—Structural Effects and Professional Behavior," in *Medical Men*, Freidson and Lorber, eds., pp. 267–283.

5. Wilensky, "Professionalization," p. 157.

6. On accountancy, see J. L. Carey, *The Rise of the Accounting Profession* (New York: Amer. Institute of Certified Public Accountants, 1969). The "professionalizing" efficacy of trust, emphasized by Goode in "Theoretical Limits," operates differently in engineering and accountancy. Trust in the engineer is inevitable because of the esoteric nature of the skills and knowledge involved. The technical supervision of engineers in the process of production is entrusted, thus, to people with engineering competence. At least in the beginning, accountancy was based on rather simple arithmetics. A major factor in the professionalization of accountancy and its independence from the large corporation was the public audit of the finances of corporations instituted during the Progressive Era: the independence of the professional scrutinizer was valuable to the corporations, in that it relieved them of potentially broader and still more "independent" audits by the government. (This point was brought to my attention by Professor Leon Mayhew, University of California at Davis.)

7. Lubove, *Professional Altruist*, p. 20.

8. *Ibid.*, p. 150.

9. On the early training programs in social work, see *ibid.*, pp. 124ff and 141ff.

10. *Ibid.*, p. 6.

11. On this point see Davis, *Spearheads*, which illuminates the conflict between professionalizing social workers and the settlement workers during the Progressive Era. See also Frances Fox Piven and Richard Cloward, *Regulating the Poor* (New York: Vintage, 1971), chap. 1.

12. Lubove, *Professional Altruist*, p. 10.

13. *Ibid.*, p. 19.

14. *Ibid.*

15. See Piven and Cloward, *Regulating*, chaps. 2 and 3.

16. Michael Katz, *Class, Bureaucracy and the Schools*, (New York: Praeger, 1971), p. 72.

17. On this subject, see Raymond Callahan, *Education and the Cult of Efficiency* (Chicago: Univ. of Chicago Press, 1962), pp. 217–220.

18. Elwood Cubberley, quoted by Callahan, *Education*, p. 217.

19. Callahan, *Education*, p. 209.

20. Katz, *Irony*, pp. 154ff.

21. Quoted by Callahan, *Education*, p. 218.

22. On teachers' unions, see S. Cole, *The Unionization of Teachers* (New York: Praeger, 1969); and Wesley A. Wildman, "Teachers and Collective Negotiations," in *White Collar Workers*, Albert Blum et al., eds. (New York: Random House, 1971), pp. 126–165. See also, for comparison, J. M. Clark, *Teachers and Politics in France: A Pressure Group Study of the Fédération de L'Education Nationale* (New York: Syracuse Univ. Press, 1967). On semi-professions in general, see Etzioni, ed., *Semi-Professions*.

23. See, for instance, the study by Eugene Litwak, "Models of Bureaucracy which Include Conflict," *Amer. Jour. Soc.*, 67 (1961): 177–184, focusing on the organization itself; see also, on accountants firms, Paul Montagna, "Professionalization and Bureaucratization in Large Professional Associations," *Amer. Jour. Soc.*, 74 (1968): 138–145; and "The Public Accounting Profession," in *American Behavioral Scientist*, 14 (1971): 475–491; on legal firms, see Smigel, *Wall Street*, pp. 275–286.

24. Richard Scott, "Reactions to Supervision in a Heteronomous Professional Organization," *Admin. Sci. Quart.*, 10 (1965): 65–81.

25. See Freidson, *Profession*, in particular pp. 185ff.

26. Marshall, *Class, Citizenship*, p. 172.

27. *Ibid.*, pp. 176 and 179.

28. See empirical studies by Bernice Fisher, "Claims and Credibility: A Discussion of Occupational Identity and Agent-Client Relationships," *Social Problems* (Spring 1969); Haug and Sussman, "Professional Autonomy"; Bradley Rudin, "Industrial Betterment and Scientific Management," *Berkeley Jour. of Soc.*, 17 (1972–1973): 59–77; Walsh and Elling, "Professionalization and the Poor."

29. Jamous and Peloille analyze two cases which redefined the orientation of French medicine: the first was the 1958 Debré Reform, a "coup de force" from above, which involved heretofore "marginal" physicians (researchers and practitioners excluded by the clinical establishment of the hospitals and the Faculté), lay representatives from the Sécurité Sociale, and representatives of the government. The second case was the reform of medical education following the crisis of May 1968: here "general assemblies" which debated the existing situation and the needed changes included "students from other fields . . . workers, nurses, ward orderlies, etc." (Jamous and Peloille, "Changes," pp. 144–145.) Always in the field of medicine, accountability to the client and client participation are the guiding principles—as well as the sources of conflict—for the alternative clinics that sprang up in some urban areas of the United States and also around the farmworkers movement in California in the late 1960s and early 1970s.

30. Elliott A. Krause, "Functions of a Bureaucratic Ideology: 'Citizen Participaton'," *Social Problems* (1968), p. 139.

31. In the Office of Economic Opportunity, which espoused the actual involvement of the poor at local levels, the ideology of citizen participation radicalized the agency's personnel and its activities: the federal headquarters rapidly quashed such successful, but conflict-producing participation. See Krause, "Functions." See also Peter Bachrach and Morton Baratz, *Power and Poverty* (New York: Oxford Univ. Press, 1970); and William Kornhauser, "The Politics of Confrontation: Crisis of Authority," in *The New American Revolution*, R. Aya and N. Miller, eds. (New York: Free Press, 1971).

32. See Carole Joffee, *Friendly Intruders: Childcare Professionals and the Family* (Berkeley: Univ. of California Press, 1976).

33. For empirical evidence on the academics' attitudes toward their clients, see Daniels and Kahn-Hut, eds., *Academics;* Joseph Schwab, *College Curriculum and Student Protest* (Chicago: Univ. of Chicago Press, 1969); and John P. Spiegel, "Campus Conflict and Professional Egos," *Trans-Action* (October 1969): 41–50.

34. See Maurice R. Berube and Marilyn Gittell, eds., *Confrontation at Ocean Hill-Brownsville: the*

New York School Strikes of 1968 (New York: Praeger, 1969); Frances Fox Piven, ''Militant Civil Servants in New York City,'' *Trans-Action* (November 1969): 24ff; and Miriam Wasserman, *The School Fix: New York City, U.S.A.* (New York: Outerbridge and Dienstfrey, 1970).

35. For concrete examples of the conflict between professionalism and advocacy, see Richard Cloward and Richard M. Elman, ''Advocacy in the Ghetto,'' *Trans-Action* (December 1966): 27–35; Neil Gilbert and Joseph W. Eaton, ''Who Speaks for the Poor?'', *Jour. of the Amer. Institute of Planners*, 36 (1970): 411–416; Lisa R. Peattie, ''Reflections on Advocacy Planning,'' *Jour. Amer. Instit. Planners*, 34 (1968): 80–87; Henry Resnik, *Turning on the System: War in the Philadelphia Public Schools* (New York: Pantheon, 1970); and Robert Rossner, *The Year Without an Autumn* (New York: Richard W. Barton, 1970).

36. An interesting conflict took place in 1974 between the A.M.A. and a group of consumer advocates, which had published a directory of physicians for Prince George County in Maryland, each doctor's fee scales, whether he prescribed drugs considered dangerous by the F.D.A., whether he ever made house calls, and so on. The A.M.A. attempted to enjoin publication of the directory, threatening the 25 percent or so of the county physicians who had cooperated in its compilation with as much as loss of their licenses.

37. See, for instance, Joseph Ben-David, ''The Professional Role of the Physician in Bureaucratized Medicine,'' *Human Relations*, 2 (1958): 901–911; Alvin Gouldner, ''Cosmopolitans and Locals,'' in two parts, *Admin. Sci. Quart.*, 2 (1957–1958): 281–306 and 444–480; Robert Merton, ''Bureaucratic Structure and Personality,'' Social Forces, 17 (1940): 560–568; and Mills, *White Collar*.

38. Kornhauser presents the following table on the development of salaried versus self-employed professionals:

Selected Professions Classified by Increase in Size
and Proportion Salaried

Proportion salaried, 1950	Increase in Size (1900–1950)		
	Large (>300%)	Medium (100–300%)	Small (<100%)
High (>80%)	scientists engineers professors accountants	teachers journalists	clergymen
Medium (40–80%)	—	artists architects	musicians pharmacists
Low (40%)	—	dentists physicians	lawyers

SOURCE: William Kornhauser (with Warren Hagstrom), *Scientists in Industry: Conflict and Accommodation* (Berkeley: Univ. of California Press, 1962), p. 5.

39. See, for instance, Mills' powerful polemic in *White Collar*, pp. 112–141. Or, in a more academic key, see Goode, ''Theoretical Limits,'' p. 267; and Wilensky, ''Professionalization,'' pp. 146ff.

40. See Gouldner, ''Cosmopolitans''; Merton, ''Bureaucratic Structure.'' See also the similar elaboration in Amitai Etzioni, ''Authority Structure and Organizational Effectivenes,'' *Admin. Sci. Quart.*, (1959): 42–67.

41. Freidson and Rhea, ''Processes of Control,'' p. 185.

42. On socialization into a profession, see the studies on physicians by Howard S. Becker and James Carper, ''The elements of identification with an occupation,'' *Amer. Soc. Rev.*, 21 (1956): 341–347; Howard S. Becker and Blanche Geer, ''The Fate of Idealism in Medical School,'' *Amer. Soc. Rev.*, 23 (1958): 50–56; Howard S. Becker, Blanche Geer, Everett C. Hughes, and Anselm Strauss, *Boys in White* (Chicago: Univ. of Chicago Press, 1961); Howard S. Becker and Anselm Strauss, ''Careers, Personality and Adult Socialization,'' *Amer. Jour. Soc.*, 62 (1956); Robert K. Merton *et al.*, eds., *The*

Student Physician (Cambridge, Mass.: Harvard Univ. Press, 1957). On lawyers, see Jerome E. Carlin, *Lawyers on their Own* (New Brunswick, N.J.: Rutgers Univ. Press, 1962) and Dan C. Lortie, "Laymen to Lawmen: Law School, Careers and Professional Socialization," *Harvard Educ. Rev.,* 29 (1959): 363–367. On dentists, see D. M. More and Nathan Kohn, Jr., "Some Motives for Entering Dentistry," *Amer. Jour. Soc.,* 66 (1960): 48–53.

43. Arthur L. Stinchcombe, "Bureaucratic and Craft Administration of Production," *Admin. Sci. Quart.,* (1959): 168–187. On Weber's ideal-type of bureaucracy, see the penetrating comments by Stanley Udy, "Bureaucracy and 'Rationality' in Weber's Organization Theory," in *The Formal Organization,* Richard H. Hall, ed. (New York: Basic Books, 1972), pp. 17–25.

44. Scott, "Reactions," p. 66.

45. See Peter Blau, *The Dynamics of Bureaucracy* (Chicago: Univ. of Chicago Press, 1963 ed.); S. Box and S. Cotgrove, "Scientific Identity, Occupational Selection and Role Strain," *Brit. Jour. Soc.,* 17 (1966): 20–28; Kornhauser, *Scientists;* and Scott, "Reactions."

46. It is interesting to note that the positive correlation of autonomy with technical competence is very weak (.121 rank order correlation). This suggests that the professional concern with autonomy always goes beyond the strict area of technical control. See Richard H. Hall, "Some Organizational Considerations in the Professional-Organizational Relationship," *Admin. Sci. Quart.,* 12 (1967): 461–478; and "Professionalization and Bureaucratization," *Amer. Soc. Rev.,* 33 (1968): 92–104.

47. A. Hastings and C. R. Hinings, "Role Relations and Value Adaptation: A Study of the Professional Accountant in Industry," *Sociology,* 4 (1970): 353–366.

48. See Stinchcombe, "Bureaucratic," pp. 183–186.

49. Hall, "Professionalization," p. 104.

50. See Michael Aiken and Jerald Hage, "Organizational Alienation: A Comparative Analaysis," *Amer. Soc. Rev.,* 31 (1966): 497–507.

51. Wilensky, "Professionalization," p. 153.

52. George A. Miller, "Professionals in Bureaucracy: Alienation among Industrial Scientists and Engineers," *Amer. Soc. Rev.,* 32 (1968): 755–768.

53. See Becker and Carper, "Elements of Identification"; and Perrucci and Gerstl, *Engineers.*

54. See, for instance, Luca Perrone, "Information Technology in Industrial Bureaucracies," unpublished paper, Berkeley, 1972.

55. Fred Goldner and R. R. Ritti, "Professionalization as Career Immobility," *Amer. Jour. Soc.,* 72 (1967): 489–502.

56. Stinchcombe, "Bureaucratic," p. 186.

57. Goldner and Ritti, "Career Immobility." Management often has much more obvious reasons to encourage "professionalism": a study of engineering unions reports that, in more than one case, engineers threatened by nonprofessional union organizing in their plants went to management for advice! Management encouraged them to form *professional* unions. Later, management was actively dealing with two of the largest engineering associations (the National Society of Professional Engineers and the Engineers Joint Council) "to persuade them to drop their former sponsorship of collective bargaining." See James Kuhn, "Engineers and their Unions," in *White Collar Workers,* Blum *et al.,* eds., p. 93.

58. See Kornhauser, *Scientists;* and Simon Marcson, *The Scientist in American Industry* (New York: Harper and Row, 1960).

59. Hall, "Some Organizational Considerations," p. 477.

60. Kornhauser, *Scientists,* pp. 192–194.

61. See Peter Blau, "The Hierarchy of Authority in Organizations," *Amer. Jour. Soc.,* 73 (1968): 435–467; and Peter Blau *et al.,* "The Structure of Small Bureaucracies," *Amer. Soc. Rev.,* 31 (1966): 179–191.

62. Perrone, "Information Technology," p. 50.

63. *Ibid.*

64. Stinchcombe, "Organizations," p. 163.

65. See Joffe, *Friendly Intruders.*

66. See Freidson and Rhea, "Processes of Control"; and also Smigel, *Wall Street.*

67. In a study comparing physicians in three work settings (with "low bureaucratization" or solo practice, "moderate bureaucratization" or private clinic, and "high bureaucratization" or large government-affiliated hospital), Engel reports some interesting results: if the physicians' perception of their work autonomy is divided into autonomy of practice and autonomy of research, practitioners in the most bureaucratized settings do, in fact, report low autonomy *of practice* much more often than the other two types (64.9 percent in the hospital versus 37.9 percent among solo doctors and 16.2 percent among private clinic M.D.'s). However, they also report high autonomy *of research* in a much larger proportion (40.5 percent in the hospital versus 22.4 percent among solo doctors and 28.2 percent in the clinic). The moderate bureaucratic characteristics of the clinic do not impair the autonomy of the physician: on the contrary, being on a salary, rather than dependent on client fees, enhances autonomy of practice (or rather, the perception of it). For physicians interested in research, the most bureaucratic work setting offers, undoubtedly, the most freedom of research (68 percent of the hospital M.D.'s engaged in research, versus 38 percent among solo doctors and 42 percent in the clinic.) See Gloria Engel, "Professional Autonomy and Bureaucratic Structure," *Admin. Sci. Quart.*, 15 (1970): 12–21.

68. See Charles Perrow, "A Framework for the Comparative Analysis of Organizations," *Amer. Soc. Rev.*, 32 (1967), pp. 194–195.

69. *Ibid.*, pp. 195–196. Litwak deals with this aspect of the work of organizations in terms of *uniform* tasks (recurrent and important, as opposed to a task or problem that is completely standardized) and *non-uniform* tasks (presenting many exceptions). See Litwak, "Models of Bureaucracy."

70. Bendix, *Work*, p. 336.

71. Nothing can be more illuminating than managerial encouragement for the professionalization efforts in one of the most discretionary of occupations: that of the private "executive secretary." Freidson and Rhea point out that reliance on prior normative socialization is very high in autonomous bureaucracies (that is, bureaucratic organizations run by the professionals who work in them), since sanctions are informal, largely symbolic, and slow in coming. They write: "In a very basic sense, the system depends upon recruiting into it properly socialized workers . . . not merely well-trained, but also responsive to the values of their colleagues." Freidson and Rhea, "Processes of Control," p. 98.

72. See Alfred D. Chandler, Jr., *Strategy*.

73. In what regards engineers, see Calvert, *Mechanical Engineer*, pp. 143ff.

74. There are suggestions that growing organizational rigidity appears at the level of the creation *and use* of information. See Harold Wilensky, *Organizational Intelligence* (New York: Basic Books, 1967).

75. Rueschmeyer, "Doctors," p. 19.

76. For an analysis of the effects of the bureaucratic mode of employment on family and on child-rearing patterns (and therefore, presumably, on personality), see D. Miller and Guy E. Swanson, *The Changing American Parent* (New York: John Wiley and Sons, 1958).

77. See Fritz Machlup, *The Production and Distribution of Knowledge in the United States* (Princeton, N.J.: Princeton Univ. Press, 1972), and Stinchcombe, "Organizations," pp. 163–165.

78. William Sewell, "Inequality of Opportunity and Higher Education," *Amer. Soc. Rev.*, 36 (1971), p. 796.

79. See Randall Collins, "Functional and Conflict Theories of Educational Stratification," *Amer. Soc. Rev.*, 36 (1971): 1002–1018; Christopher Jencks *et al.*, *Inequality: A Reassessment of the Effect of Family and Schooling in America* (New York: Basic Books, 1972); and Sewell, "Inequality."

80. Perrucci and Perrucci, "Social Origins," p. 461.

81. Montagna, "Professionalization," p. 144.

82. For a vivid description of such specialization among lawyers, see Smigel, *Wall Street*.

83. On the emergence of specialties in the medical profession, see Bucher, "Pathology"; and Bucher and Strauss, "Professions in Process."

84. For excellent descriptions of medical careers, see Hall, "Informal Organization"; "Stages"; and "Types."

85. For typical examples, see Bernard Barber, *Science and the Social Order* (New York: Collier Books, 1962), pp. 195ff; and "Some Problems." See also Goode, "Community."

86. A clearcut example is that of Internal Revenue Service officials who leave civil service for

work in the tax departments of corporations (or become independent consultants during the period of intermission prescribed by civil service regulations).

87. Parsons, "Social Structure," p. 35.

CHAPTER 12. MONOPOLIES OF COMPETENCE AND BOURGEOIS IDEOLOGY

1. On the methodological concept of genealogy in Marxist analysis, see Etienne Balibar, "Sur les Concepts Fondamentaux du Matérialisme Historique," in *Lire le Capital,* Louis Althusser *et al.* (Paris: Maspero, 1970), Vol. 2, pp. 182–192.

2. Marx, *Capital,* vol. 1, p. 104, italics mine.

3. *Ibid.,* p. 36.

4. *Ibid.,* p. 88.

5. *Ibid.,* p. 109.

6. *Ibid.,* p. 45.

7. *Ibid.,* p. 39.

8. *Ibid.,* p. 170, note 1.

9. *Ibid.,* p. 168.

10. Polanyi, *Transformation,* p. 72.

11. On the extension and use of credentialing see, in particular, Ivar Berg, *Education and Jobs; the Great Training Robbery* (Boston: Beacon Press, 1971), chaps. 2 and 3.

12. That this is not a self-evident proposition is illustrated by the example of the French system of Grandes Ecoles, founded by Napoleon: the students, recruited by contest, are completely subsidized by the state (and often board in the school as well). They *owe their services to the state* at least for a period of time on completion of their studies. Private industries who wish to employ the members of this selected elite have to "buy them back"—that is, to financially compensate the state for the expenses of their education and the loss of their services.

13. I do not intend to enter the controversy that exists in Marxist theory about which kinds of labor are productive or unproductive (on this, see Ian Gough, "Marx's Theory of Productive and Unproductive Labor," *New Left Review* November–December 1972: 47–72). I believe that the issue becomes a matter of pure exegesis when (1) large proportions of heretofore "unproductive" workers now sell their labor to capitalist firms; and when (2) the production and realization of surplus value increasingly depend on scientific and technological services, on the integration of distribution and supply with production, and also on a large range of governmental services. I will merely use the terms "productive" and "unproductive" as symbolic references to the different kinds of link that different kinds of professional labor form with the production of surplus value.

14. Karl Marx, *Theories of Surplus Value,* Part I (Moscow: Foreign Language Editions, 1969), vol. 1, p. 157. Professional labor of this kind—if it was not exchanged on a market of services—could be considered akin to the labor of small peasants or craftsmen, which is "neither productive nor unproductive," according to Marx.

15. Marx, *Theories,* p. 404.

16. *Ibid.,* p. 152.

17. Marx, *Capital,* vol. 1, p. 509.

18. Marx, *Theories,* p. 157.

19. Ernest Mandel, quoted by Gough, "Marx's Theory," p. 71.

20. See Chapter Eleven for a discussion of managerial encouragement of professionalization by employees.

21. Claus Offe writes: "The services performed by the bureaucratic worker are based on a social relation in which value expansion through surplus value production does not take place . . . and [they] are directly absorbed by social consumption. They have no market. This means that the conditions under which such labor power is socially put to use are not determined by the criterion of the production and

realization of surplus value. Such labor is *concrete,* not "abstract," it is not a commodity and produces no commodities. The social utilization of this kind of labor is determined by its *concrete results;* it is deployed with regard to its use value and to the use value of its performance and not, as in the case of abstract labor, with regard to its exchange value, where use value is not the primary factor, but only a necessary by-product." And he adds, "of course, such concrete labor can and does enhance the productivity (*i.e.,* the surplus value yield) of other kinds of labor eventuating in exchange value." Claus Offe, "The Abolition of Market Control and the Problem of Legitimacy," *Working Papers on the Capitalist State,* 1 (1973): 109–116, pp. 109, 110.

22. This tentative classification, quite unorthodox from the strict Marxist point of view, incorporates in rough form some dimensions outlined by Gough, "Marx's Theory," pp. 60 and 67.

23. On the hopes for a political role of the engineer, see Veblen, *Engineers,* and Layton, *Revolt.* On the inherent structural subordination of the engineer, see Chapter Three.

24. See Chapter Five.

25. See Weber, *From Max Weber,* pp. 186–188.

26. These comments are based on the classic works by Elie Halévy, *The Growth of Philosophic Radicalism* (Boston: Beacon Press, 1966); and C. B. MacPherson, *The Political Theory of Possessive Individualism* (New York: Oxford Univ. Press, 1962). The quotation in the text is from MacPherson, *Political Theory,* p. 263.

27. In Hobbes' thought, for instance, "the model of the self-moving, appetitive, possessive individual and the model of society as a series of market relations between these individuals, were a sufficient source of political obligation. No traditional concepts of justice, natural law, or divine purpose were needed." (MacPherson, *Political Theory,* p. 265.) Locke, however, refused to "reduce all social relations to market relations and all morality to market morality." His thought presents interesting analogies with the professions' combination of traditional and bourgeois legitimations for their own market project. (See MacPherson, pp. 269ff.)

28. *Ibid.,* p. 269.

29. For a discussion of the intellectual influences on the "professional ideal" of the middle class, see Perkin, *Origins,* pp. 252–270.

30. Halévy, *Growth,* p. 478.

31. *Ibid.,* p. 477.

32. *Ibid.,* p. 506.

33. *Ibid.,* p. 507.

34. Sennett and Cobb, *Hidden Injuries,* p. 256.

35. Halévy, *Growth,* p. 502.

36. John Stuart Mill deserves to be quoted for his clarity in formulating the articulations of liberal Utilitarianism. In a discussion of voting, he wrote: "When two persons who have a joint interest in any business differ in opinion, does justice require that both opinions should be held of exactly equal value? If with equal virtue, one is superior to the other in knowledge and intelligence, or if, with equal intelligence, one excels the other in virtue, the opinion . . . of the higher moral or intellectual being is worth more than that of the inferior. . . . The only thing which can justify reckoning one person's opinion as equivalent to more than one is *individual mental superiority; and what is wanted is some approximate means of ascertaining that. If there existed such a thing as a really national education or a trustworthy system of general examination, education might be tested directly.* In the absence of these, the nature of a person's occupation is some test. An employer of labour is on the average more intelligent than an ordinary labourer, and a labourer in the skilled trades than the unskilled. A banker, merchant or manufacturer is likely to be more intelligent than a tradesman, because he has larger and more complicated interests to manage. . . . Subject to some such condition [of successful performance], two or more votes might be allowed to every person who exercises any of these superior functions." John Stuart Mill, *Considerations on Representative Government* (Indianapolis: Bobbs Merrill, 1958 ed.), pp. 135–138, italics mine.

37. On ideological processes, see Thomas Herbert, "Remarques pour un théorie générale des idéologies," *Cahiers pour l'Analyse* (Summer 1968): 74–92.

38. See Althusser, "Idéologie," pp. 29–33.

39. Freidson, *Profession,* p. 171.

40. See Durkheim, *Division,* pp. 1–38.

41. Tawney, *The Acquisitive Society* (New York: Harcourt, Brace and Co., 1948), pp. 93–94.

42. Hughes, *Sociological Eye,* p. 353.

43. See the interesting thesis on the changing power structure of American medicine in Health PAC, *Health Empire.*

44. One author puts it candidly: "It became obvious that a high level of remuneration implies a public recognition of status, in that the most certain way of attaining the latter is to press for the former." Bernard R. Blishen, *Doctors and Doctrines: the Ideology of Medical Care in Canada* (Toronto: Univ. of Toronto Press, 1969), pp. 15–16. Material rewards are thus an indication of excellence which does not cease to operate at the threshold of the "company of equals."

45. Stinchcombe, "Organizations," pp. 181–182.

46. On the meaning of work, see Robert Blauner, *Alienation and Freedom* (Chicago, Univ. of Chicago Press, 1964); Harry Braverman, *Labor and Monopoly Capital* (New York: Monthly Review Press, 1975); N. C. Morse and R. S. Weiss, "The Function and Meaning of Work and the Job," *Amer. Soc. Rev.,* 20 (1955): 191–198; and Adriano Tilgher, "Work through the Ages," in *Man, Work,* Nosow and Form, eds., pp. 11–23.

47. See, for instance, Barber, "Some Problems"; Goode, "Community"; Greenwood, "Attributes"; and Walter L. Slocum, *Occupational Careers* (Chicago: Aldine, 1966).

48. See the work of the Chicago school on the culture and socialization processes relative to occupations and professions. In particular, see the work referred to throughout this analysis by Howard S. Becker and his associates, by Freidson, by Oswald Hall, and of course by Everett C. Hughes.

49. Incidentally, the same notion of "heavy investment" tends to weaken colleague control. Freidson's studies of medicine show that colleagues tend to encourage the culprit to "resign from their company"— to bar him, that is, from the informal networks, rather than expel him from the profession. The latter is a last recourse, forced by publicity given to a gross offense. Otherwise, the rationale tends to be "to avoid ruining a man's life." See Freidson, *Profession,* pp. 181–183; and Freidson and Rhea, "Processes of Control." The reactions of the organized profession to the case of a New Jersey surgeon who was clearly suspected of murdering a number of patients were neither rapid nor unambiguous, until the *New York Times* exposed the case of "Dr. X." The case came to a head in February and March of 1976.

50. Stinchcombe, "Bureaucratic," p. 186.

51. Wilensky, "Careers," p. 555.

52. See Peter Berger, "Introduction," *The Human Shape of Work,* Peter Berger, ed. (New York: Macmillan, 1964); William H. Form and D. C. Miller, "Occupational Career Pattern as a Sociological Instrument," *Amer. Jour. Soc.,* 54 (1949); Touraine, *Sociologie de l'Action;* and Harold Wilensky, "Measures and Effects of Social Mobility," in *Social Structure and Mobility,* Smelser and Lipset, eds., pp. 98–140.

53. Freidson and Rhea, "Processes of Control," p. 198.

54. Goode, "Theoretical Limits," pp. 282–283.

55. See Marx, *Capital,* vol. 1, chap. 14.

56. Hughes, *Sociological Eye,* p. 376.

57. Sennett and Cobb, *Hidden Injuries,* p. 227.

58. In this respect, see the interesting study of nuclear technologists by Howard Vollmer and Donald Mills, "Professionalization and Technological Change," in *Professionalization,* Vollmer and Mills, eds., pp. 22–28.

59. Weber, *General Economic History,* p. 115, italics mine.

60. One important structural reason into which I cannot enter here is not related to the need for ideological legitimacy, but directly related to the impossibility of employing the full labor surplus, in particular the young, in advanced capitalism. See Robert B. Carson, "Youthful Labor Surplus in Disaccumulationist Capitalism," *Socialist Revoltion,* 2 (1972): 15–44.

61. Kornhauser, *Scientists,* pp. 4–5, italics mine.

62. See Appendix Table 5.

63. See Albert J. Reiss, "Occupational Mobility of Professional Workers," in *Professionalization*, Vollmer and Mills, eds., pp. 73–81.

64. See Blau and Duncan, *Occupational Structure*, p. 27.

65. The tendency is much more marked in the other two categories involving proprietorship—proprietors and, especially, farmers (the inflow percentages in the same category of occupation as one's father were, respectively, 16.3 percent and 82 percent). Blau and Duncan's study also shows the high *stability* of professional work: 53.5 percent of the men whose first job was in the category of self-employed professional were in the same occupational status in 1962; 25.5 percent had moved to the salaried professional category. Only 21 percent had moved out of the professional categories altogether, and of these 1.8 percent had become managers and 4.7 percent "salesmen or other." Among the men who started out as salaried professionals, 54.5 percent were in the same category in 1962, only 16.5 percent had become self-employed and 12.3 percent managers. Blau and Duncan, *Occupational Structure*, Tables 2 and 4, p. 31.

66. See Blau and Duncan, *Occupational Structure*, pp. 39 and 32.

67. Preliminary observations in a union of architectural employees suggest that this tendency is present at all levels, both leadership and rank-and-file.

68. "Technicians and the Capitalist Division of Labor," *Socialist Revolution*, 2 (1972), pp. 79–81.

69. On the "new working class," see Herbert Gintis, "The New Working Class and Revolutionary Youth," in *Socialist Revolution*, 1 (1970): 13–43; Jim Stodder, "Old and New Working Class," in *Socialist Revolution*, 3 (1973): 99–110; and Albert Szymanski, "Trends in the American Working Class," *Socialist Revolution*, 2 (1972): 101–122. More recently, see Braverman, *Labor and Monopoly Capital*.

70. On the European approach to the new working class, see André Gorz, *Strategy for Labor* (Boston: Beacon Press, 1967); Giovanni Jervis and Letizia Comba, "Contradictions du Technicien et de la Culture Techniciste," *Temps Modernes* (April 1970): 1601–1612; John Low-Beer, *The New Working Class in Italy*, unpublished Ph.D. dissertation, Harvard University, 1974; Serge Mallet, *Essays on the New Working Class*, Richard Howard and Dean Savage, eds. (St. Louis, Mo.: Telos Press, 1975); and Alain Touraine, *The May Movement* (New York: Random House, 1971).

71. Blauner, *Alienation*, p. 29.

72. See, for instance, the report of the Special Task Force for the Secretary of Health, Education and Welfare, *Work in America* (Cambridge, Mass.: MIT Press, 1973).

73. Jervis and Comba, "Contradictions," my translation.

74. Besides the recent work I have cited, S. M. Lipset and Mildred A. Schwartz draw on almost all the sociological work published before 1968. See "The Politics of Professionals," in *Professionalization*, Vollmer and Mills, eds., pp. 299–310.

75. Sennett and Cobb, *Hidden Injuries*, p. 265.

76. Hence the often heard exaggeration among low-paid professionals (I heard it from an architect): "the man who pushes the broom can earn more than the fellow who designed the building." This observation should be read in conjunction with the intimate relation between personal worth, social esteem, and money that is manifest everywhere in our society.

77. Engineering professional associations were convinced by management to abandon their former sponsorship of collective bargaining: "The societies now argue for commitment to a professionalism that excludes any kind of collective bargaining. *By stressing the differences between professionals and workers and by urging management to emphasize and respect these differences*, they have tried to make engineering unions unnecessary." (Kuhn, "Engineers," p. 93, italics mine.) The "professional" union of Italian pilots, independent of the large union confederations, repeatedly goes on strike against the state-owned airlines (forcing the services to stop a large percentage of flights) because they do not want to sign collective contracts with the other categories of workers, but want the right to renegotiate differentials in between general contracts. (See, for instance, the strikes of August 1975 and May 1976.) So much for the "professional" defense of the public interest!

78. On strikes by professionals see, among others, Daniels and Kahn-Hut, eds., *Academics;* Haug and Sussman, "Professionalization"; Kuhn, "Engineers"; Prandy, *Professional Employees;* and Wildman, "Teachers."

79. Robert Merton, "The Machine, the Worker, and the Engineer," in *Man, Work,* Nosow and Form, eds., p. 86. For a development on "technocratic irresponsibility," see Sarfatti-Larson, "Notes."

80. "Technicians," p. 76.

81. *Ibid.,* p. 76. The quotation in the text is from Merton, "The Machine," p. 87.

82. Marx, *Capital,* vol. 1, pp. 367–368.

83. Ralph Dahrendorf, "The Service Class," in *Industrial Man,* Tom Burns, ed. (Baltimore: Penguin, 1969), p. 146, italics mine.

84. Dahrendorf, "The Service Class," p. 148, italics mine.

85. Althusser, "Idéologie," p. 18, translation mine. The above comments on ideology are based on his analysis.

86. See Blau and Duncan, *Occupational Structure,* pp. 165–171 and 199–205; and Herman Miller, "Income and Education," in *The Logic of Social Hierarchies,* Edward O. Lauman *et al.,* eds. (Chicago: Markham, 1970), chap. 24.

87. See Jencks *et al., Inequality.*

88. Berg, *Education and Jobs,* p. 32, italics mine.

89. John K. Folger and Charles B. Nam, *Education of the American Population, 1960 Census Monograph* (Washington, D.C.: U.S. Government Printing Office, 1967), p. 169.

90. *Ibid.,* p. 173.

91. In 1950, writes Berg, "59 percent of all persons 17 years or older had graduated from high school; by 1964, the figure was 76.3 percent. Americans spent $9 billion on education in 1950, $29 in 1963, and nearly $49 billion in 1966–67 . . . whereas slightly more than 20 percent of the students who completed fifth grade in 1944 and went on to college, more than 40 percent of fifth graders in 1957 eventually entered college, a remarkably high 'school retention' figure." (Berg, *Education and Jobs,* p. 1). See also the study by the Carnegie Commission on Higher Education, *College Graduates and Jobs* (New York: McGraw-Hill, 1973); and Carson, "Youthful Labor Surplus."

92. Berg, *Education and Jobs,* p. 12.

93. *Ibid.,* p. 41, italics mine. What evidence there is contradicts the manager's assumption that the best employees are also the most educated (if "best" means the most stable, productive, and loyal). See Berg's chaps. 5 and 6. See also the analysis by Collins of the "fit" between employers' and employees' "culture," in "Functionalist and Conflict Theories."

94. *Ibid.,* p. 185.

95. *Ibid.,* p. 69. On the subject of marginality and dual labor markets, see James O'Connor, *The Fiscal Crisis of the State* (New York: St. Martin's Press, 1973); and Michael Reich, David Gordon, and Richard Edwards, "Dual Labor Markets: A Theory of Labor Market Segmentation," *American Eco. Rev. Proceedings,* 63 (1973).

96. See, for instance, Eli Chinoy, *Automobile Workers and the American Dream* (Boston: Beacon Press, 1955), p. 112; and Sennett and Cobb, *Hidden Injuries.*

97. Althusser, "Idéologie," p. 20, translation mine.

98. Sennett and Cobb, *Hidden Injuries,* p. 153, italics mine.

99. *Ibid.,* italics mine.

100. See Studs Terkel, *Hard Times* (New York: Avon, 1971).

101. Peter Bachrach, *The Theory of Democratic Elitism* (Boston: Little, Brown, 1967), p. 2.

102. "Technicians," p. 82.

Selected Bibliography

I have quoted in the Notes and footnotes all the sources I consulted. I list here those I find more directly relevant for the study of professions, as well as those that informed my theoretical approach. Unless they are particularly significant, articles which appear in readers or edited books will not be listed separately here; the book will appear under the name of its editor(s).

BOOKS

Becker, Howard S., Blanche Geer, Everett C. Hughes, and Anselm Strauss. *Boys in White*. Chicago: University of Chicago Press, 1961.

Ben-David, Joseph. *The Scientist's Role in Society*. Englewood Cliffs, N. J.: Prentice-Hall, 1971.

Bendix, Reinhard. *Work and Authority in Industry*. New York: Harper and Row, 1956.

Bendix, Reinhard, and S. M. Lipset, eds. *Class, Status and Power*. New York: Free Press, 1966, rev. ed.

Berg, Ivar. *Education and Jobs: the Great Training Robbery*. Boston: Beacon Press, 1971.

Blau, Peter, and Otis Dudley Duncan. *The American Occupational Structure*. New York: John Wiley & Sons, 1967.

Blauner, Robert. *Alienation and Freedom*. Chicago: University of Chicago Press, 1964.

Blaustein, Albert P., and Charles D. Porter. *The American Lawyer*. Chicago: University of Chicago Press, 1954.

Blum, Albert *et al*. *White Collar Workers*. New York: Random House, 1971.

Boulding, Kenneth. *The Organizational Revolution*. Chicago: Quadrangle, 1968 ed.

Briggs, Martin S. *The Architect in History*. Oxford: Clarendon Press, 1927.

Calhoun, Daniel. *The American Civil Engineer: Origins and Conflict*. Cambridge, Mass.: MIT Press, 1960.

———. *Professional Lives in America: Structure and Aspirations, 1750–1850*. Cambridge, Mass.: Harvard University Press, 1965.

Callahan, Raymond. *Education and the Cult of Efficiency*. Chicago: University of Chicago Press, 1962.

Calvert, Monte. *The Mechanical Engineer in America; 1830–1910; Professional Cultures in Conflict*. Baltimore: Johns Hopkins University Press, 1967.

Carey, J. L. *The Rise of the Accounting Profession*. New York: American Institute of Certified Public Accountants, 1969.

Carlin, Jerome E. *Lawyers' Ethics*. New York: Russell Sage, 1966.

Carr-Saunders, A. M., and P. A. Wilson. *The Professions*. Oxford: Clarendon Press, 1933.

Chandler, Alfred D., Jr. *Strategy and Structure*. Cambridge, Mass.: MIT Press, 1962.

Clark, Sir George. *A History of the Royal College of Physicians of London*, 2 vols. Oxford: Clarendon Press, 1964.

Cook, Blanche W., Alice K. Harris, and Ronald Radosh, eds. *Past Imperfect*, 2 vols. New York: Knopf, 1973.

Davis, Lance E. *et al*. *American Economic Growth; An Economist's History of the United States*. New York: Harper & Row, 1972.

Durkheim, Emile. *The Division of Labor in Society*. New York: Free Press, 1964.

Etzioni, Amitai, ed. *The Semi-Professions*. New York: Free Press, 1969.

Flexner, Abraham. *Medical Education in the United States and Canada*. New York: Carnegie Foundation, Bulletin no. 4, 1910.

_____. *Medical Education in Europe*. New York: Carnegie Foundation, Bulletin no. 6, 1912.

Freidson, Eliot. *Profession of Medicine*. New York: Dodd & Mead, 1970.

_____, ed. *The Hospital in Modern Society*. New York: Free Press, 1963.

_____. "Professions in Contemporary Society." Special Issue of *American Behavioral Scientist* 14 (1971).

Freidson, Eliot, and Judith Lorber, eds. *Medical Men and their Work*. Chicago: Aldine-Atherton, 1972.

Gilb, Corinne Lathrop. *Hidden Hierarchies; The Professions and Government*. New York: York: Harper & Row, 1967.

Gramsci, Antonio. *Prison Notebooks*. Quintin Hoare and Geoffrey Nowell Smith, eds. New York: International Publishers, 1971.

Haber, Samuel. *Efficiency and Uplift*. Chicago: University of Chicago Press, 1964.

Health PAC. *The American Health Empire*. New York: Vintage, 1971.

Hobsbawm, Eric. *The Age of Revolutions*. New York: Mentor, 1962.

_____. *Industry and Empire*. Baltimore: Penguin, 1969.

Hofstadter, Richard, and Walter P. Metzger. *The Development of Academic Freedom in the United States*. New York: Columbia University Press, 1955.

Hughes, Everett C. *The Sociological Eye*, 2 vols. Chicago: Aldine-Atherton, 1971.

Hurst, James Willard. *The Growth of American Law: The Lawmakers*. Boston: Little, Brown & Co., 1950.

Kaye, Barrington. *The Development of the Architectural Profession*. London: Allen & Unwin, 1960.

Kett, Joseph. *The Formation of the American Medical Profession*. New Haven: Yale University Press, 1968.

Kuhn, Thomas S. *The Structure of Scientific Revolutions*. Chicago: University of Chicago Press, 1970 ed.

Layton, Edwin T., Jr., *The Revolt of the Engineers*. Cleveland: Case Western University Press, 1971.

Lubove, Roy. *The Professional Altruist: the Emergence of Social Work as a Career*. Cambridge, Mass.: Harvard University Press, 1965.

Marx, Karl. *Capital*, 3 vols. New York: International Publishers, 1967.

Meyers, Marvin. *The Jacksonian Persuasion: Politics and Belief*. Stanford, Ca.: Stanford University Press, 1957.

Mills, C. W. *White Collar*. New York: Oxford University Press, 1956.

Moulin, Raymonde *et al. Les Architectes*. Paris: Calmann-Levy, 1973.

Parsons, Talcott. *The Social System*. Glencoe, Ill.: Free Press, 1951.

_____. *Essays in Sociological Theory*. New York: Free Press, 1954.

Perkin, Harold. *The Origins of Modern English Society, 1770–1880*. London: Routledge & Kegan Paul, 1969.

Perrucci, Robert, and Joel E. Gerstl. *Profession without Community: Engineers in American Society*. New York: Random House, 1969.

Polanyi, Karl. *The Great Transformation*. Boston: Beacon Press, 1957.

Prandy, Kenneth. *Professional Employees*. London: Faber & Faber, 1965.

Reader, W. J. *Professional Men*. London: Weidenfeld & Nicolson, 1966.

Reed, Alfred Z. *Training for the Public Profession of the Law*. New York: Carnegie Foundation, Bulletin no. 15, 1921.

Rothstein, William. *American Physicians in the Nineteenth Century*. Baltimore: Johns Hopkins University Press, 1972.

Rueschmeyer, Dietrich. *Lawyers and their Society*. Cambridge, Mass.: Harvard University Press, 1973.

Sennett, Richard, and Jonathan Cobb. *The Hidden Injuries of Class*. New York: Vintage, 1973.

Shryock, Richard. *The Development of Modern Medicine*. New York: Knopf, 1947.

———. *Medicine in American History*. Baltimore: Johns Hopkins University Press, 1966.

Smigel, Erwin. *The Wall Street Lawyer*. New York: Free Press, 1964.

Special Task Force for the Secretary of Health, Education and Welfare. *Work in America*. Cambridge, Mass.: MIT Press, 1973.

Stevens, Rosemary. *American Medicine and the Public Interest*. New Haven: Yale University Press, 1971.

Veblen, Thornstein. *The Engineers and the Price System*. New York: Harcourt, Brace and World, 1963 ed.

Veysey, Laurence R. *The Emergence of the American University*. Chicago: University of Chicago Press, 1965.

Vollmer, Howard M., and Donald L. Mills, eds. *Professionalization*. Englewood Cliffs, N.J.: Prentice-Hall, 1966.

Weber, Max. *Max Weber on Law in Economy and Society*. Max Rheinstein, ed. New York: Simon and Schuster, 1954.

———. *From Max Weber*. Hans Gerth and C. W. Mills, eds. New York: Oxford University Press, 1959.

———. *General Economic History*. New York: Collier Books, 1961.

Wesley, Edgar B. *NEA: The First Hundred Years: The Building of the Teaching Profession*. New York: Harper and Bros., 1957.

Wiebe, Robert H. *The Search for Order: 1877–20*. New York: Hill and Wang, 1967.

ARTICLES

Aiken, Michael and Jerald Hage. "Organizational Alienation: A Comparative Analysis." *Amer. Soc. Rev.* 31 (1966): 497–507.

Althusser, Louis. "Idéologie et Appareils Idéologiques d'Etat." *La Pensée* 151 (June 1970): 3–38.

Auerbach, Jerold S. "Enmity and Amity: Law Teachers and Practitioners, 1900–22." *Perspectives in American History* 5 (1971): 551–601.

Becker, Howard S., and James Carper. "The elements of identification with an occupation." *Amer. Soc. Rev.* 21 (1956): 341–347.

Blumberg, Abraham. "The Practice of Law as a Confidence Game: Organizational Cooptation in a Profession." *Law and Society Review* 1 (1967): 15–39.

Box, S., and S. Cotgrove. "Scientific Identity, Occupational Selection and Role Strain." *British Jour. Soc.* 17 (1966): 20–28.

Chapoulie, Jean-Michel. "Sur l'analyse sociologique des groupes professionnels." *Revue Franc. Sociol.* 14 (1973): 86–114.

Engel, Gloria. "Professional Autonomy and Bureaucratic Structure." *Administrative Science Quart.* 15 (1970): 12–21.

Faunce, William, and Donald A. Clellan. "Professionalization and Stratification Patterns in an Industrial Community." *Amer. Jour. Soc.* 72 (1967): 341–350.

Freidson, Eliot. "Client Control and Medical Practice." *Amer. Jour. Soc.* 65 (1960): 374–382.

Freidson, Eliot, and Buford Rhea. "Knowledge and Judgment in Professional Evaluation." *Administrative Science Quart.* 1 (1965): 107–124.

———. "Processes of Control in a Company of Equals," in *Medical Men and their Work*, Eliot Freidson and Judith Lorber, eds., pp. 185–199. Chicago: Aldine-Atherton, 1972.

Goldner, Fred, and R. R. Ritti, "Professionalization as Career Immobility." *Amer. Jour. Soc.* 72 (1967): 489–502.

Goode, William J. "Community within a Community: the Professions." *Amer. Soc. Rev.* 22 (1957): 194–200.

_____. "Encroachment, Charlatanism and the Emerging Profession: Psychology, Sociology and Medicine." *Amer. Soc. Rev.* 25 (1960): 902–914.

_____. "The Theoretical Limits of Professionalization," in *The Semi-Professions,"* Amitai Etzioni, ed., pp. 266–313. New York: Free Press, 1969.

Hall, Oswald. "The Informal Organization of the Medical Profession." *Canad. Jour. of Eco. and Polit. Sci.* 12 (1946): 30–44.

_____. "The Stages of a Medical Career." *Amer. Jour. Soc.* 53 (1948): 327–336.

_____. "Types of Medical Careers." *Amer. Jour. Soc.* 55 (1949): 243–253.

Hall, Richard H. "Professionalization and Bureaucratization." *Amer. Soc. Rev.* 33 (1968): 92–104.

Hastings, A., and C. R. Hinings. "Role Relations and Value Adaptation: A Study of the Professional Accountant in Industry." *Sociology* 4 (1970): 353–366.

Hays, Samuel P. "The Politics of Reform in Municipal Government in the Progressive Era." *Pacific Northwest Quart.* 55 (1964): 157–169.

Jamous, Haroun, and B. Peloille. "Changes in the French University-Hospital System," in *Professions and Professionalization,* J. A. Jackson, ed., pp. 111–152. Cambridge: Cambridge University Press, 1970.

Johnson, William R. "Education and Professional Life Styles: Law and Medicine in the Nineteenth Century." *History of Educ. Quart.,* Summer 1974, pp. 185–207.

Ladinsky, Jack. "Careers of Lawyers, Law Practice and Legal Institutions." *Amer. Soc. Rev.* 27 (1963): 47–54.

Markowitz, Gerald E., and David Karl Rosner. "Doctors in Crisis: A Study of the Use of Medical Education Reform to Establish Modern Professional Elitism in Medicine." *American Quart.* 25 (1973): 83–107.

Merton, Robert K. "Bureaucratic Structure and Personality." *Social Forces* 17 (1940): 560–568.

Miller, George A. "Professionals in Bureaucracy: Alienation among Industrial Scientists and Engineers." *Amer. Soc. Rev.* 32 (1968): 755–768.

Perrow, Charles. "A framework for the comparative analysis of organizations." *Amer. Soc. Rev.* 32 (1967): 194–208.

Scott, Richard. "Reactions to Supervision in a Heteronomous Professional Organization." *Administrative Science Quart.* 10 (1965): 65–81.

Stevens, Robert. "Two Cheers for 1870: the American Law School." *Perspectives in Amer. History* 5 (1971): 405–548.

Stinchcombe, Arthur L. "Bureaucratic and Craft Administration of Production." *Administrative Science Quart.* 4 (1959): 168–187.

_____. "Social Structure and Organizations," in *Handbook of Organizations,* James G. March, ed., chapter 4. New York: Rand McNally, 1965.

Szymanski, Albert. "Trends in the American Working Class." *Socialist Revolution* 2 (1972): July–August.

"Technicians and the Capitalist Division of Labor." *Socialist Revolution* 2 (1972): May–June.

Wilensky, Harold. "Work, Careers and Social Integration." *International Social Science Jour.* 12 (1960): 543–560.

_____. "The Professionalization of Everyone." *Amer. Jour. Soc.* 70 (1964): 137–158.

_____. "Varieties of Work Experience," in *Man in a World at Work,* Henry Borow, ed., pp. 125–154. Boston: Houghton-Mifflin, 1964.

Index